W9-ABQ-051

PUBLICATIONS OF THE CENTER
FOR JAPANESE AND KOREAN STUDIES

CHONG-SIK LEE, *The Politics of Korean Nationalism.* 1963.

SADAKO N. OGATA, *Defiance in Manchuria: The Making of Japanese Foreign Policy, 1931-1932.* 1964.

R. P. DORE, *Education in Tokugawa Japan.* 1964.

JAMES T. ARAKI, *The Ballad-Drama of Medieval Japan.* 1964.

FRANK O. MILLER, *Minobe Tatsukichi: Interpreter of Constitutionalism in Japan.* 1965.

Ōkubo Toshimichi—the Bismarck of Japan

Published under the auspices of
The Center for Japanese and Korean Studies
University of California, Berkeley

大久保利通

MASAKAZU IWATA

ŌKUBO TOSHIMICHI

THE BISMARCK OF JAPAN

University of California Press
Berkeley and Los Angeles 1964

University of California Press
Berkeley and Los Angeles, California
Cambridge University Press, London, England

Library of Congress Catalog Card Number: 64-25533
Printed in the United States of America

To my parents
Yasujirō and Tatsue Iwata
who as *Issei* pioneers came to America
and sank their roots deeply
into her soil

The Center for Japanese and Korean Studies of the University of California is a unit of the Institute of International Studies. It is the unifying organization for faculty members and students interested in Japan and Korea, bringing together scholars from many disciplines. The Center's major aims are the development and support of research and language study. As part of this program the Center sponsors a publication series of books concerned with Japan and Korea. Manuscripts are considered from all campuses of the University of California as well as from any other individuals and institutions doing research in these areas.

Acknowledgments

A work of this nature necessarily involves the aid of many persons too numerous to mention here. I wish, however, to express particular gratitude to Professor Yu-shan Han who gave ungrudgingly of his time to discuss my problems and to offer invaluable advice. Through his recommendation a University of California, Los Angeles research grant was made available which enabled me in 1958 to visit the various centers for Oriental research in the United States. I would also like to express appreciation to Professor Robert A. Wilson for his suggestions and encouragement, as well as to the late Professor David B. Bjork, and Professors Ensho Ashikaga, Brainerd Dyer, Clifford H. MacFadden, and Stanley Wolpert, all of whom read the work and made helpful comments.

Others have also read the manuscript and made valuable suggestions, many of which have been adopted. I regret, however, that the element of time and the limitation of energy at this particular juncture preclude any additional revisions that may be warranted. I assume sole responsibility for whatever imperfections are contained in this work, including errors in translation and judgment.

I also wish to extend my appreciation to the librarians and staff members connected with the Oriental collections of the following institutions for their assistance and hospitality: University of California at both Los

Angeles and Berkeley, Honnold Library (Claremont), Library of Congress, Harvard University, Columbia University, University of Michigan, and Stanford University. Finally, it would be remiss if mention were not made of the one person without whose encouragement and assistance this work would not have been possible—my wife, Doreen.

MASAKAZU IWATA

Contents

I

Spirit and Structure of Old Japan

In history there are few recorded instances of overnight transformation of relatively backward countries into modern states. Two classic examples of this phenomenon are, of course, Russia and Japan. The transition of the former has taken place in this generation and hardly needs comment. Japan's leap from feudalism to modernism nearly a century ago was at least as swift and dramatic as that of Russia. In a short span of thirty years or less Japan emerged from a feudal state to become a progressive nation with a parliament, a modern defense force, an industrial base, and a national educational system.

Thoughtful Western students of Japan have written copiously and convincingly about the interaction of economic, political, and social conditions that made change inevitable in mid-nineteenth-century Japan. Hence to contemporary scholars, such as G. B. Sansom and E. Herbert Norman, Japanophiles owe a debt of gratitude for elucidating the significance of these forces in effecting the transformation.

If, however, it is true that not only do forces generated by the environment act to create history but that human beings can and do direct these forces to an extent, then it is logical to study in detail the lives of those outstanding individuals who have modified and guided the direction of history. Until recently, not a great deal had been written in English concerning the lives of the pioneers in the modernization of Japan, aside from summary treatment given to them in historical literature dealing with Japan. The writings of Charles Lanman and J. Morris contribute sketches of the more important figures of the Meiji period (1868-1912), but the brevity of the treatment imposes limitations and provides little more than a superficial knowledge of the men who have influenced the course of modern Japanese history. Fortunately, more extensive studies of Restoration statesmen are being made by scholars, as witness works that are either slated for publication or have already been published: Roger F. Hackett, *Yamagata Aritomo* (Harvard University Press, 1961), and Marius B. Jansen, *Sakamoto Ryōma and the Meiji Restoration* (Princeton University Press, 1961). In Japanese, there is certainly no dearth of biographical material on most prominent Restoration statesmen; the Japanese are voracious readers of all types of literature, among which biographies occupy a favored position inasmuch as the nation has had an inclination toward hero-worship.

Although a historian would be criticized for accepting in toto Emerson's statement that "all history resolves itself very easily into the biography of a few stout and earnest persons," this view is particularly applicable to Japan during the Restoration period—a period beginning November, 1867, and extending through the years of reform in the 1870's and 1880's. This was an era during which the country was blessed with an abundance of gifted leaders, among whom were "a few stout and earnest persons," great geniuses, whose keenness of mind and force of character set them apart from other personalities of the age. Such men influenced to a great degree the events of the time. Though children of their age, they were "precocious" enough to mold society to conform to their will, aided the while by external forces beyond their own control.[1]

Among the galaxy of leaders Japan produced during the hectic and troublesome mid-nineteenth century, three were singularly outstanding for their valuable contribution to the work of the Restoration. They were Kido Kōin, Saigō Takamori, and Ōkubo Toshimichi, who deservedly have been named the "triumvirate of the Restoration." Because of his liberal ideas and the ideological heritage he has left to Japan, Kido is an interesting figure and has become a topic of recent study by an American scholar.[2] The life of Saigō, the military hero of the Restoration, has been portrayed for the Western student of Japan in a translation of a work by a Japanese novelist.[3] But the third member of the triumvirate, Ōkubo, has not as yet been given more than superficial treatment by Western historians, except by the French writer, Maurice Courant.[4]

It is indeed difficult to understand why a personality as important in Meiji history as Ōkubo has not thus far been studied in greater detail by American scholars. The ubiquity of Ōkubo in Restoration and Meiji history is unquestioned. In fact, it is Courant who states that one cannot pick up any piece of literature dealing with the Meiji period without finding the name of Ōkubo mentioned in it.[5] His connection with almost every facet of Japanese political life during this period indicates the prestige he enjoyed and the power he wielded. Obviously, he was one of the most prominent leaders of the Restoration movement and certainly the most influential among those who guided and directed the course of the new imperial government after its establishment.

Ōkubo's rise to national prominence as a statesman can be attributed to his mental acuity and persistence, his willingness to tergiversate and even to resort to devious means in order to attain his ends. By catering to the *daimyō* of Satsuma, in whose government he served, Ōkubo rose rapidly. Once in position of power, he influenced the policy of the Satsuma *han* and instituted progressive reforms which he considered indispensable, especially after Satsuma felt the full impact of Western military might when the English bombarded Kagoshima in 1863. Prior to the Restoration, Ōkubo's political ideology shifted from one of court-Bakufu union to one of opposition to and finally overthrow of the Tokugawa government. He was one of the key figures in the movement to restore to the emperor his prerogatives as the sovereign of Japan.

As a policy-maker in the Meiji government after the Restoration, Ōkubo expended his energy in the Westernization of Japan, the specific purpose of which was to create a strong economic and military foundation for the state. He became the head of the important Finance Ministry in 1871 and, together with Kido and Saigō, was instrumental in obtaining the surrender of the feudal fiefs to the government as a prelude to the establishment of prefectures. In 1873, he began an extensive tour of the United States and Europe as a member of the Iwakura mission, but before the mission was completed Ōkubo was recalled to Japan to deal with the military faction within the government which, in the absence of the key leaders, had begun to advocate war with Korea. Taking the leadership of the opposition, he won a resounding victory for the peace faction as the result of which every member of the military clique within the government resigned. Consequently, he was able to form the so-called Ōkubo government composed of men in sympathy with his peace and industrialization policy. This action enabled him to consolidate his authority and marks the beginning of his career as the most powerful of the early Meiji bureaucrats. In 1874 he became the first chief of the Home Ministry, a position that facilitated the implementation of his policy of modernization. His enemies, however, opposed the government's policy and soon manifested their feelings in violence. Despite his position as the chief of a civilian ministry, Ōkubo himself took to the field and resolutely suppressed the Saga rebellion. During the same year he was compelled to sanction the Formosan expedition as a means of relieving the explosive domestic situation created by samurai unrest. This adventure abroad caused friction between China and Japan and ultimately Ōkubo was sent to China where he played a decisive role in the settlement of the Formosan question. Many of his countrymen, however, were dissatisfied with the settlement, and as a result increasing criticism was leveled against him. Again in 1877 he was forced to contend with rebellion when the samurai of his own *han* of Satsuma rose up in arms against his government. Directing the affairs of state from Ōsaka, Ōkubo once more took an active part in crushing the Satsuma rebellion led by his onetime friend and colleague, Saigō Takamori. For this action, Ōkubo was branded traitor to the *han*, and it won for him added enemies among the samurai class in general. The authoritarian methods he freely utilized to attain his objectives eventually led to his assassination in 1878, ironically at the hands of samurai, of whose class he himself was a member.

In dealing with human greatness, two distinct types may be discerned. There is the herculean architect, the person whose drive is of such force that he hurls the world into a new orbit, whose achievements are plainly seen but who is often overshadowed by his accomplishments. He is the doer. The second is the man who deals with the intellect of man, the thinker. Ōkubo clearly falls into the former category. It is hoped that this study will establish the validity of the thesis that the type of personality epitomized by Ōkubo was a sine qua non in the effectuation of the Restoration of 1868 and the unification of Japan under the new Meiji government.

While tracing the direction of the social, political, and economic changes that took place during Ōkubo's time—changes as profound and far-reaching as any in Japanese history—this study will focus on several important aspects of Ōkubo's historical influence. Was he the chief architect of modern Japan, the central pillar of the early Meiji administration? What was his influence upon Japan's foreign and domestic policies during this period? What is his relative position in world history? Can Ōkubo be compared with men who set the world afire as the result of a fever of the soul, like the great religious leaders of history, or was he rather the kind of man whose impulse was reasoned conviction? Even more significant than these questions is the one posed by contemporary scholars of the Restoration period such as Tōyama Shigeki and Hattori Shisō: Was Ōkubu (with his colleagues in the Meiji government) the architect of Japanese "absolutism"? Was he basically sympathetic to despotism, or were circumstances largely responsible for the absolute government with which his name is associated? Also, what was the nature of the leadership and alliances of the Restoration movement? Was it accomplished by lower samurai without outside aid, as many traditional historians have contended, or were they supported by such classes as the urban industrial and commercial groups and/or the peasantry? What were the true motives of the Restoration leaders? Such questions will be touched upon in this work although space limitation will not permit treatment in depth.

It is my belief that as the centennial year of the Meiji Restoration approaches, there is a definite need to "resurrect" some of the outstanding figures of the Restoration and Meiji periods and to reassess their roles in Japanese history.[6] A great American statesman, Thomas Jefferson, said: "History, by apprizing [men] of the past, will enable them to judge of the future; it will avail them of the experience of other times and other nations; it will qualify them as judges of the actions and designs of men; it will enable them to know ambition under every disguise it may assume; and knowing it, to defeat its view." [7] Almost a century ago Japan's policy, shaped by such men as Ōkubo, successfully established a foundation upon which Japan modernized and militarily strengthened herself sufficiently to prevent dismantling by foreign powers. This policy, although a wise one at the time, ultimately made for Japanese aggression and finally for Japan's defeat in 1945. As the nation rebuilds itself once more, it is a worthwhile task to compare those leaders who established the fundamental policy for Japan at the beginning of its first century as a modern state with the country's present leaders and ideology, thus to make a more intelligent prognosis for Japan's orientation in its second century as a modern nation.

Spirit and Structure of Tokugawa Japan

Ōkubo Toshimichi spent his early years in a rigid, feudalistic society that was arbitrarily molded to serve the purpose of the Tokugawa family. It was a period when political, social, and economic tremors were already causing definite cracks in the once granitic foundation stones of the Bakufu. Ōkubo's life, much of which was spent actively driving penetrating wedges into these cracks, culminating in the complete destruction of the Tokugawa edifice, cannot be fully understood without preliminary knowledge of the political and social environment in which he was placed and by which he was nurtured.

Japanese society in the second quarter of the nineteenth century was an anomoly. For over two centuries prior to the arrival of Commodore Perry's "Black Ships" in Edo Bay in 1853, the Japanese lived in an isolated world of their own, successfully preventing any large-scale impingement of foreign influences upon themselves and preserving a feudal system the counterparts of which had long since been outmoded and abolished in most European countries. Japan had no ruling sovereign, no parliament, no national military forces; neither did she have large-scale industries, complex commercial enterprises, nor widespread communication systems. These were not to come until after the Meiji Restoration in 1868.

Basis of Tokugawa Power

The Tokugawa Bakufu, the de facto military government devised by Tokugawa Ieyasu in 1603, developed gradually over a period of two and a half centuries. Feudalistic to the extent that it sanctioned the existence of nearly three hundred semiautonomous *han*, each under a feudal baron, the Bakufu was essentially a highly centralized form of government. At the height of its power it could expect complete compliance with its orders; the feudal lords realized that power resided in the Bakufu. To compensate for their absolute submission to the Edo regime the feudal lords were allowed relative freedom in ruling their domains. The long existence of the Bakufu attests to the thoroughness with which its founder built his system of government.

Once having gained control of Japan and established the Bakufu, Tokugawa Ieyasu and his successors oriented their policy toward strengthening Bakufu power at the expense not only of the other feudal lords, but also of the imperial family. The ruling Tokugawa family was intent upon benefiting itself, not the country. The *shōgun* therefore viewed with suspicion every *han*, and even the branch families of the Tokugawa, considering them potential enemies.

Occupying a position at the apex of the feudal pyramid, the Tokugawa *shōgun* exercised authority over several categories of vassals: the *daimyō* (*fudai daimyō* and *tozama daimyō*),[8] whose annual revenue exceeded 10,000 *koku* of rice; [9] below the *fudai daimyō* the *hatamoto*, the direct retainers of the *shōgun* receiving less than 10,000 *koku*; [10] and subordinate to the *hatamoto* a class of samurai called *gokenin*.[11] The *shōgun* thus had available the combined military force of his direct retainers as well as that of the various *daimyō* who owed fealty to the Bakufu.

The Bakufu was economically powerful during its early phase, with an annual revenue of some four million *koku* of rice from its own holdings. Its other sources of income were the annual and seasonal tributes of gold presented by its vassals, which augmented the store of precious metals from the Tokugawa mines in Sado, Satsuma, Izu, Buzen, Suruga, and Tajima. Between 1624 and 1631 these mines produced 48,000 *ryō* of gold.[12] Significantly, for the first century or more of its existence the wealth of the Tokugawa Bakufu was so enormous that it was unnecessary to impose taxes upon the *daimyō*, a situation which tended to keep dissatisfaction among them at a minimum.

The wealthy house of Tokugawa had a half-dozen related families which have figured prominently in Japanese history. These were the *daimyō* of Owari (Nagoya), Kii (Wakayama), and Hitachi (Mito), collectively designated the *Sanke*, or the Three Houses, from which was chosen the successor of a *shōgun* in the event that he died without a male heir. The Tayasu, Hitotsubashi, and Shimizu branches of the Tokugawa family comprised the *Sankyō*, or the Three Branch Families, none of which possessed a provincial castle, each instead living in Edo with its provincial domain in the care of managers.

Administrative Machinery

The administrative machinery of the Bakufu was specifically designed to give the Tokugawa absolute control over the entire land, regulating the life of every individual from the emperor at the top to the lowest commoner at the bottom of Japanese society. The *shōgun*'s position was preëminent although he was not always the most powerful figure in the Bakufu. During times of emergency a *tairō*, or great elder, was appointed first minister and given unusual power in the direction of foreign and domestic affairs. His decision was usually final. The Council of State, normally composed of five *rōjū*, or elders,[13] dealt with matters pertaining to the court, *kuge* (court nobles), and the various *daimyō*. The Junior Council, composed of from three to nine *wakadoshiyori*, or junior elders, exercised control over the *hatamoto* and the samurai.[14] To these councils were attached agents referred to as *metsuke* to act as the eyes and ears of the Bakufu.[15]

Subordinate to the councils were various administrative, executive, and judicial officers called *bugyō*, or commissioners. For example, the *machi bugyō*, or commissioners of cities, appointed to municipal areas such as Edo, Kyōto, Ōsaka, and Shumpu (Shizuoka), were powerful Bakufu functionaries with administrative and judicial authority. The similarly powerful *kanjō bugyō*, or commissioners of finance, numbering from two to four, handled financial matters and exercised supervision over the governors of the *shōgun*'s domain. During most of the Tokugawa period, when Japan was isolated from the rest of the world, there was no need for a special office dealing with foreign affairs, but as pressure from the outside began to mount the Bakufu saw the wisdom of appointing *gaikoku bugyō*, or commissioners of foreign affairs.[16] This committee system of government is an interesting aspect of the Tokugawa administrative system. The commissioners, numbering from two to four depending on the office, performed their duties in rotation, each serving a month at a time. With several officers occupying each office there was less likelihood of any one man's monopolizing authority, but the disadvantage in this arrangement lay in the fact that it was conducive to the passing of responsibility from one functionary to another.[17]

The Tokugawa administrative system included other influential offices, such as the *sobayōnin*, or personal secretaries of the *shōgun*, and the *sōjaban*, or supervisors of ceremony and etiquette.[18] The former served as the medium of communication between the *shōgun* and the members of the Council of State while the latter had the task of arranging for appointments with the *shōgun*. The *sobayōnin* often wielded influence as great as the eunuchs of the Byzantine Empire.[19]

Other significant offices of the time were the *jōdai*, or governors, of the castles of Nijō (the *shōgun*'s Kyōto headquarters), Ōsaka, and Shumpu. Another high office established early in the Tokugawa period was the Kyōto *shoshidai*, the personal representative of the *shōgun* at Kyōto. He was to exercise surveillance over the emperor and the court nobles as well as to judge lawsuits.

Laws Governing the Imperial Household

As a means of preserving the interests of the Tokugawa overlords, one of the early measures the Bakufu initiated was the strict regulation of the functions and behavior of the emperor and the court families in Kyōto. Outwardly, Tokugawa Ieyasu displayed reverence for the emperor; he rebuilt the palace in Kyōto and increased the revenues of the imperial household.[20] In actuality, however, his intention was to control the court. To this end, in 1613 the Bakufu promulgated the *kuge hatto*, or laws governing the conduct of the court, an unprecedented move inasmuch as no other military government in Japanese history had ever attempted to regulate the internal affairs of the imperial household.[21] The law of 1613 and subsequently revised codes stipulated among other things that the emperor and his courtiers must refrain from pursuing studies related to politics and that no appointments and dismissals of high court officials could be made without Bakufu sanction.[22] Then, to add insult to injury, the emperor was placed under surveillance by the *shōgun*'s representative in Kyoto—whose headquarters at Nijō castle were fully garrisoned; this was done nominally to protect the emperor but actually to overawe the court.[23] To make guardianship certain, one of the imperial princes was forced to live in Edo as a hostage for the imperial family. In this manner the prerogatives of the emperor were usurped by the Tokugawa family and the throne utilized to serve the purpose of the Edo government. Many of the thoughts and much of the effort of Restoration figures, such as Ōkubo Toshimichi, were eventually to be centered upon destruction of the power of the Tokugawa usurpers.

In comparison with the court, the feudal lords enjoyed great freedom; they were allowed a full measure of autonomy in the administration of their domains. They had their own administrative machinery modeled after that of the Tokugawa, they raised their own revenue, maintained their own military establishments, and were free to exercise their own judgment in matters pertaining to moral teaching. Among the wealthy and influential *daimyō* were Maeda of Kaga, with an annual revenue of one million *koku,* closely followed by Shimazu of Satsuma, Date of Sendai, and Mōri of *Chōshū.* Powerful and progressive *han,* such as Satsuma and Chōshū, together with their leading retainers—Ōkubo Toshimichi, Kido Kōin, and others—were to figure prominently in the Meiji Restoration drama.

Safeguards against the Daimyō

The Bakufu, being aware of the capabilities of these powerful *han,* did not neglect to take appropriate measures to prevent possible hostile actions of the *daimyō* class. To lessen the danger of surprise flank or rear attacks against the Tokugawa capital of Edo, Tokugawa Ieyasu reallocated the fiefs of the less trustworthy *tozama daimyō,* assigning them estates in areas of minimum strategic importance from the standpoint of Bakufu security. Wherever possible the domains of the more trustworthy *fudai daimyō* were interspersed between those of the *tozama daimyō.*[24] Furthermore, the Bakufu maintained *kammon,* or barriers, at various locations along the land routes to the capital, the Edo authorities being especially careful to guard against the "outward flow of women and the inward flow of guns." The assumption was that a dissident vassal planning a revolt would most likely try to slip his hostages out and weapons into the Tokugawa territory.[25] To render the *daimyō* less likely to raise the standard of revolt, the Bakufu encouraged matrimonial alliances between members of the Tokugawa family and the great feudal lords, a measure which in time succeeded in bringing practically all the *tozama daimyō* into a marriage alliance with the Tokugawa family. To weaken the economic power of the *daimyō,* the Edo government forced them to contribute men, material, and money to public works projects of various kinds. The effectiveness of this measure may be inferred from the fact that some of the *daimyō,* like Hosokawa, drained of their resources, were forced to ask the Bakufu for loans to meet their public works obligations.[26] To limit the sea power of the feudatories, the Bakufu in 1609 ordered all ships of war in excess of 500-*koku* capacity (one *koku* = one-tenth of a ton) to be destroyed.

Laws Governing the Military Household

As a further step in preserving peace and order among the feudal domains, the Tokugawa government issued regulations controlling the conduct of the *buke,* or military families. The *buke hatto,* or laws governing the military household, promulgated in 1615, formed the model for all subsequent laws relating to the military houses. They ordered the *daimyō* class to pursue the arts of war and peace; forbade any but legal residents of a fief to reside therein; prohibited the construction of any new castles and the repair of existing strongholds without Tokugawa sanction; disallowed unauthorized marriages; and frowned upon the appointment or dismissal of high *han* officials without previous Bakufu consent.[27]

Sankin Kōtai *System*

The *buke hatto* issued in 1635 instituted the *sankin kōtai* system, or system of alternate attendance, under which each *daimyō* was compelled to maintain a residence in Edo for his wife and children, who served as hostages, while he himself usually alternated his term of residence every other year, remaining one year at the capital and one year in his fief. When in Edo he was obliged to perform various administrative duties for the Bakufu. When living on his domain he could not leave the confines of his fief.[28]

Not only did the *sankin kōtai* system effect regimentation and centralization of authority, but it also had economic ramifications. As the Bakufu intended, the *daimyō*'s finances ultimately were adversely affected since he was forced to maintain two residences and to defray the entire expense of traveling between his fief and Edo. The system was obviously inequitable; it placed a greater financial burden on those living at a distance from the Tokugawa capital. The inequity was not a Tokugawa oversight; the Bakufu was fully aware that the fiefs of the more loyal *fudai daimyō* were located relatively near Edo while those of the great *tozama daimyō* were often a great distance away. For example, Ōkubo's feudal lord, Shimazu of Satsuma, whose fief was located at the extreme southern tip of Kyūshū, was forced to travel 411 *ri* (one *ri* = 2.4403 miles) by land and sea between Kagoshima and Edo.

The *sankin kōtai* system also benefited the country's economy by stimulating the development of land and sea communications. This in turn facilitated the fusion of the cultures of such cities as Edo and Kyōto with those of the outlying provinces, and the intermixing of people in these cities served to increase the spirit of unity among the Japanese, a significant factor in the later nationalization of Japan.[29]

Confiscation of Fiefs

A final means by which the Bakufu exercised control over the *daimyō* was through its authority to reduce or confiscate fiefs in the event that (1) a feudal lord died leaving an heir who was a minor, or leaving no recognized successor, or (2) he violated the laws of the Bakufu. That the Bakufu exercised its prerogative is evident; during the first sixteen years of the seventeenth century the Tokugawa reduced or confiscated the fiefs of ten military families, each of whose total yearly revenue amounted to 640,000 *koku,* because they had failed to meet the conditions with respect to the heir. Between 1615 and 1647 forty-eight families with yearly revenues totaling 3,250,000 *koku* had their domains confiscated or reduced for the same reason. Violations of Tokugawa law among those in the latter group also included such transgressions as making unauthorized repairs on castles, failing to adhere strictly to the *sankin kōtai* law, and hiding criminals on the fief.[30]

Under this peculiar and repressive administrative system the Tokugawa Bakufu established in Japan what Japanese historians consider an almost completely centralized feudal system.[31]

Isolation of Japan

The most noteworthy aspect of the Bakufu's foreign policy is that it ultimately called for the exclusion of nearly all foreigners from Japan and the nearly total isolation of the country for over two hundred years from the rest of the civilized world. It is generally conceded that the motivating factor behind the Tokugawa decision to clear the country of foreign traders and missionaries in the third decade of the seventeenth century was the desire to steer clear of the danger of political control by Europeans, either through trade or through machinations of Catholic missionaries.

The isolation policy that the Bakufu successfully imposed and maintained for over two centuries was bound to have various significant effects on Japan, both good and bad. Politically the closure of the country aided in maintaining tranquillity. Japan was spared the experience of having an invading army follow the footsteps of the missionary vanguards. On the other hand, it has been argued that Japan's withdrawal into her shell was disadvantageous to her expansion in that it caused the various Japanese settlements in such places as the Philippines, Siam, and Java to wither and die when the channel to the source of new settlers was obstructed. Expansionists have contended that, had emigration to these areas continued after the seventeenth century, Japan most likely would have established a firm foundation for colonies much earlier than it did. But whether Japan, lacking military and economic strength, was in a position to maintain extensive colonies is debatable; without sufficient economic and political basis colonies can have only a debilitating effect on the mother country.[32]

Economically the isolation policy aided Japan by checking the outflow of precious metals, a phenomenon related to Japan's unfavorable balance of trade. Arai Hakuseki estimated that the amount of gold exported from Japan during the sixty-one years after 1648 amounted to over two million *ryō*, in contrast to double this amount exported during the forty-seven years prior to 1648.[33] The Bakufu's radical foreign policy, furthermore, served to protect home industries which, during the Edo period, developed without foreign competition.

Lastly, isolation benefited Japan culturally; the long period of peace gave people time to devote to cultural pursuits. This, combined with government encouragement of cultural attainments, set the stage for the dramatic development of scholarship, thought, art, and manners that were peculiarly Japanese in character. As an era of assimilation of the cultures of the East, the Edo period is comparable to the Fujiwara epoch, when art flowered and attained its apogee of development, as well as to the Kamakura period, when religion enjoyed its halcyon days. It was out of this cultural milieu that the leaders of the Restoration emerged.

The adverse effects of the Tokugawa policy were not so much in the decrease in trade, the cessation of the inflow of cultural influences from abroad, or the decline of Japanese settlements in the south, as in the stagnation and debilitation of the Bakufu and the impoverishment of the peasantry, the largest of the several rigidly stratified classes in Japanese feudal society.[34]

Social Stratification

Throughout the long period of enforced isolation the Tokugawa rulers were able to maintain a society frozen in a rigid hierarchical mold. In time, however, economic factors were responsible for the thawing process that led to the gradual blurring of class lines, especially between the samurai and the merchant classes.

At the apex of the social pyramid were the two orders of the aristocracy, the court nobles who had prestige but no political power, and the feudal lords who constituted the governing class. Although the Bakufu forbade direct communication between the *daimyō* and the court, some intercourse was carried on between these groups. In fact, through the collusion of the *kuge* and the more powerful western *daimyō* and their subordinates, the groundwork was laid for the successful coup d'etat of 1868 which culminated in the imperial Restoration.

Below the *kuge* and higher samurai who made up the aristocracy was a middle class of samurai, a proud, privileged caste of military men whose symbol of position in society was a pair of swords carried at their sides.[35] During the earlier period of decentralized feudalism most samurai received land from their lords and cultivated their fields when not fighting for their masters. Later, however, with the advent of firearms and the need for strong castle defenses, these fighting men were assembled in castle-towns and the raising of crops was left to the peasantry.[36]

The samurai class furnished the personnel of the *han* governments. But even within this military caste there was a hierarchical order, and as a consequence only the senior vassals, the *karō*, were allowed to fill the higher positions within the feudatories.[37] In many instances, however, a young samurai of exceptional ability and character was promoted and attained an influential status in the *han* officialdom, attesting to the fact that in time personal merit often served as a key to open doors to vertical mobility within the class. Ōkubo, Saigō, and other relatively low-class samurai of the Restoration period used this key.

By the eve of the Restoration such able, low-ranking samurai officials of the *han* were the actual powers behind their respective *daimyō*. Most of the feudal lords and their hereditary councilors, descendants of active warriors and statesmen of Ieyasu's time, had been reduced to positions of nonentities, weakened politically and physically as a result of generations of secluded, pampered, and intemperate living. In contrast, as the actual administrators of districts and villages within their feudatories, the lower samurai functionaries gained invaluable insight into the intricacies of *han* administration as well as experience for leadership which made them indispensable to the feudal lord. The samurai's ability to fight and to command men was the primary factor that brought them eventually to positions of authority. They were the educated men of Tokugawa society; the pursuit of education as well as the military arts was decreed by the Bakufu.

Samurai Training

The Tokugawa policy of encouraging education, both military and academic, was responsible for the great number of schools in Japan at the end of the Edo period. One source indicates that there were about sixteen thousand educational institutions of various types.[38] There is undoubtedly a correlation between the plethora of educational institutions in this period and the amazing number of young and highly intellectual samurai leaders who came to the forefront during the Restoration era. Ōkubo Toshimichi, like others of his class, was nurtured in the educational environment of the times.

Military education for the samurai class included *kendō*, or fencing; the manipulation of the *yari*, or spear, and the bow and arrow; and horsemanship. During the Edo period only the lowest-ranking samurai were trained in the use of the muzzle-loader; the samurai elite did not condescend to handle guns. *Jūdō*, called *jūjutsu* in the Edo period, was also considered a mean art. Although Ōkubo was exposed to these arts there is no evidence that he was trained to use the muzzle-loader. The *daimyō* of each *han* maintained exercise halls, called *dōjō*, for the military arts.[39]

Besides the military training halls, there were institutions for the education of samurai youth in the arts of peace, maintained by both the Bakufu and the *daimyō* of the various *han*. The *han* schools, numbering close to 250 at the close of the Tokugawa period, were often originally private schools specializing in Chinese learning called *kangaku juku* to which the *daimyō* gave official recognition and support. Once these institutions became *han*-supported they were referred to as *gakkō* or *gakkan*, both terms meaning either academy or school.[40] These institutions were primarily for the education of the sons of samurai, who attended tuition-free, although commoners were sometimes admitted to a few of them.

The Bakufu encouraged the *han* schools so long as they conducted themselves in accordance with Tokugawa principles.[41]

The learning the Bakufu officially promoted was Chinese, and as a result the samurai were for the most part well read in the Chinese classics, Chinese history, and Chinese poetry. History was considered an important subject because, in accordance with the Chinese concept of history, "it illuminated the way through truth." Many of the samurai scholars studied Chinese history as an aid to the study of the philosophies of Confucius and Mencius.[42] The Confucian philosophy, in fact, achieved a position of an established religion in the early Tokugawa period; the Bakufu realized that Confucianism's stress on such concepts as peace, order, loyalty, filial piety, and continence, as well as its emphasis upon adherence to the social code of etiquette and music, would add support to the feudal structure.[43] Confucianism, in short, was a useful ideological tool with which the Bakufu could adjust the thinking of the people to harmonize with its own political and social philosophy.

Orthodox Confucianism, however, did not remain a permanent institution. A reaction against things Chinese caused its decline and served to revive an interest in the history, literature, and religion indigenous to Japan. Under the leadership of the *wagakusha*, or national scholars, of which Yamazaki Anzai is representative, a program of study of the ancient Japanese literature and chronicles was inaugurated, the significant consequence of which was the revival of Shintōism, the cult over which the imperial family presided. The findings of the anti-Chinese school of scholars revealed that the *shōgun* was exercising undue authority—authority which rightfully belonged to the emperor. In the 1860's the anti-Bakufu elements in Japan were thus furnished a strong political weapon; the findings of the national scholars legitimatized the movement to overthrow the Bakufu and restore the emperor.

Socioeconomic Changes

The penetration of money economy in Japan gradually forced the samurai, who had long enjoyed a monopoly of social and political power, to surrender to the wealthy *chōnin*, or merchant class.[44] As the barter system was supplanted by money,[45] the fortune of the despised mercantile class improved in proportion.[46] Its commercial ventures—real estate, small industries, and fishery—produced increasing profits. In time the *daimyō* and samurai classes, receiving their incomes in rice, found it necessary to convert rice into money in order to keep up with the luxurious urban life to which they had become accustomed during the centuries of peace. Many of them were compelled to borrow money at usurious rates from these merchants.[47]

The social repercussions of the rise of the merchant-capitalist class were significant. Impoverished warriors in time swallowed their pride and entered the ranks of the merchant class either through marriage or adoption, and wealthier merchants were even adopted into samurai families.[48] Moreover, as rice stipends were reduced by financially embarrassed *daimyō*, many of their retainers severed their ties of allegiance and became *rōnin*, or masterless samurai.[49] The more ambitious among them migrated to the cities where they studied Western languages and science while the majority, resentful of being placed under constant surveillance by Bakufu agents, became enemies of the Tokugawa and ardent supporters of the imperial cause.[50]

Plight of the Peasants

The peasants, occupying a position below the samurai in the social scale, were, like their superiors, confronted by hardship. Comprising between 80 and 90 per cent of the population, the peasants bore the burden of heavy taxation; although the annual tribute was established by custom, they were often forced to present whatever amount the lord deemed necessary. Over and above the customary annual tribute paid in grain, the peasants were obligated to pay miscellaneous taxes called *komononari*, mostly in currency. These were levied on the revenues drawn from forests, ponds, rivers, seas, and so forth. The farmers, moreover, were expected to perform corvée labor which in time was commuted to money or rice payments. They were greatly restricted in their actions; they could not move freely from one place to another, change their occupations, plant what they wished, nor dispose of land as they saw fit.[51] The increasing financial difficulties of the *daimyō* class also had their effects upon the peasantry. In the attempt to improve their economic situation, the *daimyō* tended to place greater exactions upon the farming class in the form of higher taxes.[52] In the meantime, the wealthy farmer-merchants and money-lenders progressively acquired consolidated land which resulted in the decrease of acreage available to the peasants. In some areas the decrease in the size of plots reached the point where it became unprofitable to work, forcing many peasants to part with their land and join the ranks of the poverty stricken. To make matters worse, crop failures and resultant famine took an unusually heavy toll of lives during the Tokugawa period.[53]

The intolerable economic condition in the rural districts caused the peasants to react both negatively and positively. Negatively the peasants resorted to *mabiki*, or "thinning" of the rural population through birth control (abortion and infanticide). Many peasants, moreover, reacted to their plight by moving out of their native villages to seek a livelihood elsewhere.[54] Both practices represented passive peasant revolt against authority inasmuch as birth control and fleeing one's native village were specifically forbidden by Bakufu law.

In the positive category, peasant reaction took a more aggressive form, usually open revolt. Over six hundred uprisings occurred during the two hundred years of the Tokugawa period, most of them provoked by excessive taxation. *Gōso*, or appeal to arms, was the most prevalent form of these revolts, in which the rebels banded together, fought the samurai, and outraged the village officials and the wealthy in order to force compliance to peasant demands.[55]

Decline of the Bakufu

During the nineteenth century, one of the most serious domestic problems with which the Tokugawa regime was confronted was that of agriculture. The poor harvests of 1832-1833, coupled with the debasement of the coinage, raised the price of rice and resulted in hardship for all. People died of starvation in Edo, and in 1837 over a thousand dead were left unburied in the city of Nagoya.[56] In that year the samurai joined the commoners of Ōsaka in violent protest against the high cost of living, a situation they attributed to Tokugawa maladministration. Bakufu impotence resulted in general lawlessness; highwaymen harassed travelers without fear of being apprehended.[57]

The Bakufu's weakness bred contempt, and consequently an increasing number of people of all classes denounced the Edo regime's policy of exclusion, restriction of foreign studies, excessive taxation, and regimentation of the people of all classes. The merchants spoke out against trade restrictions, and the *tozama daimyō* of Satsuma, Chōshū, Tosa, and Hizen, never completely loyal to the *shōgun*, chafed under measures designed to keep them in submission to the Tokugawa. Bands of distressed *rōnin* roamed the countryside, inciting the distraught peasantry and engaging in subversive activities against the Bakufu. Together with the lower samurai, many of whom were by this time highly placed officials of the western *han* with ambitions to play more important roles on the political stage, they were to become the most active elements in the Restoration movement.[58]

Menaced by these formidable domestic enemies, who were rallying around the more powerful *tozama daimyō*, and faced with the bleak prospect of imminent bankruptcy, the Bakufu could make only futile attempts to maintain a semblance of control. In the end, failure to cope successfully with the foreign invasion exposed the absolute incompetency of the Tokugawa regime; within a short time it was to be shorn of its authority.

Foreign Pressures

Feudal Japan, after more than two centuries of isolation, was once more, toward the end of the eighteenth century, forced to concern itself with foreign problems as Russia moved down into Sakhalin, thereby posing a threat to Yezo (Hokkaidō). Thereafter other foreign powers pounded on the closed doors of Japan: England, France, and the United States.

To the Japanese rulers and intellectuals the tide of Western imperialism seemed to reach awesome proportions with the appearance of Commodore Matthew Calbraith Perry's men-of-war in the harbor of Uraga on July 18, 1853. His instructions were to obtain safeguards for the natural rights of shipwrecked seamen, permission for American vessels to obtain supplies, food, and fuel at one or more Japanese ports, and a port of entry for commercial vessels.[59] Judging from Perry's instructions and the letter he delivered to the Japanese emperor from President Fillmore,[60] it seemed that the mission was motivated only by a desire for friendship and commerce with Japan. But both Fillmore and Perry were children of their times and, as such, believed in manifest destiny and were exponents of a greater America.[61]

Division over Foreign Policy

With this threat from without, the question of foreign policy became the paramount issue in Japanese politics by the beginning of the second half of the nineteenth century. Although unanimity was achieved concerning the need for bolstering defenses to meet the foreign threats, Japan's leaders were divided on other matters of foreign policy. The two prevailing schools of thought were the *kaikoku,* which advocated opening the country to foreigners, and the *jōi,* which advised expelling them.[62] Pressured by both factions, the Bakufu vacillated, finally deciding to follow the former policy and open the country to foreign trade, a decision owing, in no small measure, to the persuasive tactics of Townsend Harris.[63] In 1858, strong-willed Ii Naosuke, the Bakufu's first minister, without imperial sanction concluded comprehensive treaties of amity and commerce with the United States, Great Britain, Holland, Russia, and France.[64] These treaties, which were of no specified duration, provided for extraterritoriality and a fixed customs tariff at a low rate. Their obvious inequity created resentment among the Japanese and subsequently led to outbreaks of antiforeign sentiment.[65]

The imperial court at Kyōto, on the other hand, unlike the Bakufu, which, in the face of foreign threats, had been forced to take a realistic approach in its international dealings, maintained an unrealistic position by adhering to the *jōi* policy of expulsion. Ii's arbitrary decision caused extreme consternation among the loyalists who supported the imperial cause. Up to this point neither the *jōi* nor the *kaikoku* forces had any real intention of overthrowing the Edo government, but during and after 1858 the *jōi,* as well as a segment of the *kaikoku* thinkers who objected to the manner and implications of the Bakufu surrender to the foreigners, began to ally themselves with parties whose interests were primarily political. Thereafter the term *kaikoku* was to signify support of the Bakufu and its policies and *jōi* was to symbolize opposition to the Tokugawa government.[66] The cry of *sonnō jōi,* or "revere the emperor and expel the barbarians," was increasingly heard as the loyalist movement to institute political change got under way.

Within a decade after 1858 the various forces within and without Tokugawa Japan combined to topple the Bakufu. In November, 1867, Tokugawa Keiki, the last of the *shōgun,* relinquished both his administrative authority and the hereditary military title of generalissimo.[67] On January 3, 1868, the court issued a proclamation restoring imperial rule, and on the following day it accepted Keiki's resignation, thus bringing to a close a fascinating epoch of Tokugawa domination—an age that molded Ōkubo and the other Restoration leaders and one they helped to terminate.

II
Ōkubo's Formative Years

Ōkubo Toshimichi [1] was born on September 26, 1830, in Kajiyamachi, a section of the castle-town of Kagoshima in Kyūshū, comprising about eighty samurai households clustered together along the east bank of the Kōzuki River which flowed through the town.[2] Kajiyamachi not only produced two members of the Meiji triumvirate, Ōkubo Toshimichi and Saigō Takamori, but also other distinguished civil and military leaders of modern Japan. There were Murata Shimpachi, a prominent loyalist, and several outstanding military figures who participated in the Russo-Japanese War of 1904-1905—Field Marshal Ōyama Iwao, supreme commander of the Japanese forces in Manchuria; Admiral Tōgō Heihachirō, commander of the combined Japanese fleet; and General Kuroki Tamesada, commander of the First Army in Manchuria.[3]

Historians of the Meiji period have been struck by the fact that it was the remote Satsuma region, which seemingly offered poor ground for the nourishment of modern ideas, that gave mid-nineteenth century Japan her most outstanding leaders. Paradoxically, it was the Satsuma men who assumed the leading role in the movement for nationalism, centralization, and modernization, despite the fact that geographically Satsuma was far removed from the seat of the central government at Edo and the hubs of culture of Edo and Kyōto. The enigma is the more striking inasmuch as these Satsuma leaders who were to guide the Restoration movement came from one of the most feudalistic *han* in Japan. The social, geographic, and political conditions of this *han* ordinarily would have been more conducive to the nurturing of political atomization than to centralization.[4]

Satsuma

Kyūshū as a whole, and particularly the southern part of this island where Satsuma *han* was located, has always occupied a peculiar position in Japanese history. Situated between latitudes thirty and thirty-four north (latitude thirty-three north approximately bisects Los Angeles), Kyūshū is blessed by good climate, soil, and situation, facing as it does toward China and Formosa. Also, both by means of commerce and through the medium of the Christian missionaries, Kyūshū was brought into contact with the Occident long before the rest of the country. These early advantages left tangible results. Kyūshū's civilization was developed earlier, its customs bore the stamp of a marked individuality, its *han* were better organized, and their chiefs possessed greater enterprise than those of any other *han* of Japan.[5] The three *kuni*, or provinces, of southern Kyūshū, namely Satsuma, Ōsumi, and Hyūga, formed a region of special significance throughout Japanese history: they were, successively, the original home of the imperial house; the habitat of the early invaders from the south, the Kumaso; and the location of the largest fief held for the longest time in feudal Japan by a line of powerful lords, the Shimazu.[6]

The Satsuma *han*, held by the Shimazu family, was among the last of the *han* to accept the supremacy of the imperial government after the Restoration, and J. H. Gubbins, writing in the year 1879, rightly noted that "until the year before last she [Satsuma] was an *imperium in imperio*." [7] The men of the *han* were not only famed for their military prowess [8] but were also hardy navigators, many of whom were numbered among the corsairs who pillaged the maritime provinces of China and Korea in the fifteenth and sixteenth centuries.[9]

Shimazu Family

The illustrious Shimazu family of feudal lords, who controlled and molded their domain into one characterized by the intrepidity of its subjects, had as its progenitor Shimazu Tadahisa. Tadahisa was Minamoto Yoritomo's illegitimate son by a sister (a professed nun) of one Yoshikazu, Yoritomo's trusted captain.[10] In 1187 Minamoto Yoritomo, the first *shōgun* in

Japanese history, appointed Tadahisa concurrently *jitō*, or steward, over the greater part of the Fujiwara *shōen*, or manor, of Shimazu, and *shugo*, or military commissioner, of the three provinces of Satsuma, Ōsumi, and Hyūga, which comprised the *shōen*. Arriving in southern Kyūshū about 1196, Tadahisa took up residence for a time near the present city of Miyakonojō, after which he settled at Kimure in northwest Satsuma. Kimure remained the headquarters of the Shimazu for four generations until the family occupied Kagoshima in the third quarter of the fourteenth century. The Shimazu's rise to power had its beginning during the Mongolian war in the last quarter of the thirteenth century when they received the *shōgun*'s mandate to supervise the conduct of special military services that were required of their *gokenin*, or men of the lord's household, in the three provinces.[11] During the Sengoku period (1480-1570), a century of almost continuous feudal warfare which culminated in the unification of Japan at the beginning of the seventeenth century, the family was involved in a continuous struggle for ascendancy with the various territorial lords. Toward the end of the period, the field of military operations widened from the southern section of Kyūshū to the whole of that island; within the decade 1577-1587 the Shimazu lords conquered the greater part of six *kuni* to the north.[12] But their gains were far from permanent; with dramatic rapidity they were driven back into their own southern holdings by the new suzerain, Toyotomi Hideyoshi, the regent.[13] The Shimazu eventually surrendered to Hideyoshi and swore fealty to him. Hideyoshi, interestingly, displayed extraordinary generosity toward his defeated enemy. Dividing the conquered territory among the local chieftains and his own vassals, Hideyoshi gave to the Shimazu as new grants in fief the whole of Satsuma, nearly all of Ōsumi, and portions of Hyūga, specifically Sadowara and Murakata *kōri*.[14] Shimazu Yoshihiro thereafter rendered service to Hideyoshi during his Korean expeditions of 1592-1593 and 1597-1598 by leading Satsuma contingents of ten thousand and fifteen thousand respectively.[15]

After the death of Hideyoshi in 1598 most feudal lords of Japan allied themselves with either the party supporting his son, Hideyori, or the Tokugawa Ieyasu faction. The rivals met in decisive battle at Sekigahara in October, 1600. Although Shimazu Yoshihiro fought against the victorious Ieyasu, the two came to an eventual understanding whereby Yoshihiro was recognized as the lord of his old domain, the revenue of which totaled 605,000 *koku*.[16]

From this time until the death of Ieyasu, the houses of Shimazu and Tokugawa remained friendly. In fact, Shimazu Iehisa received Ieyasu's permission to send a punitive force of three thousand troops to the Lūchū (Ryūkyū) Islands whose capital, Naha, was captured in 1609 and the king seized and brought as a prisoner of war to Japan. The Lūchū Islands thenceforth came under Satsuma domination, and the *han*'s revenue was thereby increased by 123,700 *koku*. The acquisition made it possible for Japan to establish indirect commercial relations with China through the Lūchū Islands, an arrangement that mainly benefited the Shimazu.[17]

Satsuma was not noted for its culture. There was little luxury, refinement, or elegance in the life of the *han*. Its spirit was rather characterized by the robust energy of youth. The men lived a Spartan life. The women were subordinate to their men. The arts and industries, however, were not neglected. Satsuma porcelain, known the world over as *satsuma-yaki*, was exported throughout Japan and later the world. Nor was such a basic institution as education neglected.

Satsuma Education

Encouraged by Tokugawa policy and even more by the favorable attitude of the Shimazu lords who appreciated education's practicality, schools were early established under *han* auspices. Shigehide (1745-1831), the twenty-fifth in the Shimazu line of lords, was especially active as a patron of learning. Interested in Western science, he personally went to Nagasaki in 1771 to acquire knowledge from the Dutch. He returned inspired and impressed by Western progress and resolved to make Satsuma the "most enlightened *han* in Japan." [18] To this end he imported books from Holland while, at the same time, encouraging Chinese studies. His respect for scholars and learning manifested itself in tangible form with the projection in 1773 of the *han* training schools for samurai, the Embukan and the Zōshikan. Shigehide was also instrumental in establishing the Igakuin, a school for the advancement of medical knowledge, as well as the Meijikan, a school of astronomy. Moreover, as a result of his encouragement numerous district schools were built throughout the *han*.[19]

The Zōshikan in Kagoshima was situated in the southern part of the city and had a shrine to Confucius and an enclosure for military exercises. When the school was dedicated in August, 1773, with Confucian ceremonies, rules, posted in the hall, offered a guide to its educational philosophy.[20] First, the textbooks were to be the *Shishō*, the *Gokyō*, the *Shōgaku*, and the *Kinshiroku*. The *Shishō*, or the Four Books of the Confucian Classics, include the *Analects*, the sayings of Confucius as recorded by his disciples; the *Great Learning*, written after Confucius' death by Tseng-tzu; the *Doctrine of the Mean*, attributed to Confucius' great-grandson, Tsu-ssu; and the *Book of Mencius*, written in the third century B.C. by the disciples of Mencius, one of Confucius' successors. The *Gokyō*, or the Five Classics, include the *Book of Changes*, the *Book of History*, the *Book of Poetry*, the *Book of Rites*, and the *Spring and Autumn Annals*, a brief history of the state of Lu. These nine works are known as the Confucian Classics, and the ideas of ethics and of social morality contained therein exerted not only tremendous influence within the Satsuma *han*, but upon Japan as a whole, and contributed in no small measure to the establishment of a well-ordered society during most of the Tokugawa period.

The rules of the Zōshikan specified that the interpretation of the Chinese Classics was to be that of the Chinese sage, Teishu. The students were warned, furthermore, not to place their own interpretation against the accepted interpretation of the school. They might consult upon questions of difficulty but must yield to recognized explanation. They were told to be polite and diligent in study, avoiding frivolity. Ability, it was stressed, would be honored. Even the poor, if earnest, were promised admission to the school. Finally, the rules stated that respect should be paid to papers bearing the written characters, that is, books, and that these should be guarded against fire.[21]

Obviously, the Chinese influence was strong in Japanese education. This explains the similarity of many of the values held by the Japanese and Chinese. The strength of Chinese influence in Japanese education indicates, moreover, to what extent the Sinicization process had proceeded during the Tokugawa period under the aegis of the Bakufu and through the medium of the *kangakusha*, or Chinese scholars, who staffed the schools in the various *han*.

Shimazu Nariakira, the *daimyō* who governed Satsuma (1810-1858) during Ōkubo's formative years, maintained a keen interest in education. Nariakira was responsible for establishing the Rangaku Kōshūjo, a school for the study of the Dutch language and Western culture.[22] In 1854 he published new regulations urging the practice of virtue as taught in the

Classics. He is said to have personally visited the Zōshikan and called upon students to explain before him the meaning of the Confucian texts. To the most outstanding students he gave awards, and allotted four *koku* of rice annually to needy scholars. In March, 1856, he issued further instructions for the encouragement of the study of Dutch and arranged for the examination and support of students desiring to further their education in Edo, the seat of the Tokugawa military government. His educational aim was that each Satsuma youth be taught to master himself, rule his home wisely, preserve national peace, and trust the universal power. He considered education without morality no education at all, and believed that the teachings of Confucius supported the Shintō faith.[23] Nariakira was reflecting the thinking of many of the scholars of the time who were beginning to utilize Confucian ideas to support Shintōism. Earlier, Fujiwara Seiga (1561-1619), the first great exponent of Chu Hsi in Japan, said that although Shintō and Confucianism do not bear the same name, the truths they express are the same. Hayashi Razan (1583-1657) expressed the same thought when he said that Shintō is *ōdō*, or virtuous rule, and *ōdō* is Confucianism.[24]

The Japanese identified the Chinese virtue of filial piety with the Shintō virtue of loyalty. Writing in the ninth century, Sugawara Michizane said that loyalty and filial piety were the same; from the home where filial piety is upheld come the most loyal sons; therefore, the duty of a subject and that of a son is identical.[25] Nakae Tōju (1608-1648) expressed the same view, as did Ninomiya Sontoku (1787-1850).[26]

The sense of loyalty to the sovereign was intensified among the intellectuals of Japan during the eighteenth and nineteenth centuries, primarily as the result of the work of the Mito scholars. The *Dai Nihon Shi* (History of Japan), compiled under the direction of Tokugawa Mitsukuni, the *daimyō* of Mito, was merely intended to clarify the respective positions of the throne and the Tokugawa regime and thus establish the relationship between the two on national foundations. The Mito scholars, in delving into the Japanese past, succeeded, however, in establishing the historical fact that sovereignty rested upon the imperial house. The implications of this idea led to the development of the strong current of criticism against the existing political situation under the Tokugawa Bakufu.[27] The Mito school of thought exerted a powerful influence throughout Japan, arousing national consciousness and reverence for the emperor. The growing importance of *kinnō*, or loyalism, made necessary the attempt to use Confucian philosophy to support Shintōism. Nariakira's sentiments reveal that the spirit of Mito philosophy was felt strongly by those in Satsuma.

In Satsuma, education was looked upon essentially as a means of strengthening the power of the *han* through instilling in its subjects the spirit of loyalty to authority—a policy, significantly, later adopted by the Meiji leaders to enhance their own power and that of the national government. Consequently, the Confucian virtues of loyalty, intrepidity, self-respect, friendliness, self-sacrifice, chivalry, optimism, reverence, filial piety, respect for elders, gratitude, and propriety were constantly impressed upon the Satsuma lad. The Satsuma girl was expected to comport herself in a manner worthy of a daughter or wife of a warrior as well as to fulfill her duty of producing male issue to carry on the family line.[28]

Confucianism, as the chief guiding force for morality in Satsuma, was far more influential than Buddhism, whose prestige declined rapidly after Hideyoshi's campaign against the Shimazu; at that time Buddhist priests were suspected of spying for Hideyoshi.[29] Moreover, Christianity, which established hardy roots in central and western Kyūshū, failed to develop in Satsuma. Shimazu Takahisa (1514-1571) had requested the settlement of Jesuits on his fief, but this was not because he wished them to Christianize his domain. Economic motives were behind his request for missionaries, as he expected that trading ships would soon follow.[30] On September 29, 1549, Francis Xavier was given an audience with Takahisa, who granted him the right to preach the Christian laws to his subjects—an authorization confirmed by an edict issued a few days later.[31] Only 150, however, were baptized during Xavier's stay in Satsuma, and proselyting received a sudden check in 1550 when Takahisa issued another edict that, according to Charlevoix, the Jesuit historian, ordered the people to renounce on pain of death the cult of God in the domain.[32] Takahisa's successors relaxed the proscription, but Christianity on the whole continued to be discouraged.[33] The naïve samurai were constrained to worship in the temple dedicated to the ancestors of the Shimazu family.

Early in the Tokugawa period the Satsuma *han*, led by the Shimazu family, had crystallized into a distinctive entity, powerful and self-sufficient. The successive line of strong feudal lords ruled the domain with a firm hand, and through Spartan training they produced a hardy, courageous, and loyal group of followers. The fact that their soil was the original abode of the imperial family stimulated the increasing sense of loyalty of the Satsuma people not only to their own *han,* but to the emperor as well. Accordingly, Satsuma in time was to claim for itself the honor of being the birthplace of the *kinnō* spirit.[34] Its situation and circumstances, furthermore, enabled the *han* to savor the intellectual and material offerings of China during the very period when the rest of Japan was isolated from the world at large. Socially, the distinction between the native of Kagoshima and a northerner became clearly defined until it found expression in the saying that "a Satsuma man is first a Satsuma man and then a Japanese." [35] A proud breed, the Satsuma people could not forget the unfavorable events of the past. Twice defeated and humiliated by the northerners, history undoubtedly furnished the Satsuma *han* with justifiable reasons for displaying antagonism toward the Tokugawa regime in the nineteenth century.

Ōkubo Family

Ōkubo Toshimichi spent his formative years in this provincial environment. As the only son in a family of seven, he was reared in strict conformity with the traditions of the Satsuma samurai.[36] The family, though far from affluent, was of distinguished origin and was generally thought to have been descended from the noted Fujiwara house,[37] which came to Satsuma during the end of the sixteenth century and settled at Kawakami in the village of Ichiki. Later the family divided, and the branch to which Toshimichi belonged came to Kagoshima and established a home in the *hōgiri,* or district, of Kajiyamachi.[38]

Toshimichi's father, Ōkubo Jūemon,[39] was classified as a *koshōgumi,* or bodyguard, among the Shimazu retainers and received less than 150 *koku* of rice, an allowance which kept the family in straitened circumstances until he was given a minor position in the *han* government.[40] After he became a *tsuke yaku,* a minor official in the section dealing with Ryūkyūan affairs, the fortunes of the family improved.[41] Short of stature, robust, and light complexioned, Jūemon was a high-spirited man of unusual character. Though without much formal education, he made a serious study of the philosophy of Ōyōmei (Wang Yang-ming) and Zen Buddhism.[42] He was an egalitarian in a society where class cleavages were sharp, associating widely with samurai, merchant, and peasant, and dealing with them on an equal basis.[43] As a father he took a similarly tolerant attitude toward his children; he is said to have seldom scolded his son, despite the boy's propensity to prankishness, saying that a parent need not be anxious about a mischievous child, that only malevolence was intolerable.[44]

Toshimichi's father was a man of strong conviction and determination. As a loyalist and a member of the reform party in the *han*, Jūemon in 1849 participated in a movement to oust the reactionary advisers surrounding the *daimyō*, Shimazu Narioki, and intent upon naming Narioki's illegitimate son, Saburō (better known in history as Hisamitsu), as heir.[45] The progressives who opposed the move were just as determined to have Nariakira, the legitimate son of Narioki, succeed his father as soon as the latter decided to relinquish his authority. An attempt by the reform group to assassinate some of the conservatives was abortive and resulted in the capture and chastisement of many who were involved in this "family conflict" to which Japanese historians refer as Takasaki Kuzure. Takasaki Goroēmon, a scholar and chief instigator of the reform movement, and thirteen of his lieutenants were ordered to commit *hara kiri*. Jūemon and nine others, however, were more fortunate; they were exiled to an island, Okinoerabujima.[46]

As a child, Ōkubo Toshimichi was influenced greatly by his maternal grandfather, Minayoshi Hōtoku, a noted Satsuma physician. An unusually intelligent man, Hōtoku had studied for ten years at Nagasaki and Edo and was counted among the first intellectuals to gain a considerable knowledge of Western technology and science. Hence he became acutely aware of Japan's inadequacies, especially in maritime activities such as shipping, which Tokugawa decree had limited to the coastal trade. He contended that larger and more modern ships were necessary if the empire were to see future commercial progress. Subsequently, after studying Dutch books on marine architecture and navigation, Hōtoku constructed a miniature Western ship approximately six feet long and three feet wide. Using this as a model he later built a full-scale vessel, the "Iroha Maru," the first Western-type ship built in Japan. The Satsuma *han* used it in its Ryūkyū trade.[47] Besides such ingenuity, Hōtoku possessed a sturdy character. Like his son-in-law, Ōkubo Jūemon, he had become involved in a *han* conflict and was censured, after which he declined to continue his duties as *han* physician. His indomitable character and progressive ideas compare with those of Ōkubo Toshimichi's father.[48]

Toshimichi's Education

Ōkubo Toshimichi lived in the main castle-town of Kagoshima where the Satsuma authorities showed a greater interest in the training of its samurai youth than elsewhere. As a *jōka no shi,* or a samurai of the castle-town, he received very good schooling in comparison with the *tojō no shi,* or samurai of the outer castle.[49] Between the ages of seven and fourteen he, along with others of his peers living in the district of Kajiyamachi, attended the *gōchū,* a self-governing association or fraternity for young boys, one of which was maintained by each district of the city. In these institutions, peculiar to Kagoshima, the young Satsuma lads expended their energies in play, study, and military training, guided by members of the *nisaishū,* which included older youths ranging in age from seventeen to twenty-three. Men over twenty-four years of age, comprising the *osegumi,* acted as advisors to the *gōchū.*

The young samurai went to school at eight o'clock in the morning, each wearing two swords at his side to signify his social position. He returned home for lunch, and then went back to school. Once in school a boy could not leave even to go to a relative's home without being accompanied by a senior boy. All activities at the *gōchū* were oriented toward fostering military courage as well as literary proficiency. There was therefore the practice of *jūjutsu* and the playing of outdoor games such as *taishō fusegi,* a game involving mock battle. Reading matter consisted not only of books relating to exploits of loyal samurai and heroic generals of history, but of the Confucian Classics and the history and literature of Japan. Besides attending the *gōchū,* Toshimichi, being the oldest son of a samurai, was entitled to go to the Seidō, a *han*-operated educational institution. He spent his day between the two schools, going to the Seidō in the morning and then attending the *gōchū* in the afternoon.[50]

In addition to the formal education he received at these institutions, Toshimichi undertook special training in the military arts. His uncle, Minayoshi Kinroku, supervised his lessons in *jūjutsu* while Umeda Kyūnojō trained him in the use of the spear. Although Toshimichi was conscientious in the practice of the military arts, his frail constitution prevented him from excelling in them.

To compensate for his physical limitations, Toshimichi concentrated on literary pursuits. He was a voracious reader, ranging widely and deeply in the materials that were accessible to him. As the result of his wide knowledge and mental acuity, he had few peers as a debater. Even as a youth this ability was apparent and won for him the admiration of Saigō, who was three years Toshimichi's senior.[51]

The two boyhood friends studied Zen Buddhism and the Ōyōmei school of philosophy under such teachers as Itō Moemon and Musan Oshō, a Buddhist priest.[52] Zen Buddhism was introduced from south China at the end of the twelfth century and derived its name from the Chinese word *zenna,* which is in turn a transcription of the Sanskrit *dyhana,* signifying contemplation.[53] The true follower of Zen seeks enlightenment not through the reading of scriptures or by observation and experiment, but by direct intuitive perception.[54] Zen appealed to the samurai because it served to sustain them in their profession as fighting men: it sustained them morally because it taught that one must never look back once a course of action is decided upon; philosophically, because it treated life and death indifferently. Again, Zen's stress on asceticism and self-discipline attracted the warriors. Furthermore, the Zen sect very early in its history made Kamakura, the military capital of thirteenth-century Japan, its center of activity and thereby won many samurai adherents.[55] Finally, the fact that Zen had always shown itself friendly to Confucianism, which had long served as a religious philosophy for the military class, facilitated its ready acceptance by the samurai.[56]

The Ōyōmei school of philosophy, rival of the Chu Hsi school, stressed introspection and the rule of conscience and also won numerous samurai adherents.[57] Indeed, after the seventeenth century, the decided similarity between the Ōyōmei philosophy and Zen served to attract samurai intellectuals to the former school of thought. Like Zen, the Ōyōmei philosophy rejected the authority of scripture, adhered to a practical subjective morality, and taught that truth could be perceived through intuitive perception—self-study and self-control were necessary in attaining truth. Because the Japanese were free from traditionalism, such ideas had always appealed to the most resolute and thoughtful among them. The followers of Ōyōmei were generally men of reforming spirit, such as Yoshida Shōin and Ōshio Heihachirō, the revolutionary leader who attacked Ōsaka at the head of a mob in 1837.

Being a vigorous and thoughtful personality, young Ōkubo Toshimichi was drawn to the Ōyōmei philosophy as well as to that of Zen. That he was zealous in his literary pursuits may be inferred from the fact that at the age of sixteen he was given a position in the *kirokusho,* or archives, of the Satsuma *han*. The appointment as *kakiyakujo*, or archivist's aide, brought only a meager salary, but it was definitely a signal honor for the youngster since literary accomplishments were a prerequisite for the work.[58] The position gave Toshimichi further opportunities to sharpen his intellectual faculties. For the moment the future looked bright.

Aiding Rebellion

In 1849, however, the Takasaki uprising in which his father was involved changed Toshimichi's outlook for the future from bright to gloomy. The incident was to affect the fortunes of the entire family. Not only was his father exiled, but Toshimichi himself was relieved of his position as an aide in the archives and placed under domiciliary arrest for six months. He was accused of acting as a messenger between his father and the other conspirators during the uprising. Being young and without great influence, he had not taken a major role in the plot. His part had been only to join Saigō Takamori in petitioning Kuroda Nagahiro, the lord of the Fukuoka *han*, requesting his personal support for Nariakira over Hisamitsu as the successor to Narioki.[59]

The Ōkubo family was thus deprived of both its head and all normal means of income. The burden of supporting his mother and sisters fell upon Toshimichi's shoulders, a load he bore courageously during the four years of his father's banishment.[60] These were years of dire poverty for the family, evidence of which is to be found in the papers of Toshimichi. For example, a promissory note made out to one Moriyama Yohei, dated July 26, 1851—signed by Ōkubo Toshimichi and countersigned by his uncle, Minayoshi Kinroku—reveals that Toshimichi had borrowed about fourteen *ryō* to keep the family in food and shelter. This debt was to be paid off in three years at the rate of five *ryō* annually.[61] Again, in a pleading letter to his brother-in-law, Ishihara Chikamasa, Ōkubo requested a loan of eight *ryō*, stating that "no amount seems sufficient for our present needs," but "if it is impossible to spare eight *ryō*, then even five *ryō* would help." [62] If Shakespeare were right when he philosophized: "Sweet are the uses of adversity, which like the toad, ugly and venomous, wears yet a perfect jewel in its head . . . ," then the difficult years from 1849 to 1853 should have served to polish and round out Ōkubo's character. Adversity, however, had a negative effect upon him; he was to emerge from his trying experiences a cold and reserved individual.[63]

More prosperous days were to come for the Ōkubos and the progressive faction within the Satsuma *han*. As a consequence of the Takasaki affair, the movement to force the resignation of Narioki and the appointment of Nariakira as his successor gradually gained momentum. In 1850 the new and influential leader of the Fukuoka *han*, Kuroda Narimori, journeyed to Edo and conferred with Tokugawa Nariaki, Matsudaira Yoshinaga, and Date Munenari and was able to persuade the Tokugawa *rōjū*, Abe Masahiro, to suggest to Shimazu Narioki that he relinquish his position in favor of Nariakira. Accordingly, the Bakufu sent Narioki a letter of commendation for his long years of faithful service, along with gifts of an *ake no koromo*, a red robe traditionally worn by a person going into retirement, and a *cha-ire*, a tea canister. Quick to understand the purport of the Bakufu's action, Narioki resigned, and in 1851 Nariakira became the new head of the Satsuma *han*.[64]

Nariakira

As a *daimyō*, Nariakira was not in the usual run of feudal lords of the period, who were mediocrities if not nonentities. Nariakira was an active reformer of unusual caliber who not only was to be responsible for launching Ōkubo Toshimichi on a career as a *han* official, but was also to influence his thinking to a great degree.

The twenty-eighth in the line of Satsuma lords, Nariakira was born and reared in the stimulating environment of the city of Edo where he received training in the traditional arts of war and peace. He took particular interest in Western learning.[65] Although he spent the greater part of his life outside Satsuma, he nonetheless retained a consuming interest in its well-being. He kept well-informed about its activities by associating and conversing with Satsuma samurai who sojourned in Edo. Hence when he assumed leadership of Satsuma at the age of forty-three, he was fully cognizant of its problems and prepared to undertake the task of reforming it, a task to which he was to devote the next eight years of his life.

The reforms which Nariakira undertook were widespread. He initiated steps to improve the systems of both government and military defense, the latter being given the greater stress.[66] Wary of England and France, whose ships posed a threat to his Ryūkyū holdings, he established an arsenal and gave it his personal supervision—although there is no information to indicate whether Nariakira employed foreigners in the operation of the arsenal as was done in China's Foochow arsenal. Evidence does indicate, however, that he sent his retainers to Nagasaki to learn from the Dutch the art of shipbuilding. A vigorous advocate of a navy, after the arrival of Perry in 1853 he endeavored to impress upon the Bakufu the urgent need of constructing warships. Even before this he established a navy yard for the Satsuma *han* at Sakurajima, where the students who were sent to Nagasaki returned to put to use the knowledge they had acquired. Here in 1853 several Western-type warships were constructed. Each of them mounted from eight to twelve guns and was designed specifically for use in guarding Satsuma's Ryūkyū possessions. As for the other branch of the military service, the army, Nariakira emphasized the training of officers and initiated annual field maneuvers which were conducted regularly during the spring and autumn months. He also created a cavalry styled after that of the West.[67]

Nariakira encouraged the increase in production of the existing industries and the establishment of new ones. Although he realized the significance of foreign trade and cultural exchange, he nevertheless held a seemingly incompatible *kaikoku-teki jōi* view toward foreign relations, calling for opening the country until such time as it would be strong enough to expel the foreigners.[68] Thus, on September 2, 1853, after Perry's arrival in Japan, Nariakira expressed the opinion that the Bakufu should try to obtain some three years' grace, which, he felt, ought to give the *daimyō* adequate time to prepare their military defenses. He believed that Japan would thereafter be in a better position to implement successfully an expulsion policy, should the Bakufu so decide. Again, on June 8, 1858, he advised the Bakufu, at the time divided over whether it should ratify the draft treaty with the United States, to ratify the document; this, he contended, would give the country a breathing spell during which its internal reorganization and unification program could be completed. Once this was accomplished, he was certain that the foreigners could be expelled if necessary.[69]

Nariakira's foreign and domestic policies were oriented essentially to achieving *fukoku kyōhei*, or a rich country and strong defense, on a local scale. Nariakira's objective is interesting inasmuch as it was to become that of the national government after 1868 when, for the first time, the slogan *fukoku kyōhei* was used and popularized. That there should be such a striking resemblance between the objectives of some of the progressive western *han* and later the Meiji government is no coincidence; in the main it was a small group of low-ranking samurai from the western *han* which was to fashion the Meiji government and its policies.[70] During the mid-nineteenth century the problems of the semiautonomous *han,* such as Satsuma and Chōshū, were similar to those which were to confront the Bakufu and later the new Meiji regime, and the policies the western *han* formulated to meet their own pressing economic, political, and international problems were, through the instrumentality of the early Meiji leaders, transferred to the national stage. In this light, Nariakira's accomplishments take on added luster and he well deserved the plaudits given to him by one Western biographer who describes him as the foremost leader to advocate the restoration of the emperor and the adoption of the new order of things from abroad. His ideas became the foundation stones of the new Meiji government.[71]

Nariakira and Ōkubo

Significantly, it was Nariakira who was to recognize Ōkubo's talents and ability, and under whose aegis he was to rise rapidly within the *han* officialdom. Although Nariakira was progressive in most respects, he at first displayed a definite conservative bent with respect to personnel affairs of the *han.* For example, the reform party had hoped that he would divest himself of all the former Shimazu advisers who had hindered progress, but he retained these tradition-bound officials in high posts while no move was made to pardon the political prisoners who were incarcerated for advocating reforms. Indeed, it was not until the pressures from abroad compelled him to make a more realistic appraisal of the new situation that Nariakira made any attempt to recruit officials on the basis of merit. Subsequently, talented young low-ranking samurai were selected for important positions.[72] Toshimichi was not overlooked; he was given his pardon in 1853 and assigned again to the archives in his former capacity. This marked the beginning of brighter days for the entire Ōkubo family. The following year Toshimichi's father was pardoned, and he returned home from exile in 1855.[73] Three years later, in 1858, both Ōkubo and Saigō were advanced to the rank of *kachi metsuke.* Within a few more months Ōkubo was made a *kura yaku,* with responsibilities of receiving, storing, and distributing tribute rice sent in from the outlying districts of Satsuma. Nariakira established him in this position in order to better the finances of the Ōkubo family which, up to this time, had been at exceedingly low ebb.[74]

Ōkubo was grateful to Nariakira for displaying such interest in his personal welfare, but his gratitude did not in the least lessen the dissatisfaction that he and other young radicals felt toward the lord for his failure to dismiss Shimazu Bungo, a *karō*, and other carry-overs from the *ancien régime*. The radicals therefore, with the coöperation of Saigō who was in Edo at the time, undertook to remove all conservative *han* advisers. Their plan was to work through the Bakufu, a tactic previously used successfully in the ouster of Narioki. Nariakira, although undoubtedly sympathetic with the motives of the young reformers, opposed the move, arguing that it would create unrest and a possible conflict within the *han* which would reflect unfavorably upon the Shimazu prestige. The Satsuma *daimyō* was clearly for maintaining the status quo in this respect, a stand he was forced to take as the result of the pressure applied upon him by his reactionary father, Narioki; filial piety took precedence over a policy that he believed would benefit the *han*.

Nariakira's passivity to this phase of the reform movement, referred to by Japanese historians as the O-Yura Seibatsu, or the chastisement of O-Yura,[75] caused considerable agitation among the hot-blooded young samurai radicals. A number of them argued for taking direct action against the ultra-conservative advisers, but Ōkubo's remonstrance against any rash or premature action prevented an incident. Ōkubo checked his reckless colleagues in deference to Nariakira, for whom he had high respect and admiration, despite their differences of opinion over *han* policy.

Ōkubo, however, shared Shimazu Nariakira's views on the ideal polity for Japan. This question was pondered and debated by all thoughtful men of the period. Nariakira, as already seen, was a *kinnōka*, or a proponent of the doctrine of reverence for the emperor. His predisposition to the *kinnō* doctrine can be explained partly by Satsuma's tradition of reverence for the imperial house and partly by the close family ties of the Shimazu with the prestigious Konoe family, a *kuge*. Nariakira's family also was related to the Tokugawa house through his wife's connection with the Hitotsubashi family, an offshoot of the Mito branch of the Tokugawa clan.[76] Hence during the lustrum (1853-1858), when the efficacy of the Bakufu leadership was being increasingly questioned, Nariakira advocated a progressive, irenical policy for Japan which would maintain the traditional political dualism in Japanese political life—that of the existing court in Kyōto and the Bakufu in Edo—but with greater emphasis upon the role of the emperor, who hitherto merely reigned while the Tokugawa ruled.[77] In effect, Nariakira was for a closer working partnership of court and Bakufu—for *kōbu gattai*, or court-Bakufu unity. Just prior to his death, Nariakira divulged to Hisamitsu (the father and guardian of Nariakira's successor designate, Tadayoshi) that he had secretly recommended to the authorities in Edo the policy of *kōbu gattai* as the one that would most effectively serve to preserve Japan's prestige abroad.[78]

After 1858, the *kōbu gattai* reform faction clasped hands with those comprising the *jōi* party, primarily for the sake of expediency. It was thought that the union of the two groups would serve to thwart the attempts of the *kaikoku* party under Hotta Masayoshi to open Japan's ports to foreigners before the necessary reforms had been completed and national unity achieved. The newly united group embraced reformers of diverse political complexions.[79] Among them were many extremists comprising the low-ranking and economically harassed samurai who would not be content with anything short of a thorough reformation of Japanese politics and society. Ōkubo's desire for *han* reform was stimulated by the same conviction.[80] He firmly believed that the new age called for a drastic change from conservatism to progressivism and that the failure to make the change would result in the eventual ruin of the state. His indirect participation in the Takasaki incident as an incipient revolutionist, and more directly in the O-Yura affair, reveals his aversion for the entrenched traditionalism of the times, an aversion that applied no less to traditionalism on the national level. Satsuma was soon to feel the impact of Ōkubo's reforming zeal, and before too many years his burning energy was to be directed to the reformation of Japan itself.

The Takasaki and O-Yura affairs, as well as other political conflicts within Satsuma, were by no means peculiar to this particular *han*. During the second quarter of the nineteenth century many of the other *han* were experiencing tensions, and reform movements were vigorously supported in Tosa as well as in Chōshū.[81] Historians have attached considerable significance to these movements which usually brought the conservatives and the progressives into confrontation. The factional struggles involved the competent and practical lower samurai, who were intent upon bringing about economic and military reforms, and the upper samurai clique, whose purpose was to preserve the status quo. From the fires of political conflict emerged a new type of leader described by Tōyama Shigeki as *zettai shugi kanryō*, or absolute bureaucrats. He contends that their *han* reform programs tended to be arbitrary and antifeudal in nature and that it was these self-same officials who were later to establish the "absolute" Meiji government.[82] Does Ōkubo's career bear out this thesis?

Temporary Misfortune

Before Ōkubo could begin his reform activities in Satsuma, he and the other members of the reform faction were to suffer a rude jolt when the conservatives made a strong comeback. It was the unfortunate death of Shimazu Nariakira in 1858 which adversely affected the fortunes of the progressives and allowed the conservatives to strike out at their political enemies with a vengeance.

The Shimazu *daimyō* had become ill while reviewing his troops in Kagoshima on August 24 in preparation for a march to Edo. His intention was to counter the influence of Ii Naosuke, the *tairō*, whose arbitrary and strong-arm measures aimed at silencing all opposition to the Bakufu's signing the treaty with the United States was resented not only by Nariakira, but by others of varying political hues. The *jōi* faction looked upon the Bakufu action as a negation of everything for which it stood; the *kaikoku* group felt that the move was not a matter of choice, but rather one that was forced upon Ii Naosuke, and they therefore lost confidence in him as a leader; the *sonnō* party was angry because he signed the treaty without imperial approval. Ii therefore lost all his friends. As a result he was compelled to depend upon the exercise of arbitrary authority to maintain himself in power.[83] Nariakira was hopeful of persuading the Bakufu to institute reforms that would establish more intimate relations between the court and the Bakufu, and of working for some understanding with regard to the treatment of the foreign powers.[84]

The death of Nariakira had repercussions everywhere. In Kyōto the members of the loyalist party among the *kuge* and samurai had been anticipating the arrival of Nariakira and his Satsuma troops. They had felt that his objective was to chastise the Bakufu and force the imposition of the *jōi* policy,[85] and they were deeply shocked and disappointed over his death.

Ōkubo's shock and disappointment were profound; he had lost an understanding patron and fellow thinker. Now twenty-eight years of age, Ōkubo's hope for a promising future under the patronage of Nariakira was shattered. In Satsuma, a conservative counterreaction swept all progressives aside and Ōkubo and Saigō found themselves again without employment. The attempted suicides of Saigō and Gessho, a Buddhist priest, took place soon afterward.[86] Depressed and forlorn over the sudden turn of events, the two, while returning to Satsuma from Edo, made a pact to cast themselves into the sea. Ōkubo, after hearing of their unsuccessful attempt at suicide, met with Saigō and persuaded him to abandon his plan. This episode reveals the contrast in character of the two eminent future Restoration figures. One would yield to circumstances but the other would persist in molding circumstances to his own advantage.

Ōkubo was to persist. His way was to forget those things that were behind and to press single-mindedly toward the goals he had in view. The adversities to which Ōkubo was exposed during these years undoubtedly affected the character of the budding leader. It is a truism that hardships can make an individual either sympathetic and compassionate or cold and indifferent toward others. They can instill in one a tremendous drive to accomplish, to overcome the obstacles of life, and to achieve success; or they can imbue him with a spirit of defeatism and despondency. Within Ōkubo a core of coldness developed, and an obsessive desire to forge ahead in life regardless of difficulties. His personal trials, stemming from the Takasaki affair, fanned the spark of rebellion within him, and by the time he was twenty-eight he had been transformed into a serious, determined, calculating enemy of traditionalism, a reformer, psychologically prepared to achieve his objective by any means that would assure success.

III
Rebel Turns Moderate

Ōkubo's experiences during his formative years sharpened his wit, and his actions during the next several years reveal a degree of the sagacity, persistence, and guile that were to be developed in subsequent years.

The death of Shimazu Nariakira in 1858 left unfinished his plan to lead troops to Edo and force the Bakufu to carry out reforms. But those dedicated to his ideals in Satsuma could not idly sit back and observe the brash actions of Bakufu's chief minister, Ii Naosuke, as he continued to spread a reign of terror in Edo and Kyōto. Ōkubo and some of the bolder samurai resolved to take matters into their own hands. They determined to leave the *han* and, as *rōnin,* conduct a war against the tyrant. Their overall proposal was to win the support of samurai loyalists of other *han* for the execution of the plan to attack the Kyōto *shoshidai,* the official representative of the *shōgun* at Kyōto; remove Kujō, the *kampaku;* attack Ii Naosuke at Edo; and compel the complete reformation of the Bakufu.[1]

The program was both ambitious and dangerous, and no one realized its scope better than Ōkubo. Before proceeding, he decided to consult with his childhood friend, the dedicated loyalist Saigō Takamori. Saigō was at this time on his way to exile on the island of Ōshima. In the letter to Saigō, Ōkubo explained in detail the political situation at home and his plan to strike out against the Bakufu independently of the *han.*[2] Saigō's reply was forthright; he advised immediate action, saying that "he who would vacillate at this time lacks the sense of loyalty." [3] At the end of his letter Saigō listed the names of eight samurai of various *han* who would, he thought, coöperate with Ōkubo.[4]

The group was formed around a hard core of samurai loyalists, among whom Iwashita Hōhei (Masahira), Ijichi Masaharu, Yoshii Tomozane, Saishō Atsushi, Narahara Kizaemon, Arima Shinshichi, Ōyama Tsunayoshi, Narahara Shigeru, Kaeda Nobuyoshi, and Moriyama Shinzō were most prominent.[5] Ōkubo, who founded the party, thinking in terms of maximum discipline within an organization composed of radical warrior elements, recommended Iwashita, of higher social status than the others, as leader.[6] Clearly this move indicated Ōkubo's thorough understanding of Japanese psychology, a knowledge that was to prove invaluable to him throughout his career as a political strategist.

Ōkubo was well aware that well-conceived strategy, good leadership, and determination were in themselves not sufficient to assure success for a revolutionary venture. Monetary backing was essential, and it devolved upon Ōkubo to secure the necessary funds. Fortunately, Moriyama Shinzō (Tōen), a Kagoshima merchant, consented to accommodate the loyalists and immediately placed at their disposal two fishing boats and the services of a sea captain, one Tanaka Shimpei. Moriyama was a *gōshi*, or farmer-samurai, turned merchant, who had accumulated great wealth. Although he was scorned by most samurai in Kagoshima because he had entered the samurai register by devious means—offering money and grain to the Shimazu *daimyō*—Ōkubo's father had felt no compunction in associating with him and Moriyama had become a good friend of the family.[7] The underlying motives for Moriyama's action are worthy of study because throughout the pre-Restoration period the lower samurai-merchant coalition was a factor in the consummation of the subsequent politico-socioeconomic transformation in Japan. Moriyama's actions were undoubtedly induced by many factors, such as his friendship for the Ōkubos, his loyalty to the imperial house, which was enhanced by the arbitrary behavior of the Bakufu, and economic considerations. Moriyama not only acted out of friendship, but he was also no doubt loyalist; his son died for the loyalist cause. But it is difficult to believe, as Katsuda implies, that Moriyama's wealth was accumulated solely to aid the *han* in time of real need, the implication being that he had no selfish motive in offering his resources to the Satsuma activists. It is important to bear in mind that the *chōnin* were aware of the advantages in aiding samurai causes, as already noted. Moriyama's role in this one instance, moreover, should not lead to the inference that merchant support of the progressive cause was the rule in Satsuma; there is little evidence that the merchants participated to any great extent. Their apparent apathy may be explained partly by their disinclination and/or inability financially to support the anticonservatives. In Satsuma especially the merchants lacked power inasmuch as the reforms of the second quarter of the nineteenth century culminated in the total repudiation by the *han* authorities of the enormous debts owing to their own merchants, an action that would cause a reduction in the *chōnin*'s total assets as well as an increase in their legitimate resentment. This policy understandably dealt a staggering blow to the Satsuma merchant class, but a near coup de grace was administered when the *han* established rigid state-operated monopolies covering sugar and a variety of other products.[8]

Although adequate financial support was available from Moriyama to send the fewer-than-fifty men formed around Ōkubo to Kyōto, it is inconceivable that the radical loyalists, composed of *rōnin*, could have achieved their objective alone, without the patronage of some powerful *han*. Did Ōkubo realize the full import of his decision to launch the venture without such support? This is a matter of conjecture. His judgment of the situation may well have been affected by his intense animosity for the Tokugawa.

Might Ōkubo have gained the support of the Satsuma *han* for his independently conceived project? There was sympathy with his aims but not unqualified backing. In time, this became obvious. One of Shimazu Tadayoshi's attendants, with whom Ōkubo had casual contact, secretly communicated the loyalist plot to his lord, who was stunned by the news. The Satsuma *daimyō*, after consulting with his father, Hisamitsu, on November 28, 1859, personally composed a letter to the radical Satsuma loyalists discouraging the anticipated move. Indicating that an opportunity would surely come to effectuate the late Nariakira's project, Tadayoshi urged the group to reconsider and wait for a more favorable time to act. This personal letter from a member of the house of Shimazu to a group of his retainers was unprecedented. It was addressed to the *seichū shi*, or "loyal retainer." Ōkubo's group adopted the term and thenceforth called itself Seichu Gumi, or Loyal Party.[9] In reply to Tadayoshi, Ōkubo promised to defer to his suggestion but at the same time implored him to strengthen Satsuma's military defenses, arrange an alliance with Mito,

Echizen, and other *han* in order to advance the *kinnō* cause, and order Saigō home from exile.[10]

The waiting for an opportune time apparently tested Ōkubo's patience; again, several months later, in March, 1860, he advocated the dispatching of one hundred Satsuma troops to Kyōto and a like number to Edo "under the pretext of protecting against the imminent attack from abroad and the dangers inherent in the restless state within the country." [11] The real purpose was to have these forces unite with Mito troops to rid the Bakufu of Ii Naosuke and his henchmen, after which it was hoped a government capable of executing the imperial will could be established.

One of Ōkubo's letters reveals his political orientation at this juncture in his life. That he was definitely for *kōbu gattai,* the union of court and Bakufu, as was Hisamitsu, may be gleaned from his use of the phrase *tenchō gokōfuku,* or the restoration of the imperial house.[12] The two men differed only with respect to the importance to be given the components of the union. Whereas Hisamitsu, wishing primarily to save the institution of the Bakufu, advocated a *kōbu gattai* that would find the Bakufu predominant, Ōkubo wanted to see the primacy of the court over Bakufu. He thus held the view of the late Nariakira, but went a step further in that he would have the emperor rule actively through the Bakufu.[13]

Ōkubo and his party of reformers presented several more petitions to the Shimazu requesting that Satsuma dispatch troops to Kyōto. When these produced no tangible results, the loyalists decided to send Ōyama Kakunosuke and Kodama Yūichirō to meet with Shimazu Hisamitsu personally. While the two men were on their mission, about thirty of their comrades gathered in Moriyama's home to await the return of their representatives. Feelings ran high, and the majority of the *intransigeant* were impatient for immediate action. Ōkubo, however, advised against abandoning the *han* until they learned of Hisamitsu's stand. The two spokesmen eventually returned. They entered the house and, catching Ōkubo's eyes, motioned to him to step outside. There they informed him that Hisamitsu was unmoved by their request. The three men, after urgent consultation, finally concluded that without Satsuma support their cause would fail and that the only alternative now would be to await a propitious time; any rash move, they felt, would prove dangerous and abortive. When the others were informed of the decision, there was vociferous opposition. The meeting was obviously beginning to get out of hand when Ōkubo demanded attention. Speaking quietly and deliberately, he told the gathering that he expected them to do as they were told. If, he warned, any of them insisted upon acting contrary to his order, they must do so after first cutting him down. He argued that the scheme to reform the Bakufu was contrived by him, and hence there was no one more anxious to act than he, but to do so independently and against the express wishes of the *daimyō* would prejudice their chance for success. He insisted that it was not the proper season to act.[14] He placated his aroused followers by reiterating the promise of eventual action in concert with the Satsuma *han* and thereby prevented a division in the camp.

Ōkubo's reluctance to act at this time indicated that the master schemer had not considered the full consequences of his earlier plan of action. Had he done so, it is unlikely that he would have stirred up the passion of his followers by insisting that the time was ripe for a *coup de main*. As early as March of 1860 he had misgivings because he notes in his diary that "even if our party abandons the *han*, with such small numbers there would be no likelihood of success in restoring imperial prestige." [15] His final decision, however, was probably based upon several factors. First, Ii Naosuke possessed the power to bring retribution upon the Satsuma *han* for any actions of its samurai that he deemed detrimental to the Bakufu. Furthermore, he was in a position with his network of spies to arrest the movements of forty or fifty *rōnin* without too much difficulty. Another possible reason for Ōkubo's decision to change his initial plan to force a reform of the Bakufu in alliance with other *rōnin* loyalists was the change he noted in Hisamitsu's attitude. Shimazu Hisamitsu, the father of the Satsuma *daimyō* Tadayoshi, had begun to show a willingness to aid the loyalist cause. Hence Ōkubo may have decided to utilize the combined prestige of Hisamitsu and Tadayoshi to attain his objective.

Ōkubo exposed himself to criticism because he displayed a lack of conviction, a quality contradictory to the spirit of a samurai to whom temporizing was a sin once a course of action was decided upon. Saigō, the Hotspur of Japanese history, undoubtedly would have accepted the majority opinion and immediately abandoned the *han* if he had been in Ōkubo's place; but Ōkubo, the opportunist, could disavow a prior judgment if circumstances later dictated a change. In the present situation he retracted his original promise and waited to strike at a more advantageous time. He meanwhile sought a modus operandi whereby he might successfully influence the Shimazu to lend the power and prestige of the *han* to the embryonic revolutionary movement.[16]

Winning Influential Backing

To win the sympathy of Hisamitsu who wielded the real power in Satsuma, Ōkubo considered it imperative to establish closer personal relations with him and to imbue him with enthusiasm for the *kinnō* cause. Unlike Nariakira, however, who often met informally with Saigō and others in the confines of his garden for discussions, Hisamitsu was infinitely more ceremonious and hence difficult to approach.[17] Ōkubo resorted to subterfuge. Knowing that Hisamitsu was addicted to the game of *go,* or Japanese checkers, which he played regularly with Jōgan, a priest connected with the temple called Kisshōin, Ōkubo made an arrangement with his close friend, Saishō Atsushi, who was Jōgan's brother, to ask the priest to teach him the finer points of the game. The priest consented, and in a short time he and Ōkubo were playing *go* regularly. During the course of these sessions Ōkubo steered the conversation toward the topic closest to his heart. He expounded his political views and aspirations, and related to Jōgan the activities of his fellow loyalists. As anticipated, the priest unwittingly served as intermediary between Ōkubo and his superior and Ōkubo's opinions began to reach Hisamitsu's ears. Ōkubo also used other avenues to reach Hisamitsu. On one occasion, learning that Saishō was forwarding to Hisamitsu a copy of Hirata Atsutane's *Kōshi Den,* Ōkubo wrote the names of the members of the Seichū Gumi and outlined his own political ideas on a slip of paper and inserted it between the pages of the book, knowing that Hisamitsu would discover and read it.[18] By such schemes as these Ōkubo made himself better known to Hisamitsu who promised to meet him personally, in time.

Ōkubo's patently undignified if not perfidious actions won for him the distrust of his fellow samurai.[19] Many of them wondered if he had no other alternative than to demean himself by catering to a once-hated enemy. Had he not had sufficient reason for harboring malice toward Hisamitsu? The conflict centering around Hisamitsu, it will be recalled, had resulted not only in the four-year exile of Ōkubo's father, but in his own arrest and loss of employment as well. Ōkubo's driving ambition always had been to extirpate the conservatism from the *han,* an ideology Hisamitsu symbolized. Indeed, on one occasion he had even considered assassinating Hisamitsu.[20] Why then this paradoxical conduct now? Although Nariakira, whom Ōkubo respected, had held Hisamitsu in high esteem,[21] there undoubtedly were more basic reasons for Ōkubo's apparent servility in the face of abuses heaped upon him by his peers. There is evidence to indicate "method in his madness," that he believed Hisamitsu's friendship would accrue to the benefit of the loyalist cause. Like Machiavelli, he may well have felt that the end justified the means. This is the thesis accepted by the majority of Ōkubo biographers. It is quite possible that Ōkubo was moved by a high sense of loyalty in adopting a seemingly dishonorable means to achieve his end, but the question of self-promotion should not be overlooked. Being an aggressive, realistic leader with vaulting ambitions, he certainly must have considered Hisamitsu's friendship in the light of what it might mean to his future advancement in *han*—and perhaps national—politics. A reasonable conclusion, however, would be that Ōkubo was animated by conviction and a sense of duty coupled with a strong desire for self-advancement.

Soon after Ōkubo had dissuaded his followers from abandoning the plan to leave the han and strike out as *rōnin*, he requested permission to visit Edo to discuss with Satsuma samurai there the recent developments in Kagoshima and, if possible, to halt their proposed attack against Ii Naosuke, the *tairō*. Ōkubo had apparently received a secret communication from Edo notifying him that his comrades there were planning to attack Ii in collusion with *rōnin* of Mito. Ōkubo realized that such a move would have adverse repercussions in Kagoshima among members of his Seichū Gumi, making them difficult to control. He thus felt that his presence in Edo was imperative, but the Satsuma authorities, harboring suspicion as to his real motive, denied his request to leave.[22] He thereupon sent others to the Tokugawa capital with his message urging restraint but, lacking modern transportation, his agents arrived too late. On the morning of March 24, 1860, Ii Naosuke had already met his fate at the hands of eighteen disgruntled Mito and Satsuma *rōnin*.[23] It was not until twenty days later that the news of this incident reached Kagoshima.[24]

The Satsuma and Mito samurai used assassination to achieve a revolutionary objective. But what of its efficacy? Shimada Saburō has presented an interesting view on the matter. He points out that normally two methods are employed to reach such goals: war, as resorted to by the English in the Great Revolution and the Americans in the War of

Independence; and assassination. War, he contends, is the most effective; murder fails to produce desired results. Hence he considers the attack upon Ii Naosuke as having been extremely injudicious and unfortunate.[25] But the Japanese, down through history, have relied consistently upon assassination in their attempts to effect political change. Ōkubo, Itō, and other Meiji statesmen were eventually themselves to die at the hands of assassins. The Chinese, on the other hand, have been much more realistic and pragmatic in this respect; war, in most instances, has served as their chief instrument for gaining revolutionary ends.

The lone Satsuma participant in the plot to assassinate Ii Naosuke played a leading part in the attack. Arimura Jizaemon was responsible for beheading him. Soon after he accomplished his gory mission, Arimura commited suicide while still in possession of the head of his victim carefully wrapped in a *furoshiki,* or cloth wrapper.[26] His brother, Arimura Yūsuke, who was of but not in the attacking party on the fateful day, escaped to Kagoshima where he related the details of the incident to Ōkubo.[27] Ōkubo then conveyed the account to the Satsuma authorities after which he paid a visit to the home of Arimura. The Satsuma authorities considered Arimura Yūsuke's involvement in the Sakuradamon affair as *kokka fuchū,* or disloyalty to the state, and ordered him to commit *hara kiri.*[28] Ōkubo, obviously in sympathy with Arimura Yūsuke's fundamental motives, endeavored to have his life spared, but when it became evident that the officials were not going to change their decision, he consoled the condemned assassin and urged him to accept the punishment without rancor.[29]

Perhaps Arimura could be urged to accept his fate without bitterness, but the Seichū Gumi could not. The men considered the judgment an injustice to their compatriot and went so far as to offer their own lives in his stead in an effort to win leniency for him. It was unavailing.[30] In the end, Arimura, "attired in a clean garment, bowed low toward the east [in the direction of Kyōto], uttered a prayer to his ancestors, and then saying farewell to his comrades, calmly ended his life at the age of twenty-six." [31]

It was just prior to Arimura's death that Hisamitsu granted Ōkubo his first audience, at which time Ōkubo again pressed upon his lord the urgency of establishing Satsuma influence at Kyōto.[32] He argued that if this were done Hisamitsu would be in a favorable position to participate actively in the affairs of state. "At present," Ōkubo said, "when the relation between the court and the Bakufu and the attitude of the *daimyō* are unstable, it behooves the greatest *han* of Kyūshū to exercise its right of actively directing the affairs of the country." [33] Ōkubo, in voicing his opinion, was cognizant of the political instability throughout Japan after the assassination of Ii Naosuke. Those who advocated the expulsion of the foreigners were increasingly vociferous. In the fall of 1860 a group of thirty men came to the Satsuma *yashiki*, the residence of the Satsuma *daimyō* in Edo, imploring the *han* to give them support in the movement against the Bakufu, which seemed to be buckling under foreign pressure. The Satsuma *han* pacified them and gave them lodging for a while. Such attempts at restraint were not completely effective; it was early the following year, on January 14, 1861, that H. C. J. Heusken, the secretary of the American Legation, was murdered in Mita.[34] Also, Ōkubo was especially anxious at this time over the Chōshū *han*'s increasing influence in national affairs. He reasoned that if Satsuma did not make its presence felt at the imperial capital, Chōshū would very likely shape to its own mold the thinking of the feudal lords of the country. Hisamitsu nevertheless temporized. Unlike Nariakira, he did not relish the thought of acting the part of an aggressive leader; being a conservative, he found it difficult to accept Ōkubo's advanced ideas and recommendations.[35]

Thus for Ōkubo this meeting with Hisamitsu produced no tangible results. In the long run, however, it proved beneficial because from this time forward Hisamitsu made increasing use of Ōkubo's services. In March, 1860, he was promoted and given the impressive title of *gokanjōkata kogashirakaku*, or assistant superintendent of the treasury. Less than two years later, in November, 1861, he rose to the rank of *okonando*, and for the first time he became a powerful figure in the Satsuma government. This was a remarkable accomplishment inasmuch as no other lower samurai before him had ever attained this position in Satsuma.[36] Normally the highest rank a lower samurai could hold was *kachi metsuke*. In attaining the position of *okonando*, Ōkubo did in less than two years what usually took more than ten.[37] Eventually he was to be elevated to the office of *soba yaku*, or adviser.[38]

As a newcomer within the ranks of the Satsuma council, Ōkubo immediately launched upon a program to sell himself and his ideas to his colleagues. He established rapport with the senior *soba yaku*, Nakayama Chūzaemon, for whom he had great admiration, and with Komatsu Tatewaki, a man from a distinguished family and of unusual influence.[39]

By winning their coöperation and establishing close contact with Hisamitsu, Ōkubo was to enable the progressive elements within the *han* to realize their aspirations.

Calling for Han *Reform*

One of the urgent demands of the progressives within the Satsuma *han* was for reform in government leadership. At the end of 1859 Ōkubo had conveyed the sentiments of his party to the Shimazu in a petition saying that "the need of the moment is to consider popular sentiment and bring into government leadership a person who is favorable to the people. We request that Shimazu Saemon be given the position of *karō* [senior minister] as soon as possible." [40] This demand was ultimately met, although Hisamitsu evidently offered objections to it initially. According to Matsumura Junzō, Hisamitsu, in voicing his disapproval of the contemplated scuttling of the inefficient "old guard," heatedly told Ōkubo: "If they are not doing what is expected of them, teach them how things should be done." [41] Ōkubo, however, remained unperturbed, and before long the conservative Shimazu Bungo was relieved of his position as *karō* and given a sinecure. He was replaced by Shimazu Shimofusa, a former *karō* under the late Nariakira. There were, moreover, several other resignations among the conservative officials, two of whom, Niiro Suruga and Tateyama Buhei, later worked through an agent in Edo, ultimately to bring down the Shimofusa government. Consequently, by 1860 the "Nariakira progressives" were once more enjoying power in Satsuma. Although the conservatives went into political retirement, Ōkubo and the progressives continued to be resisted by the middle-of-the-road gradualists. Moreover, harmony was not the rule within the progressive camp itself because there were those who adhered to Arima Shinshichi's *sokkō ron,* or immediate-action theory, and others who advocated Ōkubo's *jichō ron,* or cautious-action theory.[42]

Besides being instrumental in having the conservatives purged from the *han* government, Ōkubo succeeded in initiating other significant reforms. Among them was the abolition of ten or more *dejō,* or outer castles, situated in Hyūga, Ōsumi, and Satsuma. These fortifications, around which administrative districts were centered with the *jōshu* as the administrative officers, were originally established to facilitate the enforcement of a seclusion policy—to keep the feudal society undisturbed by outside influences.[43] It is obvious that the preservation of these semi-autonomous outer castles would also preserve political decentralization of the *han* as well as a condition in the rural areas in which the lot of the peasants was little better than that of what Tōyama describes as "slaves." Tōyama contends that the outer castle system was utilized by the feudal overlords to maintain strict control over the peasants.[44] The abolition of these outer castles, however, was effected primarily to unify the fief and thereby establish political centralization and not as a conscious step in the direction of freeing the peasants from "bondage." But the policy met with resistance. The samurai of Miyakonojō were so aroused over it that many came out with spear in hand ready to resist the enforcement of the abolition order.[45] Yet Hisamitsu surprisingly allowed his new leadership to take this basic step in centralization.

It is interesting to note that the centralization of the Satsuma *han* was in microcosm the basic reform that was to be effected on a national scale after the Restoration. This and other projected reforms, however, did not issue from a body of ideal theory. In most instances they were dictated by necessity and expediency. The Japanese, unlike the Chinese scholar-gentry who resisted change at every turn, were realistic enough to foresee the danger inherent in maintaining the status quo. Ōkubo and other young, intelligent, and energetic future leaders of the Restoration sensed the imperative need for drastic alterations in the military, political, and economic aspects of *han* life if the threats of foreign domination were to be successfully met. For example, as early as 1857 Satsuma and Chōshū had reëvaluated and thoroughly revamped their military organizations, establishing modern foundries, arsenals, and shipyards.

It would be a mistake to assume, however, that national concerns were paramount in the reform programs of the *han* leaders. The reforms initiated in Satsuma and Chōshū, for example, were designed more specifically to better the military position of each *han* in the impending realignment of political power within Japan.[46] That this was Ōkubo's primary motive for reform may be inferred from his earlier statement to the Shimazu with respect to stationing Satsuma troops in Kyōto.[47] Ōkubo perceived the shape of things to come and did not intend to miss any opportunities that would place Satsuma in the forefront of national politics. He played his hand well; when the opportunity came, Satsuma was powerful enough to seize the dominant role in national affairs and, in the Meiji era, to apply the principles of *han* unification in the centralization of the Japanese state.[48] Ōkubo, along with other farsighted young progressives of the Satsuma, Chōshū, Tosa, and Hizen *han*, was in a very real sense an early contributor to the development of modern Japanese nationalism.

By 1861 Ōkubo's influence upon Hisamitsu had increased considerably, one gauge of which was the consummation of the various *han* reforms. By this time the Shimazu Shimofusa government had fallen, after it had attempted to hinder the Ōkubo policy, and had been replaced by a government more amenable to Ōkubo's plans. Among the members of the new council were Kiiri Settsu, *karō;* Komatsu Tatewaki, *soba yaku;* Nakayama Shōnosuke, Hori Jirō, and Ōkubo Toshimichi, *okonando;* Arimura Shunsai (Kaeda) and Yoshii Tomozane, *kachi metsuke.* Saigō was still in exile.[49] The same year, Hisamitsu acceded to the Ōkubo recommendation that Satsuma troops under Shimazu leadership be sent to Kyōto. Up to this point Hisamitsu had refused to consent to the request of the radicals because to have done so would have been "unprincipled." In the meantime, a subtle change had taken place in Ōkubo's thinking. Aware of his lord's determined frame of mind, Ōkubo had begun to adhere more and more to the Shimazu viewpoint. His original zeal for reform had cooled in inverse ratio to his advance in official rank, a development that created dissatisfaction among the extreme wing of the progressive party under Arima Shinshichi.[50]

This faction, however, was pleased to learn that Hisamitsu had consented to send Satsuma contingents to the imperial capital. As a preliminary step, Hori Jirō was dispatched to Edo to meet with representatives of the Chikuzen and Echizen *han* as well as with officials of the Bakufu and members of the Nambu and Konoe families. Hori's purpose was to take soundings of their attitude toward Satsuma's proposal. Next, in view of Hisamitsu's contemplated march to Kyōto in 1862, the Satsuma men evolved a plan to burn down a part of the Satsuma residence in Edo in order to force a postponement of Shimazu Tadayoshi's scheduled trip to the Tokugawa capital under the *sankin kōtai* system. On December 19, 1861, Ōkubo wrote to Hori that "if the novel scheme should succeed, I would consider it very fortunate." [51] Whether Ōkubo was the author of this scheme is conjectural, but he definitely was party to it, a fact that reveals his willingness to resort to the most drastic measures to achieve his objective.

The plan to put fire to the Satsuma *yashiki* was executed on January 6,

1862. The Bakufu, however, always suspicious when vassals were absent from Edo for any reason, took measures to rebuild immediately. It presented the *han* with a grant of three thousand *ryō* for this purpose. This display of Bakufu "generosity" benefited the Satsuma plotters. It gave Hisamitsu an ostensible reason for making the anticipated trip to Kyōto without arousing the suspicions of the Bakufu; he publicly announced that his purpose in going was to thank those concerned for the monetary grant and for allowing the postponement of the scheduled trip of the Satsuma *daimyō* and his retinue to Edo for alternate residence.

To prepare the way for Hisamitsu, Ōkubo left Kagoshima for Kyōto on January 24, 1862, commissioned to persuade the court to give the Shimazu an imperial mandate to reorganize the Bakufu. The proposed mandate was to include the appointment of Hitotsubashi Yoshinobu (Tokugawa Keiki) as guardian of the *shōgun*, the appointment of Matsudaira Yoshinaga as *sōsai*, or supreme executive officer, and the complete reform of the Bakufu.[52] Before his return to Kagoshima on March 1, 1862, Ōkubo had exchanged with Konoe Tadahiro, Konoe Tadafusa, and others information on conditions in Kyōto as well as in Satsuma.[53]

As the date for Shimazu Hisamitsu's northward march to Kyōto drew nearer, there was an increasingly vociferous demand for the pardon of Saigō, whom friends considered indispensable to the loyalist cause. During Saigō's exile Ōkubo had shown much solicitude for him. Evidence indicates that through Ōkubo's intercession the Saigō family received monetary aid from the Shimazu *daimyō*. For example, Ōkubo's entry in his diary for March 17, 1860, says that the *daimyō* had granted the Saigō family the sum of twenty-five *ryo*.[54] There is also reason to believe that Ōkubo worked persistently for his friend's pardon. Thus on March 14, 1861, Saigō, in a letter to Saishō and Ōkubo, expressed his gratitude for their efforts in his behalf. "I wish to thank you," Saigō said, "for your continual concern for me." [55] This perseverance eventually bore fruit. Working through Komatsu Tatewaki, Ōkubo and his colleagues finally convinced Hisamitsu of the wisdom of having the exiled warrior return home. On March 12, 1862, Saigō once more set foot on Satsuma soil.[56]

After Ōkubo welcomed Saigō home, the cordial relationship between the two leaders was put under severe strain. Their political differences became increasingly obvious, and many clashes ensued. The basic makeup of Ōkubo and Saigō may help to explain why the two began to drift apart.

Tokutomi contrasts these two Restoration figures, revealing their fundamental dissimilarities, in the following words:

> The character of Kōtō [Ōkubo] and that of Nanshū [Saigō] differed in that the latter was determined to follow undeviatingly a course of action once decided upon; for him there was only one right way. Kōtō, on the other hand, would not hesitate to resort to an alternative course if an obstacle were to block an original one. In other words, Nanshū would rather do a thing resolutely and well or not at all; Kōtō in undertaking a thing desired to do it well, but if he could not achieve his purpose in one way, he was willing to take other steps.[57]

If a parallel were to be drawn, Saigō might be compared with a Chiang Kai-shek, uncompromising, unyielding, inflexible; Ōkubo to a Henry Clay, compromising, yielding, flexible. One was a soldier through and through and the other a leader who bent to situations if to do so would mean the eventual attainment of a particular goal. Given two such diverse personalities, opinions were bound to differ and conflicts occur.

In 1858 the two men held similar political ideas; by 1862 these had undergone transition. Saigō maintained an extreme view—one generally held by the *rōnin*—that of taking immediate action for the extension of the imperial prerogatives, but Ōkubo's thinking had become much more moderate. Extremely devoted to Nariakira and his ideals, Saigō could not help contrasting him with Hisamitsu, whom he found markedly inferior. Saigō called the latter a bumpkin, a *seitei no kawazu,* or a frog in a well (a person with narrow views), and declared that little could be accomplished by having Hisamitsu lead Satsuma forces to Kyōto and Edo as proposed.[58] Ōkubo, now close to Hisamitsu and therefore a proponent of the plan, strongly insisted that with Saigō's coöperation he could subtly guide Hisamitsu toward the *kinnō* objectives in a more positive manner. After considerable persuasion, Saigō finally consented to make the trip north with Hisamitsu. Saigō was commissioned to leave ahead of the main party in order to feel the political pulse of Kyōto and was told to meet the Satsuma group at Bakan (Shimonoseki).

Temper of the Country

Meanwhile, the temper of the country was becoming increasingly tense as the movement to "revere the emperor and expel the barbarians" gained momentum. After the death of Ii Naosuke the mantle of Bakufu leadership fell upon the shoulders of Andō Nobuyuki, the lord of Tsushima, who in 1861 obtained imperial sanction for the marriage of Princess Kazu, Emperor Kōmei's younger sister, to the *shōgun*, Iemochi. Andō had argued that the nuptials, symbolizing the union between court and Bakufu, would bring unity to the divided land, a prerequisite for the expulsion of the foreigners which he thought could be accomplished within a decade.[59] Andō had also hoped that the marriage would assure the pacification of the restive samurai, but this was not to be. During this period the samurai deserted their *han* in increasing numbers. They joined with *rōnin* from other parts of the country and raised the cry of *sonnō jōi*, causing ferment throughout the empire. In March, 1862, the still-cautious house of Shimazu published a proclamation to its samurai, expressing approval of the imperial cause, but forbidding the Satsuma samurai to unite with the *rōnin* of other *han* for the advancement of the *sonnō jōi* objectives, or to do anything without the approval of the Satsuma authorities. Hisamitsu made this proclamation through Ōkubo. The text states in part:

> Since the Year of the Horse [1858] when commercial relations were established with foreign nations there has been unrest among the people. It has been brought to our attention that there are those in various *han* calling themselves patriots who, in the name of *sonnō jōi*, are advocating violence in collusion with others throughout the country. There are those in Satsuma who have joined such elements through the means of correspondence. Although this is a result of a deep feeling of loyalty to the Emperor, to unite in undertaking any rash actions with the *rōnin* would obviously be harmful to Satsuma, cause a conflict involving the entire empire, and plunge it into a period of intense rivalry among different contending leaders. To cause such a situation would be an act of disloyalty and unrighteousness, a thing not to be taken lightly. We also have intentions of working for the union of court and Bakufu but will not associate with such elements mentioned above. . . . You are ordered not to associate with these *rōnin* here or in Edo. If you are inevitably forced to mingle with them, do not enter into discussion with them. Punishment for those disobeying these orders will be meted out unhesitatingly.[60]

During this tumultous period, there was, in addition to the *daimyō* of Mito, a group of men actively working against the interest of the Bakufu. Among them were the former *daimyō* of Owari, Echizen, Tosa, and

Uwajima, who, in 1859, were forced by the Bakufu to surrender their positions as *daimyō* to their respective sons. These men were accused, first, of having conspired with Mito to have Tokugawa Keiki adopted by the head of the Tokugawa family so that he might eventually succeed Tokugawa Iesada as *shōgun*, and, second, of having denounced the Bakufu for misgovernment and thereby failing to show due respect to the emperor.[61]

The Bakufu was forced to contend with the spirit of rebellion in other sections of the country as well. There was ferment in Chōshū, one of the most important *han* in Restoration history.[62] Influenced by Yoshida Shōin, an ardent advocate of *sonnō jōi* who had been executed in 1859 for his anti-Bakufu activities, the Chōshū samurai were strongly *kinnō* in sentiment. Just as Satsuma suspected Chōshū of conspiring to play a leading role in national affairs at Satsuma's expense, so Chōshū believed that Satsuma was secretly organizing a great effort to bring the Bakufu into collision with the foreign barbarians, thereby rendering the Bakufu vulnerable to attacks from within. The Chōshū extremists were determined that their *han*, and not Satsuma, should take the most prominent part in the task of overthrowing the Bakufu. The Chōshū councilors, however, were conservative and tended to move in submission to the Bakufu. Mōri Takachika, the Chōshū lord, was warned of the possibility of the *rōnin* transferring their support to some of the powerful *daimyō* of the west in an effort to gain control of the throne and to use imperial prestige to expel the foreigners, if not to overthrow the Tokugawa government.[63] Mōri thereupon took steps to prevent such possibilities. He advised the Bakufu to work for a conciliation with the court, stating in his letter to the Edo authorities that he hoped the *shōgun* would recognize the supremacy of the emperor so that harmony between the two would be evident.[64] *Kōbu gattai,* he felt, would end the violent protests of the people against the Bakufu as the result of its conclusion of treaties with foreign powers. The inability of Mōri to obtain a Bakufu promise to expel the foreigners, although it was agreeable to the idea of court-Bakufu unity, caused the extreme loyalists to lose faith in his leadership. The *rōnin,* for the time being, ceased to rely upon Mōri and began to look to Shimazu Hisamitsu of Satsuma.

Hisamitsu's Mission

On April 14, 1862, Shimazu Hisamitsu, along with Ōkubo Toshimichi and a thousand leading patriots, embarked for Kyōto.[65] The Satsuma force arrived in Shimonoseki on April 26, a day of rain according to Ōkubo's diary.[66] That evening Ōkubo received several callers with whom he discussed the critical political situation of the land.[67]

One of the persons upon whom Ōkubo expected to rely in the execution of his policy was Saigō, who was to meet the Hisamitsu party at Shimonoseki. Ōkubo looked for him but he was nowhere to be found. To the punctilious Hisamitsu, Saigō's absence was an intolerable breach of faith. To Ōkubo, who had persuaded Hisamitsu to give the exiled Saigō his freedom, it was embarrassing. There was no alternative but for Ōkubo to go and search for the errant samurai. He put to sea for Ōsaka on the twenty-eighth, and during the course of the journey, as a typical Japanese who possesses a streak of sentimentality behind the most practical exterior, he was to wax poetic: "Kono hi Akao no shiro wo haruka ni mite, / Kono shiro no ne ni oritaru ōishi no / Ugokanu michi wo yo ni terasu kana." (This day as we gaze upon the castle of Akao in the distance, / The "great stone" at its base, steadfast and immovable, / Symbolizes for all the immutability of the Way.)[68] At the time he wrote, Ōkubo was at Akao in the province of Harima west of Ōsaka. In the poem he makes a significant play-on-words. "Ōishi," or great stone, here alludes to Ōishi Kuranosuke, leader of the famous Forty-seven Rōnin, who was considered the epitome of unselfish loyalty. "Way" may mean duty or moral principles, but in this instance most likely alludes to duty in relation to the emperor. That Ōkubo was a Japanese loyal to his sovereign there is no doubt.

Leaving Akao, Ōkubo arrived in Ōsaka on May 3, but left the following day for Fushimi where he had hoped to find Saigō at the temporary residence of the Satsuma *han*.[69] He discovered, however, that Saigō was not there. Again frustrated, he joined friends for a round of drinks and serious consultation. Here he learned that Saigō, true to his promise, had arrived at Shimonoseki for the meeting with Hisamitsu and the Satsuma force, but that the more Saigō had thought of the political situation the more restive he had become. He had become increasingly aware of the conflict between Hisamitsu, who continued to cling to the concept of *kōbu gattai* as the formula for the restoration of unity in the empire, and the *rōnin,* with whom he had been in consultation in recent days and who were determined on *tōbaku,* or overthrow of the Bakufu. Although in full accord with the extremists, Saigō was nevertheless a retainer of the Shimazu, and he felt constrained to allay the restless feelings of the *rōnin.* Therefore, instead of waiting for the Satsuma party to arrive, he immediately set out for Kyōto, only to find the situation there beyond control. The radical loyalists were seething with excitement. It was while Saigō was discussing the new developments with Murata Shimpachi, Moriyama Shinzō, and others over cups of *sake,* or rice wine, that Ōkubo's messenger arrived requesting Saigō's return to the Satsuma residence at Fushimi. There, Saigō and Ōkubo engaged in a heated argument over the former's failure to meet Hisamitsu at Shimonoseki. But when Ōkubo fully understood his friend's motives and dilemma, he could only sympathize with him. For the rest of the evening, according to Ōkubo, the group sang and drank, the gaiety lasting until the early hours of the morning.[70]

After this meeting with Saigō, Ōkubo set out to locate the Satsuma party, which by this time was in the general area of Hyōgo. He eventually joined it at Ōkuradani where he reported to Hisamitsu the events that had transpired during the previous week, making it a point to clarify the reasons for Saigō's recent behavior.[71] During their conversation, however, Ōkubo sensed that Hisamitsu had already decided the warrior's fate, having based his decision upon intelligence indicating that Saigō had been acting in concert with the radical *rōnin.* For example, one report had noted that Saigō ridiculed the idea of *kōbu gattai* to which Hisamitsu tenaciously adhered. To Hisamitsu, Saigō's alleged action was an affront and in wrathful indignation he had ordered Saigō's arrest. The specific charges against Saigō included: (1) connivance with *rōnin* of various *han,* (2) inciting young samurai to extreme action, (3) retarding Hisamitsu's trip to Kyōto, and (4) disobeying Hisamitsu's orders and leaving Shimonoseki for Ōsaka.[72]

Later, while a worried Ōkubo pondered the possible effects of the arrest of Saigō on the loyalist movement, Saigō, on the afternoon of May 7, unexpectedly appeared at Ōkubo's inn in Hyōgo. Being aware of Hisamitsu's extreme antagonism toward Saigō, Ōkubo frankly admitted to his friend that he saw no hope of winning any leniency for him. Ōkubo was certain that Hisamitsu would demand Saigō's life. Ōkubo therefore suggested that they die together by applying the sword to each other.[73] To his credit, however, Saigō demurred, arguing that the loyalist cause would suffer little from his absence but that it would experience a profound loss if Ōkubo were to die. Saigō implored him to abandon the plan, promising to give himself up to Hisamitsu regardless of consequences. Ōkubo finally acceded to Saigō's pleas. He then reported Saigō's sentiments to Hisamitsu who, instead of issuing an order for Saigō to commit *hara kiri,* called only for his banishment.[74] Saigō's apparent sincerity and conviction, his close friendship with Ōkubo, and the fact that he had been one of Nariakira's favorite retainers were considerations that induced Hisamitsu to deal leniently with him. Also, Hisamitsu was undoubtedly aware of the dire consequences of putting Saigō to death. By destroying the very symbol of radical reform, the adherents of which were increasing in influence and numbers, Hisamitsu would inevitably bring down upon himself the wrath of the reformers. Although his life was spared, Saigō had to return to exile again after savoring only four months of freedom since his departure from Ōshima in March of 1862. On July 14 he was sent to Tokunoshima where he remained until his transfer to Okinoerabujima two months later.[75] Thus a sincere but impetuous warrior was placed in a position where he could be of only minimum use to the cause he championed.

It was fortunate for Japan that neither Ōkubo nor Saigō carried out the double suicide plan. They, along with Kido Kōin, were to form a triumvirate to spearhead the drive to unify Japan. They were to give guidance to the Restoration movement and to the subsequently established Meiji government. The force of these vigorous leaders, each complementing the others, gave impetus in the Meiji period to a modernization process, the rapidity of which had no equal until recent times. By 1878 the triumvirate was gone. But by that time Japan had gained enough strength to be spared the humiliating lot that fell to nineteenth-century China.

Obtaining Bakufu Concessions

Shimazu Hisamitsu and the Satsuma contingent, which had been proceeding from Kagoshima to the imperial capital, reached Ōsaka on May 8, 1862. Leaving half of his men at the Satsuma residence in that city, Hisamitsu pushed on to Fushimi and then to Kyōto, arriving there on the fourteenth.[76] As for the Bakufu, always anxiously on guard against attacks by the powerful *han*, it was greatly relieved to discover that Satsuma forces were not contemplating an assault against it. Hisamitsu had other plans. In Kyōto he promptly called upon Konoe Tadafusa at whose home other court nobles were gathered. Hisamitsu addressed himself to this small group of notables, pointing out the universal unrest caused by the Bakufu's policy to open Japan to foreign intercourse. He then denounced the Bakufu's harassment and arrest of various *daimyō* who opposed its policies, and stated that his mission was to fulfill his late brother's dream of initiating a reform movement for the sake of the country.[77] Finally, Hisamitsu presented to the assembled *kuge* a nine-point program calling for the issuance of a court edict for the complete overhaul of the Bakufu.

Among the Satsuma recommendations were: (1) that all court nobles and *daimyō* who were victims of the wrath of the Bakufu (Ansei purge, 1858) be freed of all penalties; (2) that the ex-lord of Echizen, Matsudaira Yoshinaga, be made *sōsai*, and Konoe Tadahiro be named *kampaku;* (3) that Tokugawa Yoshiyori be relieved of the guardianship of the *shōgun;* (4) that Andō Nobuyuki, a *rōjū*, be formally dismissed; (5) that Kuze Hirokane, a *rōjū*, be ordered to Kyōto; (6) that Tokugawa Keiki be made guardian of the *shōgun;* (7) that two or three *daimyō* be ordered to intervene should the Bakufu fail to obey the imperial edict; and (8) that there be no indiscriminate reliance on the opinions of the *rōnin.*[78] Here, spelled out, was the Hisamitsu brand of *kōbu gattai* with which Ōkubo was in complete agreement. The first seven points related to the reform of the Bakufu, and the final item pertained to the control of the radical *rōnin*. The Hisamitsu-Ōkubo policy called for the reform of the Bakufu but not for its destruction as the radicals increasingly advocated, and it preached moderation at a time when the country was in danger of being irrevocably split by exponents of the several ideologies.[79]

The Satsuma leaders were intent upon maintaining this policy of moderation. Hisamitsu's firm attitude toward the anti-Bakufu Satsuma radicals at the Teradaya inn indicated that no extremism would be tolerated. The Satsuma *rōnin*, congregated in the Ōsaka-Kyōto area, had hoped that Hisamitsu, while on his mission to Kyōto, would receive imperial sanction to capture the Ōsaka castle, rout the Bakufu garrison in the Nijō castle in Kyōto, take Hikone castle, and expel all the Bakufu officials in the imperial capital. They were also hopeful that Satsuma would take the initiative in freeing the political prisoners incarcerated by the Bakufu, and in persuading the Emperor to accompany a punitive expedition, composed of elements from various *han,* against the Bakufu.[80] The aspirations of the *rōnin* reveal that they were now clearly and openly advocating *tōbaku,* or overthrow of the Bakufu, a thought that was not expressed at all prior to 1859 and which very few were courageous enough to air while Ii Naosuke was alive.

The advocates of *tōbaku* were deeply disappointed when they learned of the moderate tone of Hisamitsu's proposals made before the Konoes and the other *kuge.* Disappointment turned to bitterness, and the *rōnin* reacted violently. Some of the Satsuma *rōnin* who had been left in Ōsaka started for Kyōto to remonstrate, but Shimazu was forewarned of their move and emissaries were sent to intercept them. On May 21, Ōkubo noted in his diary that "an emergency occurred today." Describing his own response to the situation, he wrote that "upon learning of the arrival of Takasaki Satarō, I immediately went to the lord's residence where I was informed that a group of Ōsaka and Satsuma *rōnin* from Edo numbering thirty or forty, including attendants, left this morning for Kyōto after conspiring to attack the Kyōto *shoshidai.* Takasaki had hastened here to warn us of this." Measures were forthwith taken, and he continues: "Since the lord's wish is to check them [the conspirators], the following men were sent to Fushimi: Suzuki Yūemon, Ōyama Kakunosuke, Narahara Kihachirō, Michijima Gorōbei, Ena Chūzaemon, Yamaguchi Kinnoshin, Morioka Zensuke, and Uedoko Gensuke."[81] These eight men, ironically, were members of Ōkubo's Seichū Gumi. They met with the insurgents at the Teradaya, an inn at Fushimi, and when the rebels refused to comply with Hisamitsu's orders the agents suddenly attacked and killed eight of them outright, including the extremist leader Arima Shinshichi, one of the original members of Ōkubo's Seichū Gumi.[82]

Ōkubo later went to Fushimi to deal with the rebels, which he did firmly but not unreasonably. By May 26 all of the recalcitrant *rōnin* involved were either ordered to leave for their homes or handed over to their *han* authorities.[83] In effect, the radical loyalists, who had relied heavily upon the support of Hisamitsu's reform group, were betrayed. Later, lamenting the hypocrisy evident in the actions of men of supposed integrity, Saigō wondered in whom one could place one's faith when those considered closer than blood brothers could not be trusted.[84] Needless to say, after the Teradaya incident Satsuma's prestige declined in the eyes of the radical *rōnin* who had turned to it for leadership.

That Ōkubo was entrusted with the task of dealing with the Teradaya affair is testimony of his growing influence and the trust that Hisamitsu placed in him. While in Kyōto, Ōkubo was used more and more as a *han* plotter and policy-maker. Soon after the Teradaya incident, Ōkubo was delegated to meet with influential *kuge* to discuss plans and aspirations common to Satsuma and the court nobility. In the course of such meetings, he became acquainted with some very influential people. Thus on June 3, his diary notes that he met with several nobles, among whom was Iwakura Tomomi, later to become one of Ōkubo's closest political allies.[85] The two men were drawn together because of their common political aspirations, that of realizing *kōbu gattai.*[86] Hisamitsu, in recognition of the value of his adviser, Ōkubo, on June 17 promoted him to the rank of *okonando tōdori.*[87]

Early in June, the draft of the imperial mandate to be presented to the Bakufu had been accepted by those concerned, and the court ordered Shimazu Hisamitsu to escort to Edo the imperial messenger, Ōhara Shigenori, who was commissioned to deliver the rescript to the Bakufu. The mandate represented the Satsuma recommendations in modified form. Changes to the original were made necessary because of the pressures exerted by Satsuma rivals. Fearful of Satsuma's possible monopolization of political influence in Kyōto, other *han,* notably Chōshū and Tosa, had by this time oriented their own policies to enable them to compete more favorably with their strong rival. Thus Chōshū, besides having instituted various domestic reforms and made an effort to gain the support of the *rōnin* for its *sonnō jōi* policy, succeeded in obtaining access to court circles through Ōgimachi Sanjō Sanenaru.[88] The imperial order demanded that the *shōgun* come to Kyōto in person "together with various *daimyō* in order to preserve the peace and tranquility of the country . . ."; that the appointments as *tairō* (Hideyoshi had several chief ministers) of Shimazu, Mōri, Yamanouchi, Date, and Maeda, *daimyō* whose territories lay on the coast, be made "to administer the government and defend the coasts of the land"; and that the appointment of Tokugawa Keiki as guardian of the *shōgun* and Matsudaira of Echizen as *tairō* be effected.[89]

The objective of these three measures was the renovation of the institutions created by the founder of the Tokugawa line, Ieyasu, and the promotion of effective administration.[90] An amalgam of the views of several factions, article one of the rescript represented the principles supported by Kido Kōin and Chōshū, article two that of the imperial house, and article three that of Satsuma.[91]

Armed with the mandate, Ōhara, accompanied by Hisamitsu, Ōkubo, and a Satsuma contingent, arrived in Edo on the afternoon of July 3.[92] The imperial orders were conveyed to the proper authorities for study, and a meeting between Bakufu officials and the imperial messenger was scheduled for July 22. At this time both Ōhara and Ōkubo were fully prepared to resort to violence should the *rōjū* refuse to submit to the imperial will. Ōkubo's diary reveals that he called on Ōhara at his residence just prior to the conference and informed the envoy that "if the *kakurō* [*rōjū*] should fail to accept the imperial order, I am determined not to allow them to return home." [93] In other words, if the Bakufu representatives failed to consent to the reformation proposal, Ōkubo was prepared to put them to the sword. The plan was to station three men outside the conference room and, if the *rōjū* failed to submit, Ōhara was to step out of the meeting. This was to be the signal for the attack on the assembled Bakufu officials.[94]

Fortunately, there was no need for implementing this ruthless plan, although its existence gave the imperial negotiators confidence and boldness. Intimidated by the fierce determination of their opponents, the *rōjū* eventually agreed to the first and third articles of the mandate.[95] Especially significant was the Bakufu's acceptance of the order for the *shōgun* to go to Kyōto to achieve a complete understanding with the Emperor. As a result, for the first time in 230 years, since Iemitsu had last observed this practice, a *shōgun* was to visit Kyōto. In the spring of 1863, Tokugawa Iemochi, accompanied by three thousand men, arrived in Kyōto. Tokugawa Keiki became guardian to the *shōgun* on August 1, 1862, and Matsudaira Yoshinaga became chief minister on August 4 of the same year. These were all concessions reflecting the weakened position of the once mighty Tokugawa regime.

Through the Tokugawa concessions the *kōbu gattai* fashioned by Hisamitsu and his advisers was largely achieved, but only after the Bakufu officials had been browbeaten and intimidated by those who believed in negotiating on the basis of force, not reasoned persuasion. History has also accused Japan of resorting to such tactics in its international relations in more recent times. Ōkubo himself was to set the pattern for such diplomacy in the modern period when as minister plenipotentiary he dealt with China over the Formosan question—less than a decade after he aided in winning concessions from the Tokugawa Bakufu. In all fairness to Japan's policy-makers and diplomats down through history, let it be said that the philosophy of "might makes right" is as old as mankind itself. No one nation has had a monopoly on it. It has often proved an effective, if not ethical, means of gaining an objective, and Ōkubo, being a proponent of *realpolitik,* applied it often to attain his goals.

The Richardson Affair

Upon the successful conclusion of their mission to Edo, the Satsuma party departed for Kyōto on September 14, 1862.[96] The *daimyō* procession had scarcely left the city when, in the village of Namamugi, between Kawasaki and Kanagawa, a party of Englishmen on horseback was attacked by Satsuma swordsmen, killing one of their number, C. L. Richardson. One explanation for the attack is that Hisamitsu left Edo smarting under the ill treatment he had received from the Bakufu and therefore allowed his retainers to attack the English party in order to create an international incident that would embarrass the Edo government.[97] The more likely reason is that the foreigners unwisely neglected to dismount when the procession passed by and do obeisance to the *daimyō* as required by Japanese law and custom. Ōkubo and Komatsu, in reporting the incident to the Bakufu, attempted to absolve the Satsuma retinue of blame. They stated that the assailant of the Englishman was Okano Shinsuke, a Satsuma samurai who had abandoned the *han* and was now a *rōnin.* Wishing to view the colorful procession of his former lord, Okano had come to Namamugi. When he observed the apparently disrespectful behavior the English displayed toward the Satsuma *daimyō,* his blood boiled. He therefore ran forward and cut down Richardson.[98]

Although Okano Shinsuke may have been directly responsible for the murder of Richardson, this does not entirely absolve the Satsuma *han* from blame; members of the retinue actively participated in the attack against the English. After the Englishmen had dispersed, Narahara Kizaemon, Arimura Shunsai, and others clamored for permission to attack the English homes in Kanagawa immediately, rather than wait for the inevitable skirmish with English troops. If a clash of arms were to take place, they argued, Satsuma, with inadequate manpower, would most certainly face defeat and dishonor. The majority of the men favored taking the offensive, but Ōkubo raised a dissenting voice. After commending them for their determination, he urged that sober consideration be given to the situation. Pointing out that the foreigner was killed merely for indiscreetly cutting across the path of the procession, he contended that the English would adjudge this insufficient grounds for the Japanese to have resorted to such drastic action. He advised against an attack on the English residences and suggested that the cortege move on immediately to the next *eki,* or post station. Thus by the time the English cavalry arrived on the scene of the murder, only Takasaki Isoroku and several others who had remained behind to handle the situation were present.[99] Little did Ōkubo realize at this time the tremendous impact the Richardson affair would have upon the basic thinking of Japanese leaders, and therefore upon the history of Satsuma and Japan as a whole.

Resurgence of Radical Influence

After the Richardson incident, the Satsuma party's journey to Kyōto proved uneventful. When it finally reached Kyōto, however, toward the end of September, it found the whole political complexion of the capital drastically changed. While Ōhara, Hisamitsu, and Ōkubo were making their influence felt in Edo, the radical elements, whom Hisamitsu had supposedly suppressed by his action at Teradaya, had stepped up the pace of their activities. Joining forces with members of the extreme wing of the *kuge* and the Chōshū *han,* the radical coalition had begun a campaign of vilification and terror against the moderates. Iwakura's *kōbu gattai* faction as well as the foreigners in Japan became objects of fresh attacks by the adherents of *sonnō jōi.* The Tōzenji affair of June 26, 1862, in which a Japanese British Legation guard, Itō Gumpei, murdered two English marines, was a result of the growing feeling of hostility engendered by the radicals.[100] Iwakura was to be deprived of office as a result of the disruption of the political power equilibrium in Kyōto.[101] Ōkubo discovered that other *kuge* with whom he had freely consulted a scant six months earlier, just before his departure for Edo, no longer enjoyed positions of influence. As a reaction to this new situation, Satsuma and Aizu entered into an alliance in the hope of offsetting the growing power of Chōshū and Tosa.[102] Tension mounted and, on October 16, Shimazu Hisamitsu, genuinely disgusted over the turn of affairs, quit Kyōto and returned to Kagoshima. He was also concerned over the reaction of the English to the Richardson affair. There was a strong possibility that the British would attack Kagoshima in retaliation, and Hisamitsu wanted to be in Kagoshima when and if such an attack came. Even the weather seemed to favor the decision to go home. According to Ōkubo, "since the day before yesterday rain has continually fallen until this morning when the sky cleared up by departure time." As Hisamitsu and his liegemen left the city, "there were enormous crowds viewing the procession up to about Yojō [name of a thoroughfare], while many people continued to line the road as far as Fushimi." [103]

Arriving home at the end of October, Ōkubo had reason to look back upon the accomplishments of the past six months with considerable satisfaction. His lord took cognizance of his services on behalf of the *kōbu gattai* movement by presenting him with various gifts.[104] These were gratefully received, to be sure. But perhaps the news of additional reform measures effected by the Tokugawa government, which struck at the very base of the Tokugawa control system, was for Ōkubo most rewarding of all. Ōkubo's diary carries the following entry for November 4, 1862:

> Since a cold is bothering me, I did not go to work today. Kamada has come here with the news of the reformation in Kantō, according to the advice I received from Uchida Nakanosuke. The *daimyō* are now required to remain in Edo for only one hundred days every three years under the *sankin kōtai* system. Wives and children may be taken home to their own *han*. *Daimyō* who are already on their way to Edo may return home immediately upon being advised of the change in the law. With reference to dress, moderation is to be effected. . . . The above is in substance what I have heard. This is the manifestation of Lord Saburō's [Hisamitsu's] efforts for which I am grateful.[105]

By displaying what amounted to false humility, Ōkubo was observing the propriety expected of a Japanese. No subordinate in Japanese official life would openly attribute to himself achievements he might know belonged to him; traditionally his superior expects and usually takes the credit. For subordinates, such as Ōkubo, to have accepted credit for an achievement undertaken in the name of his lord would have been considered disrespectful. The importance the Japanese have attributed to headship, whether in family, *han*, or nation, may be responsible for this attitude. Whatever the reason, it would be erroneous to give Hisamitsu all the credit for prodding the Bakufu to move toward reform. Only with the guidance of an adviser such as Ōkubo could Hisamitsu have accomplished many of the things that history has ascribed to him.

Ōkubo's talents were honored. His star continued to ascend; within the year he was given a higher preferment in the *han.* Made a *goyō toritsugi minarai* in November, he soon was handling *han* duties on the highest level. On November 24 he began his new duties, which involved dealing directly with the *karō,* the senior minister.[106]

IV
Champion of the Restoration

The war between Satsuma and England, growing out of the Namamugi incident, was of utmost significance to Ōkubo, since it was to alter his basic thinking concerning foreign policy from one of *jōi* to that of *kaikoku.* It also impressed upon him the urgency of strengthening the economic, military, and political structures of the country. And although Ōkubo was a moderate who had hitherto endeavored to establish the union of court and Bakufu, his sympathy for the hopelessly impotent military government in Edo was to dissipate when he realized that a united front against the West could not be formed under its feeble leadership. In time, Ōkubo was to shift from a *kōbu gattai* position to one of *hambaku,* or opposition to the Bakufu, and finally to that of *tōbaku,* or overthrow of the Bakufu. The latter was the ideology of the Chōshū extremists which he had previously opposed, but once he accepted the *tōbaku* position Ōkubo worked relentlessly for its realization and the restoration of imperial rule. In fact, he was to sever the alliance with Aizu because it no longer served his purpose and, furthermore, he was to cement a political and military union with Chōshū, a traditional Satsuma enemy. The Ōkubo strategy, although completely opportunistic, was to serve his purpose well; by January 3, 1868, he, along with his colleagues, was to succeed in preparing the ground for the historic decree that would restore the rule of the emperor.

Mission to Kyōto

After his return to Kagoshima in the fall of 1862, Ōkubo was kept busy with *han* affairs until January 8, 1863, when he once more left for Kyōto as a Satsuma representative. He was commissioned to arrest the growing influence of the *kuge* extremists, who were *kokuji goyōgakari,* or officials of the court designated to advise the throne on national affairs. This body of advisers was created on January 28, 1863, specifically to attend to the increasing number of petitions and suggestions presented to the court by the various *daimyō* as the result of the growing complexity of the political situation after 1860. The members, numbering twenty-nine, were to deliberate on all proposals submitted to them before presenting their recommendations to the throne for decision. The original appointees were competent men chosen without consideration for their lineage or official rank. Naturally, the moderates became anxious as the strength of the radical faction increased; they feared that the extremists would gain complete control of the newly created consultative council and, through it, the court itself.[1] Those most concerned with the growing prestige of the Chōshū- and Tosa-supported extremists at court were the Bakufu and Satsuma, who, as adherents of the moderate *kōbu gattai* policy, feared the antithetical *sonnō jōi* stand of the extremists.

The Bakufu and Satsuma had ample reason to be concerned over the *sonnō jōi* movement, which had its beginning around 1861. By 1863 it had gained tremendous momentum. Although the Teradaya incident temporarily checked its forward thrust, it soon regained its former vigor. The extremists among the minor *kuge* were intent upon gaining control of the court with the aid of other radicals, all of whom looked to Chōshū for leadership, and then, under imperial prestige, working for *ōsei fukko,* or the restoration of imperial rule.[2] The movement met resistance from the Bakufu and its allies, but it nevertheless continued to move ahead and eventually proclaimed the doctrine of *tōbaku,* a concept that had germinated in the minds of thinkers prior to the period 1861-1863.[3]

The authorship of the *tōbaku* doctrine is generally ascribed to Yoshida Shōin, who made it implicit in his *Jisei Ron* (Essay on the Spirit of the Times) which appeared in 1859. In this essay he alluded to the supplantation of the Bakufu by an imperial government.[4] The most outspoken proponent of the *tōbaku* doctrine, however, was Yoshida Shōin's contemporary, Maki Izumi, who wrote the *Keii Gusetsu,* in which he expressed restoration sentiments and espoused the implementation of various large-scale reforms. In his *Daimuki,* Maki more specifically outlined his *tōbaku* program by calling for the expression of imperial wrath over the Bakufu's inept handling of foreign policy. He suggested that the emperor personally lead a force to Edo to judge the crimes of the Bakufu officials, from *tairō* on down to the lesser functionaries, and mete out death penalties to the guilty. Furthermore, he advocated the relegation of the Tokugawa from the position of *shōgun* to *daimyō*.[5]

Influenced by Maki's doctrine, the *sonnō jōi* adherents after 1861 attempted to rally the sentiments and forces of the various *han* against the Tokugawa government by stressing the record of the Bakufu in foreign relations. In order to realize their ultimate objective of restoring the monarchy and expelling the foreigners, they had first to destroy the Bakufu, and hence, with the Bakufu's progressive enervation after Ii Naosuke's assassination in 1860, the *sonnō jōi* party made increasing use of *tōbaku* as its clarion call.[6]

Satsuma's opposition to the radical doctrine was both ideological and practical. To prevent the radical-supported Chōshū *han* from supplanting it in national leadership, Satsuma had to weaken the influence of the radicals in Kyōto. Satsuma's plan was to work in collusion with the Bakufu in an attempt to dislodge Chōshū from its entrenched position in the imperial capital, thereby isolating the radical *kuge* elements and nullifying their influence. The Bakufu, being more than amenable to the plan, ordered Hisamitsu to be in Kyōto by March 9, 1863, where, together with Matsudaira Yoshinaga, the Bakufu minister, and such friendly *kuge* as Konoe, he might formulate a common plan of action. Having plans of his own, however, Hisamitsu did not immediately comply with the Edo order. Hisamitsu wanted to enter Kyōto only after radical influences had languished from lack of support of such *han* as Chōshū and Tosa, whose power was dominant there. He suggested that all *daimyō* then present in Kyōto be ordered to return to their respective domains where they could concentrate their energies upon bolstering their own defenses against external danger. Only after these *daimyō* had quit the imperial capital should the other lords be summoned to the city. Hence he requested a postponement of his departure for Kyōto. Also, the Satsuma authorities wanted to postpone the scheduled visit of the *shōgun,* Iemochi, to Kyōto later that spring; they believed that his presence in the imperial city would place him at the mercy of the extremists.[7]

Given the task of gaining these Satsuma objectives, Ōkubo left Kagoshima early in January, 1863. There is no question that he was instrumental in formulating Satsuma policy and was therefore thoroughly familiar with its objectives; at this time Ōkubo was the most important person among the leaders of the *han*, and his opinion represented that of Satsuma.[8] Arriving in Kyōto on February 8, he presented Hisamitsu's memorial to Konoe, the *kampaku*.[9] It stated that preparations for defense against a possible English attack in retaliation for the murder of Richardson necessitated Hisamitsu's presence in Kagoshima for several months after the date set by the Bakufu for his departure. It also argued that the *shōgun*'s visit to Kyōto would be inexpedient as the nature of the international situation made it imperative for Iemochi to remain in Edo, and that his travel expense of about eight hundred thousand *ryō* could more beneficially be utilized for defense purposes. It also stressed the urgency of applying the *jōi* policy.[10]

Clearly, the Satsuma proposal was in opposition to the scheme of the *sonnō jōi* party to compel Tokugawa Iemochi to come up to Kyōto, which would symbolize the fact that the Bakufu conceded subordination to the court. For Satsuma to advocate the postponement of the *shōgun*'s visit to Kyōto would be construed as an abandonment of the *kōbu gattai* policy nurtured by Tokugawa Keiki and Shimazu Hisamitsu and founded upon the theory that neither court nor Bakufu would retain dominant administrative authority. To prevent certain provocation of public sentiment against Satsuma, Ōkubo requested his *kuge* associates to refrain from disclosing the source of the new proposal.[11] This in effect was asking the court nobles to be responsible for the Satsuma-conceived plan, a pusillanimity occasioned by his knowledge that he was really attempting to annul what was basically a Chōshū policy.

After winning the agreement of Konoe and other *kuge* to the Satsuma plan, Ōkubo, on February 13, 1863, wrote to Nakayama Chūzaemon reporting his progress and indicating that he was departing that day for Edo to win Bakufu approval of the proposals.[12] Reaching Edo a week later, Ōkubo discovered to his dismay that the date for Tokugawa Iemochi's visit to the imperial capital had already been set and that Tokugawa Keiki was just then en route to Kyōto. The Bakufu, however, assured Ōkubo that it was in general agreement with the Satsuma plan.[13] On this note, he left Edo and hurriedly returned to Kyōto, arriving there on March 4.[14] There, through court channels, he made one more attempt to have the *shōgun*'s visit postponed by imperial decree, but the strength of the radical influence was so great that the Satsuma plan was foiled.[15]

Contemplating the Use of Force

Having failed through peaceful means to gain his objective, Ōkubo was prepared to use force to suppress the radical party. While in Edo he had consulted with Yamanouchi Toyoshige and Matsudaira Yoshinaga and informed them of his secondary plan, namely that, after all *daimyō* were ordered from Kyōto and before the arrival of the *shōgun*, Tokugawa Keiki, Matsudaira Yoshinaga, Yamanouchi Toyoshige, and Shimazu Hisamitsu would enter the capital and fix state policy.[16] Ōkubo now felt that circumstances dictated positive action. He suggested in a letter to Nakayama Chūzaemon that Hisamitsu bring with him on his next trip to Kyōto a military force capable of overwhelming all opposition. Stressing the importance of Hisamitsu's presence under the existing situation, Ōkubo wrote:

> As I observe the unsettled situation here, it is impossible for me to predict when it will improve. Thus we hope that the lord will come to Kyōto. I am certain that the entire *han* will be consolidated and of a mind not to tolerate any outrages, and I urgently request that a plan be formulated to overpower the various *han* [that are opposed to the *kōbu gattai* policy].[17]

The political stage in Kyōto at this time was dominated completely by the extreme *kuge* who, with the backing of Chōshū military might, had ejected their more moderate colleagues. The Sanjō Sanetomi–Anenokōji Kintomo faction forced the resignation of such moderate court nobles as Nakayama Tadayasu and others. Konoe, the *kampaku*, was forced to retire and was replaced by Takatsukasa. Although Tokugawa Keiki, Yamanouchi Toyoshige, and Matsudaira Yoshinaga arrived in Kyōto on February 22, March 14, and March 22, respectively, they could do nothing to frustrate the actions of the extremists.

Dejected over the seriousness of conditions in Kyōto and the failure of his mission, Ōkubo, on March 12, boarded a ship for Kagoshima. Misfortune continued to pursue him; that same night his vessel struck a treacherous reef, and both he and his traveling companion, Komatsu Tatewaki, barely escaped with their lives.[18] Once home, however, Ōkubo's gloom was somewhat dissipated by the honors that came to him. On

March 10 he and Nakayama Chūzaemon were made *soba yaku* while yet retaining the posts of *okonando tōdori*. Ichiki Shirō noted in his diary that people were amazed to see the rapid advancement of Ōkubo, who, only several months previously, had been made *goyō toritsugi*. His rise was phenomenal.[19]

In Kyōto, agitation for the early expulsion of the barbarians was daily increasing in intensity, and the *rōnin* and low-ranking samurai clamored for the immediate establishment of a specific date for the exploit. The seriousness of the situation forced a party of thirteen *kuge*, headed by Sanjō and Anenokōji, to rush for consultation to the home of Takatsukasa, who had become the *kampaku* in the summer of 1862; there it was decided that Tokugawa Keiki should be pressed to fix the date at once. He and Matsudaira Yoshinaga temporized, asserting that that could only be done after the arrival of Iemochi, the *shōgun*.[20]

Tokugawa Iemochi and a retinue of three thousand arrived in Kyōto on April 21, 1863. Although the *shōgun* intended to remain no more than ten days, he was detained nearly a hundred days, until July 24, by the extremists who, now determined to overthrow the Bakufu, realized the advantage of having him under their control.[21] Matsudaira Yoshinaga, who had been under pressure to have a date set for the expulsion of the foreigners, and knowing the difficulty involved in this matter, on May 8 resigned his office as *sōsai*, furtively left the capital, and returned to his province of Echizen.[22] Early in June Emperor Kōmei announced that on June 25 all foreigners would be expelled and ports closed to them.

In Edo the absence of the *shōgun* was keenly felt as the English demanded settlement of the problems stemming from the murder of the two English marines and the Namamugi outrage. The British, on December 4, 1862, had demanded ten thousand pounds for the death of the sentries, and, on April 6, 1863, had demanded an apology from the Bakufu and an indemnity of one hundred thousand pounds for the Namamugi incident. Furthermore, the assassins were to be brought to justice and twenty-five thousand pounds more transferred to the British for distribution among Richardson's relatives and companions who had been attacked.[23] The Bakufu, perceiving that further procrastination would lead to war, decided to clear its reputation and then put an end to foreign intercourse.[24] The day before the date fixed for the expulsion of foreigners, on June 24, it paid the sum of one hundred and ten thousand pounds.[25] Caught between external and internal pressures, the Bakufu officials had been placed in an almost impossible position.

In Kyōto, Emperor Kōmei also had his problems. Although antiforeign, he was concerned over the growing power of the radical elements whose rashness he feared. Their objective was to overthrow the Bakufu, whereas the Emperor wished for the union of court and Bakufu, believing that only a united country could hope to ward off foreign aggression.[26]

Discredited as they were, the *kōbu gattai* faction, persisting in attempts to make a comeback, urged Shimazu Hisamitsu to return to Kyōto. He had arrived in the imperial city on May 1, while Ōkubo remained in Kagoshima preparing safeguards against the expected attack of the British.[27] Hisamitsu met with Takatsukasa, the *kampaku;* Matsudaira Yoshinaga, the *sōsai;* Tokugawa Keiki, Yamanouchi Toyoshige, and other fellow thinkers, and urged strong and drastic measures against the extremists. He advised against the immediate expulsion of the foreigners; demanded the removal of all radical *kuge,* the punishment by the Bakufu of radical *rōnin,* and the reinstatement of Konoe Tadafusa, the former *kampaku,* and Prince Nakagawa. He also recommended that administrative authority be vested in the *seii taishōgun* and that a mandate be issued ordering all *daimyō* and retainers to return to their provinces.[28] But Hisamitsu perceived that his policy of repression could only be effected by utilizing the entire armed might of Satsuma, which at that time was imperatively needed at home.

After a brief sojourn of less than a week he left for Kagoshima, the Satsuma capital, against which the British were preparing to launch an attack. It was reported that criticism by other *han* in Kyōto, aimed at Hisamitsu's excessive control over state affairs, had led to his decision to leave. This is borne out by his memorial to the Emperor in which he stated that he had criticized the political situation and offered his opinion to the throne. But the tongue of slander had effectively prevented his suggestions from being carried out. He felt that if he remained in Kyōto he would be justifying the slanders uttered against him and some disaster might result. He therefore asked the Emperor to grant him a few months' leave of absence, during which time he could prepare for the attack by the English.[29]

Striking at the Extremists

In Kagoshima, Hisamitsu was not allowed to concentrate his efforts solely on *han* affairs; the imperial house insisted on his support in reëstablishing political equilibrium in Kyōto, where the clamor by the *sonnō jōi* party for the establishment of imperial rule and the early expulsion of foreigners was daily mounting. Through the intermediary of Prince Nakagawa the Emperor transmitted to Satsuma a secret message requesting Hisamitsu's return to Kyōto to restore the prestige of the *kōbu gattai* faction. Ōkubu, however, advised his lord against an early departure, stressing that with insufficient planning and inadequate forces the presence of Hisamitsu in Kyōto might prove to be more harmful than beneficial to their cause. As an alternative he suggested that Shimazu Shigetomi, Tadayoshi's brother, immediately lead a force, composed of samurai, from Miyakonojō to Kyōto. Ōkubu recommended that Hisamitsu request of the court a postponement of his departure until the early part of September and that three groups of *hatamoto* be dispatched under him at that time.[30] He further emphasized that Prince Nakagawa and Konoe Tadafusa should be notified not to relinquish their positions under any circumstances, and reassured them that Satsuma was prepared to come to their aid. Ōkubo apparently was determined to employ the full force of the Satsuma military power in reëstablishing control of Kyōto by the *kōbu gattai* adherents. The target date for the coup d'etat was to have been in mid-September, but the English bombardment of Kagoshima in August forced a change in plans. Preoccupied with pressing problems of the *han*, the Satsuma leaders were unable to leave for Kyōto with the main body of troops as anticipated.

In the meantime, the *daimyō* of Aizu had received word that Kusaka Genzui, the Chōshū loyalist, and his fellow extremists were prepared to seize control of the Emperor. The scheme was to kidnap him while the imperial procession proceeded to the Yamato shrines. The radicals, furthermore, had made it known that the Emperor was willing to take the field in person to drive out the foreigners. This, however, the Emperor had no intention of doing, at least at the time the radicals had set. The growing arrogance of the radicals and the startling new developments stemming from their actions induced Princes Nakagawa and Konoe to consult with the Emperor on September 28 and again on the following day to arrange for a countercoup. On the night of the twenty-ninth the troops of Matsudaira Katamori, military commissioner of Kyōto, were stationed within the castle while those of Satsuma, Aizu, Bizen, and Inaba took their assigned posts. All the gates to the palace were firmly shut. Meanwhile, at a palace conference, several proposals were agreed to: (1) the postponement of an imperial expedition against the foreigners,

(2) the arrest of Sanjō Sanetomi and other *kuge* who favored the Chōshū policy, and (3) the relief of the Chōshū forces from the duty of guarding the Sakimachi gate. The Chōshū contingent, in the face of the overwhelming military superiority of their adversaries and in obedience to an imperial mandate, reluctantly withdrew without resistance on the afternoon of September 30. Seven low-ranking *kuge* extremists left for Chōshū on October 1 and were later deprived of their titles and honors.[31]

The coup d'etat, which drove out the extremists from Kyōto and restored the prestige of the *kōbu gattai* faction, changed the political complexion of Kyōto within a day. Although the radicals were not completely defeated, there was a temporary power vacuum in the capital which Satsuma feared might be filled by Aizu. Furthermore, there was the real fear that, with Aizu's support, the Bakufu could, under the circumstances, afford to attempt a reassertion of its former authority. This, however, Satsuma and other like-minded *han* were to succeed in preventing.[32]

Defying the British

The ejection from Kyōto of the Chōshū faction on September 30, 1863, occurred two weeks after the bombardment and destruction of a large portion of Kagoshima by an English squadron. This was a significant engagement since British naval strength was to impress and humble an otherwise haughty and smug Ōkubo who believed in the invincibility of his *han* and its defenses. In a letter to Komatsu Tatewaki, dated May 11, 1863, Ōkubo had reported with pride the satisfactory progress of defense preparations, stating that the batteries were being restored with the aid of five hundred men and women workers who would complete their task at an early date.[33] Although the Bakufu had paid indemnities and submitted its written apology to England over the murder of Richardson at Namamugi, the British were unable to compel Shimazu to afford full justice by sending the perpetrators of the murder to Edo as demanded.[34] Therefore on August 3, 1863, the British chargé d'affaires, Colonel St. John Neale, notified the Bakufu that within three days he would proceed with a squadron under Vice-Admiral Kuper to prefer the remaining demands of the British government. Weighing anchor at Yokohama on August 6, the squadron arrived in Kagoshima Bay on the night of August 11.[35] Early the next morning two Satsuma officials boarded the British flagship and, after interrogating the visitors, returned to shore. A few hours later the squadron moved to a position off the batteries of the city, at which time a second boat with four Japanese officials came up to the flagship. They were handed the British demands calling for the immediate trial and execution, in the presence of one or more British naval officers, of the chief perpetrators of the murder of Richardson, and the payment of twenty-five thousand pounds sterling. The Satsuma officials thereupon went ashore and returned a few hourse later to invite Neale and Kuper to meet with the Satsuma council, since the "Prince of Satsuma" was not then in Kagoshima. The British, however, declined the offer.[36] Then, on August 13, several officials came alongside the flagship, accompanied by a retinue of forty men, which the British allowed to come aboard only after taking precautionary measures against any attempt to attack and kill Neale or Kuper.[37] But the officials, instead of meeting the British demands, this time sheltered themselves under the plea that their *han* was subject to Bakufu authority and hence could neither accept nor refuse the demands.[38]

This continued uncompromising Satsuma attitude led Admiral Kuper to resort to preliminary measures of coërcion, namely, the seizure of three Satsuma steamers that were then lashed alongside three of his own ships; it was Kuper's intention to retain them "until such time as the Prince of Satsuma should either comply with the demands made upon him or should make advances with a view to their settlement." This was hostile action and naturally the Satsuma batteries opened fire. When they did, the Admiral charged the Japanese with initiating hostilities, saying that on August 15 the batteries opened fire on the squadron, "an act which it became necessary immediately to resent." [39] The British attack set flame to half the town and destroyed an extensive arsenal, gun foundry, and five large Ryūkyū junks, in addition to the three steamers mentioned above.[40] A heavy typhoon which blew throughout the night aided the British operations, and Kuper could say with a great deal of satisfaction that "there is every reason to suppose that the palace has been destroyed, as many shell were seen to burst in it, and the fire, which is still raging, affords reasonable ground for believing that the entire town of Kagoshima is now a mass of ruins." [41]

The official Satsuma report to the Bakufu regarding the British attack concurs in detail with the British account, although the "palace" to which Admiral Kuper alludes in his statement was in reality one of the temples in Kagoshima. The gist of the Satsuma report is as follows:

> On August 11 at 5:00 P.M. (*nanatsu-han doki*), seven ships of the British squadron arrived and anchored off Taniyama Nanatsujima. On the following day, August 12, at 10:00 A.M. (*yottsu doki*), it cast anchor off Jōkamae. We sent a boarding party to interrogate the English who demanded compensation for the family of the foreigner who was killed during the Namamugi incident. If a satisfactory answer did not come within twenty-four hours, the British threatened to resort to coërcive measures. As we reported to you last year, however, we have endeavored to locate the perpetrators of the killing without success; we have done the utmost to resolve this problem peacefully. Before dawn on August 15 the English besieged with five of their ships three Satsuma steamers anchored off Shigetomi and after boarding and attaching lines to them, towed them out into the Bay. We offered pursuit unsuccessfully. Orders were thereupon issued to open fire upon the foreign ships; five Jōka batteries continued firing from 11:00 A.M. (*yottsu-han doki*) to before 12:00 noon (*kokonotsu doki-mae*). The British ships to which our steamers were lashed were anchored off Koikemura on Sakurajima. The British returned the fire of the island batteries. The firing continued all day. Tsukujimachi was set ablaze, and whipped by a strong southeast wind, the flames destroyed half of Kamimachi and a quarter of Kamibushikōji. Jōkomiyōji, Fudankōin, and Kōkokuji were likewise razed. The Shūseikan and some adjacent buildings were destroyed. Five Ryūkyū junks, a native vessel anchored off shore as well as three steamers were destroyed. A British ship ran aground off Gionnosu, but it was towed off by other ships in the squadron. About noon the following day the British ships changed anchorage while the Jōka batteries withheld fire because the targets were beyond their range; two batteries on Sakurajima were damaged slightly. The small cannons were ineffective. Firing was directed at the enemy from both the Jōka Kawajiri and the Okikōjima batteries. The enemy ships directed intense firing against us off Okikōjima. The squadron anchored off Taniyama Nanatsujima, and left this area on the same day.[42]

During the bombardment Ōkubo was in Kagoshima and observed the shelling of the city from atop a roof of one of its buildings. As he viewed the shells landing and the flames destroying the flimsy structures, Ōkubo suddenly lost his footing on the tile, slippery from rain. Crying out, he fell to the ground below. Some of those who witnessed this accident thought that Ōkubo had lost his balance because he was seized by fright and therewith branded him a coward.[43] However, his subsequent behavior under similar circumstances was to prove that he did not lack courage.

Besides Ōkubo's wounded pride after tumbling off the roof, there were real casualties on both sides as the result of the British bombardment. The Japanese claimed that the enemy lost over sixty men killed or wounded, including Captain Josling and Commander Wilmot who were killed when a shell struck the bridge of the flagship "Euryalus." [44] Japanese losses were comparatively small, with ten men killed and eleven wounded, although property losses were enormous.[45] Many native historians have credited the Satsuma *han* with a glorious victory, claiming that the British China squadron was crippled to the point of being unable to continue operations and thus failed to fulfill its intended mission.[46]

The British bombardment nevertheless had a profound effect on Satsuma. Tokutomi, for example, states that the war between England and Satsuma eventually resulted in mutual coöperation between the two parties. He further states that the war served as a test of strength, its outcome giving the Satsuma samurai confidence in their military power.[47] Francis Ottiwell Adams, former British chargé d'affaires and secretary of legation at Edo, stated that the bombardment of Kagoshima was the turning point as far as Satsuma was concerned. It was then that the samurai first became convinced that Japan was not the most powerful country in the world and that there were other nations stronger and perhaps more civilized. It was from that time that the leaders ceased to look upon the foreigners with contempt and began to open their *han* to foreign influences. They subsequently introduced modern machinery and other inventions, took the lead in employing European technicians to teach them their use, and became inspired to rival foreign nations in the arts of war as well as peace.[48]

This conclusion is supported by the less nationalistic Japanese scholars. Shirayanagi Takeshi definitely states that the thinking of both Hisamitsu and Ōkubo, and therefore that of the *han*, was changed because of the encounter with British naval power.[49] Another writer implies that the entire Satsuma *han* was forced to recognize the superiority of the West in naval architecture and tactics.[50] The Japanese have also asserted that by vigorously expelling the English, Satsuma in effect supported the *jōi* position, which won for Satsuma admirers among the ranks of the extremists and increased its influence.[51] The fact is that the Satsuma leaders were at the time against the expulsion of foreign influences and for their introduction, that is, against *jōi* and for *kaikoku*. For example, Shimazu Hisamitsu and Ōkubo Toshimichi, recognizing the need for adopting the best ideas of the West in order to compensate for the *han*'s lack of strength, prevailed upon the Satsuma *daimyō* to establish the Kaiseijo, an institute for Western studies.[52]

British policy was also to undergo a change after the British-Satsuma incident. Before this, England had looked upon the Bakufu as the most promising stabilizing force for Japan and had lent it her support while, at the same time, attempting to suppress the *jōi* clique operating in the name of the Emperor. However, when it became apparent that the Edo regime was neither genuinely desirous of developing commercial relations nor capable of controlling the antiforeign faction, the British policy gradually veered from its original course to that of supporting the anti-Bakufu faction. The British realized that the progressive party led by Satsuma and Chōshū wielded de facto power. They also realized the political significance of the imperial house with which this progressive faction was associated, and were to dangle the bait of trade and profit before the various antiforeign *daimyō* in an attempt to destroy the basis for the *jōi* sentiment. By 1866 British-Satsuma relations had improved to the point where Satsuma students were being sent secretly to England. One of these students, Terajima Munenori, no doubt instructed by the *han*, conferred with Lord Clarendon, the British foreign minister, urging that England conduct her diplomatic dealings through a conference of *daimyō* under imperial aegis rather than with the Bakufu.[53]

Bending to British Will

That the Japanese were highly impressed by Western naval might can also be inferred from the willingness on the part of the Satsuma leadership to settle their differences with the British. Realistic thinkers within the *han* council, such as Niiro Tatsuo, who foresaw a possible British occupation of Satsuma and disaster for a disunited Japan, advised initiating negotiations with the English.[54] Ōkubo, one of the ablest among the *han* councilors, was sent to Edo at the head of a commission including Takasaki Isoroku and Shigeno Aneki to direct secret discussions with the British representatives. Having decided to pay the indemnity, Ōkubo guilefully approached Itakura Katsukiyo, a *rōjū*, and insisted that the Bakufu lend Satsuma the money demanded by the British. Itakura, however, was loath to make such a commitment in view of the embarrassed state of the Tokugawa finances. Ōkubo nevertheless pressed his argument unremittingly, reminding him that his failure to concede would result in a rupture of Anglo-Satsuma negotiations, which would in turn threaten the peace of the land.[55] Finding Itakura an obstinate opponent, Ōkubo finally sent two young swordsmen to the official's home to inform him of their intent to embarrass the Bakufu by killing the British chargé d'affaires if Itakura did not agree to the Satsuma request. Faced with this, Itakura promised to acquire the sum from the house of Mitsui.[56] Thus, by December 13, 1863, the Richardson affair was settled amicably with the payment of a hundred thousand dollars and Satsuma's promise to "use every diligence" in searching for the assassins of Richardson.[57] Once more Ōkubo gained his objective by intimidation, compelling the Bakufu to underwrite an obligation for which it was never to be recompensed. Perfidious Albion perhaps little realized that it had its equal in Ōkubo.

Winning Prestige

During the months in which Ōkubo was dealing with the Richardson affair, domestic problems accruing from the coup d'etat of September 30 also absorbed his attention. On October 13 he had written to Okabe Bungō, *karō* of the Echizen *han*, that the circumstances were favorable for the moderate faction to act and that Hisamitsu would leave for Kyōto on October 24.[58] What Ōkubo had not anticipated was the sudden resurgence of the radical party in Satsuma. Stimulated by the determined resistance the *han* had offered the British in August, the extremists regained enough influence to have Nakayama Chūzaemon, Ōkubo's colleague and a *han* policy-maker, removed from office and sent to an isolated section of Sakurajima. The Japanese have contended that a man with less fortitude and faith in his cause than Ōkubo would have become discouraged in the face of such constant opposition.[59] Ōkubo, however, maintained his composure and resolution. On October 24, in company with Shimazu Hisamitsu and twelve companies of samurai, he left for Kyōto.[60] En route, the party was on constant alert against any retaliatory action by enemies, but it reached its destination without incident on November 13.[61] Four days later, Ōkubo was ordered to Edo to induce Tokugawa Iemochi and his guardian, Tokugawa Keiki, as well as several major *daimyō* of the *kōbu gattai* faction, to come to Kyōto.[62] The proposed visit of Iemochi, intended to symbolize a close relationship between the imperial house and that of the Tokugawa, was in keeping with the proposed realignment of court and Bakufu.

After having successfully completed his mission to Edo, Ōkubo returned to Kyōto on December 25, a day before the arrival of Tokugawa Keiki. Matsudaira Yoshinaga of Echizen, Date Munenari of Uwajima, and Yamanouchi Toyoshige of Tosa had already established themselves in the city along with the central figure of the *kōbu gattai* coalition, Shimazu Hisamitsu. As the trusted adviser to the Shimazu, Ōkubo Toshimichi was one of the chief policy-makers in Kyōto at this time.[63] The scope of his responsibilities was indicative of his competence and a reflection of his growth in political stature. Only thirty-three years old, this low-ranking samurai from Kagoshima was already involved in the most intricate affairs of state.

Assuming an Anti-Bakufu Position

The political control in Kyōto reëstablished by the court-Bakufu faction was to engender clashes of opinion within the party. The Shimazu Hisamitsu-Ōkubo Toshimichi faction, laying primary stress upon the internal development of Japan, called for a realistic foreign policy based upon the defensive potential of the country. It took the position that Japan's weakness would make it foolhardy for the country to follow an aggressive policy toward the West. On the other hand, the opposing Tokugawa Keiki-Matsudaira Katamori clique, contending that the foreign question was in itself responsible for the decline in Tokugawa prestige, advocated a strong attitude in this sphere and urged the conclusion of treaties for the closure of the ports. On the domestic scene it wanted to reëstablish the Bakufu to its former position of undisputed authority.[64] In an attempt to conceal the breach and make a token show of unity, Satsuma, through Hisamitsu, suggested the plan to appoint Tokugawa Keiki, Matsudaira Katamori, Matsudaira Yoshinaga, Yamanouchi Toyoshige, and Date Munenari to the post of *chōgi sanyo,* or imperial councilor. On February 7, 1864, Hisamitsu, the father of the Satsuma *daimyō* and a man without rank or title, was made a court councilor.[65]

The superficial unity symbolized by the appointment of Hisamitsu as *sanyo* from the *kōbu gattai* party was destroyed by the Keiki-Katamori Bakufu partisans whose propaganda succeeded in associating the Satsuma *han* firmly with the *kaikoku ron,* or the doctrine of opening the country.

Consequently, the radicals, the *sonnō jōi* adherents, became bitterly resentful of Satsuma, which came to occupy an unenviable position between two unfriendly factions, namely, the pro-Bakufu conservatives and the *sonnō jōi* extremists of the Satsuma and other *han*.[66] Ōkubo, in reporting the general situation to Niiro Tatsuo in Edo, criticized Keiki's conversion to conservatism.[67] The latter had contrived to dissolve the *kōbu gattai* coalition, and, while rendering token loyalty to the court, hoped to reëstablish Bakufu domination of national affairs. For Keiki this was the logical attitude to assume since his interests were being threatened by the extremists who were determined to destroy the Bakufu. As for Satsuma, it was faced with the decision of joining either the conservatives or the radical camp; to have remained independent would have meant certain defeat in the power struggle.[68] Ōkubo, who had worked tirelessly for the union of court and Bakufu, sided with those associated with the *ōsei fukko* movement to restore imperial rule. Henceforth his objective was the subversion of the Tokugawa Bakufu. Once more he became imbued with revolutionary zeal.[69]

Ōkubo's sudden change from the moderate *kōbu gattai* stand to that of the radical *tōbaku* was motivated more by expedience than conviction; by this time public opinion was definitely balanced in favor of the *sonnō jōi-tōbaku* party, and for Ōkubo to have effected a union with the losing faction would have been detrimental not only to his *han*, but also to his career. Here again Ōkubo, the inveterate opportunist, adapted his actions to circumstances.

Recalling of Saigō

Meanwhile, the Satsuma extremists, represented by Kuroda Kiyotsuna and Ijichi Masaharu, impatient to bring about a favorable development in the political situation, approached Komatsu Tatewaki and Ōkubo to discuss the feasibility of having Saigō recalled from exile. The plan was brought to the attention of Hisamitsu, who was reluctant to agree but finally did so since Tadayoshi, the Satsuma *daimyō*, concurred with the idea. Hisamitsu must have realized also that there was no other alternative than to relent and allow the return of the chief Satsuma loyalist; with Saigō's return to political life the control of the extremists might be facilitated.[70] Consequently, Saigō, after leaving Okinoerabujima and visiting Murata Shimpachi who was then in exile on Kikaigashima, arrived home on April 4.[71] A few days after his return he was ordered to report to Kyōto where, on April 23, he was commissioned as a *gunkubariyaku*. Saigō, the malefactor, became within a period of days a highly placed administrator.[72] He seemed to display unusual constraint. No doubt his experiences in exile had mellowed the impulsive warrior. For this Ōkubo was thankful.[73]

Saigō soon discovered that he was to be entrusted with great responsibilities in the imperial capital where political calm appeared to have returned with the arrival, on February 22, of the *shōgun*, Iemochi. Instead of the animosity that greeted him on his earlier visit to Kyōto in 1863, Iemochi was cordially welcomed in 1864 with an imperial rescript expressing a spirit of concord between court and Bakufu: "The *shōgun* and every *daimyō* and *shōmyō* [a smaller landholder than the *daimyō*] are our children. We desire that together we shall reform the affairs of the country. . . ." [74] Nevertheless, there were rumblings of discontent. Shimazu Hisamitsu and Matsudaira Yoshinaga were dissatisfied with the machinations of the pro-Bakufu faction aimed at the recovery of Bakufu dominance. The Satsuma leaders therefore received imperial permission to take their troops and return home to concentrate on strengthening the *han* for its ultimate struggle against the Bakufu. On May 23, 1864, Ōkubo and Hisamitsu left for Kagoshima, leaving behind Saigō, Komatsu Tatewaki, Ijichi Masaharu, and a token force of guards.[75] Significantly, each of the leaders who was left behind was a proponent of the *tōbaku* policy. They were charged with the task of implementing the newly adopted pro-court policy.

Chōshū and the radical elements in Kyōto saw in the replacement of Ōkubo with Saigō a modification of Satsuma policy to one more in conformity with their own. Saigō was repeatedly approached by extremist representatives and asked to discuss a *rapprochement*, but he purposely gave equivocal replies. Saigō's equivocation, according to his report to Ōkubo in Kagoshima, aroused much disapproval among the extremists in Kyōto.[76] Satsuma at this juncture could not afford to side precipitately with any one *han*; it was intent upon effecting a union with those who would give Satsuma the maximum support in the implementation of its newly adopted anti-Bakufu and pro-court policy. It had to make decisions cautiously.

Nevertheless, with the change of Satsuma leadership in Kyōto, the Chōshū extremists considered the time opportune to strike at the Bakufu clique, which was consolidating its position at court. Although by now the *shōgun* had been reduced to his real status of a vassal, the court had entrusted him with full power. This was a bitter disappointment to the extreme loyalists. The Chōshū samurai were indignant also over the failure of the officials surrounding the Emperor to heed their petition for the reinstatement of their lords (the Mōri) in the favor of the court and the restoring to rank and office of the seven banished nobles.[77] Rallying around Maki Izumi and Kusaka Genzui, the radicals moved into Kyōto intending to set fire to the windward side of the palace on a blustery day, seize Prince Nakagawa as he hurried to the palace, kill Matsudaira Katamori, and regain control of the court.[78] The Satsuma-Aizu coalition engaged the radical loyalists in battle on August 20, 1864, during the course of which the Chōshū loyalist Kusaka lost his life; Maki was to die some time later by his own hand.[79] When Tokugawa Keiki appealed to Saigō and Komatsu for aid against the radicals, they at first refused to commit Satsuma, viewing the conflict as one that concerned only Aizu and Chōshū. They made it clear to Keiki that Satsuma forces would be committed only upon orders from the court, a declaration clearly reflecting an attitude of emancipation from the control of the Bakufu.[80]

Softening toward Chōshū

Precisely what attitude was Ōkubo to take relative to the chastisement of Chōshū? In a memorial he drafted and addressed to the court in September, he opposed a punitive expedition against Satsuma's rival. In view of the threats from without, it was wiser, he counseled, to observe the situation a while longer.[81] In proffering this advice, Ōkubo was motivated by his belief, by this time greatly strengthened, in the practicability of joining forces with Chōshū in a common action against the Bakufu. Thus, despite his indignation over Chōshū's attempt to gain control of the Emperor by attacking the imperial palace, the thought of Chōshū's potentialities as a future ally was alluring enough to temper Ōkubo's wrath.

It would not have taken Ōkubo's gift of shrewdness and foresight, however, to realize the need of strengthening the military potential of Satsuma in the unsettled political milieu of Japan of the 1860's. Whether Satsuma's future enemy was to be Chōshū or the Tokugawa, only complete military preparedness would offer assurance of victory. After the

British bombardment of Kagoshima, Ōkubo appreciated more than ever the perspicacity of Nariakira who had laid the groundwork for the *han*'s modern military facilities and methods which, however, after his death, had been allowed to become obsolescent. Therefore upon his return to Kagoshima, Ōkubo turned his attention to the renovation of the *han*'s military establishments, and to acquire the latest gunnery techniques Kuroda Kiyotaka and Ōyama Iwao were sent to study at an institute in Edo, the Egawa Juku. Furthermore, the *han* subsidized the work of Murata Tsuneyoshi who, while advocating a policy of progressively decreasing reliance upon foreign weapons, had been experimenting with a breech-loading rifle. Ōkubo, who saw great potentialities in Murata, was instrumental in influencing Hisamitsu to establish an armory where Murata breechloaders were designed and manufactured.[82] Students were sent to Katsu Kaishū's naval training center where the services of the castaway, Nakahama Manjirō, were retained to teach the navigational techniques he had acquired while in the United States. Ōkubo seriously discussed plans to have these men engage in training cruises to the Ryūkyūs.[83] Also, as part of Satsuma's program to adopt Western science, ten men were sent to England for study.[84]

Growth of Bakufu Ambitions

Saigō returned to Kagoshima on February 10, 1865, where, in consultation with Ōkubo, it was decided that Satsuma should oppose the Bakufu in any attempt to chastise Chōshū.[85] In Edo the Bakufu, gloating over the defeat of the mainstay of the extreme loyalist movement, accelerated its drive to regain its former power. It openly planned to reinstate the *sankin kōtai*, the Tokugawa control measure that the *kōbu gattai* party had succeeded in abolishing, and to order the Chōshū leaders, Mōri Takachika and Motonori, and five *kuge* extremists who were in Chōshū, to be brought to Edo. The gravity of the national situation forced Ōkubo to leave for Kyōto on February 20, together with Yoshii and Saishō, for the express purpose of settling the question of the disposition of the five *kuge*, of preventing the rejuvenation of the Bakufu, and of forming a coalition of *han* to implement the Satsuma program.[86]

Upon arriving in Kyōto on March 4, Ōkubo discussed his mission with Prince Nakagawa and later with the Konoe, father and son, telling them that in his opinion the only effective means of discouraging the Bakufu's aspirations was to secure an imperial command against their activities.[87] The *kuge* were receptive to this scheme and readily adopted it. They also informed Ōkubo that Honjō Munehide and Abe Masatō, both Tokugawa *karō*, were at the head of troops marching to Kyōto with specific orders to prevent the indiscriminate entrance of the various *han* representatives into the imperial capital; the Bakufu was fearful that its enemies would so dominate the court as to endanger the position of the Edo government. After ridding the city of undesirable rivals, according to the informants, the Bakufu intended to reëstablish itself as the guardian of the emperor.[88] The attitude of the Edo government, reminiscent of that during the height of Ii Naosuke's dominance, was the natural consequence of the earlier defeat of the extremists that had created a power vacuum the Bakufu was now doing its utmost to fill—a vacuum Satsuma itself had also helped to create. Fortunately, however, a strongly-worded imperial mandate issued in accordance with Ōkubo's suggestion—in which the *shōgun* was again ordered to appear in Kyōto—served notice to the Bakufu of the true imperial will, and proved effective in dampening its zeal. The two Tokugawa *karō*, rebuffed, were forced to return to Edo.[89] Ōkubo, satisfied that his mission was accomplished, in turn left for home on April 17.[90]

Back in Satsuma, Ōkubo worked arduously to achieve *fukoku kyōhei*, or the establishment of a rich country and strong defense.[91] His primary interest at this time centered on the military aspect of this policy. In a memorandum to the Satsuma *gunyaku kata*, the official in charge of military affairs, Ōkubo pressed for answers to such questions as: "Is it adequate to maintain the same number of men as heretofore in the field artillery corps in view of the gradual change in methods of open warfare?" "Are the tactics employed in military drills adequate in view of the urgency of the times?" [92] Again, in a letter to Ijichi, who was in Nagasaki preparing for the arrival of Satsuma trainees in gunnery tactics and the purchase of steamers and small arms, Ōkubo requested that, for the Shūseikan, his colleague employ two Dutchmen who were connected with an iron foundry in that city.[93] One important reason for the accelerated military program was the need to make Satsuma militarily self-sufficient so that its policies might be implemented independently and with greatest assurance of success. More specifically, Ōkubo was aware of the intended Bakufu punitive action against Chōshū and he wished to pursue a *kare wa kare, ware wa ware* (he-for-himself, I-for-myself) line of action vis-à-vis the Bakufu and thus gain benefits for Satsuma at the expense of the Tokugawa regime. In fact, it is contended that the Satsuma (and Chōshū) policy of strengthening its economic and military power under the pretext of defending Japan against foreign aggressors was in reality a move designed to contend for the political control of Japan.[94] With this thought in mind, Ōkubo again headed for Kyōto on June 14, 1865.[95]

At the imperial capital Ōkubo found a worsened situation. The military power of Aizu and Kuwana, he reported to Komatsu Tatewaki, was now of such magnitude around Kyōto that it was "indeed beyond description." As for the court, he described it as "almost helpless at present because of the tremendous authority of the Bakufu." With the aid of his allies, Tokugawa Keiki was trying to prevent any influence detrimental to his own cause from being exerted upon the court.[96] Under these circumstances Ōkubo realized the imperative need of Satsuma to continue increasing its military strength; only in this way could the Bakufu's encroachment upon affairs in Kyōto be checked. He therefore suggested to Komatsu that a naval vessel be purchased through the British Harrison Company.[97] The significant portion of Ōkubo's letter to Komatsu is his frank request that he be given a free hand in dealing with the situation in Kyōto, an attitude reflecting a confidence and independence of spirit which Ōkubo displayed more and more.[98]

Ōkubo's role as one of Satsuma's chief representatives in Kyōto involved increasing responsibilities. On June 15, 1865, Tokugawa Iemochi, accompanied by a large force, arrived in Kyōto for the punitive campaign against Chōshū, and also for the purpose of consolidating the Bakufu's position in the imperial capital. In a memorial to the court he charged that Chōshū had "sent its vassals abroad and purchased in quantity weapons such as cannons and rifles." Chōshū was indeed guilty of this and other charges; secret trade was being carried on under the direction of Takasugi Shinsaku and Ōmura Masujirō.[99] These accusations did not, however, deter Tosa's Sakamoto Ryūma, who believed deeply in the necessity for a Satsuma-Chōshū union, from meeting with Kido Kōin at Shimonoseki to discuss the matter.[100] Nor did they serve to browbeat the Chōshū samurai into inactivity. More of them joined the extreme party of Kido and Takasugi and strongly insisted that if the Mōri were not absolved of the Bukufu charge of treason, Chōshū should resort to war. Satsuma's reaction was just as strong; it unequivocally opposed a Bakufu punitive action against Chōshū, and was later joined in this by Owari, Echizen, Kaga, and Tosa. But in spite of growing antagonism toward its policy, the Bakufu continued its preparations. In these circumstances Ōkubo once more returned to Kagoshima on September 3, ready to recommend the withdrawal of Satsuma men from Edo and Kyōto.[101]

Growing Anti-Bakufu Sentiment

Ōkubo was determined to pursue a course which would establish the predominance of the court. His antagonism toward the Bakufu's policy vis-à-vis Chōshū was a reflection of his total anti-Bakufu sentiment. To what degree this attitude had solidified may be judged from a letter dated September 23, 1865, dispatched by Ōkubo to Ishigaki Einosuke and Ueno Ryōtarō, two Satsuma samurai studying in England at the time. He wrote in part:

> Since the Chōshū war the so-called extremists have generally had their eyes opened and now discern the impossibility of maintaining a *jōi* position. Consequently, they have become advocates of opening the country to foreign trade. Naturally, the more enlightened *han* [Saga, Echizen, Tosa, and Uwajima] have tended to favor such things as the enforcement of commercial law. If anticlimatically the *shōgun* should return to Edo, his orders would increasingly be disobeyed. The ability of the various *han* to maintain their freedom from central government control cannot be doubted. Consequently, there is no alternative than to aim for the fundamental policy of protecting the court and establishing imperial prestige abroad by resorting to the energetic execution of *fukoku kyōhei*.[102]

The use at this early date of the term *fukoku kyōhei*, rich country and strong defense, is one indication that many *han* policies conceived prior to 1868 by such progressive *han* officials as Ōkubo were to be duplicated in the Meiji period. The same letter deals in some detail with the threatening gestures of the foreigners and indicates the seriousness with which he viewed their behavior.[103]

In Kyōto once more, Ōkubo soon became deeply involved in the foreign problem, which had become inextricably interwoven with domestic politics. On November 4, 1865, a combined British, French, and Dutch squadron, with the representative of the United States on board, had arrived at Hyōgo. Sir Harry Parkes, the British minister who initiated the entire plan of dispatching the ships to Hyōgo, had hoped that by negotiating with the Japanese in relative proximity to the imperial city he could more easily procure the Emperor's sanction to the treaties of 1858 (previously ratified only by the Bakufu) and the immediate opening of Hyōgo to foreign commerce.[104] The Edo regime, pressed by the determined foreigners, finally, on November 9, moved to have Tokugawa Iemochi approach the court and request the imperial sanction not only of its Chōshū policy, but also of the opening of the port of Hyōgo.[105]

Ōkubo was against the court's compliance with such requests. On the same day, consulting with members of the upper *kuge*, he expressed disapproval of both Bakufu proposals. Through Konoe, he recommended that a council of great feudatories should be convoked to deal with these matters, but the Bakufu argued that the problems were so pressing that there was not time to call such a conference. In the meantime, Ōkubo had gone to Fukui to urge Matsudaira Yoshinaga to come to Kyōto and had sent messengers to Date Munenari of Uwajima, Yamanouchi Toyoshige of Tosa, and Shimazu Hisamitsu of Satsuma, asking them to proceed at once to the capital.[106]

The burden of foreign and domestic affairs was weighing more and more heavily upon the Bakufu. Tokugawa Iemochi, caught on the horns of dilemma, requested that he be allowed to resign his office in favor of Tokugawa Keiki. Ōkubo urged the *kuge* to accept the resignation and to have the court assume the direction of affairs. But this the court refused to do, urging Iemochi instead to settle the Chōshū affair without delay.[107] Thus, despite his direct appeal to some of the most influential *kuge*, Ōkubo failed to have the Bakufu's Chōshū policy nullified. Moreover, the Emperor, on November 22, sanctioned the foreign treaties, but only after Iemochi's promise had been obtained that the port of Hyōgo would never be opened to foreign trade.[108]

What were Ōkubo's motives in opposing the Bakufu proposals? It was obvious to Ōkubo that a defeat of Chōshū would mean one less enemy for the Tokugawa regime and, by the same token, one less ally for Satsuma. Apparently Ōkubo's strong remonstrance against the opening of Hyōgo was dictated by the fact that he had intended to use the Hyōgo-Ōsaka area as a base of operations for the attack he was considering against the Bakufu.[109] It is also likely that his dedicated opposition to all Bakufu proposals at this time stemmed from his desire to embarrass the Edo government by having the court disregard its will; for the throne to have done so with regard to the treaties, for example, would have meant that the already perplexed and encumbered Bakufu would have reaped the further wrath of the British and their allies.[110]

Casting Aizu Aside

When Ōkubo's harassment of the Bakufu proved abortive, he resorted to other methods to undermine the Edo regime. He proceeded to weaken the prestige and power of Aizu, the chief supporter of the Tokugawa government, by dissolving the Satsuma-Aizu alliance. Aizu realized that its policy was no longer in harmony with that of its ally, but it nevertheless hoped to preserve the coalition and commissioned Sotojima Kihei to confer with Ōkubo on the possibility of renewing it.[111] After consultation with his colleagues, the Satsuma official, in a letter to Sotojima dated November 30, 1865, rejected the suggestion, giving as his reason Satsuma's desire to formulate its future policy on an independent basis.[112] Satsuma felt that the alliance had outlived its usefulness. Its continuance, in fact, might obstruct the new policy Satsuma was trying to implement. The Satsuma-Aizu alliance, erected on the loose sands of expediency, was as easily destroyed by its conceiver as it was made. Ōkubo considered most matters of policy in terms of what they could render to the fortune of the Satsuma *han*. To Ōkubo this was the attitude of realistic statesmanship, the benefits derived from which far outweighed the moral issues involved. Completely estranged from the Bakufu, and its ties in turn severed with Aizu, Satsuma under Ōkubo's guidance could now freely set a course in the direction of a Chōshū *rapprochement*.

Developing Sat-Chō Unity

The Satsuma-Chōshū, or Sat-Chō, alliance was in the process of formation as early as the summer of 1865 when Sakamoto Ryūma and Nakaoka Shintarō arranged a meeting between Saigō Takamori of Satsuma and Kido Kōin of Chōshū. However, because of Saigō's uncompromising attitude, no understanding was reached at that time.[113] Undismayed, Sakamoto continued to work toward this objective. He procured weapons and ammunition from an English merchant and had them sent to Chōshū by a Satsuma steamer for future use against the Bakufu's punitive forces.[114] Later, in January of 1866, the Satsuma authorities, believing the time opportune for a Sat-Chō union, dispatched Kuroda Kiyotaka to Chōshū to persuade Kido to come to Kyōto for a conference. He came reluctantly; the Chōshū leaders were strongly suspicious of Satsuma's intentions in view of its history of Machiavellian conduct, and the memory of their defeat at the hands of the Satsuma-Aizu coalition on September 30, 1863, was still vivid. Nevertheless, through the good offices of Kido and Saigō, the two *han* were finally drawn together by a secret understanding reached on March 7, 1866.[115] The first of the six provisions of this agreement stated that "with the commencement of hostilities [Satsuma agrees] to muster about two thousand troops to be dispatched to Kyōto, supplementing forces already there, and another thousand or so to be sent to Naniwa for the defense of the Kyōto-Ōsaka position." [116] Satsuma had gained an ally whose antagonism toward the Bakufu would facilitate the implementation of Satsuma's new policy, while Chōshū leaders complimented themselves for having won the friendship of a potential enemy. On March 17 Ōkubo returned to Kagoshima to report to Hisamitsu and Tadayoshi the details of the alliance and the general political situation in Kyōto.[117] Some historians state that this formulation of the Sat-Chō alliance marks the beginning of the Restoration period.

In Satsuma, Chōshū was to have a strong and progressive ally. Satsuma had undergone drastic transformation since its leaders had set their course in the direction of reform. Yokoi Shōnan noted that after Satsuma had launched its *fukoku kyōhei* policy it had procured Western weapons of war as well as technicians to train its military forces. He further observed that customs had been changing. The younger men of the *han* were generally dressed in Western clothes and had their topknots cut off. Travelers, who had been forbidden to enter the Satsuma domain in the past, were now allowed to visit not only Kagoshima, but other parts of Satsuma as well. As a result, traders from various *han* were seen in increasing numbers in the Satsuma capital. He also observed a noteworthy change in *han* opinion, which seemed to be much less divided.[118]

In April, Ōkubo was again back in Kyōto where he was called upon to deal with the insistent demand that Satsuma participate in the punitive expedition against Chōshū which the Edo authorities were contemplating. The Bakufu, after destroying the Chōshū *han* and reëstablishing its own authority, intended to establish a more centralized form of government—a *gun-ken,* or county-prefecture system of administration—with the presidency to be held by a member of the Tokugawa family.[119] This plan for administrative modification based upon a suggestion made by M. Roches, the French minister to Edo. France, at this time having confidence in the authority of the *shōgun,* supported the Bakufu. In 1866, for example, Roches expressed his reluctance to conduct diplomatic negotiations with the court on the grounds that it did not have the necessary resources to form a new government. The French minister continued to encourage the Bakufu with promises of military supplies and arms even after its forces had been defeated by the imperial army at the battle of Toba-Fushimi. It is conceivable that this attempt on the part of France to bolster the sagging authority of the Tokugawa Bakufu would have ended in failure because French power was weak in the Far East. The other foreign powers probably would have successfully isolated France had she succeeded in exercising dominion over the Bakufu, and the Bakufu itself did not have the resilience to reassert itself and to exercise complete domination over Japan.[120]

Satsuma, in any event, was not inclined to emulate France and give the Bakufu its support, and Ōkubo was not at all subtle in making Satsuma's position known. He told the Tokugawa authorities quite plainly that they could not expect help from Satsuma. This message was conveyed in a letter he composed but which was signed by Koba Dennai, another Satsuma official. It stated that Satsuma could not furnish troops for a cause that seemed to violate *tenri,* or the laws of nature.[121] Thereupon Itakura Katsukiyo, the Tokugawa *kakurō,* still unaware of the new relationship between Satsuma and Chōshū, requested a conference at his Ōsaka castle with an authorized Satsuma representative. Despite the fact that Iwashita Masahira, a Satsuma *karō,* was in Kyōto as the senior official and would ordinarily have represented Shimazu on matters of great import such as this, it was Ōkubo who was chosen to go to Ōsaka with full authority to deal with the Bakufu in the name of the Satsuma *han.* His strategy was well conceived; he feigned deafness. After the initial greetings were concluded, Ōkubo informed Itakura that he was bothered by otorrhea and, being hard of hearing, would appreciate his speaking loudly and distinctly. Itakura then began explaining the reasons for the Bakufu's decision and stressed the close ties between the Shimazu and Tokugawa families. In view of these considerations, Itakura said, he was confident that Satsuma would place troops at the Bakufu's disposal. Ōkubo, pretending to have misunderstood the meaning of this statement, gave Itakura a look of complete incredulity and asked him for the reasons for the projected attack upon "Satsuma," whereupon Itakura hastily attempted to correct him by saying he had meant "Chōshū," not "Satsuma." Still feigning deafness, Ōkubo this time conveniently heard the word "Chōshū" as "Bakufu." Without allowing the Tokugawa *kakurō* time to reëxplain, Ōkubo launched into a vociferous protest against Satsuma's participation in an ignominious plot to wage war against the "Bakufu." Finally, however, pretending to understand the full import of Itakura's repeated explanation of his statement, Ōkubo demanded: "Is it your intention to force us into a punitive war on the basis of the Shimazu friendship with the *shōgun?* If you are to launch a campaign against Chōshū, then in the name of justice, state the crimes upon which you base the charge of insurgency against that *han*. The mind of the Satsuma *han* is fixed; it is not to move a single soldier without ample justification." Without giving the venerable Tokugawa official an opportunity to say another word, Ōkubo stood up and stalked from the room.[122] For the display of "good judgment and courage" on this occasion, Saigō later wrote a laudatory letter and informed Ōkubo that the Shimazu, both Hisamitsu and Tadayoshi, had expressed their gratitude for the fine accomplishment.[123]

Motivated not so much by self-confidence as by self-interest, the Edo government resolved to prosecute the war against the bitterly anti-Bakufu Chōshū *han* despite Satsuma's refusal to contribute aid. The conflict began on July 18, 1866, with the shelling of Chōshū territory by a Bakufu warship.[124] Being well aware of the close relationship between the Bakufu and France, Ōkubo and his colleagues schemed to counteract the coalition by giving Chōshū not only moral support, but also more tangible aid.[125] In accordance with the terms of the Sat-Chō treaty, Satsuma moved troops into Ōsaka while its representatives at the same time took the initiative in circulating a declaration, which stated the Bakufu and Chōshū positions, among the thirty-odd *han* represented in Kyōto.[126] Satsuma, moreover, made an attempt at this time to win the support of England, a logical step since France was supporting the Bakufu. Sir Harry Parkes, the British minister, accepted the Shimazus' invitation to be their guest in Kagoshima; and when he arrived there, about the end of July, he was given a royal reception, the visit "concluding with a grand hunt in a forest full of deer, wild boar, and monkeys." [127]

Feigning Loyalty

Ōkubo's primary objective was to destroy the Bakufu institution as it was, and an event favoring this achievement occurred on August 29, 1866, when Tokugawa Iemochi died at Ōsaka at the age of twenty-one.[128] The most likely successor to Iemochi was Tokugawa Keiki, the late *shōgun*'s guardian, but Keiki declined the office, stating that he would accept the headship of the Tokugawa family but not the position of *shōgun*. Keiki, in effect, seemed to be favoring the abolition of the Bakufu and the restoration of the monarchy. He may have felt that the future of the current Edo government was not bright; he was undoubtedly aware of the mounting opposition to it and the persistent demands of influential figures calling for the formulation of policy by a conference of *daimyō*. His coyness, on the other hand, may have been a part of his political strategy, that of daring the Sat-Chō elements who were attempting to usurp the Bakufu's authority to come in and take over. Also, his action may have been meant as a tactic to disturb the conservatives within the Bakufu who, with the prospect of being left leaderless in an extremely critical juncture in history, would either have to give Keiki more coöperation than he was getting or be deprived of his leadership.[129]

Tokugawa Keiki's attitude presented Ōkubo with an opportunity to call for the destruction of the Bakufu system. On October 16, he wrote to Saigō emphasizing that the appointment of the *shōgun* ought not to be considered until a conference of the great *daimyō* was convoked, at which time, in adherence to the fundamental *kyōwa*, or "republican" policy, the *shōgun* could be elected by the *han* representatives. Obviously, if such a policy were sanctioned by imperial decree it would place the fate of the Bakufu in the hands of the powerful *daimyō*. By this device, Ōkubo anticipated the "destruction of the authority of the Bakufu and the affirmation of the principle of the elevation and extension of imperial prestige." [130]

To avoid misunderstanding, a clarification should be made of Ōkubo's use of the term *kyōwa*, or *kongho* in Chinese. Its derivation is traceable to the early period of Chinese history. According to Ssu-ma Ch'ien, the "father of Chinese history," *kongho* was the term originally used to designate the period 841–828 B.C. when the Dukes of Chao and Tcheou served as regents during the time Emperor Li was in exile and while the heir presumptive to the throne was in his minority. *Kongho* was the name applied to the regency of these court nobles who established a *commune harmonie*. A contradictory thesis is that Kong was the name of a fief and Ho the count of the domain. Thus, according to this view, Ho, the count of Kong, was the one who exercised the regency during the era in question and not the Dukes of Chao and Tcheou. Modern historians, however, have adopted Ssu-ma Ch'ien's version.[131]

The Japanese knew this term and its derivation through their knowledge of Ssu-ma Ch'ien's *Shih Chi*, describing a *kyōwa* polity as a monarchless country ruled coöperatively by two or more court nobles, as with the aforementioned regency in China. In 1845 a Japanese translation of a Dutch book was published in which the term *kyōwa* was used to describe the polity of the United States. It called the United States a *kyōwa seijishū*, or a republic.[132] The Japanese apparently used this Chinese term to describe a state in which the sovereignty resided in the people and the administration lodged in officers elected by and representing the people, or a representative democracy.

It is difficult to ascertain precisely what meaning Ōkubo attributed to *kyōwa*. Although he was not a political liberal, his ideas nevertheless were in advance of the general thinking of the age. To conclude, however, that his advocacy of a *kyōwa* policy implied an inherent desire on his part to establish the basis for a representative democracy in the Western sense of the term would be wrong. He did not believe that such a concept of government was feasible or practical for Japan in the nineteenth century. Thus it is probable that he interpreted *kyōwa* in a broad sense as meaning a political framework within which the great nobles would have the right to express their views in directing the course of national affairs, and on such matters as the selection of a new *shōgun*. This interpretation is supported by Ishii Takashi in his work on the Meiji Restoration.[133] Ōkubo apparently wanted a government in which the administrative functions would temporarily if not permanently be placed in the hands of the feudal nobility, the *daimyō* and their officials. By working through a conference of the great feudatories, Ōkubo and his fellow thinkers hoped to manipulate decisions in favor of the *han*; for Ōkubo this meant his own *han*. Had the Bakufu not become aware of the intentions of their opponents and hastily induced Tokugawa Keiki to assume the office of *shōgun*, Ōkubo's plan would have materialized, and the election of Hisamitsu as *shōgun* would not have been impossible. Thus such terms as *kyōwa* in its broad sense; *hambaku*, or anti-Bakufuism; and *ōsei fukko*, or imperial restoration, assume less significance. They appear to have been merely shibboleths utilized by ambitious *han* and their officials, by men such as Ōkubo, to enhance their own political positions.

Dealings with Iwakura

Ōkubo's own prospects improved about this time with the acquisition of a friend with whom he was destined to share the political limelight for the next decade. He was Iwakura Tomomi, a *kuge,* whom Ōkubo had met for the first time five years earlier in 1862. As an ardent adherent of *kōbu gattai,* Iwakura had arranged the marriage of the Emperor Kōmei's sister to the *shōgun,* and for this he had afterward been degraded and sentenced to perpetual seclusion. He was an able court noble who impressed others by his political astuteness.[134] Realizing the impossibility of continuing government by the Bakufu, he became an advocate of *tōbaku,* believing this to be the surest means of attaining the restoration of imperial rule. Since the overthrow of the Bakufu would require the aid of the powerful *han,* Iwakura first contacted Ōkubo, who thereafter paid surreptitious visits to his retreat at Iwakura-mura.[135] It was here that Iwakura and Ōkubo, together with Saigō of Satsuma, Kido of Chōshū, Sakamoto of Tosa, and Kitajima of Mito made definite plans for the Restoration movement. Being aware of Iwakura's importance to the cause, Ōkubo went to the extent of having the *kuge* guarded by samurai each night without Iwakura's knowledge.[136] As in his friendship with Hisamitsu, Ōkubo, undoubtedly a genius in the judgment of character, was shrewd enough to attach himself to the individual most likely to prove useful to him in the achievement of his immediate objective. Ōkubo's selection of Iwakura as a partner was to pay profitable dividends, especially after the latter was pardoned in the fall of 1867 and once more became active in politics.[137]

On February 3, 1867, three weeks after the formal investiture of Tokugawa Keiki as the new *shōgun,* Emperor Kōmei died of smallpox (succeeded by Mutsuhito whose posthumous name is Emperor Meiji) and the court ordered the Chōshū struggle to be halted during the fifty days of mourning. Emperor Kōmei has been given little notice for his role in the Restoration story. He was naturally eager to see the restoration of imperial rule but could hardly be called an extremist. He favored the moderate *kōbu gattai* position over that of *tōbaku,* represented by Ōkubo and Iwakura, and, had he not died, the history of the Restoration might have been different. Despite his influence at court, Iwakura would not easily have been able to change the will of the Emperor. With his demise, however, Iwakura was given a free hand to force the Ōkubo-Iwakura *tōbaku* policy upon a less resistant court.[138]

Despite the death of the Emperor, the anti-Bakufu conspiracy continued. Saigō endeavored in Kyōto to win over to his camp both Aki and Uwajima. He then hastened to Kagoshima to urge Shimazu Hisamitsu to go to the imperial city. Hisamitsu agreed, and on June 7 met with Matsudaira Yoshinaga, Date Munenari, and Yamanouchi Toyoshige and their chief retainers and discussed the matters of opening the port of Hyōgo and arranging an amnesty for Chōshū.[139] In the meeting, Ōkubo resolutely stated that the Hyōgo problem should not be settled prior to a debate by a conference of feudatories, but he advocated, just as strongly, the early pardon for Chōshū; this would enable that *han* with which Satsuma had a secret understanding to enter Kyōto once more. Despite Satsuma opposition, however, the court issued an edict on June 26, 1867, annulling the second and third clauses of the decree of November 22, 1865, which ordered the treaties amended and the question of the opening of Hyōgo dropped. Another decree recommended a lenient settlement of the Chōshū case.[140]

During the June conference of the four most powerful *han*, Satsuma expressed the intention of overthrowing the Edo government at all costs, an idea that ran counter to the more conservative thinking of Yamanouchi Toyoshige of Tosa who retained traditional respect if not admiration for the Bakufu. Differences over this and other matters eventually forced the breakup of the four-*han* conference.[141] Although the conference was fruitless in most respects, it did have significance for the anti-Bakufu movement. Ōkubo and Saigō, while listening to the debates regarding the Bakufu's attitude on the Hyōgo question, became fully convinced that the regime could be destroyed only by resort to arms. Ōkubo's revolutionary position is evident in a letter he wrote in July, 1867, requesting the dispatching of Satsuma troops to Kyōto. Charging that the Bakufu had endeavored to overpower the innocent *han* by exerting its authority and attempting at the same time to secure control over the court, Ōkubo wrote that drastic measures would be required to correct the situation. He suggested that arrangements be made to operate with Chōshū "because without provisions for the use of military power, moral support, and a determined policy, rendering aid to the court will be difficult." He further outlined a specific program to be followed. One *daitai*, or battalion, of Satsuma troops was to be transported aboard three warships to Kyōto at a time that Saigō would determine after consultation with Chōshū. Finally, Ōkubo had the audacity to name Shimazu Bingo as his choice as commander of this force.[142]

Sat-Chō Military Alliance

Instead of resentfully ignoring his subordinate's dictatorial attitude, Shimazu Hisamitsu followed Ōkubo's advice. Hisamitsu sent for and received in audience on July 17, 1867, two representatives from the Chōshū *han*, Yamagata Aritomo and Shinagawa Yajirō, and informed them that Satsuma was ready to work closely with the Mōri for the restoration of imperial rule.[143] The developing military alliance was further strengthened a few days later when, on July 23, Ōkubo, Komatsu, and Saigō of Satsuma conferred with Nakaoka, Sakamoto, Gotō, and Teramura of Tosa at an inn in Kyōto and signed a treaty binding Satsuma and Tosa together.[144] Significantly, the official text stressed *ōsei fukko* as the primary aim of the signatories. It stated in part that "a country does not have two monarchs, a home does not have two masters; government devolves on one ruler. . . . The full authority to rule the land rests in the court." [145] The author of the treaty is not known, but the opinions expressed in it are those of Gotō Shōjirō and Sakamoto Ryūma. The Restoration movement was beginning to gain momentum. It was now necessary to formalize the understanding between Satsuma and Chōshū.

The task of negotiating the Sat-Chō military alliance against the Bakufu fell to Ōkubo. On October 12 Hisamitsu left for home to recuperate from an illness and was replaced by Shimazu Bingo, who arrived in Kyōto on October 14 with a force of one thousand men.[146] Upon assuring himself that adequate Satsuma troops were available in the Kyōto area, Ōkubo left for Yamaguchi where, also on the fourteenth, he met with Kido Kōin and, on the following day, with the Mōri to whom he disclosed Satsuma's plans to mass troops in sufficient strength to overthrow the Bakufu and at the same time guard the imperial household. He pointed out, however, that the forces of one *han* would be inadequate for this plan and that he had therefore come to request Chōshū's participation. The very nature of Chōshū's attitude toward the Bakufu, rancorous and vengeful as it was, made Ōkubo's mission an easy one; on October 16 the Satsuma and Chōshū representatives signed a pledge to contribute troops for the loyalist cause. Having secured the pact, Ōkubo next conferred with Ueda Otojirō of the Aki *han* at Hiroshima and reached a similar understanding with him before returning to Kyōto on October 20.[147]

Readying for a Showdown

The objectives of the pact signed by Satsuma, Chōshū, Tosa, and Aki were not to be attained without difficulty. Opinion within each *han* was far from united. Chōshū was ready to have recourse to arms, but there were those among its leadership whose faith in Satsuma's integrity continued to waver and who therefore urged vigilance in dealing with its newly acquired ally. In Ōkubo's own *han*, moreover, an opposition party centering around Narahara Kizaemon attempted to obstruct the Ōkubo war policy while a large segment within the Aki and Tosa *han* advocated a more pacific approach in dealing with the Bakufu. Fortunately for Ōkubo and the extremists, Shimazu Hisamitsu accepted their view and was prepared to resort to warfare if necessary to restore administrative authority to the court.[148] In an attempt to unify conflicting opinions within the coalition, the three *han* of Satsuma, Chōshū, and Aki met on November 3, 1867, and, after successfully persuading Aki's Tsuji Shōsō to accept the *tōbaku* policy, drew up a declaration reaffirming their pledge to work together for the common cause. The pact pledged the signatories to render determined aid to the court and empire. One of the clauses stated that the parties to the pact would not be swayed by rumors that might tend to cast suspicion upon any of the other signatories. The provisions were made known to Iwakura and the friendly *kuge* who were pleased with the implications contained therein.[149] Also, on the same day, Ōkubo presented to the court his petition, cosigned by Komatsu and Saigō, which requested the issuance of an imperial decree calling for the overthrow of the Bakufu and the restoration of imperial rule.[150] Conveniently appended to this was a long list of grievances stressing the Tokugawa usurpation of imperial authority upon which Ōkubo and his colleagues expected the decree to be based.[151] On the following day Ōkubo consulted Iwakura who, deeming the time propitious for action, consented to draw up the *Ōsei Fukko Gi*, the Proposal for the Imperial

Restoration, which was forwarded secretly to Prince Nakayama. The proposal reviewed the world situation and pointed out that Japan's present governmental structure was incompatible with its rightful and traditional national polity. It concluded by calling for a reformation reëstablishing imperial authority.[152] On November 9, Ōkubo and Hirozawa of Chōshū were given imperial orders to overthrow the Bakufu.[153]

At the same time loyalists holding more moderate views had been working just as frantically to effect a restoration without an appeal to arms. Gotō of Tosa, who was definitely against a policy of bloodshed, accepted Sakamoto Ryūma's suggestion that "the danger of hostilities might be averted and Tokugawa prestige saved if the *shōgun* could be induced to tender his resignation voluntarily." He prevailed upon Yamanouchi Toyoshige to memorialize the *shōgun*. On October 27, after some difficulty, Gotō presented the petition to Itakura, the Tokugawa *rōjū*. The *shōgun* presented his surrender of administrative authority on November 9, expecting that it would not be accepted. The court, however, accepted it without hesitation on the following day.[154] As a result of the *shōgun*'s surrender of his administrative power to the throne on November 16, a court order temporarily halted the implementation of the secret imperial decree issued on November 9 to the Sat-Chō *han*.[155]

Restoring Imperial Rule

Ōkubo, however, had already left Kyōto by the time the latest decree was issued. On November 14, he and other representatives of Satsuma and Chōshū, armed with the secret order to overthrow the Bakufu, had left Ōsaka for their respective *han* to make arrangements for the movement of troops to Kyōto.[156] Ōkubo arrived in Kagoshima on November 21 where he met with the Shimazu, Hisamitsu and his son, Tadayoshi.[157] On November 24 the Shimazu decided that Tadayoshi would go to Kyōto, setting December 3 as the day on which they would move troops to the imperial capital.[158] On November 26 they communicated their intentions to the Satsuma council.[159]

Ōkubo left Kagoshima on December 5 and, after consulting with Yamanouchi Toyoshige in Kōchi, returned to Kyōto on the tenth.[160] There he was confronted with a dangerous political situation. The conservatives were highly agitated by Tokugawa Keiki's surrendering his administrative authority. There was even a movement afoot to have

Keiki, who was in Kyōto at the time, return immediately to Edo. Under these conditions Ōkubo felt that the lives of the *kuge* who were members of the reform faction were in danger, and he furnished Iwakura and others with small arms.[161] This undercurrent of political unrest was not to be ameliorated until the arrival of Satsuma troops, after which the position of the reformers became much more secure.[162]

Ōkubo, who was determined to force the issue with the Bakufu, had reported the results of his Kagoshima mission to Iwakura Tomomi, Nakayama Tadayasu, and Ōgimachi Sanjō Sanenaru. He voiced his fear that unless drastic action were taken soon vis-à-vis the Bakufu, the *shōgun* would very likely reassume his administrative role. Ōkubo told the *kuge:*

> Although Tokugawa Keiki has already surrendered his administrative authority and expressed his feeling of loyalty [to the sovereign], the real intentions of the Aizu and Kuwana *han* are not clear. I fear that they will conspire to have Keiki reassume his administrative power. It is therefore necessary to have the court maintain a firm stand in dealing with this matter. If in fear of the Bakufu's power the imperial council should be forced to change its position, the great task [of the Restoration] would immediately come to a halt.[163]

The Satsuma troops, three thousand strong, entered Kyōto on December 8, 1867, and those of Aki on December 22. The Chōshū vanguard reached its destination on December 23.[164] Meeting secretly with Iwashita Masahira, Shinagawa Yajirō, and Saigō Takamori, Ōkubo discussed the immediate course to be followed. The men decided that it was imperative to prod the court into action.

Ōkubo, therefore, personally approached the court. On December 24 he conferred with Ōgimachi Sanjō Sanenaru and notified him that Satsuma troops were ready to aid in a restoration effort. Ōkubo then made it very clear that all opponents of the movement for imperial restoration would be annihilated. Highly impressed, Ōgimachi Sanjō Sanenaru met that same evening with Nakayama Tadayasu and Iwakura Tomomi and discussed the aims of the loyalists as outlined by Ōkubo. Iwakura was for the plan but Nakayama was reluctant to accept it. The latter's obstinacy was not long-lived. On December 26 Ōkubo had a heart-to-heart conversation with Nakayama and finally convinced him that the time was opportune for positive action. The necessary preparations were now completed to set the wheels of the Restoration plan into motion: the Emperor would be asked to sanction a proclamation restoring imperial rule, all court officials below the rank of *sesshō* would be forbidden to attend the court, Satsuma and Chōshū would be given the assignment of guarding the nine gates of the imperial palace, the Tokugawa would be relegated to the status of *daimyō,* and an imperial government composed of members of the anti-Bakufu party would be established.[165]

Although the lower samurai leaders of the Satsuma and Chōshū *han* had met and decided on the Restoration proclamation, differences in opinion arose as to when it should be issued. Earlier, Satsuma's Ōkubo, Saigō, and Yoshii and Chōshū's Yamada and Shinagawa had fixed January 2, 1868, as the date for the proclamation. Iwakura consented to this.[166] On December 28, Ōkubo and Saigō called upon Gotō and informed him of the nature of their Restoration scheme and asked for Tosa's coöperation in its execution. Gotō was startled by the scope of the plan and was reluctant to commit his *han,* stating that he was in no position to speak for Tosa.[167] Fearful of being termed a rebel, however, Gotō finally agreed to the idea, but made it known that the matter should be taken up again with Yamanouchi Toyoshige after his arrival in Kyōto on January 2. On December 30, Gotō notified Ōkubo that the date should be extended until January 4. He made the same suggestion on the following day.[168] Saigō, however, was anxious to act on the date originally set; as a military strategist, he was fearful that any delay would give the Aizu and Kuwana *han,* the main supporters of the Bakufu, an advantage over the loyalist forces of Satsuma, Chōshū, and Aki.[169] The court, on the other hand, through a letter dated January 1, 1868, from Iwakura to Ōkubo, informed the reformers that it could not complete its preparations for the Restoration proclamation any earlier than January 3.[170] Iwakura's letters written to different individuals just prior to January 3, 1868, reveal the uncertainty prevailing among the extremists as to when the proclamation would be issued. As late as January 1 he noted that no decision had been made as to whether "it will be on the second or the third." He then resignedly continued, "but it will probably be difficult to effect before the third. . . ." [171] In deference to the court's request, the date for the proclamation was finally changed from January 2 to January 3, 1868.

Iwakura's repeated reference to Ōkubo in his letters to Nakayama Tadayasu during this period attests to the close relationship between the two men. Ōkubo worked through Iwakura to influence the court as did Kido, the Chōshū loyalist, through Ōgimachi Sanjō Sanenaru. These *kuge* were the means through which the will of the extremists was made known to the imperial house. There can be very little doubt that Ōkubo, along with Kido and Saigō, played an important part in laying the groundwork for the coup d'etat of January 3, 1868; it was on this day that the imperial troops, composed of men contributed by those *han* supporting the *tōbaku* policy and led by Saigō, forced the Bakufu, Aizu, and Kuwana forces to withdraw to the Nijō castle, and a new Meiji government was proclaimed which supplanted the Tokugawa Bakufu.[172]

Forces behind the Restoration Movement

Various forces interacted to bring about the downfall of the Bakufu. The seeds of destruction were contained in the very policy of the regime itself. The rigid control over the social, political, and economic life of the country instituted as a means of preserving Tokugawa feudalism reacted adversely against the Bakufu. The establishment of a rigid class structure prevented social mobility and stifled the spirit of freedom, especially among those in the lower classes. The reactionary policies followed by the Tokugawa leaders—most of whom were unimaginative, unprogressive, and often incompetent—did not help their own cause in a time of political, economic, and social ferment. The Bakufu's unrealistic economic controls, for example, stifled production during a period when the Japanese were beginning to feel the impact of the spirit of capitalism.[173]

According to one view, it was the common people, the townsmen and the peasant as well as the samurai class, who recognized the contradictions in the decaying Tokugawa feudalism and desired to gain freedom from its oppression. The merchants wanted to trade freely and the peasants likewise wished to be freed of restrictive laws on production.[174] The discontent among the common people manifested itself in the form of *hyakushō ikki* and *uchikowashi*, or revolts among the peasants and townspeople, respectively. The immediate demand of the peasants was the reduction of rice tribute, and that of the townsmen for relief from the high cost of rice, but the basic demand of both these dissident classes was for the abolition of feudal control. The proponent of this thesis, Hani Gorō, states that "the occurrence of *hyakushō ikki* and *chōnin uchikowashi* in open opposition to the fundamental laws of the Bakufu and the *han* which positively prohibited conspiracy—*gōso* and *tōsan*—was to shake the foundations of Bakufu and *han* feudalism." [175] Hani states that the historical concept that considers the Meiji Restoration an accomplishment of a handful of distinguished retainers in which the peasantry and townsmen stood by in stupid indifference, or a movement that was led by the lower samurai, is a feudal one.[176]

Other Japanese scholars, however, although recognizing the significance of the roles played by the merchants and peasants in the Restoration, hesitate to subscribe unconditionally to Hani's thesis. Horie Yasuzō, for example, points out that although the support given by the farmers and merchants contributed greatly, their support was in general neither active nor positive. He states:

> Although the foundations of the feudal system were shaken in these circumstances, the farmers' movements of opposition did not . . . constitute any positive attempt to revolutionize the existing order of things. The same may be said of the *chonin*, that is, [that] although they reached the point when they no longer meekly obeyed the orders of their feudal lords by reason of their amassed wealth, and while some merchants even attempted secret foreign trade in defiance of Shogunate orders, they were too powerless and too deficient in self-consciousness to take any active part in the Restoration movement. Generally speaking, it meant the bankruptcy of the commercial class itself to attempt in any way to overthrow the feudal order of society, and moreover, few merchants possessed any modern knowledge. They did not, therefore, take any active part in the Restoration movement. The fact nevertheless remains that the accumulation of wealth by this commercial class dealt a fatal blow to the economic basis of feudal society. Nor can it be denied that their financial power contributed greatly to the success of the Meiji Restoration. . . .[177]

Both scholars agree, however, that the action of the common people was sufficient to shake the foundations of the feudal system; these disturbances were exploited by the samurai in their attempts to overthrow the oppressive Bakufu and to reëstablish the rule of the emperor.

An American scholar, Thomas C. Smith, believes that the *gōnō*, or wealthy peasant entrepreneurs, played a more dramatic role in the Restoration than they are generally given credit for by most historians. He contends that loyalist sympathies were common among the educated class of the village and that a number of peasants were given court honors for their part in the Restoration.[178] This thesis is in line with that presented by the Japanese scholar, Fujita Gorō, who maintains that after the Tempō era (1830–1844) the rural "bourgeois landlords" accumulated wealth through the manufacture of small articles of commerce. Naramoto Tatsuya and Hattori Shisō also argue that the more common elements of society—the bourgeois landlords composed of the *gōnō*, *gōshi* (peasant-samurai), and *chūnō* (middle-class peasants)—were significant components of the Restoration movement.[179] The peasantry supported the samurai leaders, the majority of whom were lower samurai, although the leadership included men of the upper samurai class as well. Those in the latter category would include such men as Gotō Shōjirō and Itagaki Taisuke of Tosa and Takasugi Shinsaku of Chōshū.[180] Hattori's contention is that the bourgeoisie of the Bakumatsu-Tempō era (1830–1868) were still closely tied to the land (bourgeois landlords) and that therefore the period can only be characterized as "a manufacturing era in the narrowest sense of the term." [181] Tsuchiya Takao takes exception to this viewpoint, arguing that commercial capitalism, as opposed to early industrial capitalism (local production), had its origin much earlier in the Tokugawa period. He points specifically to the well-developed economic institution, the *tonya* (commission merchants), as evidence.[182] Tsuchiya contends that the economic difficulties confronted by the samurai toward the close of the Tokugawa period created dissatisfaction and eventually a rebellious mood aimed at the Bakufu.[183] The samurai were supported by the *chōnin*.

It is Hattori who first argued that the Meiji Restoration signified the establishment of "absolutism" in Japan, a concept adopted by the Marxist school of Japanese historians of which Tōyama Shigeki is a member.[184] Tōyama indicates that the Restoration was a class revolution of a limited nature which was utilized by the samurai leaders of the strong western *han*, represented by such political entities as Satsuma and Chōshū, in order to establish their hegemony over Japan. According to Tōyama, the overthrow of the old feudal order of high-ranking samurai by an alliance of lower samurai and an emerging class of local producers gave rise to absolutism.[185] The Restoration, for this school of thinkers, was not motivated primarily by a spirit of loyalty to the imperial house; indeed, many of the samurai participants, it is contended, brazenly used in conversation such cryptic phrases as *tama wo ubau* (steal the jewel)—the "jewel" being an allusion to the emperor, and the phrase connoting usurpation of the throne.[186]

The Bakufu's policy of encouraging scholarship contributed, ironically, to the undermining of the Tokugawa political foundation. The studies of the *wagakusha,* or national scholars, of the early history of Japan resulted in weakening the position of the Bakufu by taking the philosophy of loyalty to its logical conclusion, applying it to indigenous institutions and thus revealing the usurpation of imperial authority by the Bakufu. Moreover, scholars specializing in Western learning brought the Bakufu's raison d'etre under scrutiny and question. In addition, the spirit of Western science, which placed value on the freedom to search for the truth, was applied by the *rangakusha,* or Dutch scholars, to their study of the indigenous culture, and thereupon revealed the unprogressive and contradictory nature of feudal society under the rule of the *shōgun.*[187] Finally, Confucian scholars inadvertently contributed to the ideological currents that swept around and weakened the basic supports of Tokugawa feudalism by their study of the *gun-ken,* or county-prefecture, administrative system of the Chinese sages. This system, called *chun-hsien* in Chinese, had been used in China to combat feudalism.[188] This concept of state, developed toward the end of the Tokugawa period, played a part in the Restoration movement and the final destruction of Tokugawa feudalism.[189]

The role of the national scholars was especially important because they laid the ideological basis for the *sonnō ron,* or imperialist theory.[190] The loyalist movement, which attained its apogee toward the end of the Tokugawa period, drew its inspiration from the findings of the Japanese classical scholars. According to Tōyama Shigeki, the *sonnō* ideology was not originally intended as an instrument for the restoration of imperial authority. Rather, the Mito branch of the Tokugawa family, the prime espousers of the ideology, had planned to use it to restore the Tokugawa regime to its former state of glory. Since the Mito ideology was based upon the Confucian concept of loyalty, the assumption was that each social stratum—commoners, *han* retainers, *daimyō,* and *shōgun*—as it showed loyalty to the emperor, would in turn display loyalty toward its immediate superior. It was therefore hoped that a call for reverence toward the emperor would ameliorate the anti-Bakufu sentiment among the *kuge* and maintain the loyalty of the various *daimyō* toward the Tokugawa government. Ironically, the ideology of the Mito scholars was eventually used by the radical loyalists as a political weapon against the weakening feudal regime in Edo.[191]

Watanabe Ikujirō believes that one of the basic loyalist motives behind the destruction of the Bakufu was to restore the land to its original political structure. He contends that the objective of the Meiji Restoration was to realize the implication of the *sonnō* concept and to establish Japan in a position of equality in international relation; the purpose of the *sonnō* movement was to reëstablish Japan's original polity by abolishing the feudalistic military government and restoring the personal rule of the emperor.[192] Watanabe strongly believed that every important participant in the Restoration movement was motivated by a burning loyalty to the emperor. Thus he states that "direct rule by the emperor was the life of the Meiji Restoration and its spirit, and hence Sanjō, Iwakura and the others who rendered distinguished service to the movement had this as their purpose and consequently exerted their utmost effort to realize it." [193]

There is no doubt that the Japanese had great loyalty for their sovereign, and that reverence for the emperor and the expulsion of foreigners had strong emotional force, but the immediate objective of the movement appears to have been the destruction of the Bakufu and the overthrow of an oppressive military regime. The movement to expel the foreigners was exploited by the anti-Bakufu forces to achieve their end. The reformers, noting the growing unpopularity of the Bakufu among the people, took up the slogan to expel the foreigners and by subtly associating it with the doctrine of reverence for the emperor carried on their movement with vigor.[194]

A final factor that proved disadvantageous to the Tokugawa regime was the political and economic pressures of the foreign capitalist nations that, combining with internal pressures built up by the political, social, and economic forces of the time, tended to create problems with which the Bakufu was unable to cope.[195]

The question of leadership and class alliances with reference to the Restoration has become a subject for heated debate among historians, especially since World War II. It is apparent that the leadership of the movement remained not with the *daimyō* class but with their retainers—men such as Ōkubo Toshimichi and Saigō Takamori of Satsuma, Kido Kōin and Takasugi Shinsaku of Chōshū, and Nakaoka Shintarō of Tosa —who had experience as *han* administrators. It is equally true that not all retainers active in the movement were so-called lower samurai. Among them were men from the upper samurai class, as Komatsu Tatewaki of Satsuma, who worked closely with Ōkubo and Saigō in planning the alliance with Chōshū and the destruction of the Bakufu; and Gotō Shōjirō,

Itagaki Taisuke, and Fukuoka Kōtei from Tosa's "middle-upper" samurai class, who worked for the Restoration cause.[196]

Many of these loyalists were *han* retainers, but a number of others were *rōnin,* or masterless samurai, who also played a prominent role in the Restoration. The *rōnin* had a background of political action; during the early years of the Tokugawa period they opposed the establishment of the Bakufu. Their activity waned, however, in inverse ratio to the growth of Tokugawa power. They were under control until the Bakumatsu era when the weakness of the Bakufu once more brought them back to the political stage. They were deeply involved, as has been seen, in the major anti-Bakufu incidents prior to the Restoration, the Teradaya and Sakuradamon incidents being cases in point. Hirao Michio says that the *rōnin* were not simply the opponents of the existing order but were also forerunners of the new Restoration era. Sakamoto Ryūma, the Tosa loyalist and *rōnin,* was instrumental in bringing Satsuma and Chōshū together in an alliance against the Bakufu.[197] Generally in straitened circumstances, and oppressed as a class, the *rōnin* became active politically, especially after 1860. Under the slogan of "Revere the emperor and expel the barbarians," they campaigned against the Edo government, aided significantly, by money often exacted from the wealthy *chōnin.*[198]

Important *rōnin* of the caliber of Sakamoto Ryūma, Nakaoka Shintarō, and Ōhashi Shintarō worked closely with another group of loyalists, the *kuge,* or court nobles. Among the latter, Iwakura Tomomi, Anenokōji Kintomo, and Sanjō Sanetomi are the most representative. It is clear that the leadership of the Restoration was mainly in the hands of the samurai, both upper and lower classes, and in those of a few radical courtiers. The importance of the *daimyō* was primarily that of lending prestige and influence to their retainers who were in the forefront of the movement.

Besides the support from the anti-Bakufu *han* in western Japan, what other sources of help did the Restoration leaders have? It would be difficult to disprove, for example, that the Restoration cause was ignored by the wealthy merchants, the *chōnin.*[199] Hirao Michio, basing his conclusions on the records of the Mitsui family and the studies of the Japanese economic historian Honjō Eijirō, states that "the wars for the Restoration were fought and won with the funds supplied by the *chōnin* contributed through coercion," whereas E. H. Norman believes that the *chōnin* willingly aided the cause; their own interests were involved inasmuch as the merchants lived off the interest on loans to *daimyō* and samurai.[200]

Others, as already noted, have discussed the role played by the peasantry, pointing out that the peasant revolts, like their *chōnin* counterparts, were manifestations of discontent with oppressive Bakufu regulations and taxation. Tōyama Shigeki indicates that the basis of the Restoration was a struggle between the coalition of wealthy merchants and peasants led by the lower samurai on the one hand and the feudal Tokugawa regime on the other.[201] He suggests that the basis for the samurai prestige and power was primarily the backing they received from their respective *han*, a conclusion which seems valid.[202]

Although scholars have attempted to explain the Restoration in simple terms—for example, that it was primarily the culmination of social resentment, or that it was motivated wholly by samurai loyalty to the imperial house, or that it was the inevitable result of the power struggle among the feudal factions—a study of the period reveals a variety of interacting forces in operation. It is just as much a mistake to accept completely the Tōyama thesis that the Restoration was a socioeconomic struggle involving the *ancien régime* and the burgeoning merchant and peasant classes as it is to adhere strictly to the traditional school of thought that patriotism was the only motive force. In assessing the various viewpoints, one must be aware of the social and political milieu in which a particular Japanese historian worked. During the Meiji and Taishō eras, Japanese society was completely permeated with the idea of loyalty to the emperor, and historians, knowingly or unknowingly, were influenced by this climate of thought. Since World War II, however, with the emergence of a more democratic environment in Japan, thinkers who have heretofore been intellectually shackled are free to expound whatever view they hold. The postwar trend has been in the direction of Marxist thinking—a manifestation of extreme reaction to the ultraconservatism of the past. The intellectual pendulum in time is certain to swing back to a middle ground and to what will probably be a more correct position.

In evaluating the Restoration forces, an eclectic approach is plausible, as the Restoration was, after all, the result of various interrelated factors. The *rōnin*, for instance, had real and abiding grievances against the Bakufu whose lack of sympathy for their economic and social distresses aroused resentment. The *chōnin* also had sufficient grounds for antagonism against a feudal regime which harshly regulated economic life and arbitrarily utilized the merchants' wealth for its own purpose. It was inevitable that the awakening political consciousness [203] of the urban merchants would thrust this class into the role of supporters of the samurai leaders although monetary aid was often not given entirely of the *chōnin*'s own volition. There is also reason to believe, as indicated by Thomas C. Smith, Hani Gorō, and Tōyama Shigeki, among others, that the wealthier peasants played an important role in the Restoration along with their wealthy city cousins, a thesis that in recent times has been vigorously refuted by such American historians as Albert M. Craig and Marius B. Jansen. The development among the samurai of a sincere feeling of loyalty to the imperial house, resulting from their exposure to the Mito school of thought, to Confucianism, to Japan's past history, and to their reëxamination of Shintoism, undoubtedly spurred many to work for the loyalist cause. Patriots also sensed the danger to their homeland from external forces if the weakened Tokugawa government were to continue in power. A love of country—a land free from foreign domination—was a strong force, as strong as that which impelled the Minutemen back in '76. A final and very significant explanation for the Restoration is purely Machiavellian in basis, namely, that the movement was a definite attempt by the western *tozama han* to overthrow their feudal overlord, the Tokugawa, and to gain for themselves hegemony over Japan. It was a culmination of a power struggle, led by young samurai *han* leaders who, thrusting forward under the slogan of *sonnō jōi,* utilized whatever support they could muster, either voluntary or enforced, from any and all classes in order to grasp the reins of authority for their side—and ultimately for themselves. Ambition is part of men and politics whether in Japan or in Kuwait.

The study of Ōkubo Toshimichi should bring to light some of the interacting forces that have been mentioned. He is typical of many of his peers. He was for the most part sympathetic to the distressed samurai class, generally loyal to the imperial house, deeply anxious about his homeland under Tokugawa rule in the face of foreign pressures, without any consuming fondness for the feudal master in Edo, and filled with tremendous ambition for personal power. Who would isolate any one of these several characteristics and dogmatically say that this particular characteristic consistently impelled Ōkubo to work for the loyalist cause? By the same token, it would be difficult to point to any one factor—

social resentment or loyalty—as the dynamo of the Restoration movement. As a whole, causes like this, as the American Revolution, are backed by individuals for varying reasons that drive men to action: social, political, economic, intellectual, selfish and unselfish.

At any rate, by the mid-nineteenth century the Bakufu had become a symbol of reaction, oppression, and inept leadership. People of every class, *kuge* and samurai as well as townspeople and peasants, desired a change. The leadership of the movement to overthrow the Bakufu in the name of restoring the political authority to the throne was assumed in the main by the aggressive, educated, progressive, and generally court-oriented samurai functionaries of the western *han*. As has been seen, one of the most progressive and powerful among these *han* was Satsuma, and undoubtedly the most outstanding among its leaders was Ōkubo Toshimichi. A lower-class samurai, Ōkubo was not only among those most deeply involved in the overthrow of the feudalistic Tokugawa regime, but also subsequently in the creation of the new Meiji government and a modern Japan.

Meiji Government

The composition of the group at the initial meeting on January 3, 1868, of the new Meiji government portended the power alignment that was to prevail during the early days of its existence. On the evening of January 3 the Kogosho was the scene of an impressive assemblage of court nobles as well as the *daimyō* of Echizen, Tosa, Bizen, Aki, and Satsuma with their chief retainers. It was apparent that the dominant *kuge* in attendance was Iwakura and one of the most influential samurai was Ōkubo. These two men helped set the tone for the evening and perhaps for a decade to come. When Matsudaira Yoshinaga of Echizen and Yamanouchi Toyoshige of Tosa insisted that the ex-*shōgun* as head of the Tokugawa family be granted a position in the new government, there were angry outbursts from both Iwakura and Ōkubo who declared that Tokugawa Keiki would not be admitted to a seat in the council until he had pledged his good faith by resigning his court offices and surrendering his lands and revenues. As a result, the representatives of Echizen and Owari were delegated to meet with Keiki, their mission being to inform him that his resignation of the office of *shōgun* submitted on November 19 had been accepted and that he should now resign his court offices as well as surrender his private property.[204] Obviously, Ōkubo and the extremists would not be satisfied until the Tokugawa family was shorn of all effective political and economic powers.

The superstructure of the Tokugawa military government was destroyed by the proclamation of January 3 when the offices of *sesshō*, or regent; *kampaku*, or chief adviser to the emperor; and *seii taishōgun*, or *shōgun*, were abolished. In its place was erected the *Sanshoku*, composed of three offices of government: a provisional government headed by a *sōsai*, or president, who would be assisted by a number of *gijō*, or senior councilors, and *sanyo*, or junior councilors.[205] Prince Arisugawa was selected to fill the position of *sōsai*, and the *gijō* included the five *daimyō* of Satsuma, Aki, Echizen, Owari, and Tosa. The *sanyo*, significantly, was composed of such prominent Restoration figures as Iwakura, a *kuge*, and lower-class samurai such as Ōkubo and Saigō of Satsuma and Gotō Shōjirō of Tosa.[206] The *sanyo* was a significant position, being tantamount to the later office of *sangi*. The *sanyo* superintended the actual work of the government, and therefore Ōkubo and Saigō were in positions of real power.[207] Moreover, this was the first time in Japanese history that *han* retainers achieved such high positions in imperial officialdom.[208]

A characteristic of the provisional government was the predominance of Satsuma men within its council. In fact, until January 27, 1868, there were no Chōshū men in the position of *sanyo*.[209] The reasons for the early Satsuma predominance were the plethora of capable leaders within the Satsuma *han* and the fact that Chōshū, because of past offenses against the court, had not been permitted to enter Kyōto until after the formation of the incipient Meiji government. After January 3, 1868, national leadership fell into the hands of low-ranking samurai from the several *han*, largely because of the incompetence of those who under ordinary circumstances would have gained control of the government, namely, the *daimyō*. The *daimyō* class for generations had tended to rely more and more upon their retainers to carry on the work of administering the *han*, and the samurai retainers therefore gained both administrative experience and political insight. Hence the new Meiji government, instead of being administered by the *daimyō* class, was to be controlled in the main by the lower samurai.

Katsu Kaishū, in speaking of the Meiji leaders, has pointed out that the triumvirate of the Restoration became the driving force behind the Meiji government. The decisions, he noted, were made by Ōkubo, Saigō, and Kido, the other members of the government serving merely as assistants to these men.[210] It was Katsu who, early in the Meiji period, charged that the Restoration resulted in the supplantation of the Tokugawa Bakufu by the Satsuma Bakufu, a charge supported by some later Japanese historians.[211] There is no evidence to indicate that Ōkubo had any intention of establishing a Satsuma Bakufu, that is, a dual form of government as existed during the period of the *shōgun*, but there is no doubt that his aim was to place his own *han* in a position of preëminence in national life. By utilizing its power and prestige, Ōkubo and his colleagues could gain control of the imperial government and work through it. With conditions as they were at the time of the Restoration, this was probably the extent of his ambition.

Tokugawa and the Meiji Government

The new Meiji government was soon confronted with the disposition of the vestiges of the old regime. Could Tokugawa Keiki be deprived of his private property? He was willing to forego his office of *shōgun*, but as for resigning his court offices and surrendering his lands and revenues, he was adamantly opposed; and, furthermore, the Aizu and Kuwana samurai who supported the Bakufu did not intend to allow the liquidation of the Tokugawa government. Wishing to avoid a conflict and being branded a rebel, Keiki left the Nijō castle on January 6, 1868, and went to Ōsaka where he was soon joined by the Bakufu troops from Kyōto. After a few weeks he yielded to the pressures from his subordinates and, on January 25, returned to Kyōto at the head of his forces to remove by his sword what he considered to be evil advisers from around the throne.

When Ōkubo learned that the Satsuma residence in Edo had been burned by its foes and was informed of the movements of the Aizu and Kuwana forces in the direction of the imperial capital, he immediately arranged for the issuance of an imperial decree authorizing the dispatching of punitive forces against the rebels. The troops would bear the imperial standard and be under the command of a prince. At the battle of Toba-Fushimi, which took place between January 27 and 30, the imperial forces, composed mainly of Satsuma and Chōshū troops, defeated the Tokugawa contingents.[212] For Ōkubo and the members of the new government this was a decisive battle; had the imperial forces been routed, Ōkubo and his cohorts would have been branded as rebels. Toba-Fushimi was for the Meiji government what Sekigahara was for the Tokugawa in 1600. With his army defeated, Keiki was compelled to flee to Edo. Thereafter, except for the Aizu and Kuwana forces which held out for some months in central Honshū and Hokkaidō, the whole country submitted to the rule of the new imperial government.

Ōkubo had foreseen the impossibility of achieving the Restoration without the use of arms. In the fall of 1867 he had secretly purchased from a store in Nishijin cloth to make imperial standards. He had then contacted Tamamatsu Misao who designed and completed two stands of imperial flags and twenty stands of ensigns. These were entrusted to the care of Shinagawa Yaijirō, a Chōshū extremist, who had them stored in Yamaguchi until they were used by the imperial forces against the rebels. Ōkubo thus meticulously prepared each step toward his goal, leaving nothing to chance.[213]

Not only had Ōkubo laid careful plans for a possible conflict with the Bakufu but, when war came, he was willing to accept a commission for active service. He was appointed a staff officer of the imperial forces on January 30 and went immediately to the scene of battle.[214] When he returned to Kyōto on February 1, 1868, Iwakura was highly displeased because his colleague had left him alone to manage the complex affairs of state. Pointing out that the two had pledged to work together for the imperial cause, Iwakura said that he could not afford to risk losing Ōkubo on the battlefield. Ōkubo thereupon relinquished his military commission, apparently without undue reluctance, and remained in Kyōto.[215] His decision was probably motivated primarily by his deference for Iwakura and not because he feared the dangers of war.

It was Ōkubo who was responsible for sparing Tokugawa Keiki's life when those in the new Meiji government argued for his execution. This episode occurred after Keiki's retreat to Edo. As the imperial troops pressed on toward the Tokugawa capital, one of Keiki's retainers, Katsu Kaishū, realizing that his side could not hold off against the forces under Saigō Takamori and Ōmura Masujirō, approached Saigō and requested the cessation of hostilities. Saigō returned to Kyōto where the council discussed the treatment to be accorded the ex-*shōgun*. Opinion was divided. Mōri of Chōshū favored putting him to death and obliterating the Tokugawa name. Saigō was unalterably opposed to this. It was Ōkubo who offered the compromise proposal of punishing Keiki's advisers but sparing the life of the former *shōgun*. The compromise was accepted.[216] One should not infer from Ōkubo's attitude that he was motivated wholly by compassion for an enemy; he may very well have foreseen that in sparing Keiki's life he would win for himself the support of some of his former enemies.

Ōkubo's life is a study of contradictions. Like a pendulum his ideology swung from left to right, from revolutionary to moderate and back again to extremism. But who can say that his opportunism, determination, and daring did not serve his country well? No one can deny that he played a vital role in the Restoration movement and in the establishment of the new government.[217] Although few Japanese historians would admit that a man of Ōkubo's caliber would work only for his own ends, it is difficult to agree that the members of the Sat-Chō clique who controlled the Meiji government after 1868 were allowed a free hand because the others recognized the justice and righteousness of their motives. Behind the *sonnō* facade there existed ulterior motives, considerations of power and prestige for their respective *han* if not for themselves personally. But whatever the motives, Japan was to be centralized under a single government and guided by men of unusual ability, tremendous drive, and steadfast purpose. Ōkubo and his colleagues were to adhere to a harsh and dictatorial policy, and although few favor such methods of government, for a Japan just emerging from her feudal chrysalis—weak, disunited, and unsophisticated in the ways of international relations—the leadership of proven samurai administrators was to prove a boon. Men of the stamp of Ōkubo, Kido, Saigō, and Iwakura were indispensable to the founding of Meiji Japan.

V
Architect of Modern Japan

Ōkubo was to nurture the young Meiji government just as carefully as he had helped plan and execute the detailed operations of the Restoration movement. Almost single-handedly, during the critical period from the spring of 1868 to 1871, he held the government together, coaxing and flattering jealous colleagues and suspicious *han* into devoting themselves to the national ideal. Because of his untiring efforts the Meiji government displayed sufficient unity to cope with the myriad problems, both internal and external, that beset it. Such projects as the transfer of the imperial capital from Kyōto to Edo, and the abolition of the feudal *han* and establishment of prefectures, were directed toward the strengthening and modernization of Japan. In the role of national reformer, Ōkubo was no less successful than he had been as a *han* reformer. Without these reforms, which were implemented with vigor and consistency, Japan would have been unable to rise to her subsequent height as a political power. Certainly there can be no question as to the efficacy of Ōkubo's work as one of the prime architects of modern Japan. He planned wisely. He built solidly. Like George Washington, who faced great problems in the early years of the American republic, Ōkubo and his colleagues worked under tremendous difficulties but succeeded in erecting the basic structure of the Japanese state.

One of the early problems confronting Ōkubo and the new government was that of dealing with vacillating *han*, many of which hesitated to commit their support to a yet untested government lest ultimately they be found on the side of a losing contender in the power struggle. To inspire confidence in the new administration, Ōkubo received imperial consent to display the military strength of the *han* comprising the coalition government. On January 21, 1868, he had seventy-five hundred troops of the Satsuma, Chōshū, Tosa, and Aki *han*, all drilled in Western military fashion, march in review through the streets of Kyōto, their precision and numbers "impressing the viewers." [1]

In the administrative sphere, the leaders realized the inadequacies in the *Sanshoku*, the first organization of the government.[2] On February 10, 1868, the imperial council, acting according to the recommendation of Fukuoka Kōtei, issued a decree establishing the *Shichika*, a government comprising seven administrative offices. The seven offices included those dealing with home affairs, foreign affairs, military affairs, finance, justice, laws and institutions, and Shintō.[3] Ōkubo accepted a post in the important department dealing with home affairs as a *jimu kakari*, or administrative officer, a position from which he was able to exert his influence in the formation of national policy.[4]

Moving the Capital

Ōkubo's thinking on domestic policy was thoroughly progressive. When, on February 10, Prince Arisugawa, the *sōsai*, consulted him about some initial reforms, Ōkubo advanced the startling proposition that Emperor Meiji come out of seclusion and mingle with his subjects after the manner of the monarchs of the West, breaking a practice of centuries.[5] But he did not reveal at this time his belief that Kyōto, the imperial residence since A.D. 794, should be abandoned. His first discussion of that was with Iwakura Tomomi two days later, and on the following day he mentioned the radical idea to Arisugawa. Then, on February 16, Ōkubo's petition explaining his stand was presented to the imperial council, but no decision was reached at that time.[6] The petition noted that the emperor had traditionally lived in isolation with no more than a few court nobles permitted to see him, a practice opposed to the "laws of heaven." It contended that if man reveres his superior too highly a breach is created between the emperor and his subjects, who are unable to communicate their needs to him. The petition then urged that the capital be moved temporarily to Ōsaka, a significant diplomatic, military and naval, and economic center.[7]

Ōkubo's purpose in making this suggestion was to rid the court of undesirable people who were apt to influence imperial decisions. His proposal, therefore, was opposed not only by those with vested interest within the court, but also by others on the outside. For example, Iwakura informed him that Kuga Tatemichi interpreted the plan to be a Satsuma plot to remove the Emperor to Ōsaka so that the Sat-Chō clique could exercise its authority with the least amount of resistance. Ōkubo was also told that Gotō of Tosa was of the same opinion, although he apparently did not express any objections publicly and pretended to be in accord with the idea.[8] In fact, enmities were engendered even in Ōkubo's own *han* which, according to one source, were to culminate several years later in the Satsuma rebellion and the assassination of Ōkubo.[9]

Despite opposition, Ōkubo's recommendations were adopted. The day after the proclamation of the Charter Oath on April 7, 1868, it was announced that the Emperor would leave for Ōsaka. Ōkubo noted in his diary on April 13 that the Emperor left that morning.[10] He arrived at his destination on the fifteenth and established his *anzaisho*, or place of sojourn, at the Nishi Honganji. The fact that Ōkubo and his colleagues successfully effected the transfer of the imperial capital from Kyōto to another site, a move opposed by the traditionalists, indicates the great influence they exerted upon the newly formed government.

Opinion varied as to where the permanent site of the imperial capital should be. After the defeat of the Tokugawa forces in the Kantō region and the surrender of the Edo castle to the imperial forces on May 3, 1868, that region came to be favored.[11] The Tokugawa were no longer a threat there; after surrender ceremonies, Keiki and his forces withdrew to Mito where he was apportioned a revenue of seven hundred thousand *koku*, the minimum figure Ōkubo had suggested.[12] Even prior to the fall of Edo to the imperial forces, Ōkubo had expressed an opinion favoring Kantō as the site for the new capital, justifying his position on strategic grounds. It was to acquire this region that Ōkubo first pressed for the removal of the Tokugawa from the area.[13] After the acquisition of Edo, Ōkubo went there to make necessary arrangements for the transfer of the seat of government. Arriving in Edo on August 9, he met with Iwakura Tomomi, Kido Kōin, Ōki Takato, and Ōmura Masujirō and discussed matters pertaining to changing the name of Edo, the administration of Kantō, and the sojourn of the Emperor in the newly-acquired city.[14] Ōkubo and Ōki soon returned to Kyōto where, after overcoming stubborn opposition from the conservative faction, they were able to have an imperial pronouncement made on September 3, changing the name of Edo to Tōkyō.[15] About a month later, on November 4, the Emperor left for the eastern capital for a temporary stay. In the spring of 1869 he again came up to Edo (Tōkyō), this time to make it the permanent abode of the imperial family and the seat of his government.[16]

The transfer of the capital to Edo was a logical move. Edo had long been the military capital and it supported a large population. For the new government to have overlooked it as the site of its administrative center would have worked extreme hardship upon the city. Moreover, it was strategically located where the anti-Tokugawa faction supporting the imperial government could keep a close watch over the northern *han* that were antagonistic toward Satsuma and Chōshū, whose men dominated the government. Edo was also fast becoming an important city of Japan with Yezo (Hokkaidō) acquiring increasing strategic importance because of Russia's interest in the area. Nor could the fact of Edo's valuable human resources, in the form of experienced administrative personnel left behind by the defunct Bakufu, be overlooked. Finally, there were minor considerations that influenced the decision to transfer the capital: Edo, having been a military capital, had an attraction for the Restoration leaders who were samurai; it had an established castle that could be converted into a palace, thus saving the financially embarrassed government the cost of building a new imperial edifice; and it had the prestige of being one of the great cities of the world.[17] Judging from the perspective of history there is no reason to doubt the wisdom of Ōkubo's decision.

Dealing with Foreigners

During this time, the government was busy dealing with foreign problems. On January 1, 1868, in accordance with the agreement made with the treaty powers in 1862, Ōsaka and Hyōgo were opened to trade. But with the coup d'etat of January 3 and the proclamation of the new imperial government, the Bakufu had been deprived of its authority. Ōkubo took immediate steps to have the foreign nations represented in Japan recognize the new government and the sovereignty of the throne. Satsuma's French political adviser suggested that an imperial pronouncement be made notifying the foreign representatives that the Emperor, as the head of the federated *han,* had assumed the authority previously vested in the *shōgun.*[18] Accordingly, on February 8, 1868, the Emperor announced to the foreign powers that henceforth he would exercise supreme authority both in the internal and external affairs of the nation.[19]

The *jōi,* or the antiforeign, faction was to embarrass the new government by its ruthless attacks upon aliens in Japan. Early in February, retainers of the Bizen *han* attacked foreigners in Kōbe, but fortunately there was no loss of life. The central government, unlike its predecessor, tendered its apology without quibbling and ordered Bizen to surrender the offenders.[20] Again, on March 8, 1868, Tosa samurai attacked a party of French seamen at Sakai, killing eleven of them. On this occasion, Ōkubo, although connected with the *Naikoku Jimuka,* the office dealing with home affairs, was ordered by the *Gaikoku Jimuka,* the office dealing with foreign affairs, to assist in the settlement of the incident. Arriving in Ōsaka on March 10, Ōkubo met for two days with the French representative, M. Leon Roches, aboard the "Dupleix." The French demanded the execution of all who had participated in the attack, an indemnity of one hundred and fifty thousand dollars for the families of the murdered sailors, an apology by the imperial government through the office of foreign affairs, an apology by the lord of Tosa, and the exclusion of all armed Tosa men from the treaty ports. After a consultation with Iwakura, Kido, and Hirozawa Saneomi, Ōkubo and the government accepted these demands on March 14, much to the dissatisfaction of the *jōi* faction.[21]

The willingness to settle with the foreigners represented a *volte-face* in Japanese foreign policy. This conciliation reflected Ōkubo's attitude; he was against unnecessary involvement with foreign powers while Japan was still struggling to get on her feet. His participation in the settlement of the Sakai incident indicates his versatility as a statesman and his colleagues' high respect for his judgment.

The structure of the new government underwent another change on February 25 when the *Shichika* was abolished and replaced by the *Hachikyoku.* Ōkubo, in addition to his position as *hanji,* or deputy administrator, within the *Naikoku Jimukyoku,* or the department dealing with home affairs, was subsequently given a temporary appointment as a *komon,* or adviser, in the *Sōsaikyoku,* the body that exercised supervisory control over the other administrative offices. According to Robert A. Wilson, "the actual work of administration seems to have been in the hands of the *komon* and *benji*. . . ." [22] Significantly, two of the four *komon* at this time were Satsuma men, namely, Ōkubo Toshimichi and Komatsu Tatewaki. The other two were Kido of Chōshū and Gotō of Tosa.[23]

Charting the Course of State

On April 6, 1868, the new government issued in the name of the Emperor the momentous *Gokajō no Goseimon*, or Charter Oath, outlining the future course for Japan.[24] The Charter Oath is noteworthy because of its democratic implications, for instance, the creation of an assembly, and Japanese historians have taken pains to allude to the Charter Oath as the raison d'etre for the new nation.[25] To what extent was Ōkubo responsible for this historical statement of policy? Interestingly enough, Ōkubo did not take a major part in the preparation of this fundamental document. The day on which the pronouncement was made in elaborate ceremonies performed at the Shishinden was a momentous one, but the entry of April 6, 1868, in Ōkubo's diary merely says, "Attended the meeting of the council." [26] Nothing is said about the Charter Oath. Why the apparent disinterest in such a significant event? Did he not adhere to its liberal principles?

The Charter Oath was the handiwork of several men: Yuri Kimmasa and Fukuoka Kōtei, who drew up the first and second drafts respectively, and Kido Kōin, whose third and accepted draft was in the main a revision of those of Yuri and Fukuoka.[27] The pronouncement was motivated by political and economic considerations; it manifested the aspirations of the liberals who were eager to create a more representative government through the establishment of an assembly,[28] but another factor was the provisional government's dire financial condition. Its meager revenues were insufficient to finance the civil war with the Tokugawa diehards, a fact which necessitated its securing financial aid from the wealthy landholders and merchants in the form of *goyōkin*, or forced loans. The government rightly realized that without an established long-term policy, as represented by the Charter Oath, it could not gain the complete confidence of potential creditors.[29] Also, by stressing public opinion, that is, *han* opinion, the Charter Oath was intended to prevent defection among the allied *han* waging war at the time against the Tokugawa forces. Because of this last consideration, Satsuma and Chōshū supported the Charter Oath. From this it may be inferred that Ōkubo did have more than passing interest in the pronouncement; it affected the future of the government.[30] In short, the Oath was meant to be a pledge among the *daimyō* supporting the new government and a statement of policy consciously designed to unite the whole nation behind its leaders.[31] No doubt it was also intended for foreign consumption, a tangible manifestation of Japan's eagerness to be accepted by the world as a modern nation. The Marxist interpretation, as might be expected, is cynical. According to Tōyama, the leaders of the Meiji government intended the Charter Oath to be no more than a temporary expedient; it was merely to serve as an anesthetic for any potential opponents of the new government, giving them surcease from pain during the transition phase from the old to the new order. Once the absolute authority of the new imperial government was established, the political ideals contained in the Charter were to be discarded.[32]

The varying degree of interest displayed by Ōkubo and Kido in the formulation of this idealistic policy for Japan reveals the nature of the two men. Kido, moved by idealism, envisioned a progressive country based upon the Charter Oath; whereas Ōkubo, although no less farsighted, was a pragmatist whose interests lay in the present and the immediate future—upon such matters as the settlement of the civil war, the transfer of the capital, and the selection of competent administrative personnel. The basic difference in the character of these two Restoration leaders was a source of friction between them. Kido, sensitive and emotional, could not, furthermore, forget the unpleasant aspects of past Satsuma-Chōshū relations, which tended to make him suspicious of anyone connected with Satsuma. His pride, moreover, was wounded because Chōshū seemed fated to occupy a position subordinate to Satsuma in national affairs.[33] Thus Ōkubo was burdened with the problem of placating an important colleague as well as with the numerous other difficulties related to foreign relations, the prosecution of the war, and a populace dissatisfied with its economic plight.

Ōkubo's first meeting with Emperor Meiji added brightness to his difficult life as a statesman. The audience took place at the Emperor's temporary abode in Ōsaka on May 1, and left a lasting impression upon the Satsuma leader.[34] This was the first time in history that a person of the retainer class had been so honored, and Ōkubo noted that he was "moved to tears." [35] Without attempting to be cynical, it should be pointed out that this action was less the desire of the Emperor to achieve a closer relationship with his subjects than it was the implementation of a policy prescribed by the leaders of the Meiji government—by Ōkubo himself.

Financing the Government

The financial status of the new government during the crucial year of 1868 was precarious. Like American leaders during the early years of the Revolution, Ōkubo, with insufficient funds, was responsible for maintaining the imperial troops on the field, furnishing them with military supplies and pay, and at the same time trying to increase the number of men in arms and to give adequate treatment to the sick and the wounded.[36] The government very early resorted to the printing of paper currency.[37] At the same time, it was forced to borrow from such merchant families as Mitsui, Ono, and Shimada in order to prosecute the civil war.[38] Iwakura, who was actually the one in charge of the treasury at this time, worked closely with Ōkubo and relied upon his judgment regarding financial matters. In a letter dated June 20, 1868, Iwakura requested his colleague to "come over before going to the office," and said that he wished to consult with him on the "serious" state of the finances and suggested that steps would have to be taken "to establish a firm basis for the wealth and power of the empire." [39] Soon thereafter, on July 4, the government issued the *Dajōkan* notes in denominations of ten, five, and one *ryō*.[40] By June 1, 1869, forty-eight million *ryō* in *Dajōkan* notes had been placed in circulation.[41] Ōkubo, however, even during this critical year, cautioned against a rash financial policy. In a letter written to Nakai Hiroshi on October 15, expressing gratitude for the assurance of two hundred thousand *yen* earmarked for military use, Ōkubo warned against a policy that might tend to lessen the creditors' confidence in the government.[42] Sawada Akira, an authority on Meiji finance, notes that Ōkubo was among the opponents of an inflationary policy.[43] The following table presents the overall picture of the new government's financial condition in 1868: [44]

Regular income	3,664,780 yen
Extraordinary income	29,424,533
Total income	33,089,313 yen

Regular expenditure	5,506,253 yen
Extraordinary expenditure	24,998,832
Total expenditure	30,505,085 yen

The extraordinary income included among other items the following:

Dajōkan notes	24,037,389 yen
Loans from native merchants	3,837,107
Loans from foreign merchants	894,375

The extraordinary expenditures included among other items the following:

Boshin campaign	3,348,822 yen
Industrial expansion	9,011,518

Besides the problems related to finance and to the action of the *jōi* party, whose attacks upon foreigners kept the international situation tense, Ōkubo and the new government were harassed by a segment of the *kuge*. The latter reasoned that, since the Restoration was carried out under the slogan of *sonnō* (revere the emperor), the new government should devolve around the throne with much of the administrative responsibilities placed in the hands of the court nobles. The *kuge* naturally opposed the monopolization of authority by the samurai class.[45]

Among other sources of opposition to the new government were the minor *han*, which were jealous of Sat-Chō influence. Yamanouchi Toyoshige of Tosa, for example, had charged that the Toba-Fushimi battle was a private war between the Bakufu and the Sat-Chō coalition. Indeed, this could not be denied because the so-called imperial forces, composed mainly of Satsuma and Chōshū men, were supplied by and acted upon the orders of their respective *han* and not of the Emperor; the court could not of itself have prosecuted the war without the aid of friendly *han*.[46]

Furthermore, the returned soldiers were to present problems for the national policy-makers after the termination of the civil war. By their independent and forceful actions, they tended to upset the political balance within their respective *han* while ignoring if not harassing the central government. In Satsuma they grouped themselves around Kawamura Sumiyoshi, Ishūin Kanahiro, and Nozu Shizuo and purged the more conservative members of the *han* government while instituting reforms conducive to their own well-being.[47] Circumstances such as these induced Saigō eventually to advocate a Korean expedition in the hope of diverting the samurai's attention from their problems by undertaking a foreign adventure. Kido himself seemed to have entertained a similar thought. On January 26, 1869, he noted that there were two pressing problems facing the nation, one of which was the discord and contention created by the ex-servicemen. He advocated the dispatching of a mission to Chōsen (Korea) to inquire into the matter of Korean disrespect toward the new Japanese government. If, he continued, Korea did not satisfy Japanese demands, then, after publicly announcing the fact, Korea ought to be attacked and the authority of Japan extended throughout the peninsula. Such a measure, Kido hoped, would dissipate the internal unrest, as "attention will be focused upon an objective far beyond our own boundaries. . . ." [48]

Ōkubo, however, did not concur with the Saigō-Kido policy of war for the sake of ameliorating a domestic conflict. He gave priority to the development of the country. Japan, he contended, should be strengthened before undertaking a risky foreign adventure. His solution therefore was to reorganize the servicemen and employ them as imperial troops. He did not, however, conceive of a national army raised through conscription as advocated eventually by Ōmura Masujirō. Ōkubo thought in terms of an army composed of men from different *han* and commanded by their respective officers. Thus Satsuma's force would naturally be led by Saigō.[49]

Returning the Fiefs to the Throne

The increasing suspicion of and mounting opposition to the Sat-Chō government, which was charged with emulating the Tokugawa Bakufu, compelled its leaders to demonstrate their devotion to the Emperor and nation by initiating what they hoped would be a popular reform. They proclaimed the *hanseki hōkan* movement, or the returning of the fiefs to the throne, which had the objective of yielding up the quasi-sovereign right of the *daimyō* to the imperial house. There are those who have suggested that the Sat-Chō leaders realized that for their own *han* to retain lands while having forced the Tokugawa *shōgun* to resign his court offices and surrender his land holdings to the imperial house was a contradiction of the principle of justice. For this reason, plus the fact that the financial difficulties of the various *han* created sentiment favorable to *hanseki hōkan*, the leaders decided to take the drastic step forward. Another factor was the growth of the lower samurai influence in the fiefs; these men, unlike some of the *daimyō*, were generally in favor of such a move; it was to their interest to accept such a plan. They wished to emerge from their subordinate position within the *han* and step onto the wider national political stage where the opportunities to rise to eminence were better.[50] Then there are those who believe that *hanseki hōkan* was inspired by the feeling of insecurity on the part of Chōshū, which hitherto had occupied a position secondary to Satsuma. Thus the coalition was known as Sat-Chō and never Chō-Satsu. This situation not only affected the sensitivity of Chōshū, but made for anxiety as well; Chōshū was just as ambitious to grasp and monopolize power as was Satsuma. Despite the fact that originally there was no intention among the Restoration leaders to abolish the *han* lest the action induce a dangerous reaction, the fear of Satsuma political dominance caused Kido to resort to *hanseki hōkan*, a measure he hoped would equalize the strength of the various *han* and prevent any one of them from relying upon superior material and human resources to further its own political ambitions.

It was Kido who seems to have sparked the drive for *hanseki hōkan*. He first approached his own *daimyō*, Mōri, to agree to the idea. Later, on November 2, 1868, in secret consultations, Kido won the reluctant support of Ōkubo and Satsuma, and the two men subsequently prevailed upon Tosa and Hizen to follow suit.[51] On March 2, 1869, the four *han*—Sat-Chō-To-Hi—offered up their respective lists of possessions and men to the Emperor.[52] Kido's *hanseki hōkan* petition appeared in the Official Gazette on March 5.[53] Other *han* fell into line behind these leaders, and, by April 16, 118 out of the 276 *daimyō* of Japan had consented to return their fiefs to the Emperor. Ultimately all but seventeen *daimyō* relinquished their fiefs. The *daimyō* thereafter were given the title of *chihanji*, or imperial governors of what was their former *han*.[54] This step eventually culminated in the complete abolition of the feudal institution, the *han*, and the establishment of prefectures under the control of the central government.

With respect to the *hanseki hōkan* proposal, the question arises as to why Ōkubo, an advocate of centralization as far back as his *han* functionary days, should hesitate to accept a plan that would give the new government leaders greater control over the land. This is an apparent paradox. There is evidence that Ōkubo realized the inevitability of *hanseki hōkan*. The idea germinated in 1867, about the time the question of the disposition of Tokugawa lands was being debated. In discussions with Ōkubo, Terajima Munenori, a Satsuma official, maintained that "not only should the lands and people of the Bakufu be returned to the Emperor, but those of our own Satsuma *han* as well. Should this be done, the other *han* will follow our example." [55] Terajima contended that imperial rule could result only after the abolition of the fiefs. And no less a person than Prince Saionji has stated that Ōkubo accepted this line of reasoning.[56] Why, then, did he later hesitate? Ōkubo's essential consideration was welding together a unified country. He feared decentralization and the risk of a program that would possibly cause the feudal lords to rebel against the government. He may have also hesitated for fear of being branded a traitor to the *han* by advocating the abolition of the fiefs. But certainly Ōkubo believed that a move striking at the very heart of feudalism was premature.[57]

Ōkubo's primary interest at the time was focused less upon the creation of new institutions than upon improving the quality of the personnel of the existing institutions. Even as a *han* official he was extremely conscious that institutions are effective only as those who staff them are competent and able. Therefore, with the objective of creating an efficient corps of government officials, Ōkubo recommended that a program be initiated under which promising *kuge* and samurai be selected and sent abroad for the study of world problems and foreign cultures. Writing to Iwakura, he stressed that "the choice of personnel is of fundamental importance to administration," and requested the prompt but careful selection of "three or four men from among the *kuge* and seven or eight men from the various *han* to sojourn in England." [58] Reminiscent of the Heian period when Japanese students were sent to T'ang China to absorb its culture, Ōkubo in the nineteenth century was urging a similar program of cultural adoption, this time from the progressive West. He was convinced that the establishment of the new imperial government could be assured only as Japan was successful in producing men capable of "blending together the civilization of Japan, China, and the West." [59] Accepting Ōkubo's proposal, Japan sent Saionji Kimmochi to France, Yanagibara Sakimitsu and Madenokōji Michifusa to England, and Iwakura Tomosada, the son of Iwakura Tomomi, to the United States. These men eventually became important leaders of Japan.[60]

Reorganization of Satsuma

Ōkubo had originally planned to return to Satsuma early in 1869 to explain the purpose and ramifications of *hanseki hōkan* and to initiate reforms in the *han* government to bring it into closer relationship with the central government. Thus far, with respect to local administration, the government had established the *fu*, or a metropolitan district; *han*, or fief governed by the feudal lord; and *ken*, or prefecture, created in the territory of the ex-*shōgun*.[61] The office of *kōmunin* had been created as mediator between the central and *han* governments.[62] On December 11, 1868, the *han* governments were reorganized to facilitate their control by the central government.[63] The principal officials of the *han* were the *shissei*, who were subject to imperial authority and whose duties were to assist the *chihanji* (who were usually the former *daimyō* of the *han*) and to preside over the general affairs of the *han*. The *sansei* assisted in the management of general *han* affairs, and the *kōginin*, subject to imperial authority, represented the *han* in the national deliberative assembly. Significantly, both the *shissei* and *sansei* were appointed by the lords.[64]

Ōkubo's plans to return to Kagoshima early in 1869 were disrupted, however, when, on February 15, Yokoi Shōnan, a *sanyo* in the government created under the *Seitaisho*, the Document on the Structure of Government, was assassinated. Yokoi was accused of favoring the introduction of Western learning and Christianity and has the distinction of being the first major political figure in the Meiji government to be murdered.[65]

In Kagoshima the political situation had reached a point of crisis for the once-powerful Shimazu family. The samurai party, composed of returned warriors from the civil war, and grouping themselves around Saigō, was successfully opposing the Hisamitsu party. Obviously, there was an urgent need to reëstablish accord within the Satsuma *han*, and Ōkubo's colleagues in Kagoshima began pressing him to return. He did so, but only after giving consideration to the question of his own status. Should he give the impression that he was merely a Satsuma samurai ready to return to his *han* at its will, or must he emphasize his capacity as an official of the national government, no longer under the control of the *han*? He reasoned that a situation wherein any *han* could order the return of its men serving in the national government would reflect adversely upon the prestige and dignity of the central government.[66] Hence, as a means of impressing upon the *han* its subordinate position in relation to the central government, Ōkubo requested that an imperial messenger be dispatched to Kagoshima and that he, Ōkubo, be made a member of the envoy's party. This arrangement would enable him to go home as an official with primary responsibility to the imperial government and not to the *han*. Furthermore, the honor of receiving an imperial messenger would be flattering to the Shimazu, and Ōkubo hoped that this would help in persuading Hisamitsu and Saigō to participate actively in central government affairs. Ōkubo, in the company of the imperial messenger, Yanagibara, arrived in Kagoshima on March 25.[67]

In the Satsuma capital, Ōkubo, in discussions with the powerful samurai faction, tended to align himself with the Shimazu party by calling for unity and coöperation between the two factions. This display of favoritism to the Shimazu and his nationalistic orientation combined to make him suspect in the eyes of the samurai group.[68] In the matter of *han* reform, however, both Ōkubo and Saigō were in agreement as the measures advocated were advantageous to the samurai. Thus the reform of 1869 was completed.

As the result of the reform, separate offices were created to administer matters pertaining to the Shimazu family and those of the *han* government, the *naimukyoku* and the *chiseijo* respectively. As on the national level, Ōkubo instituted a policy of equitable selection of administrators on the basis of merit. The reconstituted *han* government was composed of Katsura Hisatake as *shissei* and included such men as Ijichi Masaharu, Hishiguchi Hikoji, and other members of the samurai party as *sansei*, a position corresponding to the former office of *karō*. The Satsuma government was in fact controlled by the Saigō faction.[69] The monopoly was completed when Saigō himself assumed the position of *sansei* and exercised the power of a prime minister.[70] The diminished influence of the Shimazu in *han* affairs was resented by Hisamitsu. This circumscription of family power was a factor in his decision to leave for Kyōto early in April, a display of anger toward the opposition party. Ōkubo himself left Kagoshima on April 22, arriving in Kyōto on April 26.[71]

National Government Reforms

The national government, operating under the *Seitaisho*, a document based upon the principles laid down in the Charter Oath, was weak and far from united.[72] In analyzing the problems, Ōkubo concluded that official irresponsibility was basically at fault for the grave state of affairs. In order to obtain strong and capable officials for the important administrative posts and thereby realize a more responsible government, Ōkubo, on June 22, 1869, had the *tōhyō kōsenhō*, or a law for the election of officials by ballot, passed, under which officials above the third grade were to be elected by the *kuge* and *daimyō*.[73] This method was adopted from American election practices.[74] He also contrived to reduce the number of *gijō*, or senior councilors, from an unwieldy eighteen or nineteen to three, and he believed that six *sanyo*, or junior councilors, and one *hoshō*, or executive officer, were sufficient. Ōkubo conceived of a governing nucleus of ten strong leaders instead of the much larger number that comprised the *Seitaisho* government. Ōmura Masujirō opposed the Ōkubo plan, contending that the elective system would become a forerunner of a *kyōwa seiji*, or a government operated on republican principles.[75] In actuality, however, the plan was to decrease the number of participants in the government and was an attempt to create a tightly knit committee—an oligarchy—in which would rest the supreme authority. Although he and the Chōshū leaders had consciously taken steps to consolidate their positions of power in the government, Ōkubo ultimately realized that further concentration of power in fewer hands was necessary if the government were to be unified and strengthened.[76] The results of the election to the *Sanshoku* (three offices of the government) announced on June 24 were as follows: [77]

Position	Name	Han	Votes
Hoshō	Sanjō Sanetomi (*kuge*)		
Gijō	Iwakura Tomomi (*kuge*)		48
	Tokudaiji Sanenori (*kuge*)		
	Nabeshima Naomasa	Hizen	29
Sanyo	Higashikuze Michitomi (*kuge*)		28
	Kido Kōin	Chōshū	42
	Gotō Shōjirō	Tosa	23
	Soejima Taneomi	Hizen	31
	Itagaki Taisuke	Tosa	21
	Ōkubo Toshimichi	Satsuma	49

Ōkubo received the highest number of votes and Iwakura and Kido followed with 48 and 42 votes respectively. Itagaki received the least number of votes with 21. This is a fair indication of the relative importance of each of these individuals as judged by his superiors. And although Ōkubo's votes may reflect the fact that he was the representative of the powerful Satsuma *han*, his popularity was primarily owing to his competence and indispensability to the government. Unquestionably he and Iwakura were two of the undisputed pillars of the Meiji government at this time.

The Meiji leaders had translated the principles of the Charter Oath into tangible form by promulgating the *Seitaisho* under which an assembly was to be a prominent feature. Consequently, on June 30 the new government called a meeting of a national council, the *Jōkyoku Kaigi*, composed of members of the upper chamber of the legislative department.[78] The first convocation of an assembly in accordance with the first of the five articles of the Charter Oath was the one called the *Kōgisho*, the body consisting mostly of the representatives of the feudal lords "for the purpose of getting at national opinion and taking the advice of the ruling class." The *Kōgisho* was convened on April 18, 1869, some time before the meeting of the *Jōkyoku Kaigi*.[79] The membership of the *Jōkyoku Kaigi* was far from being representative inasmuch as it included only the princes of the blood, *kuge*, *daimyō*, and officials above the fifth grade in the executive department and in the administrative departments for Shintō affairs, civil affairs, finance, war, foreign relations, and justice.[80] The assembly was merely a consultative body to which the government presented various problems of national policy for discussion.

These discussions in the assembly, which served as a sounding board, gave the government some idea of the existing sentiment of one segment of society and facilitated the adoption of various government measures. On July 25 the Emperor at last gave sanction to *hanseki hōkan*, and those lords who had not yet offered their fiefs to the throne were now called upon to do so.[81] On August 15, moreover, a new and more authoritarian government, popularly referred to as the Two *Kan* Six *Shō*, was inaugurated. The two *kan* were the *Jingikan*, or the Department of Shintō, and the *Dajōkan*, or the Executive Department. Plainly in a regression to the ancient concept of church-state, the leaders of Japan now placed the *Jingikan* at the very apex of the new government structure, above the *Dajōkan*. Furthermore, a colonization bureau was established to deal with the affairs of Yezo (renamed Hokkaidō in September) while changes were made in other government organs.[82] The *Kōgisho* was replaced by the *Shūgiin* and the *Taishōkyoku* became the *Taishōin*.[83] These were indeed steps reverting to the traditional authoritarianism after a period of constitutional experimentation under the *Seitaisho*.

Criticizing Popular Debate

The assembly idea, advocated by such men as Fukuoka and Soejima during the early years of the Meiji period, failed to take root because the leaders in control of the government, the Sat-Chō clique, did not encourage its growth. Ōkubo, in fact, regarded the assemblies as useless organs of government which their political opponents would use advantageously.[84] Making direct reference to the *Kōgisho*, Ōkubo, on July 12, 1869, wrote to Katsura Hisatake that "many unnecessary matters are raised in the course of a debate. It [*Kōgisho*] is not suited to our present national polity so the decision has been made to abolish it." [85] Thus on July 15, 1869, the first and only session of the *Kōgisho* was brought to an end.[86] Although Ōkubo himself had insisted during the last days of the Bakufu that it convene meetings of the *daimyō* and consider their opinions before making important decision, when he was placed in a similar position of leadership the attractiveness of public debate seemed to fade. He could not tolerate opposition to the government. Obviously, these early experiments in quasi democracy convinced Ōkubo that representative government would only hinder his policies. The failure of the experiments was used to justify his later diatribes against a government of the people.

After the creations of the Two *Kan* Six *Shō* on August 15, Ōkubo and Kido were made *Taishōin gakushi*, a position in the office through which memorials from the people were channeled to the government.[87] As this was little more than a position of prestige, the opposition interpreted the appointments to mean that the two men, disgusted with the disunity within the government, were retiring from active participation in national affairs.[88] This may have been true with Kido, but Ōkubo probably accepted the sinecure as an opportunity to step into the background temporarily for psychological effect; a seasoned leader knows that well-timed retreat often increases his desirability. Having lost his two stalwart political companions, Iwakura Tomomi wrote to Sanjō strongly requesting that Ōkubo and Kido be reëmployed in a more active capacity.[89] Consequently, on August 30, 1869, Ōkubo was made a *sangi*, or state councilor.[90] Kido, however, refused the post, pleading illness, and consented to Hirozawa Saneomi's acceptance of the post in his stead.[91] The *Dajōkan*, the branch of the government in which the real power rested, was composed of the following officials prior to this latest appointment: [92]

Position	Name	Han
Udaijin (Minister of the Right)	Sanjō Sanetomi	
Dainagon (Chief Councilors of State)	Iwakura Tomomi	
	Tokudaiji Sanenori	
Sangi (state councilors)	Soejima Taneomi	Hizen
	Maebara Issei	Chōshū

With the appointment of Hirozawa, the *Dajōkan* included two samurai from Chōshū, namely, Hirozawa and Maebara. Ōkubo objected to this arrangement, and the problem was resolved by inactivating Maebara who was, however, not deprived of his position.[93]

As a *sangi,* Ōkubo immediately submitted to the council three provisions designed to stabilize the government. Ōkubo argued that the disunity within the new government resulted from the lack of a fixed objective and therefore called for the formulation of a definite statement of purpose. To preserve unity, he urged that the members of the government refrain from bending before the winds of varied opinion blowing in from all sides. He also stressed the necessity of withholding government secrets from the public. Obviously, this authoritarian policy was intended to cope with the mounting opposition against the government from the dissatisfied courtiers, samurai, and peasants. For example, an increasing number of peasant revolts occurred after 1869. The feeling of peasant insecurity engendered by the gradual dissolution of feudalism and its concomitant master-servant relationship made them sensitive and prone to react against any apparent injustice. In November, 1869, peasants of the Takasagi *han* revolted over the question of unequal taxation. When the government endeavored to lay a railroad line between Ōsaka and Kōbe, the peasants, fearing the expropriation of land, reacted violently. In most instances, the underlying motives for these uprisings were economic.[94]

The covenant of four articles that Sanjō, Iwakura, Tokudaiji, Soejima, Hirozawa, and Ōkubo signed on September 15, 1869, pledged officials (1) to maintain secrecy; (2) to submit all important matters of state to the department heads as well as to the various organs of the government such as the *Taishōin, Shūgiin,* and so on, before presentation to the Emperor; (3) to give wholehearted support to any policy once determined by the *Sanshoku,* composed of the three offices of *udaijin, dainagon,* and *sangi;* and (4) to visit the homes of the different members of the *Sanshoku* several times each month to cultivate closer friendship.[95] This was a conscious effort on the part of Ōkubo to form an efficient, unified brain trust, a powerful oligarchy, to shape the country's policies. The commanding figure within the group was, of course, Ōkubo Toshimichi himself.

Receiving a Foreign Prince

In the month of September, 1869, for the first time in the history of Japan, a foreign prince became the guest of the Emperor. The Duke of Edinburgh was most cordially received, being entertained by jugglers and acrobats, fencers and wrestlers, and shown the ancient dramatic performance of Nō during his sojourn of a week in Tōkyō.[96] As members of the government, Ōkubo, Sanjō, and Iwakura were hosts at a dinner for the Duke and they in turn were invited to the English legation in Yokohama on September 10, where they were feted and later witnessed, wide-eyed, members of the opposite sexes dancing together.[97] Had Ōkubo not exerted his influence as he did, the English prince might not have left Japan singing the praises of Japanese hospitality because prior to his arrival the *jōi* party was not at all in a mood to befriend the royal guest. As early as August 12 Ōkubo had met with the representatives of the *jōi* faction to explain the circumstances of the visit, and on the following day matters of protocol were discussed with two of their number.[98] It was ultimately decided that the government would show the prince utmost courtesy. Of interest in this connection is Sir Harry Parkes' letter to his wife in which he stated his belief that the Duke of Edinburgh would be treated better in the Japanese capital than at Peking where he was to go incognito. "I am not certain how my Japanese friends may behave, but they have commenced their preparations, and if at the last moment I see anything derogatory in their arrangements, I can decline the reception. So I have secured my vantage-ground. . . . In politics we are quiet and peaceful, but I had a good deal of work in making this government run in the right groove." From the tone of this letter it is apparent that Parkes had done his utmost to influence the Japanese to display their best behavior in receiving the English prince.[99]

Failing to Win Han *Support*

After the departure of the Duke of Edinburgh in mid-September, the fundamental question confronting the government was how to implement its program of modernization; it did not have the capability of enforcing its will upon the half-million samurai, the majority of whom were antagonistic toward the central authorities. Disaffection had been heightened by rumors of the creation of a citizens' conscript army which would obviously place in jeopardy the samurai's means of livelihood. Ōmura Masujirō, the chief advocate of military reform, was attacked in Kyōto on October 8 and later died of wounds inflicted by vengeful samurai.[100] Thus the enemies of the government were not so much the *han*, per se, but rather the samurai party whose interests were definitely crossing *han* lines. Ōkubo recognized the threat to the infant government and determined to use force against force. The force he had in mind was the combined might of the Satsuma and Chōshū *han*. He decided to return to Kagoshima once more to persuade Saigō and Hisamitsu to join the central government, and he also induced Kido to go to Yamaguchi to win the support of the Chōshū lord. Although Iwakura sanctioned Ōkubo's plan on January 4, 1870, Sanjō urged him to postpone the trip until February.[101] Ōkubo, however, felt it was necessary to go immediately. Winning his point he received an imperial order on January 6 to go to Kagoshima.[102] Kido, likewise commissioned to go to Yamaguchi, left Tōkyō on January 18, Ōkubo departing a day later.[103]

On the day of departure Ōkubo published some of his views in a statement entitled *Bōgi*. In it he expressed concern about the flaccid attitude the *han* held toward the government, contributing to its instability. He argued that it had become imperative for Satsuma and Chōshū to render military support to the central government without which the object of the Restoration, that of establishing undisputed imperial authority, could not be realized. There was no other alternative, he stated.[104] Fully aware of the important role played by these two western *han* in reëstablishing imperial rule, Ōkubo candidly stated that the early advocates of *kinnō* were Satsuma and Chōshū, the chief participants in the work of the Restoration were Satsuma, Chōshū, Tosa, and Hizen, and the first *han* to offer to return their fiefs to the throne were the same four. He pointed out that in all instances the other *han* followed the example of Sat-Chō-To-Hi. Continuing his argument, he stated that "if at present Satsuma and Chōshū, while aware of the condition of the country, were to retreat and remain indifferent to its plight, the other *han* would also follow suit and remain apathetic. If, on the other hand, Satsuma and Chōshū would step forward and accept their responsibility, the other *han* would fall in step, and there would be a manifestation of strength and unity." [105] Continuing, Ōkubo made a surprisingly un-Japanese but nevertheless realistic appraisal of the situation when he stated, "At present the *han* which have greater power than the court are Satsuma and Chōshū." [106] These were Ōkubo's reasons offered in justification of his scheme to make Satsuma and Chōshū the bulwark of the government against samurai opposition.

Ōkubo arrived in Kagoshima on February 19, 1870, after having consulted with Kido in Yamaguchi while en route.[107] The next day he reported to Shimazu Hisamitsu and the imperial governor of the Satsuma *han*, Shimazu Tadayoshi.[108] Using his power of persuasion and even employing the service of Katsura Hisatake, the chief minister, Ōkubo attempted to coax the Shimazu, father and son, to go to the capital. Tadayoshi was especially reluctant to commit himself.[109] Obviously Ōkubo no longer had his former influence over the leaders of Satsuma; he could sway neither them nor his fellow samurai.

Further evidence of his decline in stature in the eyes of Satsuma became apparent during the ensuing days of his sojourn there. On March 5, 1870, word reached Kagoshima that Chōshū samurai dissidents, fanatically opposed to the institution of military reform in that *han*, were in rebellion. Ōkubo was informed of the unsettled situation at the time he visited Kido in Yamaguchi and had promised to have troops sent in to quell any insurrection that might occur. The reason for this determined stand against insurrection becomes clear when it is realized that for both central government leaders any opposition against the new policy of modernization, even within the *han*, would be construed as being antigovernment. Ōkubo immediately requested the Satsuma authorities to dispatch necessary forces to Chōshū, and in the meantime made plans to go there in person.[110] However, he was not to be accommodated so readily. The *han*, to his astonishment, decided instead to send Saigō first to evaluate the situation and ascertain if Satsuma's aid were necessary or not.[111] To Ōkubo and Kido the situation was urgent, requiring immediate action, but to Saigō it was not of such great concern; he favored a slower course of action, much to the dismay of his two central government friends. Saigō's sympathies lay with the rebels in Chōshū who were, in effect, resisting the abolition of feudal military institutions. Therefore when Saigō returned from his mission to Chōshū he reported that since the rebellion had ended there was no need to send Satsuma troops. This, however, was not the case. Saigō, having no intention of coöperating with Ōkubo, had lied.

The friendship between these two former Satsuma men had cooled considerably. Ōkubo, the official, interested himself in modernizing Japan and Saigō, the warrior through and through, sulked in the background, getting angrier by the day as government policy threatened the feudal way of life. Ōkubo had sensed the estrangement between himself and Saigō and had not attempted to see him until about two weeks after his arrival in Kagoshima. This apparent snub coupled with the fact that Saigō no longer considered Ōkubo loyal to Satsuma further dampened relations. Ōkubo was fully aware of Saigō's role in causing the Satsuma council to overrule his suggestions. To Ōkubo this action not only indicated Saigō's unfriendliness, but also his heavy influence and the decline of Ōkubo's own authority within the Satsuma government. A further indication of Ōkubo's declining prestige within the *han* came on March 25 when Shimazu Hisamitsu, giving ill health as a reason, rejected his plea to go up to Tōkyō. Hisamitsu did not wish to join a government whose policy was eventually "to abolish feudalism and establish a *gun-ken* [county-prefecture] system." [112] Nor was Saigō allowed to leave for Tōkyō; his services ostensibly were needed at home.[113] Thoroughly rebuffed and not a little frustrated by his inability to influence those whom he once regarded as political allies, Ōkubo left for Tōkyō on March 27.[114]

The coolness and indifference with which he was received at home made a lasting impression upon Ōkubo, the samurai leader who had hitherto been able to accomplish almost any mission upon which he set out. From this time, Ōkubo became increasingly court-oriented and prone to show favor to no one *han*. His allegiance to his own *han* was superseded by a greater loyalty to the nation.[115] Ironically, this change in his attitude was hastened by the very people who were intent upon preserving the feudal concept of prime loyalty to the *han*. Ōkubo turned his entire energy to the building of a strong nation to which he would transfer his entire devotion.

The Japanese government in 1870 continued its policy of nationalization and economic development. It issued new regulations governing the *Danjōdai*, or board of censors, a pre-Meiji institution copied closely from an analogous institution in China and set up to exercise moral supervision over the acts of civil officials, both central and local.[116] As a means of tying the country together, the building of a communication system was begun. On January 7 the first message was transmitted over the telegraph line put up under the supervision of an English engineer, George Miles Gilbert.[117] A one-million-pound loan from England was approved by the council to be used to build a railway system.[118] Furthermore, motivated by the idea of universal education, a cardinal principle of the new government, elementary and middle schools were established in the metropolitan district of Tōkyō. Ōkubo's interest in education, which he deemed indispensable to the development of a modern nation, is attested by his unconditional support of the school-building investigatory program.[119] A man of his political insight could not but realize that education might serve a nationalistic purpose as well as be an agency for the training of government personnel, a subject of special interest to him. But the military program was not neglected. On May 17, 1870, the Emperor reviewed troops of the various *han* at Komabano.[120] Moreover, Yamagata Aritomo instituted military reforms that called for the organization of a standing army modeled after the French system and a navy patterned after that of England.[121]

Formulating Broad Policy

Despite this apparent progress in the direction of modernization, no one was more aware of the government's persistent weakness than Ōkubo. His resolve to achieve a secure foundation for the government is reflected in his writings, and specifically in one of the letters to Iwakura. Stating that the prosperity of the empire depended upon thorough reform, for which he was willing to sacrifice his life, Ōkubo listed for Iwakura some broad objectives.[122] Consideration, he wrote, should be given to the strengthening of the structure of the court; to the matter of leadership; to economy in the court through radical reform; to economy in the *Sanshoku* and to the encouragement of greater diligence among its members; to economy in the *benji* and the administrative departments; to the dismissal of supernumerary officials; to the employment in full-time service of a part of the *sangi*; to assuring the government's retention of absolute authority within the *Mimbushō,* or Civil Affairs Ministry, and the *Ōkurashō,* or Finance Ministry; and to the appointment of two or three *sangi* to serve in the court.[123] Ōkubo then noted that the government should give its utmost attention to the areas of finance, civil administration, foreign relations, a foreign study program, education, relief for the destitute, and the selection of civil servants.[124]

Note especially Ōkubo's concern regarding government control over the ministries of finance and civil affairs: *Minzō no ken danzen seifu ni onnigiri no koto* (The government must positively control the *Mimbushō* and the *Ōkurashō*). By controlling the *Ōkurashō* and the important *Mimbushō,* which was responsible for the census, taxes, postal service, mining, poor relief, and the care of the aged, the government would occupy an advantageous position from which to direct its modernization policy.[125] It would, for instance, have the authority to determine the fiscal policy, control important natural resources, and act as a public-welfare agency whose program could be oriented in such a way as to win the sympathies of the numerous dissatisfied and destitute elements within the country. To assure the implementation of the Ōkubo policy, moreover, the ministries of finance and civil affairs were packed with men belonging to the *yōkōha,* or the faction composed of men who had been abroad, those who were imbued with the progressive spirit of the West. The list of officials in these two important ministries included such notable as Inoue Kaoru, Itō Hirobumi, Ōkuma Shigenobu, Ōki Takato, and others of like ideological persuasion. Ōkubo formulated his objectives and selected the men willing to support them. He still required the military backing of Satsuma and Chōshū, without which the implementation of his program would be difficult.

Gaining Han *Support*

Ōkubo first endeavored to win over Chōshū by acting through Kido. The two men met in the congenial atmosphere of the Baisatei, a restaurant in Tōkyō, where Ōkubo repeatedly urged Kido to give his assent to his program. There is no evidence to indicate that they discussed the matter of abolishing the *han* and establishing prefectures at this time, but it nevertheless was definitely in Ōkubo's mind; he considered it an inevitable reform if complete imperial rule were to be established.[126] Ōkubo, after much persuasion, finally won Kido's coöperation, and the two men agreed to the appointment of Iwakura as an imperial messenger to go to Chōshū and Satsuma. The emissary's party was to include Ōkubo and Kido. Although Iwakura was ill in Kyōto at the time, he nevertheless unhesitatingly acceded to their request. Writing to Ōkubo on January 3, 1871, Iwakura opined that "if Shimazu and Mōri and Saigō were wholeheartedly to coöperate in supporting the court, anything could be accomplished. . . . Although I am ill, I shall immediately leave for Satsuma and Chōshū and pledge to do my utmost to make the mission a success, even at the risk of my life. If, however, I should fail, I am determined never to return home." [127] Ōkubo had Yamagata Aritomo, an official in the *Hyōbushō*, or the War Ministry, and a close friend of Saigō Tsugumichi, Takamori's brother, accompany the party solely for the purpose of prevailing upon Saigō to consent to come to Tōkyō.[128] Ōkubo and Kido left Yokohama aboard ship on January 19, and in Kyōto a few days later met with Iwakura.[129] The party of the imperial emissary left Ōsaka on February 4 and arrived in Kagoshima on the seventh.[130] The envoys met with Saigō four days later and received his promise to support the central government and its policies. Shimazu Hisamitsu also gave a favorable reply and stated his intent to depart for Tōkyō within a few months.[131] What Ōkubo hitherto had failed to do, the imperial mission had performed. Iwakura attributed the success of the mission to Saigō Tsugumichi, Kawamura Sumiyoshi, and, of course, Ōkubo, all of whom had contributed yeoman service on behalf of the central government.[132]

The Iwakura party, with the addition of Saigō Takamori and Ōkubo's two sons, left Kagoshima for Yamaguchi, where they met Kido on February 25, 1871. There the triumvirate of the Meiji Restoration came to an amicable understanding and the Sat-Chō union was once more established.[133] On February 28 this union was made official.[134]

During the course of their discussions at Yamaguchi, the leaders decided it advisable to include Tosa in the coalition and to proceed to Kōchi to extend their invitation to that *han*.[135] On March 3, Ōkubo, Saigō, and Kido left for Tosa while Iwakura and the rest of the party proceeded to Tōkyō. In Kōchi the Ōkubo party conferred with Itagaki Taisuke, the *shissei*, and successfully persuaded him to bring Tosa to the support of the central government. Itagaki, moreover, agreed to accompany the party to Tōkyō.[136] Having in this manner won the support of three powerful *han* for the national government, Ōkubo, very much relieved, returned to Tōkyō on March 22.[137]

In Tōkyō the members of the coalition met with Sanjō and Iwakura on March 28, on which occasion the pressing matter of acquiring adequate military forces for the court was discussed.[138] Without armed forces the imperial government could not hope to carry out its contemplated reforms. The leaders therefore petitioned the two *kuge* to arrange for the commissioning of the troops of Satsuma, Chōshū, and Tosa as imperial guards to be used for the protection of the court. An imperial decree ordering the three *han* to contribute men for the imperial guard was issued on April 2, and two days later Saigō departed for Kagoshima to lead the Satsuma contingent up to the capital.[139] On June 8, Saigō accompanied Shimazu Tadayoshi at the head of four *daitai,* or battalions, of regular infantrymen, four *shōtai,* or sections, of artillerymen, back to Tōkyō.[140]

At this juncture the question may arise as to why Saigō, whose relations with Ōkubo were strained, should have consented to support the government controlled by Ōkubo and his associates. Different explanations have been put forth, one of which, emphasizing Saigō's loyalty to the imperial government, is that he foresaw an inevitable conflict between the central government and those who opposed its reform program, especially the contemplated abolition of the *han* and the establishment of prefectures, and he therefore placed himself in a position to protect the court and pacify rebellious elements.[141] Another stresses the Ōkubo-Saigō accord in policy matters.[142] A more radical explanation is that Saigō came to Tōkyō with the specific purpose of overthrowing the new government, which was apparently centered around Ōkubo.[143] Lastly, Saigō conceivably could have been duped by his former friend into joining the government.

The first interpretation is difficult to accept. If Saigō had been so loyal to the imperial government, why had he refused to join it when he was approached earlier? Also, is it likely that Saigō was in full accord with Ōkubo's policy, especially since its implementation would have meant the obliteration of the *han* and the feudal order in which Saigō had an interest? There is some evidence to indicate that Ōkubo had learned of a possible *coup de main* by Satsuma forces against the central government. Ōkubo noted in his diary on November 3, 1870, that "a certain person of the Satsuma *han,*" implying Saigō, said in effect that, the present condition in court being intolerable, "a reformation must be carried out with the use of force."[144] This possibility may have appeared farfetched to most contemporaries of Ōkubo, but within six years' time Saigō did rebel against the imperial government. As for the last explanation, it is unlikely that a man of Saigō's discernment would have failed to note that Ōkubo's intention was to utilize Saigō to facilitate the implementation of the government's policies. Had Ōkubo failed to bring Saigō into the government, its program would have been jeopardized; only with the support of the leaders of the powerful *han* of Satsuma, Chōshū, and Tosa could it have been implemented. Therefore the most likely explanation for

Saigō's decision to coöperate with the government is that he intended to work from within to modify if not transform government policies so that they would be more in keeping with the desires of the feudal faction.

Kido left for Yamaguchi on April 13[145] and upon arrival encountered difficulty in consolidating *han* opinion in favor of the government's policy. The death on May 17 of Mōri Takachika marked a resurgence of the antigovernment party. Its antagonism toward Kido and his government party culminated in rebellion. The fact that Satsuma procrastinated in sending troops to aid Chōshū forces in quelling the rebellion offered Kido grounds for suspecting the motives of everyone connected with Satsuma, including Ōkubo. As a result, Kido made no effort to return to Tōkyō with Chōshū troops, stating that the situation in his *han* would not permit him or its troops to leave home.[146] To allay his misgivings, Ōkubo and Saigō Tsugumichi made a special trip to Yamaguchi late in June and finally coaxed Kido back to Tōkyō.[147] Highly sensitive and prone to sulk when circumstances did not favor him, Kido, at least on this occasion, lacked the resolute character necessary in a leader.

Agreeing to Kido-Saigō Leadership

Ōkubo fully recognized Kido's value to the government despite his shortcomings and therefore went to great lengths to satisfy his vanity. Ōkubo was, in fact, willing to subordinate himself to the Chōshū leader if this would assure his services for the government. Believing that a single leader would promote efficiency, Ōkubo recommended that Kido be made the central figure within the council. Iwakura, Itagaki, and Saigō Takamori were in agreement with the proposal, but when Kido was approached and offered the position, he declined. He did, however, consent to share the leadership responsibilities with another individual. Accordingly, Saigō and Kido were made *sangi* under whose guidance Ōkubo hoped the reform to abolish feudalism could be smoothly effected.[148] In the drastic council reshuffle of August 11, 1871, Ōkubo Toshimichi, Sasaki Takayuki, Saitō Toshiyuki, Ōkuma Shigenobu, and Kido Kōin resigned as *sangi*. Saigō was now newly appointed and Kido was reappointed to the position of *sangi*. Ōkubo stepped down to the position of *Ōkura Kyō*, or Minister of Finance, and had Ōkuma join him as his assistant.[149] Kido and Saigō, in order to pack the government with men more amenable to their views, attempted to have Itagaki appointed as *Hyōbu Tayū*, or Vice-Minister of War, and to have Ōki Takato, the *Mimbu Tayū*, or Vice-Minister of Civil Affairs, replaced by Yuri Kimmasa. The plan was to give Ōki a corresponding position in the *Mombushō*, or Ministry of Education. Ōkubo, however, rejected this plan and instead had Yamagata Aritomo fill the position of War Minister and opposed the appointment of Yuri Kimmasa for any office.[150] Although the reshuffle seemed to have resulted in the relegation of Ōkubo to a subordinate position, his opinion continued to be an important factor in the Council of State.

Ōkubo's apparent sacrifice of his own authority and prestige in favor of Kido cannot be explained merely on the basis of his desire to retain the Chōshū leader in the government. The action can be viewed as a concession to Kido, who had advocated the immediate abolition of the *han* even against Ōkubo's advice that the promulgation of a *hanseki hōkan* decree be made only after the consolidation and strengthening of the government's position. Kido had been reluctant to join the government because his views did not concur with Ōkubo's, and it is probable that both Iwakura and Sanjō exerted pressure to have Kido and Saigō brought into high positions in the Council of State.[151] Hence whether Ōkubo's action of "self-relegation" was one of voluntary self-denial for the sake of national welfare, as some historians have contended, is open to question.[152] Watanabe states that Ōkubo merely appeared to have relegated himself to a subordinate status, whereas in reality he had not at any moment released the reins of government but continued to wield considerable power through his control of the nation's purse strings. The *Ōkurashō*, which he headed, not only collected taxes and disbursed money, but also supervised local administration, a unique situation resulting from the temporary incorporation of the *Mimbushō* into the *Ōkurashō*.[153] Ōkubo could well permit Kido and Saigō to retain nominal authority. These two men were the helmsmen now, but Ōkubo was really the captain giving directions from the bridge. Precisely for this reason he continued to foster misgivings in the minds of the Chōshū leaders.[154]

Abolishing Feudalism

A council meeting was called on August 24, 1871, to discuss the matter of *haihan chiken*, or the abolition of the *han* and the establishment of prefectures. Only a handful of the top lower-class samurai leaders were present at the deliberations which were held at Kido's residence at Kudansaka in Tōkyō. Besides Kido and Ōkubo there were Saigō Takamori and his brother, Tsugumichi, Ōyama Iwao, Yamagata Aritomo, and Inoue Kaoru. That this meeting was monopolized by Satsuma and Chōshū leaders is as significant as was the absence of such prominent members of the *kuge* as Iwakura and Sanjō. Political power and influence in the national government had gravitated completely into the hands of the former samurai *han* officials. These men, after having fixed August 29 as the date on which *haihan chiken* would be announced, delegated Kido and Saigō to call upon Sanjō, and Kido and Ōkubo were commissioned to visit Iwakura to arrange for the execution of the plan. Sanjō and Iwakura were shocked when informed of this scheme, in whose formulation they had played no part. Iwakura hesitated to give his sanction, contending that the promulgation of a *haihan chiken* decree was premature, but he soon changed his mind and consulted with Sanjō regarding the matter. On the date set for the announcement the Emperor called together all imperial governors of the various *han* who were in Tōkyō and read a statement abolishing the feudal *han* and establishing modern prefectures.[155] That there was no unanimity of opinion for the immediate promulgation of *haihan chiken* is pointed out in Kido's diary. He states that some favored postponing it until after all the nearly three-hundred *han* governors could be assembled in Tōkyō, but the advocates of immediate proclamation won out.[156] In this manner the administration of the country was to be brought under central government control. Furthermore, all regular *han* troops with the exception of token forces were henceforth to be disbanded. A feudalistic system was to be supplanted by a nationalized state, a daring project launched and completed by men composing the core of formerly feudal Japan, the samurai themselves.

When this latest development was announced to the foreign representatives, the English minister, Sir Harry Parkes, noted that the abolition of the *han* and the establishment of prefectures was a resolute step which would accrue to Japan's benefit. He conceded that in Europe such a drastic revolution could not have been accomplished without several years of warfare. The establishment of the foundation for a unified country through government assumption of the authority hitherto exercised by the 270-odd *daimyō*, and then simply by the issuance of an edict, was, to Sir Harry, unprecedented, and he attributed this phenomenon to providence; it was to the Britisher an achievement almost beyond the power of man.[157] Parkes was impressed with the lack of overt resistance to the scheme because he did not appreciate to what extent the Japanese were conditioned to yield submissively to imperial authority, regardless of whether that authority was real or nominal. Ōkubo and his associates, on the other hand, were deeply conscious of this fact and therefore made it a practice to work through the Emperor to implement their own policy.[158]

There were reasons other than respect for imperial authority for this peaceful abandonment of the military administrative system of two-century standing. The necessity for complete unification of the state had been understood to some degree by the more influential *han* which took the initiative in reorganizing the *han* system for this purpose.[159] This was certainly the case of Ōkubo and Satsuma. Their example predisposed many other *han* to look in the direction of political unification. There was, moreover, an important economic factor that favored unification. Most *han* were so financially distressed that their situation could be relieved only by means of *haihan chiken*.[160] Under the new political structure the feudal lords were guaranteed their household and compensations, and they therefore anticipated an improved financial status after the abandonment of the *han* system.

It is true that no one leader of the new regime could claim *haihan chiken* as a personal victory.[161] Many persons were interested and involved in the plan. For example, even prior to the assumption of the leadership of the council by Kido and Saigō on August 11, Torio Koyata and Nomura Yasushi, recognizing the inevitability of establishing a *gun-ken* system of local administration, strongly advocated *haihan chiken*. They first won the support of Yamagata Aritomo and then approached Inoue Kaoru with whom they discussed means of accomplishing their purpose. Inoue suggested that Yamagata be asked to convince Saigō of the urgency of the proposal. Ultimately Yamagata succeeded in doing this. Saigō in turn influenced Ōkubo to favor the *haihan chiken* ideal and Inoue won Kido's approval without too much difficulty. It was only after preliminary agreement had been reached that the historic meeting took place at Kido's home.[162]

It is also true that Ōkubo was the person most responsible for the accomplishment of *haihan chiken*. It was he who, willingly or unwillingly, relegated himself to a subordinate position so that the Kido-Saigō government might be established to facilitate the reform program. It was he who arranged with the leaders of Satsuma, Chōshū, and Tosa to bring their troops to Tōkyō, without which drastic changes would have been difficult if not impossible to effect. And he was the master schemer who laid the groundwork for the reform, the resolute tactician who, once having agreed to the execution of the reform, worked with diligence and skill to complete it. And although Kido's role cannot be minimized, his ill health, emotional difficulties, and effeminacy precluded him from exerting the influence of Ōkubo; Kido was a dreamer, Ōkubo the implementor of dreams. In the final analysis, Ōkubo, working with a well-entrenched oligarchy, played an important role in destroying feudal home rule and unifying Japan.[163] National unity was the sine qua non for the creation of the later constitutional government.[164]

Further reshuffling within the council of the government took place after August 29, and consolidated the position of Ōkubo and his colleagues. On that date Iwakura was made *Gaimu Kyō*, or Minister of Foreign Affairs, Ōki Takato was appointed as the new *Mimbu Kyō*, or Minister of Civil Affairs, Inoue Kaoru was promoted from *Mimbu Shoyū* to *Mimbu Tayū*, or Vice-Minister of Civil Affairs, and Ōkuma Shigenobu retained his position as *Ōkura Tayū*. At the same time Itagaki Taisuke of Tosa was made a *sangi*. Some time later Saigō, still attempting to exert his authority, moved to replace Ōkuma, one of Ōkubo's trusted men in the Finance Ministry, with Yuri Kimmasa. The upshot of this move was significant; on September 11, 1871, Ōkubo had the *Mimbushō* abolished and its duties entrusted to the *Ōkurashō*.[165] Consequently, Ōki, the Vice-Minister of Civil Affairs, was appointed Vice-Minister of Finance under Ōkubo. Other Ōkubo progressives were also added to his staff in the *Ōkurashō*. These appointments included Itō Hirobumi, Tsuda Tsuru, Matsukata Masayoshi, Yasuba Yasukatsu, Shibuzawa Eiichi, and Yoshida Kiyonari. Japanese national life was controlled to a great extent by Ōkubo's Finance Ministry. In effect, this one department concerned itself with work which would ordinarily be allotted to the home, finance, agriculture, commerce, and communications ministries.[166]

Other reforms were also carried out by the new government during the course of 1871. On September 24 the *Dajōkan*, or Council of State system, was modified for more effective administration. It became the *Seiin*, or Central Board, composed of Sanjō as the *Dajōdaijin*, or First Minister; the *Sadaijin*, or Minister of the Left, left vacant at this time;

Iwakura as *Udaijin,* or Minister of the Right; Saigō, Kido, Itagaki, and Ōkuma as *sangi;* all of whom formed the council of the Emperor. This council and the chiefs of the various departments met as the *Uin,* or the Board of the Right. The *Sain,* or Board of the Left, was composed of members nominated by the Emperor and served as a privy council. Soejima replaced Iwakura in the *Gaimushō,* or the Foreign Ministry.[167]

Social reforms were not overlooked. The samurai were permitted to discontinue wearing their swords.[168] The Emperor emerged from retirement.[169] On October 1 a proclamation declared that on the following day he would go to his palace on the seashore and that the people should conduct themselves as on ordinary days; His Majesty even, unprecedentedly, left the palace in an open carriage.[170] Members of the nobility were allowed to marry commoners.[171] Women were now permitted to accompany their families abroad. Finally, the designation of *eta,* or outcast, was abolished.[172] These measures reflected the ideas of the leaders who had breathed the air of Western culture and found it good. Ōkubo was in complete sympathy with the modernizers.

However, the road to modernization was not smooth; there were many who were dissatisfied with the *haihan chiken* reform and they loudly expressed their discontent. In Kagoshima the situation was tense and serious enough for the Satsuma authorities to request that central government leaders be sent there to placate the dissidents. Even Shimazu Tadayoshi had been so bitterly opposed to the abolition of the *han* that he was at one time ready to agitate.[173] In view of the situation Ōkubo, after consulting with Saigō, sent Yoshii Tomozane, of the *Kunaishō,* or Imperial Household Ministry, and Saigō Tsugumichi of the *Hyōbushō,* or War Ministry, to Kagoshima to explain the government's resolve to carry out its program and to do what they could to lessen the tension.[174] Such opposition to the national government was not peculiar to Satsuma.

Summary

Ōkubo was the rock upon which was based the future of the young nation. Forgetting the past and ignoring the stings of criticism, he adhered closely to the blueprint he and his colleagues had drawn up. In foreign relations his course was for coöperation and amity with the more advanced Western nations. With bold disregard for tradition he embraced the civilization of the Occident, sending students abroad for study and testing foreign institutions for possible adoption by his own fatherland. But in the course of his administrative duties he tended more and more to divorce himself from his *han* and to shift his allegiance to the national government, a tendency that prompted his critics to refer to him as *chōtei-teki,* or court-oriented. At the same time the intense pressures of his duties, and especially the task of preserving cohesion within the land, exposed his authoritarian nature. Through political expedience he gathered around himself a highly competent group of administrators who pledged utmost secrecy concerning matters deemed inadvisable for public consumption and unanimity in support of established government policy. He experimented with democratic institutions, but if he found them unsuited to his concept of a paternalistic government he abolished them as he did the *Kōgisho* and the system of electing higher officials. His obsession was to maintain and consolidate his power. Therefore, even during the interim of the Saigō-Kido leadership, he retained actual control of the government from his post as *Ōkura Kyō.* His greatest contribution to Japan was his work of helping to preserve a semblance of unity in the early years of the Meiji government until it was capable of enforcing its laws and ordinances and fending off ambitious foreign colonial powers. Without the Ōkubo-dominated oligarchy as the stabilizing force there would have been little likelihood of accord; without him and his select colleagues the Meiji government might well have floundered and destroyed itself in infancy. In this respect Ōkubo Toshimichi must be considered one of the most important architects and unifiers of modern Japan, one of Japan's nation-builders—the Bismarck of Japan.

VI
Statesman and Soldier

With the abolition of the feudal *han,* domestic equilibrium was attained, at least temporarily. The leaders turned their attention to foreign relations. Hoping to renegotiate the unequal treaties of 1858, the Iwakura mission (1871-1873) toured the United States and Europe but was unsuccessful in achieving its objective. For Ōkubo and other Meiji leaders who comprised the party, however, the trip was illuminating; it revealed Japan's backwardness and served as an added incentive to Westernization. Significantly for the subsequent course of Japanese history, Ōkubo's visit to Prussia and meeting with Bismarck left a lasting impression upon him. Although Ōkubo arranged for leaders of his faction to carry out the progressive policy during his absence, the government fell under the control of Saigō and the members of the war party who vehemently advocated a military campaign against Korea. Ōkubo and Kido were called home from Europe, and Ōkubo's uncompromising stand against the opposition forced the resignation of the Saigō faction, thus enabling Ōkubo further to consolidate the power of the oligarchy. Thereafter, upon the reformation of the government, he was to assume almost dictatorial power. Ōkubo, although only a civilian functionary, exercised military powers and was personally responsible for the suppression of the Saga rebellion, a pro-war party insurrection led by Etō Shimpei.

Considering Trip Abroad

The Iwakura mission that left Japan in the winter of 1871 for the United States and Europe was primarily interested in sounding out the various treaty powers concerning the feasibility of revising the treaties that were, by their own terms, subject to revision on July 1, 1872. The Japanese were especially anxious to have the more obnoxious treaty provisions, such as the extraterritoriality clause, abrogated. The mission itself had an interesting origin. Despite the approach of the date of the treaty revision, no one in the government seemed aware of the fact that, if Japan desired to have revisions made, the treaty powers would have to be given a year's notice—until a well-informed student from Satsuma, Yoshida Kiyonari, brought this stipulation to Ōkubo's attention. Thereupon Ōkubo conveyed the matter to the council, which established the office of *Jōyaku Kaisei Goyōkakari* to deal with treaty revision and placed Ōkuma Shigenobu in charge. Yoshida Kiyonari, the student, was given a position in the new office which recommended sending the Iwakura mission abroad to lay the groundwork for the revision of the treaties.[1] The Terajima memorandum of 1871 enumerated the objectives Japan wished to attain through the proposed treaty revision. They were (1) reciprocity of treaties; (2) revision of the tariff; (3) standardization of all treaty texts; (4) substitution of tonnage dues for clearance and entrance fees; and (5) reservation of the coastal trade to Japan.[2]

A secondary objective of the Iwakura mission was to give its members an opportunity to observe and absorb the culture of the West. Emperor Meiji had stated prior to the mission's departure that Japan would have to send an expedition of observers abroad to bring back ideas and institutions that would benefit the nation. He further indicated that the Japanese lacked good institutions for high female culture, and stressed the importance of the education of women. He therefore granted wives and sisters the right to accompany their relatives on foreign tours so that they might acquaint themselves with better forms of female education that Japan could subsequently adopt.[3]

Ōkubo, of course, was in favor of the mission. As early as October 4, 1871, he had discussed with Yoshii and Saigō the possibility of his being included in the embassy.[4] There were, however, differences of opinion within the council. Itagaki and Ōkuma opposed the mission because it would deprive the country of some of its most important leaders at a time when the establishment of prefectures was still unfinished. Inoue had no objection to Kido's joining the mission but did not believe it wise for Ōkubo, the strongest pillar of the government, to leave at such a critical time. But he finally relented, on October 25.[5] However, about a month later Inoue once more voiced his objection because he thought that Ōkubo intended to leave without reaching an understanding with all concerned regarding the management of the important *Ōkurashō*, or Ministry of Finance, which dealt with the problem of local administration. Inoue felt that, as the Vice-Minister of Finance without a seat in the *Seiin*, he could not effectively carry out the established policy during the absence of his chief.[6] He was ready to hand in his resignation, but Ōkubo, Kido, and Saigō persuaded him to remain.[7]

Ōkubo was determined to go abroad despite the opposition from some of the members of the government, and for reasons beyond the stated objectives of the mission. He realized that an understanding of the cultures of the advanced nations of the world was imperative for the Japanese leaders and therefore did not intend to miss an opportunity to travel abroad. He also wished to take his two sons, Hikonoshin and Nobukuma, and to enroll them in Western schools. In this connection, a letter from Tōkyō to his wife in Kagoshima dated October 8, 1871, sheds light upon Ōkubo's feeling toward his children's education and his attitude toward Western learning. He says in part:

> A foreign tutor has been engaged for Hikonobu [Hikonoshin], who has advanced considerably in his pursuit of knowledge, and Nobukuma is also devoting himself to his books, for which I feel exceedingly fortunate. Please convey this fact to Omiwa-dono [Ōkubo's sister]. The world today differs from that of the past as night does from day. . . . It is necessary as a child to apply oneself to writing, learning, and to the acquisition of the various arts. I have therefore purposely retained the services of a foreigner to educate them. They are both doing well, and their foreign teacher has praise for them.[8]

Ōkubo also hoped by going abroad to prevent a schism within the government. Since assuming the post of Finance Minister, Ōkubo had progressively expanded both the scope and authority of the ministry, which led critics to censure the *Ōkurashō*'s monopoly of power. Itagaki, the chairman of the *Sain*, was vociferously critical of Ōkubo. Obviously, the situation was created by the juxtaposition in the government of the war party and the industrial expansionists who were controlling the *Ōkurashō*. As a safeguard against the possible destruction of his policy through internal division within the Council of State, Ōkubo considered it expedient to step out as an active participant by going abroad and allowing Saigō and his faction to assume nominal leadership in the government's program. With the strong man gone there was hope for the reëstablishment of peace among the oligarchs. In a letter of October 25, 1871, to Iwakura, Ōkubo wrote that, as he observed the present situation, he could discern a mounting opinion among the opposition in favor of decreasing the power of the *Ōkurashō* and, in view of this, he felt it an excellent idea for the top ministers to go abroad for a time.[9]

Fettering the Opposition

Ōkubo made certain, however, that in his absence the opposition could not readily assume real control and thereby seek to alter his policies. In the aforementioned letter to Iwakura, Okubo stated that the thought of his colleagues—men such as Inoue, Itō, and Yamagata—was to permit Saigō and his clique "to deal only with matters pertaining to the abolition of the *han* and the establishment of prefectures, and nothing else, while the selection of officials for the *Ōkurashō* should be left solely to the *Seiin*. The *Sain* should be all but inactivated." [10] The import of such a move is clear. Sanjō, the pro-Ōkubo chairman of the *Seiin*, would, if such a policy were instituted, exercise appointive power in the selection of functionaries for the powerful *Ōkurashō*, thereby depriving the opposing Saigō faction of the opportunity to pack this powerful ministry with its own men.

On November 9, Ōkubo met with Inoue and Saigō and won the latter's agreement to give Inoue full latitude in the *Ōkurashō* to effect the progressive policy.[11] Then, on December 18, a few days before the Iwakura mission was to leave for the United States, a twelve-point pledge was drawn up and signed by the members of the Council of State, the purpose of which was to prevent the leaders in charge from subverting the established policy during the absence of Iwakura, Kido, and Ōkubo.[12] Article one pledged the signatories to work together in unity and for the common goal. Article two required that all important matters dealing with internal or external affairs be reported to each of the signatories without delay, and a regular bimonthly report be issued. Article six promised that the government would make no drastic change in domestic policy until the return of the embassy; if, however, such a change became necessary, the ambassador would be fully apprized of it. Stating that the disposition of the *haihan chiken* matter was fundamental for the unification of internal administration, article seven pledged to forward the work. Article eight promised that no vacancies created in the ranks of the department heads would be filled by any person other than a *sangi,* and no changes would be made in the scope and objectives of the departments. Article ten stated that no foreigners besides those presently employed would be hired, but if it became necessary to do so, the reasons for it would be explained in detail and approval sought. Article eleven suspended all regular sessions of the *Uin* with the provision that, should its deliberation become necessary, the *Seiin* would so announce and set the date for each session.[13] Such, in essence, were the conditions of the vow taken by the Meiji leaders.

The pledge was the result of Ōkubo's fear, verging on the paranoic, of the samurai party leaders to whom he had entrusted the administration of the country. It was a precautionary measure, intended to preserve Ōkubo's position and policy, and indicated his thorough understanding of the intricacies of government and the ramifications of administrative authority. The first article is self-explanatory. The second clause was designed, of course, to keep the leaders abroad fully abreast of developments at home. Articles six and seven are especially noteworthy. The former was clearly intended to limit the government to the established policy, giving it no liberty for deviation, while the latter exhorted the government to bring to fruition the establishment of prefectures. In other words, Ōkubo's strategem was to have his policy carried out through Inoue under the guise of effecting the *haihan chiken* reform while, at the same time, shackling the opposition by prohibiting the initiation of any new measures of its own. Articles eight and ten were obviously planned to maintain the status quo regarding administrative personnel. Ōkubo, like some of the strong executives in the history of the United States, appreciated the significance of the power to appoint and dismiss. He had no compunction about packing the *Ōkurashō* with his own men, but while he was gone he wanted no appointments of unfriendly officials who might endanger his program. Why Saigō should have conceded to such obvious circumscription is difficult to understand. His elevation to the positions of *shuseki sangi,* or senior councilor, and *jimu kantoku,* or supervisor of administrative affairs, of the *Ōkurashō* may have served as a balm for wounded pride.[14] No man, however, with an iota of self-esteem, would have accepted such a pledge, a symbol of mistrust, without showing anger. Saigō possessed self-esteem, and therefore he must have accepted the pledge and remained in the government in order to consolidate the position of the profeudal clique.

Bound for the United States

The embassy left Tōkyō on December 21, 1871, headed by the Ambassador Extraordinary Iwakura Tomomi (the Junior Prime Minister); and four vice-ministers extraordinary, Ōkubo Toshimichi (Finance Minister), Kido Kōin (state councilor), Itō Hirobumi (Vice-Minister of Public Works), and Yamaguchi Naoyoshi (Vice-Minister of Foreign Affairs).[15] Included in the party of more than one hundred were fifty-four students, five of whom were girls, accompanied by the American minister to Japan, Charles E. De Long, and his family.[16] Ōkubo's two sons, Hikonoshin and Nobukuma, were also among the scholars going to the United States and Europe for study.[17]

The S. S. "America" carrying the embassy arrived at San Francisco on January 15, and the Japanese were given a cordial reception by Mayor William Alvord. The citizens of the city serenaded the party, which was staying at the Grand Hotel.[18] San Francisco newspapers printed glowing editorials of welcome for the Japanese. A portion of one in the *Daily Evening Bulletin* is of interest in that it presents a picture of the role played by Americans in the modernization of Japan. Stating that "Japan is today, all the circumstances of her previous condition considered, the most progressive nation on the globe," the editorial went on to discuss Japan as it was merely twenty years earlier and contrasted it with the new Japan with its new system of government, its drydocks, foundries, machine shops, forges, and railroads.[19] The editorial continued:

> The government schools at Yeddo [*sic*] contain about sixteen hundred pupils, studying foreign languages, three-fourths of whom are under American teachers, receiving an English education. The principal of this school and some twenty sub-teachers are Americans, while many subjects of other nations are employed in different capacities in other departments. An American fills the highest office that a foreigner can hold under the Japanese Government—that is,

> Imperial Councilor, whose duty is to frame codes of general laws for the empire. Four Americans compose a scientific commission, to introduce new methods of agriculture, mechanics, mining, roads, etc., while another American has been appointed to revise and organize a system of internal revenue somewhat similar to our own. In addition, during the last four years, nearly one thousand young men of intelligence and ability have been sent abroad to study the languages, laws, habits, manufacturers, methods of government, and all other matters appertaining to western civilization, the greater part of which is to be introduced into Japan.[20]

Taking note of the gradual growth of antagonism toward the Chinese immigrants, the same editorial went on to contrast the Japanese with these less desirable Orientals, little realizing that within a few decades it would be the Japanese who would bear the brunt of defamatory comment. The paper noted:

> Unlike the Chinese its people [Japanese] readily make changes in clothing, food manufactures, and modes of living, when they see improvement therein. They are, as a race, impulsive, highly intelligent, brave to rashness, cleanly in their habits, have a high sense of personal honor, and are universally polite, from the highest dignitary to the lowest in the land, and withal are kindly disposed toward foreigners, especially Americans. Unlike the Chinese, again, the people of Japan are warmly attached to their country, and will not emigrate on Coolie contracts, the thirst for knowledge being the incentive of those who seek foreign lands.[21]

The embassy left the city by the Golden Gate for Sacramento on January 31, 1872. In his diary Ōkubo noted seeing a mental hospital "at a place called Stockton." Continuing, he wrote, "Sacramento is the state capital of California with a population of approximately 35,000. The city and its shops appear to be prospering. . . ." The party visited places of interest such as the State House, the garrison, railroad shops, as well as a newspaper plant where a "steam-operated press prints 2,500 papers an hour."[22] From Sacramento the embassy went to Salt Lake City, where it was snowbound from the time of arrival, February 4, until February 21, but the members were comfortably housed and treated with utmost kindness by the authorities and citizens of the city.[23] Referring to the Great Salt Lake, Ōkubo noted its dimensions as being 148 by 60 *ri* (one *ri* = 2.44030 miles). "There are no fish [in the lake]," he wrote, "because of the excessive salinity of the water." He also wrote that "a Mormon religious leader called Young arrived here twenty-five years ago and developed this area. The polygamous Young, now seventy-one years old, has sixteen wives and forty-nine children." [24] While in Chicago the embassy presented Mayor J. Medill with a sum of five thousand dollars for the benefit of those who suffered from the great fire in that city.[25] Then on February 29 the embassy finally reached Washington, D.C., where the Congress of the United States had appropriated fifty thousand dollars for entertaining their guests.[26]

Meeting the President

On Monday, March 4, Iwakura and his aides met President Ulysses S. Grant and Iwakura presented to the President their "credential letter folded in an envelope some two feet long and six inches wide, and curiously wrought with flowers of gold." [27] The letter from Emperor Meiji to President Grant stated in part:

> The period for revising the treaties now existing between ourselves and the United States is less than one year distant. We expect and intend to reform and improve the same so as to stand upon a similar footing with the most enlightened nations and to attain the full development of public right and interest. The civilization and institutions of Japan are so different from those of other countries that we cannot expect to reach the desired end at once. It is our purpose to select from the various institutions prevailing among enlightened nations such as are best suited to our present condition and adopt them, in gradual reforms and improvements of our policy and customs, so as to be upon equality with them.[28]

A few days after the meeting with the President, the Japanese were given a reception by the Congress of the United States and James G. Blaine, the Speaker of the House of Representatives, addressed the group. The man "from the State of Maine" said in part:

> The course of migration of the human race has for many centuries been steadily westward—a course marked by conquest, and too often by rapine. Reaching the boundary of our continent, we encountered a returning tide from your country setting eastward, seeking, not the trophies of war, but the more shining victories of peace; and these two currents of population appropriately meet and mingle on the shores of the great Pacific Sea.[29]

As Ōkubo, together with his colleagues, sat listening to this speech, little did he realize that this mingling of the races on the "Pacific Sea" would one day lead to misunderstanding, war, and finally defeat for his proud fatherland.

In later negotiations with Secretary of State Hamilton Fish, the Japanese ambassadors perceived the possibility of concluding a new treaty with the United States. Iwakura hurriedly sent Ōkubo and Itō back to Japan to inform the Tōkyō government of the American proposals and to have it vest the envoys with full powers to negotiate the treaty.[30] Arriving in Tōkyō on May 1, the two messengers were to discover that a segment of the Council of State was opposed to the embassy's attempt to conclude the treaties in piecemeal fashion; it preferred to have the new treaties negotiated in Europe at a conference of treaty powers. Moreover, there were those who demanded that the mission limit its work solely to observation. Ōkubo and Itō nevertheless acquired the necessary credentials and left once more on June 22 for the United States, arriving in Washington a month later. However, when informed of the views of his government, Iwakura met with the American negotiators for a final conference on July 22 to explain Tōkyō's current attitude, after which he terminated his attempts to revise the American-Japanese Treaty.[31] The mission then left for Boston on July 27 where it boarded the English liner "Olympus" on August 6 for the trip to England.

Observing Europe

Arriving in Liverpool on August 16, the embassy spent a busy four months meeting with notables, visiting places of interest, and carefully observing the social, political, and economic life of Great Britain. Ōkubo sent home glowing reports of his personal impressions of British industrial progress after visiting such places as the shipyards of Liverpool, cotton mills of Manchester, iron foundries of Glasgow, Newcastle, and Sheffield, and the breweries of Birmingham. The great quantity of machinery interested him especially, and he attributed the wealth and power of Britain to its highly mechanized industries.[32] He also marveled at the conveniences offered travelers, saying that "there is no place that the trains do not go." And in commenting upon the British people, he said appreciatively that "the warm reception we have received wherever we have gone has not differed from that which we received in America." [33] On December 16 the Iwakura mission left England for France.

While in France the group was cordially received by the president and other state dignitaries. In Paris, Ōkubo met Ōkura Kihachirō, who had been sent abroad by the War Ministry to investigate the process and possibility of manufacturing woolen cloth in Japan for military uniforms, to replace the cotton uniforms then in use. Ōkubo, very much interested, urged Ōkura to follow through with his research because he also felt that Japan should not always rely upon imported fabrics. Ōkubo suggested, moreover, that the government should subsidize such a venture. "Since you are an entrepreneur, starting a new venture," he said, "there is the possibility of failing, in which case others who subsequently may wish to enter the field would hesitate to do so. The government should therefore aid you, and after the enterprise is well established it can be sold back to you." Ōkura was enthusiastic, whereupon Ōkubo and Kido decided to carry out the plan as soon as possible. As a result of this meeting the government subsequently sent Inoue to Germany to study the woolen textile industry and Iwayama to the United States to undertake research in sheep raising. The latter returned to Japan in 1876 and began raising sheep, but this venture failed because the animals contracted various diseases and died. Inoue returned home in 1878 and, using imported wool, established the first woolen mill in Japan.[34]

On the tour through the United States and Europe the members of the embassy had occasion to observe each other's behavior at first hand. Several have described their impressions of Ōkubo. Kumai Kunitake, Iwakura's private secretary, stated that Ōkubo was reserved and smoked continually.[35] Tanabe Yasukazu, a first secretary of the Ministry of Foreign Affairs, declared that he was very formal and difficult to approach. He would never come to the door himself when a visitor called but invariably had an aide inquire first to learn the caller's business. He was a dapper dresser and had his hair parted on one side.[36] Fukuchi Yōji, a first secretary in the Ministry of Finance, was impressed by the fact that Ōkubo very seldom smiled.[37]

Meeting Bismarck

After a visit to Holland the Iwakura mission arrived in Berlin on March 9. Ōkubo's impressions of the "Iron Chancellor" of Germany, Prince Otto Eduard Leopold von Bismarck-Shönhausen, were strong and favorable. On March 15, the Prussian statesman who was instrumental in establishing the German Reich after the Franco-Prussian War of 1871 related to his attentive guests the steps in the development of the German empire. He told them that Germany had placed no reliance upon the great powers in building up her military strength, but had relied solely upon herself. The Prussian statesman told the Japanese guests about the fickleness of the great powers which tended to abide by the law of nations only so long as it proved advantageous to them. However, when it worked to their disadvantage these powers resorted to force and intimidated the weak nations in spite of law. Consequently, Germany resolved to carry on her international relations on the basis of power. The chancellor warned the Japanese to be especially cautious in their relations with England and France, powers that had territorial ambitions inasmuch as they relied heavily upon their colonial resources. Bismarck's program for strengthening his nation was obviously motivated by the desire to safeguard Germany's national rights against these same powers, and hence the chancellor's feeling toward them is understandable.[38] Ōkubo, there can be little doubt, realized that Germany had faced and solved the very problems that were demanding solution in his own country. On March 21, Ōkubo wrote to Saigō Takamori and Yoshii Tomozane and said that "Germany differs from the other European countries in that she possesses an aspect of unusual stability. The people are placing more and more confidence in Bismarck, and I surmise that Germany will progress under his policies." [39] Bismarck's basic ideas were not new; Ōkubo had arrived at similar conclusions, and their reiteration by the German chancellor had merely vindicated his policy of *fukoku kyōhei* for Japan. If anything, Bismarck's lecture reinforced the determination of the Japanese to return home and press the program for domestic reform with added zeal.

Progressive Reforms

In Tōkyō, Inoue and Yamagata were successfully carrying out the reform policy in the absence of the Iwakura party. By January 2, 1872, three *fu*, or municipal prefectures, and seventy-two *ken*, or prefectures, were created with the adoption of the *gun-ken* system. Schools were soon to be established in these new administrative subdivisions.[40] A week later mail service was started between Tōkyō and Nagasaki.[41] As a measure to solve the unemployment problem among the nonlaboring classes of the old society, nobles and samurai were, on January 27, permitted to engage in agricultural, industrial, or commercial activities.[42] The issuance of new paper money was announced on February 5, placing in circulation in the emerging capitalistic society of Japan denominations of one hundred, fifty, twenty, five, two, and one *yen;* and fifty, twenty, ten, and five *sen.* A court of law had been established on the previous day in the Ministry of Justice in Tōkyō.[43] On March 23 the law against the sale and purchase of land was repealed.[44] Several days later the *Hyōbushō,* or Ministry of War, was abolished and separate ministries of army and navy created.[45] The old *shimpei,* or court guard, was abolished and replaced by the *konoe hei,* or imperial guard, under the command of Lieutenant-General Yamagata Aritomo. The vice-commander was Major-General Saigō Tsugumichi. Both of these men concurrently served as high officials in the Army Ministry.[46] The *Jingishō,* dealing with religious affairs, was replaced by the *Kyōbushō,* on April 21.[47] On May 4, newspapers were circulated throughout the empire.[48] Later in the same month military courts were established.[49] An educational system came into being on September 5, 1872, when the country was divided into eight *daigaku,* or university, areas with each area to have a university. These areas were to be further divided into middle and elementary school districts with such institutions to be established in their respective districts.[50] Another step in the direction of modernization was taken with the creation of a state bank on September 17.[51] On October 25 the government prohibited the private sale of arms and ammunition.[52] By way of social reform, the terms of girls employed by houses of prostitution were limited and those who had been sold into such service were to be released.[53] On November 25 the *Kyōbushō* was consolidated with the *Mombushō,* or Ministry of Education.[54] The solar calendar was adopted on December 9.[55] At the end of the year, on December 30, the universal military conscription system was inaugurated under which there was to be the regular army, the reserves, and the militia.[56] On March 14, 1873, Japanese were allowed to marry foreigners, a concession to the ardent Westernizers.[57]

Mounting Resistance

The progressive measures of the government, however, were not given wholehearted approval. Universal military conscription was a crucial issue inasmuch as it affected the samurai party members in the Council of State. Its leader, Saigō Takamori, was in favor of military reforms but had doubts whether the sons of farmers, workers, and shopkeepers could be trained to compose an efficient fighting machine. Yamagata nevertheless convinced him that this was possible and subsequently the conscript system was inaugurated.[58] Prior to its adoption on August 22, Saigō had been given the rank of marshal of the army and commander of the *konoe* troops while concurrently serving as *sangi*.[59] Whether this had any bearing on his willingness to approve the military reform is conjectural, but it is clear that he was friendly with Yamagata and did not resist the execution of his plan. Saigō, however, did not hide his antagonism to the so-called industrializers in the Ministry of Finance who were responsible for the reform program. Therefore, as a measure of opposition to the progressives, several anti-Inoue members of the government were elevated to the rank of state councilor. On April 19, 1873, Gotō Shōjirō, the *gichō*, Etō Shimpei, the Minister of Justice, and Ōki Takato, the Minister of Education and Religion, aligned themselves with the Saigō faction in opposition to the strong clique of modernizers in the Ministry of Finance. The three men were vexed because Inoue, who feared deficit spending, had refused to grant the full amount of funds they had requisitioned for their respective departments.[60] Moreover, Saigō harbored resentment toward Inoue because he opposed, on the grounds of inadequate funds, the former's plans to send a punitive expedition to Formosa. Saigō was extremely anxious to chastise the Formosan aborigines who in December, 1871, had murdered some Ryūkyū islanders who had drifted there.[61] Faced with strong opposition, Inoue Kaoru and Shibuzawa Eiichi finally presented a petition to the government revealing the actual state of the public finances.[62]

In preparing his national balance sheet, Inoue calculated that the revenue would amount to 40,000,000 *yen* while the expenditures would reach 50,000,000 *yen*, leaving a deficit of 10,000,000 *yen*. Stating their inability to balance the budget under the circumstances, the two men therewith resigned.[63] The government requested Ōkuma to check Inoue's financial report, which showed a national debt of 140,000,000 *yen*. Whether by juggling figures or the use of better judgment, Ōkuma produced a surplus of 2,141,000 *yen* in the budget and computed the national debt outstanding at only 31,224,000 *yen*. Convinced that the financial situation was not critical, the government adopted Ōkuma's budget for 1873.[64] The old *han* rivalry among members of the Meiji government had come to the fore again. Here was a case of the Hizen men, who numerically dominated the council, reacting against a Satsuma minister. The members of the Council of State at this particular time included three men from Hizen: Ōkuma, Ōki, and Etō; two from Tosa: Itagaki and Gotō; one from Chōshū: Yamagata; and one from Satsuma: Saigō Takamori.

Returning to Trouble

Along with friction among the leadership, the government was being pressed by problems relating to the Korean, Formosan, and Karafuto (Sakhalin) questions. The Tōkyō government urgently requested the return of Ōkubo and Kido from abroad to facilitate their settlement. Unfortunately, the relations between these two men while on the world tour had worsened to the point of almost total estrangement—an estrangement brought about by differences in background, opinion, and personality. Ōkubo's friendship for Itō Hirobumi, which developed as the result of their close association as members of the Iwakura mission, angered Kido, who considered Itō his own protégé. Kido feared that Ōkubo was trying to snatch Itō away from him, and therefore heaped acrimony upon Ōkubo and to some extent upon Iwakura as well. Kido also was afraid of being shunned by his colleagues.[65] Because of the strained relationship, on March 25 Kido and Ōkubo agreed to take separate routes home, the latter to precede the former.[66] Ōkubo embarked from Marseilles and arrived home on May 26, 1873.[67] Kido returned to Japan via the Suez Canal, Singapore, and Saigon, reaching Yokohama on July 23 where, among those who welcomed him, Ōkubo was conspicuous by his absence.[68] The rest of the Iwakura mission followed, arriving in Japan on September 13.[69]

The Iwakura mission, which expended over a million *yen* during its twenty-month stay abroad, failed in its primary purpose of revising the treaties. But, as Ōkuma noted, the embassy not only brought Japan an awareness of the civilization and institutions of the West, but the mission also had the effect of focusing world attention upon a heretofore little-known entity in the Far East, a country whose "polity and people were in nowise inferior to those elsewhere." [70] The sojourn abroad definitely altered the thinking of both Ōkubo and Kido. When they left Japan, Kido was much more imbued with the spirit of progress than Ōkubo; when they returned, Kido was more conservative than Ōkubo. Impressed by the prosperity of the United States and Europe, Ōkubo became a stronger advocate of progressive reform while Kido, depressed by the plight of Ireland and the fate of Poland, was less enthusiastic about Westernizing Japan.[71] Ōkubo was inspired by his contact with Bismarck; like the German empire, even Japan could become a world power if it sacrificed and built up its resources.[72] This thought became an obsession that was to remain with Ōkubo until his death.

Back in Tōkyō, Ōkubo immediately realized that with the resignation of Inoue the disunited government had come increasingly under the domination of the military party. Its members were beginning to clamor for a positive policy toward Korea. Ōkubo at first said that there was little he could do until Iwakura returned. Reporting conditions to Ōyama Iwao and Murata Shimpachi, who were then studying in Europe, Ōkubo stated that the situation at home was definitely out of hand: "It is like having a swarm of mosquitoes at your back, and it is difficult to decide just what to do. I am temporizing and waiting until all hands are available before taking any positive steps; even granting that one's intentions are good, to act now would accrue to our disadvantage. . . . I am imperturbably looking on." [73]

For the moment Ōkubo had to be patient. Hence, on August 16, he left Tōkyō for Hakone, the resort district southwest of Tōkyō, and, after climbing Mount Fuji, went on to Yamato and Kii, the present areas of Nara and Wakayama. Ōkubo returned to Tōkyō a week after Iwakura's arrival home in mid-September. With his colleagues to support him, Ōkubo was now ready to confront Saigō and the military party, the hotheads who were advocating an immediate settlement with Korea. Like a realistic strategist on the battlefield, he did not join forces with the enemy until adequate "troops" were available.

Korean Issue

To understand the background of the *seikan ron,* or the doctrine of invading Korea to which the military party adhered, a brief digression into Japan's earlier relations with that country becomes necessary. Since the failure of Toyotomi Hideyoshi to conquer Korea at the close of the sixteenth century, the relations between the two countries had been limited to the conduct of trifling trade, and formal missions of courtesy sent to announce the accession of a new emperor, or to offer congratulations on the occasion. This trade was carried on at Pusan, and the attitude of the Koreans toward the Japanese in that tiny settlement was not friendly. The Koreans continued to send periodic missions of courtesy during the Tokugawa period, but when the Restoration took place they refused to dispatch the customary envoy to Tōkyō and also declined to accept the envoy sent by the Japanese government. Korea, advised by China, desired to have no further intercourse with Japan, who had allied herself to all intents and purposes with the West by adopting a new and progressive policy. The Koreans and Chinese believed that Japan had abandoned the traditions of the East. The attitude of the Koreans was taken as an affront to Japanese dignity and created resentment throughout Japan, an unfortunate situation which developed at a time when there was much friction and ill-feeling smoldering within the government.[74]

The militarists, led by Saigō, Soejima, Etō, Itagaki, and Gotō, pressed for the immediate dispatch of a strong force to Korea. Saigō himself expected to be commissioned an envoy. This course, if followed, would have led to war. War, in fact, had been practically decided upon when propriety dictated that action be withheld pending the return home of the Iwakura mission. When the confrontation within the Council of State came, Ōkubo, Kido, and Iwakura, the leaders of the industrialization party, declared that the time was inopportune for war. The ensuing debate was long and embittered, leading to the ultimate rupture in the government, the first since the formation of the new Meiji government in 1868.[75]

Why did Saigō advocate what would have been a devastating course of action? Ōkuma believed that Saigō wished to divert the attention of the restive samurai from their plight as unemployed fighters by engaging them in a foreign campaign.[76] Chauvinism was another explanation. Saigō, it was contended, was imbued with the traditional spirit of expansion exemplified by Emperor Jimmu, the first of the Japanese sovereigns, as well as later patriots who wished to enhance the dignity of Japan through aggrandizement. Another hypothesis was that hatred and fear of foreigners who Saigō believed were scheming to conquer Korea induced him to adopt this particular viewpoint, his objective being to prevent the encroachment of foreigners into Korea. He was in essence extending the *joi* principle to cover an area in East Asia outside Japan.[77] There are historians, however, who believe that Saigō was simply reacting violently to the impelling power of the pro-Ōkubo members of the government who were imposing their progressive, antisamurai reforms upon the country while he, a member of the samurai party, was nevertheless committed to the implementation of the reform policy. He realized that his authority was circumscribed, and he was also angered by the fact that Shimazu Hisamitsu, never friendly to him, continued to attack him. Highly irritated and depressed, Saigō's drastic policy vis-à-vis Korea served as an outlet for his resentment. He had hoped that in war he might once again be able to make full use of his military talents.[78] This is a most plausible thesis.

Finally, there is the thesis that Saigō was duped into advocating war with Korea by those, led by Etō Shimpei, who wanted war in order to restrain the power of Satsuma and Chōshū. Etō, since becoming a member of the government, had had hopes of establishing Hizen as a dominant force in the Council of State. He realized, however, that Hizen could not possibly compete with Satsuma and Chōshū. In Etō's thinking, Satsuma and Chōshū were influential mainly because of their domination of the fighting forces. He therefore reasoned that in the event of a war with Korea he would have an opportunity to establish a monopoly of Hizen power in Tōkyō in the absence of the Sat-Chō forces.[79]

It is probable that a multiplicity of considerations dictated Saigō's decision to advocate a war with Korea, but that one of Saigō's stature could have been duped by Etō is difficult to believe. It is evident nevertheless that Etō and others had hoped that war would be conducive to an equation of political power in Tōkyō among representatives of the various *han*.

During the absence of Ōkubo, Iwakura, and Kido, the leaders who were left in charge of the government had discussed the Korean question as early as June 12, 1873, at which time Itagaki Taisuke urged the immediate dispatch of troops to the Korean peninsula. Saigō, however, rejected this suggestion and offered an alternative plan, that of sending an envoy whose likely assassination by the Koreans would furnish a fair *casus belli* for Japan. Itagaki ultimately agreed to this.[80] On July 29, Saigō wrote to Itagaki requesting that Itagaki recommend him for this hazardous task, saying that "although I probably cannot accomplish the diplomatic feat that Soejima could if he were to go, I am nevertheless prepared to undertake the mission and to be killed." [81] He thereafter wrote to Itagaki more than a half-dozen times pleading for the commission. Saigō was apparently fearful that Foreign Minister Soejima would be given the ambassadorial appointment. On August 16, apprehensive and restless, Saigō paid a personal call upon Sanjō and urged him to make a favorable decision before the return of Iwakura from abroad. Sanjō therefore decided to call a meeting of the council.[82] On August 17 the *Seiin* decided unofficially to dispatch Saigō as an envoy but to await the return of the Iwakura mission before an official decision was made.[83]

After having returned to Tōkyō, Iwakura, who learned that Ōkubo and Kido had not been attending council sessions since they had returned from Europe, planned to have them participate in deliberations and thereby reëstablish a degree of equilibrium within the government. Iwakura suggested that Ōkubo accept the position of *sangi*, but the latter adamantly refused, even after Sanjō and Iwakura used Itō Hirobumi and Kuroda Kiyotaka as intermediaries in an effort to break down his resistance. In his letter of September 30 to Iwakura, in which he expressed regret that he could not accede to his wishes, Ōkubo suggested that the Korean question be settled under the leadership of Kido, a *sangi*.[84] Kido at this time was ill and unable to attend council meetings, but he was strongly against the Korean adventure despite the fact that as early as 1869 he had staunchly advocated a positive policy for Korea.[85] As his diary notation of September 3, 1873, reveals, Kido's views had undergone a complete change during the preceding five years and now coincided almost exactly with those of Ōkubo, to wit, that any foreign venture at the moment would further weaken Japan and hence internal administration should receive priority over external affairs.[86] Why Ōkubo apparently shifted his own responsibility to Kido is a moot question. Did he realize that, as a *sangi*, he would surely be forced to clash with Saigō and was he trying to avoid the unpleasant consequences of such a clash? Did he wish to retain Kido as an active participant in the government? With their relationship strained almost to the breaking point, Ōkubo's assumption of this office might have forced an emotional Kido to resign. Did he hesitate because of the obvious enmity which Shimazu Hisamitsu and the Satsuma *han* displayed toward him? Or was he cognizant of the fact that if he succeeded in solving the immediate problem, there would be others for the solution of which he would be responsible? [87]

Ōkubo's reluctance to become a contender in the coming power struggle dissipated when he was assured that both Iwakura and Sanjō would inform the council at its next meeting on October 14 of their decision to postpone the plan to dispatch a mission to Korea pending the settlement of more urgent problems, namely, that of the Russian penetration of Karafuto.[88] On October 10, Ōkubo notified the two *kuge* of his intention of working with them for the common cause.[89] Although other considerations played an important role, Ōkubo had been purposely evasive in order to ascertain with what degree of determination Iwakura and Sanjō would support the antimilitary faction. On October 12, Ōkubo was raised to the rank of *sangi*.[90] Now the stage was set for the clash between two able protagonists, Ōkubo and Saigō.

On October 14 the meeting of the Council of State opened with Iwakura stating in broad terms the anti-*seikan* position. Iwakura argued that the Russian menace in the north was of such magnitude as to require first consideration.[91] Itagaki then outlined the opposing view, contending that the Korean question demanded priority. The remainder of the session was monopolized by Ōkubo and Saigō, the Satsuma warrior looking impressive in his military attire. Saigō was fervent in his argument for the settlement of the Korean issue. Ōkubo, in contrast, quietly and cogently upheld his *naichi dai-ichi shugi ron,* that is, the doctrine of devoting primary consideration to domestic policy. The line of reasoning followed by the progressives betrayed the profound influence exerted upon them by their recent tour abroad. Ōkubo, as their spokesman, stressed the need for modernization if Japan were to reach the level of Western civilization. To engage in war now would severely hamper the policy forged by the modernizers. However, despite the long debate, no decision was reached at this meeting.[92]

The debate continued the following day. Saigō was conspicuously absent although his colleagues were represented at the meeting. He did, however, present through Sanjō a demand for prior consideration for the Korean problem, and the military faction stubbornly supported their leader's view.[93] With neither side willing to relent, Sanjō realized that the upshot would be Saigō's resignation if a prowar decision were not reached. He therefore consulted Iwakura privately and won his consent to recommend to the government the adoption of the Saigō policy. When informed of this, Ōkubo, indignant over the arbitrary behavior of the two *kuge,* returned home after the meeting determined to resign rather than agree to the recommendation.[94] On October 17 he forwarded his resignation to Sanjō.[95] Kido and Iwakura were soon to follow suit.

Articulating Objections

The specific reasons for Ōkubo's opposition to the war policy are articulated in a lengthy document that he submitted to Iwakura and Sanjō.[96] It reveals Ōkubo's logic, his "cold reasoning" which won eventual victory over Saigō and the militarists. Moreover, it manifests his complete grasp of the social, political, and economic situation of Japan and the likely effects of an ill-advised war with Korea. He states in his introduction:

> The most mature consideration and forethought is essential in order to govern the nation and to protect the land and its people. *Every action, whether progressive or conservative, should be taken in response to the occasion, and if it develops unfavorably should be abandoned. This may entail shame, but it is to be endured; justice may be with us, but we are not to choose that course. We must act as our greatest needs dictate, taking into account the importance of any problem and examining the exigencies.* [Italics mine.] We have here the problem of dispatching an envoy to Korea. The reasons why I am in no great haste to subscribe to the proposal come from much careful and earnest reflection upon the problem. . . .[97]

These thoughts were formulated by a tough-minded realist; they are both practical and unemotional. Ōkubo went on to give seven reasons against any rash actions regarding Korea.

First, such action might lead to civil disturbances. Ōkubo noted that with the abolition of the feudal fiefs and the establishment of prefectures a drastic change had occurred, bringing to Japan a semblance of prosperity, especially in the capital. He warned, however, that in the provinces there were many people who had lost their homes and property as a result of the reforms and were bitter and restive. Within the past two years they had become victims of agitators because of their ignorance of the purport of government proclamations or of their misgivings about increased taxes.[98]

Second, such action might lead to economic bankruptcy. Ōkubo pointed out the budgetary deficit confronting the nation and warned that a protracted war would necessitate increased taxation, foreign loans with no prospect of repayment, and the issuance of paper notes without sufficient backing. War would be "so disastrous as to preclude any chance of salvation." [99]

Third, such action would force the abandonment of the *fukoku kyōhei* policy. Ōkubo called attention to the long-range nature of this policy, and indicated that reforms in education, justice, industry, colonization, and defense would take many years to achieve. A meaningless war would waste the government's efforts, increase expenditures, and cause the loss of lives, forcing the government to abandon the modernization program.[100]

Fourth, such action would deplete the gold reserves. Ōkubo argued that Japan's unfavorable balance of trade would worsen with the need for increased imports during wartime. Increasing amounts of gold would have to be exported to make up for the shortage in exports. The reduction of this precious metal would affect adversely the credit of the government, reduce the value of the notes, and generally create hardship among the populace. The end result would be the impoverishment of the entire nation.[101]

Fifth, such action would make Japan an easy prey for Russia. Russia, already ensconced in the north, could drive southward into Sakhalin. "Thus, should we cross arms with Korea and become like the two water-birds fighting over a fish, Russia will be fishermen standing by to snare the fish." [102]

Sixth, such action would enable England to interfere in Japan's domestic affairs. Ōkubo stated that Japan had hitherto depended largely upon England for foreign loans. A war, which would impoverish Japan, would reduce her ability to refund her foreign loans. This would give England, already poised to act at a moment's notice, a pretext for meddling in the country's affairs.[103]

Seventh, such action would divert the attention of the ministers from the urgent matter of treaty revision. The unequal treaties, Ōkubo noted, impaired the dignity of an independent nation. This was a disgrace. With the time for treaty revision near at hand, the government had a duty to evolve means by which Japan could be restored to a position of dignity. A venture in Korea should not take priority over this matter.[104]

In his concluding paragraphs Ōkubo reminded his opponents that the occupation and defense of Korea, presupposing a victory for Japan, would not be simple. Internal disturbances would create difficulties while Russia and China would pose an external threat despite formal treaties that might bind them to forsake interference in Korean affairs. "It is certainly no difficult matter," he stated, "to find an excuse to break a promise." [105] Ōkubo reached to the crux of the matter when he said:

> Some argue that the arrogance of Korea toward our country is intolerable. But as far as I can see, the reasons for the sending of an Envoy Extraordinary seem to be to look for a positive excuse for war by having him treated arrogantly and discourteously. We would then dispatch troops to punish them. If this be the case, it is clear that this venture is to be undertaken, not because the situation makes it unavoidable or because there is no other way but rather because the honor of the country will have been sullied and our sovereignty humiliated. I consider such a venture entirely beyond comprehension as it completely disregards the safety of our nation and ignores the interests of the people. It will be an incident occasioned by the whims of individuals without serious evaluation of eventualities or implications. These are the reasons why I cannot accept the arguments for the undertaking of this venture.[106]

In addition to the considerations against a Korean adventure outlined in Ōkubo's paper, there was the consideration of military preparedness as well. Yamagata himself expressed the opinion to Saigō that Japan would be in a better position to send troops abroad in a year or two after the nation's military foundation had solidified.[107]

The tenor of the document is peace. But it is important to note that nowhere in it does Ōkubo argue against war per se. He was against war at that particular time when the country, in his estimation, was not prepared for it. Thus he used such expressions as, "This is the third reason against the *hasty* commencement of a Korean war," and "To launch a meaningless war *now* . . ." [italics mine]. War was undesirable now, but the future might be a different matter. His intention was to develop Japan first before expanding outward across the waters. He cannot really be considered any less an expansionist than Saigō, Itagaki, or Soejima. Ōkubo was at heart an imperialist, but one who believed in gradualism.[108] It is difficult to defend Itō Hirobumi's statement that Ōkubo's unwillingness to see his friend assassinated by the Koreans induced him to oppose the plan to send Saigō as an envoy to Korea.[109] Friendship between the two men had deteriorated almost beyond repair, and it certainly was not an important factor influencing Ōkubo's decision to reject the policy of the military faction. It is a fact, however, that Itō and Ōkubo were close friends, and the former very likely publicized this reason to place his friend in a better light.

Scheming to Oust the War Clique

Another government crisis occurred as a result of the wholesale resignation of the progressives. The meeting of the council of October 17 found only the militarists in attendance. Highly perturbed, Sanjō, who was anxious to maintain harmony, sought and received from Saigō an agreement to postpone deliberations for one day while the former sought to reunite the ministry. But the strain of the situation was too intense for Sanjō; he collapsed.[110] This development, however, was as unfortunate for the military party as it was fortunate for the peace faction whose resignation was not accepted, since it afforded the latter the opportunity to have Sanjō replaced by a less vacillating individual—one who would side with the peace faction—at a very critical juncture. Ōkubo did not hesitate to turn the situation to his advantage. His diary for October 19 contains a cryptic entry:

> Matsukata Masayoshi, Saigō, the younger, and Iwashita Masahira were in today. Kuroda also came. He was apprehensive of the present difficulties and indicated sympathy for our position. I confided in him that I had but one plan by which we might retrieve the initiative. He agreed that it was feasible. I asked him to relay the idea to Yoshii.[111]

The plan was to have Kuroda contact Yoshii who in turn would go to Tokudaiji, the Minister of the Imperial Household, and request that he arrange for Iwakura to receive an imperial appointment to fill Sanjō's position temporarily.[112] The plan succeeded, and the peace party obtained a friendly *dajōdaijin* for the interim. The antimilitarists thereupon renewed their activities.

Ōkubo's machinations is an example of the manner in which the powers behind the Japanese throne sought to translate their will into policy or, as in this instance, block the progress of an opponent. Japan has had government by advisers from as far back as the Heian period when the Fujiwaras exerted tremendous authority over the nominal rulers of the country. Even under the relatively strong Emperor Meiji the powerful lower samurai advisers comprising the oligarchy generally determined policy, which normally reflected the ideas of the most powerful among them, that of the oligarch. During these years the oligarch with power was Ōkubo.

The militarists did not passively accept the appointment of Iwakura, who temporarily replaced Sanjō. Iwakura was put to the test when, on October 22, the four opposition *sangi*, Saigō, Itagaki, Soejima, and Etō, came to his home and demanded that the government officially sanction Saigō's mission to Korea. Iwakura, however, stubbornly resisted attempts at coërcion.[113] Saigō, the petulant samurai, angry at the rebuff, resigned the following day; and Etō, Itagaki, Gotō, and Soejima followed the example of their chief.[114] On October 24 the Emperor intervened and proclaimed that peaceful means should be employed in negotiating with Korea, thus resolving the long-standing problem of what form Japan's policy should take with respect to its neighbor.[115]

Although the earlier resignations of Sanjō, Kido, Ōkubo, Ōkuma, and Ōki were not accepted, the resignations of Saigō and the members of his clique were accepted upon the advice of Ōkubo.[116] Saigō and his colleagues were decisively defeated, and after experiencing the exalting feeling of power for a period of more than two years returned to their respective provinces, dejected and bitter.

What were the basic causes for the cleavage within the council? It is doubtful that the split was attributable ultimately to the conflict over the Korean issue. The Korean issue was merely the spark that caused the explosion. Dissension and hostility had been mounting before this time between Ōkubo and Saigō and other strong-willed members of the government. There had been a constant tug-of-war between Ōkubo and the civilian party on the one side and Saigō and the military clique on the other. The increasing antagonism between incompatibles was bound to culminate in a government split, even if the Korean issue had not come up when it did. In this early example of a struggle for power between the civilian and military factions within the government, the civilian party emerged victorious because it possessed the strongest leader of the day. Unfortunately for Japan, it was subsequently to have a dearth of leaders of Ōkubo's caliber, and, consequently, military figures were to emerge to dominate the critical periods in her history.

It was inevitable that the army would react to the resignation of the military hero, Saigō. The first indication of trouble came on October 28, the day on which Saigō left Tōkyō for Kagoshima—when Ōkubo noted that "disorder among the *konoe* troops is imminent." [117] For the next several days Ōkubo met with Saigō Tsugumichi, Yoshii Tomozane, and Tokudaiji Sanenori to discuss means to pacify the restive men. The earliest intimation of what Ōkubo had in mind as a solution is his notation for October 30: "This morning Takasaki Isoroku and Narahara came in. We discussed the Hisamitsu matter." [118] The plan was to have Shimazu Hisamitsu join the government and thereby fill the vacuum created by the resignation of Saigō. This would preserve Satsuma influence within the government and reduce the danger of a military uprising. Hisamitsu's presence in the government would serve, it was thought, to check Saigō and the military party from engaging in any open retaliation against the government. So long as the two Satsuma men, Ōkubo and Saigō, occupied the center of the political stage in Tōkyō, Hisamitsu, who had a special aversion for Saigō, had ostracized them. But with the complete severance of friendly ties between Hisamitsu's two former subordinates, there was now a possibility of Ōkubo's regaining Hisamitsu's coöperation. As anticipated, he did eventually join the government.

Forming a New Government

The formation of a new government, referred to appropriately as the "Ōkubo government," began in the fall of 1873, and it was not until the fall of the following year that all posts were filled. The completed government included the following members: [119]

Position	Name	Han	Date appointed
Dajōdaijin	Sanjō Sanetomi (*kuge*)		
Udaijin	Iwakura Tomomi (*kuge*)		
Sangi concurrently Minister of Home Affairs	Ōkubo Toshimichi	Satsuma	Appointed *Naimu Kyō*, November 29, 1873
Sangi concurrently Minister of Education	Kido Kōin	Chōshū	Appointed *Mombu Kyō*, January 25, 1874
Sangi concurrently Minister of Finance	Ōkuma Shigenobu	Hizen	Appointed *Ōkura Kyō*, October 25, 1873
Sangi concurrently Minister of Justice	Ōki Takato	Hizen	October 25, 1873
Sangi concurrently Minister of the Navy	Katsu Kaishū (former Bakufu official)		Appointed *sangi* concurrently *Kaigun Kyō*, October 25, 1873

Position	Name	Han	Date appointed
Sangi concurrently Minister of Public Works	Itō Hirobumi	Chōshū	Appointed *sangi* concurrently *Kōmu Kyō*, October 25, 1873
Sangi concurrently Minister of the Army	Yamagata Aritomo	Chōshū	Appointed *sangi*, August 2, 1874
Sangi concurrently Minister of Foreign Affairs	Terajima Munenori	Satsuma	October 25, 1873
Sangi concurrently Chief, Colonization Bureau	Kuroda Kiyotaka	Satsuma	August 2, 1874
Sangi concurrently Speaker, *Sain*	Ijichi Masaharu	Satsuma	Appointed *sangi*, August 2, 1874
Sadaijin concurrently Adviser to the Government	Shimazu Hisamitsu	Satsuma	Appointed *Naikaku Komon*, December 25, 1873; appointed *Sadaijin*, May 27, 1874

An analysis of the Ōkubo government reveals several conspicuous characteristics. It was dominated by five Satsuma men with Chōshū and Hizen contributing three and two men respectively. There were no professed opponents of the progressive policy. Hisamitsu, the only representative of the once-prominent *daimyō* class, was conspicuous among members representing in the main the samurai retainer class, the other exception being Katsu Kaishū, who was a former Tokugawa official. In accordance with Ōkubo's plan, the government was solidified by having persons of *sangi* rank assume concurrent ministerial posts, thereby enabling government decisions to be made and executed with greater dispatch. The new government was, moreover, much more amenable to the direction of the oligarch, Ōkubo; the members were mostly newer men who had yet to make a name for themselves in politics and therefore were less inclined toward independent action. The one exception was Kido, whose antipathy for Ōkubo hindered the establishment of complete unity within the government. Fortunately, however, the Korean issue had unified the government, at least for the moment, but a subsequent crisis, over the Formosan problem, was to force the confrontation of Ōkubo and Kido and the disruption of this harmony.[120]

Developing the Home Ministry

Ōkubo's authority increased with his assumption of the post of *Naimu Kyō*, or Minister of Home Affairs, on November 29, 1873. The *Naimushō*, or Ministry of Home Affairs, had been newly established two weeks earlier, on November 10.[121] As a *sangi* and concurrently Minister of Home Affairs, Ōkubo was to exercise virtually the power of a prime minister until an assassin's sword ended his career in May, 1878.[122] Although the ministry was the creation of Itō Hirobumi, it was Ōkubo who was responsible for making it the "heart and center of the domestic bureaucracy." It was eventually to exercise "controls which reached down through regional, prefectural, city, town, and village governments to the wards and neighborhoods to intrude upon, influence, and restrict the waking hours in the life of every man, woman and child in Japan." [123]

The *Naimushō* originally was formed to fulfill two basic purposes, civil control and the implementation of economic growth. To realize these objectives two special bureaus were created within the ministry and given the status of primary departments. The first was the *keihōryō*, or police bureau, whose initial supervisor was Murata Ujihisa. Anticipating internal disturbances created by dissidents, especially those within the ranks of the recently defeated military party, this department was authorized to maintain peace and order within the country. The second of these primary departments was the *kangyōryō*, or industrial promotion bureau, under the supervision of Kawase Hidekatsu.[124] This was the natural adjunct to the government policy that emphasized internal development. Ōkubo's observations abroad had convinced him that he must establish for Japan the same bases upon which the world powers of the day had founded their wealth and strength. The creation of the *kangyōryō* was an early step in the government's plan to establish manufacturing industries. Similar governmental patronage was given to education, trade, shipping, and every facet of Japanese life that could be utilized for the growth of Japan's power. Secondary bureaus in the *Naimushō* included those of topography, engineering, forestry, and census, among others. As head of the ministry, Ōkubo was described by one of his subordinates as a stickler for diligence and a chief who was not hesitant about accepting responsibility.[125] He was the epitome of efficiency and industry and deserves the encomium given him by the Western writer who said that, under the supervision of Ōkubo, the *Naimushō* vastly improved internal administration and public finances, established model enterprises and in other ways worked to increase national income.[126]

Philosophy of Government

The increasing power Ōkubo wielded after 1873 and apparently enjoyed exercising gave rise to charges by the Japanese that he was a "model for absolutism and the embodiment of a bureaucrat," accusations dismissed by Ōkubo's supporters as superficial.[127] One Western writer has more recently called him an "autocrat," [128] a characterization not incorrect when Ōkubo's career is viewed in retrospect. Some injustice is done, however, when he is described as "the defender of the absolute monarchy." [129] It is true that the conservative Ōkubo was a marked contrast to the liberal Kido, and there is no doubt that the latter, by comparison, was "the Jefferson of Japan." [130] But was Ōkubo basically an advocate of autocracy? What precisely was Ōkubo's political philosophy, his actual views on constitutional government?

He, like Kido, early favored a gradual evolution of representative government and worked toward that end.[131] In fact, both he and Kido were the early advocates of removing from the *Sain* the responsibility of formulating a draft constitution and placing it in the hands of a national agency which could "systematically and comprehensively prescribe the rights and duties of the people." [132] Itō, who was eventually commissioned to undertake studies preparatory to the framing of a fundamental law for Japan, relied heavily upon the advice of these two men.[133] It was Ōkubo who suggested to Itō that Fukuzawa Yūkichi, the outstanding liberal and educator of Japan, be associated with him in the task. Itō, however, who was more inclined toward the Prussian concept of state, appointed Terajima, who shared Itō's view.[134] There is no doubt that many of Ōkubo's ideas were used by Itō and incorporated in the Japanese constitution of 1889.[135]

Ōkubo's concept of an ideal state lay between democracy and autocracy. This is indicated in a paper expressing his political philosophy, which he forwarded to Itō in 1873.[136]

His introductory remarks leave no doubt that he definitely favored a monarchy:

> People who discuss the system of government in the world do so in terms of monarchy and democracy. Japan cannot yet adopt democracy, nor yet discard monarchy. Indeed, monarchy is rooted in the very foundation of our nation. It is the supreme type of government. If we do not establish monarchy firmly, how can we build the nation? How can we administer the affairs of state? [137]

With considerable insight, he explains the nature of democracy and its merits and limitations:

> Democracy seeks to work for the common welfare of the nation. It does not seek to make the nation the realm of any one person. Generally it signifies freedom of the people. It is a system of government perfected according to the laws of nature, but it does not ignore the principles of administration by law and the responsibility of officials. At present, it is the system of government in the United States, Switzerland, and countries in South America. This system of government can be put into operation when new nations are founded or by new nations of immigrants, but it cannot be applied to a people who are accustomed to long-standing practices based on old ways. . . . However, this system is not free from abuses! With the establishment of political parties, which gradually grow larger, political deterioration and disintegration set in. . . . One cannot say that democracy is the best system of government.[138]

Ōkubo continued by stating that a society of unenlightened people cannot have rule based upon contract and that an authoritarian rule is best suited to such a situation. The allusion here is to Japan. He felt, however, that this would only be a temporary situation and believed that a change was inevitable. Thus he said:

> But a nation cannot hold to the same kind of government merely because it is time-honored. . . . Our people are already under the influence of Europe and America, and we are already partially modernized. In the future, we will not be able to maintain the same kind of government.[139]

The type of government he desired was a limited monarchy:

> Shall the government become a government of the people? I say no. . . . Democracy must not be adopted, nor should a monarchy be retained which is not adapted to the people. We must develop a polity that conforms to the customs, feelings, and conditions of our nation, that is, a political system based upon a constitution. . . . Constitutional monarchy is a joint government of the ruler and the

> people. . . . Where ultimate power is vested . . . in both the ruler and the people, it is limited monarchy. . . . This shall be the foundation of our nation and the basis of our government.[140]

How much did Ōkubo intend to limit the power of the throne? Very little. The constitution, he said, "must maintain the emperor's position for all ages to come and make the people keep their natural order." [141] Significantly, the powers he would allot to the emperor were essentially those the throne was to enjoy under the constitution of 1889. The Ōkubo draft gave the emperor supreme power to operate the national administration, the right to hand down the throne, convene and dissolve the assembly, submit laws for discussion by the assembly, command the army and navy, confer and rescind titles. Ōkubo inserted a clause stating that the sovereign would not be responsible for political mistakes.[142]

Ōkubo's concept of an assembly was one that called for consultative responsibility only. Its composition, moreover, would be far from representative as the term is conceived in the West. It would be composed of nobles, "specially selected" representatives, and departmental ministers.[143]

It is apparent that although Ōkubo had definite autocratic tendencies—his actions loudly speak out to this effect—his political philosophy was not essentially autocratic. Indeed, it is difficult to accept the theory of "absolutism," upheld by such scholars as Tōyama, and its implication that the Restoration leaders were hard-core autocrats whose handiwork, the Meiji government, was purposely designed to be an absolute state. If the government verged on the absolute, it was not because Ōkubo and his colleagues were basically despotic and therefore premeditatively planned it to be so. Circumstances more often than not forced them to take an autocratic course, irrespective of their ideals which on occasion had to be laid aside to meet the exigencies of the times.

Ōkubo was neither a disciple of liberalism nor a defender of autocracy. He tried to follow a middle course toward a limited monarchy based upon traditional Confucian ideals, a path Itō also attempted to tread.[144] Like Kido, he was a gradualist, warning against too great haste in deciding upon the shape of the government. Although the study of Ōkubo's career as a political leader reveals him to be more of an authoritarian than a liberal, the fact is that he was one of the earliest advocates of constitutional monarchy in Japan.

Problems of Foreign Relations

While the industrializers regained control of the government with the defeat of the military party, none of the outstanding problems had been solved by the change. In foreign affairs the solutions to the Korean, Formosan, and Karafuto problems were still pending. The Karafuto question, the penetration of Sakhalin by the Russians, was a critical one. Russian exploration parties were followed by the establishment of settlements in Sakhalin, all of which disconcerted the Japanese. On January 29, 1874, Ōkubo requested that he be commissioned to negotiate a boundary settlement with Russia.[145] However, his services were more urgently needed in Tōkyō, it was argued, and, consequently, Vice-Admiral Enomoto Takeaki was made minister plenipotentiary and envoy extraordinary to deal with the Russians. As the result of negotiations a treaty was signed with Russia in 1875 by which Japan ceded the southern part of Sakhalin as Russian territory while retaining the Kurile islands for herself.[146] With respect to the remaining two questions, the government commissioned Ōkubo and Ōkuma, along with Charles W. Le Gendre, an American adviser, to study the problems and submit their recommendations.[147]

The Formosa report of the Ōkubo-Ōkuma investigation appeared under the title of *Taiwan Banchi Shobun Yōraku,* or an outline for the disposition of the problem involving the aborigines' region of Formosa. In essence, the nine-point report called for a reprisal against the murderers of the Ryūkyūans, stated that Japan's chief aim was to chastise the tribes and pacify the people, and declared that if China protested Japan's move, the government should commit itself to the argument that the aborigines' region lay outside China's jurisdiction. This report was discussed by the government on February 6 and the recommendations were generally approved.[148]

The recommendations with respect to Korea were presented to the government during the same month. Ōkubo and Ōkuma advised sending a mission to Korea to express Japan's friendship for and desire to reëstablish intercourse with the Koreans. The mission was also to be instructed to observe the general temper of the country and to ascertain the extent of its military preparations. It further recommended that agents be sent across both the Russian and Chinese borders for investigatory purposes.[149]

Ōkubo would prepare for war while waging a peace offensive—a realistic, if unethical, policy.

Suppressing Rebellion

The opposition forces did not permit the newly constituted government to proceed without resistance. On January 17 the dissidents presented to the government a formal demand calling for the establishment of a popularly elected legislative assembly. The petition was signed by eight men, among whom were Gotō Shōjirō, Soejima Taneomi, Itagaki Taisuke, and Etō Shimpei, all members of the military faction that had quit the government during the previous year.[150] Through manipulation of the legislative assembly the dissidents hoped to check the power of those in control and prevent a monopolization of authority by a limited number of former retainers of a few influential *han*.[151]

Prior to the presentation of this petition, violence had erupted on January 14, 1874, when an attempt was made to assassinate Iwakura. The assailants, nine samurai from Kōchi prefecture, attacked Iwakura "in the hope that by his murder the counsels of the government might be shaken in regard to the expedition against Korea. . . ." [152] Shortly afterward rebellion broke out in Saga, led by Etō Shimpei, one of the signers of the aforementioned petition.

The genesis of the uprising is traceable to the middle of January, 1874, when two dominant samurai political parties in Saga prefecture began to accumulate and store arms, supplies, and money. The *Seikantō*, the party advocating the conquest of Korea, numbering about two thousand, was led by Etō Shimpei, a former member of the Tōkyō government. Its objective was to force the government to sanction the conquest of Korea. Etō and his compatriots were confident that their cause would be supported by Saigō and his military party members in Kagoshima, Kōchi, and other prefectures. The *Hōkentō*, approximately one thousand strong, with Shima Yoshitake as its leader, opposed industrialization, and desired to reëstablish the feudal order. Their many grievances against the government induced them to join in the cause with Etō's group. Over 90 per cent of the officials of the prefectural government were sympathetic with these elements, and plans were made to have officials sever telegraphic and mail communications with the outside world when the order was given. There was, however, a third group in Saga which remained loyal to the central government. Sensing trouble, one of its members was dispatched to Tōkyō to report the situation.

Ōkubo was informed of the rumblings in Saga on February 3, but apparently did not realize their significance; he and Saigō Tsugumichi conferred and planned to send only a few garrison troops to suppress any uprisings that might occur.[153] Not until February 7, when intelligence reached Tōkyō of insurgent attacks upon government garrisons in Fukuoka, Hiroshima, and Nagasaki prefectures, did Ōkubo begin to appreciate the serious predicament facing the country. As Minister of Home Affairs, he was responsible for the preservation of peace and order, and he petitioned to be allowed to go to the scene of the trouble to deal with it personally.[154] By the time more specific reports from Saga began to trickle in, Ōkubo had formulated a plan of action. He was in conference with Sanjō and other high state officials when news of Etō Shimpei's attack on the Onogumi bank in Saga reached the group. After reading the message, Ōkubo gave Sanjō a memorandum advising: (1) the Home Minister should be given full authority to go immediately to Saga to deal with the rebellion; (2) troops should be dispatched at once; and (3) Major-General Yamada Akiyoshi should be placed in command and dispatched to the scene in advance.[155]

There was some reluctance to allow Ōkubo to direct the suppression of the insurrection, but he eventually received dictatorial powers and proceeded southward. Iwakura, as was his wont, at first hesitated to give his sanction, saying that Kido had earlier requested a leave of absence and that to have two of the most important members of the government away from the capital would be inadvisable. Kido, however, at Iwakura's suggestion, offered to remain in the city while his colleague was away.[156] Accordingly, on February 10, Ōkubo was commissioned to utilize military forces to capture the rebels and punish those whose guilt was clear, and to use his discretion in the imposition of the death penalty. He might send troops against any other prefecture he suspected of aiding and abetting the insurgents. He was empowered to remove officials, including those given imperial appointment, who in his opinion had abused their position and authority, and to appoint others to serve in their stead. He was authorized to reward prefectural officials who had rendered extraordinary service on behalf of the central government. His commission further entitled him to issue orders to the prefectural authorities during the emergency. Finally, he had the prerogative of calling out garrison troops in coöperation with their respective commanders and mobilizing men from adjacent prefectures.[157]

The magnitude of the power entrusted to Ōkubo indicates his influence and stature within the inner circles of the Meiji government. No one but the strongest and the most competent would have been able to acquire both civil and military authority as he did, even in this period when such arbitrary monopolization of authority was not uncommon. Sanjō had confidence in him and from the outset left the entire matter of settling the Saga question in his hands.[158] But there were more cautious, and perhaps jealous, minds which reasoned that such unusual concentration of authority in the hands of one person was dangerous. On February 23 they arranged for a member of the imperial house, Akihito Shinnō, to assume the nominal position of commander-in-chief of the punitive forces, assisted by Lieutenant-General Yamagata Aritomo, a measure taken to counterbalance the excessive powers assumed by Ōkubo.[159]

The general military strategy of the government troops was to encircle and then converge upon the stronghold of the rebels. General Nozu Shizuo's troops were dispatched to Kumamoto, to the west of Saga; General Torio Koyata held the environs of Ōsaka; General Yamaguchi Naoyoshi's troops were sent to Nagasaki; and General Yamada Akiyoshi was ordered to advance toward the enemy along the Saikaidō.[160] Kagoshima, at the very southern tip of Kyūshū, was a crucial area not only strategically, but because it was a stronghold of Saigō and his military party adherents. Consequently, Shimazu Hisamitsu, who had joined the central government, was ordered to return to Kagoshima to prevent the spread of the insurrection into his prefecture, and to watch the movements of Saigō.[161]

With the necessary groundwork for the expedition laid, Ōkubo left Tōkyō on February 14. Arriving in Ōsaka on February 16, Ōkubo was informed that hostilities had begun in earnest, and he consulted immediately with General Nozu on matters pertaining to transport of troops.[162] He then left for Shimonoseki, reaching there on February 18. On February 19 he proceeded to Hakata in Fukuoka prefecture where he established his headquarters.[163] His diary notes for February 20 that he was "greatly relieved when early today the "Hokkai Maru" arrived and disembarked troops." [164] On February 23 he "went by horseback and *jinriksha* to the scene of battle and observed an artillery engagement." [165] Finally, on March 1, the government forces succeeded in crushing the rebellion, and the work of demobilizing the troops began.

The two rebel leaders, Etō Shimpei and Shima Yoshitake, remained at large; they had evaded capture. Presuming that their destination was Kagoshima, Ōkubo sent searchers there.[166] He had guessed correctly, because a week later word arrived that the two men had reached that city.[167] Their tracks were lost, however, after they boarded a ship for some unknown destination.[168] They were finally captured in Kōchi prefecture on April 2.[169] After being returned to Saga, the two insurrectionists, along with others of their party, were tried and executed.[170] Ōkubo's scorn for Etō after listening to his statement during the trial is shown in his diary: "Etō's statement was ambiguous. It was indeed ridiculous. By it one may judge his character. Among the rebels only Soejima Yoshitake, Asakura Danzō, and Yamanaka Ichirō acted like human beings." [171]

The life of the new imperial government was secured anew. Ōkubo, one of the prime architects of the Meiji government, used the inevitable prop, force, to keep his edifice from tumbling to the ground. By taking immediate action the new government was to win the respect of the people.[172] Interestingly, the American Whisky Rebellion of 1794, which Washington crushed on the advice of Hamilton, had a similar effect with respect to the new government of the United States. Both Ōkubo and Washington acted decisively at the proper moment to maintain their policy of building an industralized nation. The parallel is striking.

VII
Statesman and Diplomat

Ōkubo's career continued to be punctuated by one crisis after another. Soon after the suppression of the Saga rebellion he became involved in the complex Formosan question. Although he had argued strongly against the conquest of Korea in 1873, a year later he was to adhere to the very policy he had so recently resisted. When Saigō Tsugumichi, disobeying government orders, directed the embarkation of troops to Formosa, Ōkubo could do very little but give sanction to the move. He accepted the entire responsibility for the punitive expedition. When China protested, he went to Peking armed with plenary powers to effect a settlement of the situation. Kido, the staunch opponent of expansion, resigned in protest against the Ōkubo policy, but the resignation simply resulted in even greater power for Ōkubo. In answer to the increasing protests lodged against the government, and more specifically against his own power, Ōkubo was to issue regulations suppressing newspaper criticism derogatory to the central government. Ōkubo, however, recognized that without the aid of key figures such as Kido the government would not be secure; Chōshū's support was indispensable. He therefore agreed to the suggestion that an attempt be made to recall Kido and other liberals. At the Ōsaka conference initiated by Itō and Inoue, Kido was persuaded to rejoin the government, but only after political concessions were made to the liberals. Ōkubo conceded to their demands for the establishment of the *Genrōin,* or Senate, the *Daishinin,* or Supreme

Court, the assembly of the *Chihōkan Kaigi*, or Conference of the Prefectural Governors, and the reorganization of the various administrative departments of the government. Ōkubo continued his crusade for industrial development through increased taxation. The peasants, who bore the brunt of taxation, expressed their dissatisfaction through revolts that forced Ōkubo to reduce the land tax. Then in 1877, the year of Kido's death, he was confronted with the rebellion of samurai in Satsuma, feudalism's final organized attempt to preserve itself. The imperial forces crushed the insurrection in which Saigō, the rebel leader, lost his life. By the end of 1877 Ōkubo was the only remaining member of the triad of the Restoration. A few months later Ōkubo joined the other two in death.

Growing Formosan Tension

The year 1874 found Ōkubo constantly preoccupied with the official duties of statesman, soldier, and diplomat. After dealing with the rebellion in Saga, he returned to Tōkyō on April 24, 1874, to be met by a solemn welcoming party who had some weighty problems to discuss with the strong man of the government. "Arriving in Tōkyō by train," he noted in his diary for that day, "I was greeted at the station by Katsu, Itō, Tokudaiji, Andō, Kuroda, and Ishūin." [1] According to Hayashi Tadashi, Itō informed Ōkubo that many government leaders believed that war with China was now almost inevitable. Being no alarmist, Ōkubo calmly expressed his opinion that there was probably some means by which the problem could be settled.[2] Indeed, as he had predicted, the Formosan problem was resolved eventually through diplomacy, but only after Japan sent a punitive expedition to the island. Had China been militarily prepared to resist Japan more vigorously, the date of the Sino-Japanese war would have been advanced by twenty years from 1894, when it actually broke out, to 1874.

In December, 1871, fifty-four Ryūkyū islanders were accidentally driven ashore on Formosa near the territory occupied by the primitive Botan race and murdered. The Japanese then dispatched an expeditionary force to the southeastern coast of Formosa. The barbarism of these tribesmen in Formosa was well known to the mariners of nearly every civilized nation.[3] In March, 1867, the entire crew of the American bark "Rover," except for a single Chinese sailor who escaped, was killed after being shipwrecked on the southern coast of the island.[4] In April of that year the United States Consul at Amoy, General Charles W. Le Gendre, tried to communicate with the chiefs of the tribes of this region to obtain pledges of security for the future, but in this he was unsuccessful. The Chinese officials on the western coast of Formosa disclaimed any direct authority over the people to the east and declared their inability to interfere. Peking, however, "expressed a disposition to inflict chastisement, in consequence of the assumption of the United States' Minister that China was responsible for the deeds of all the Formosans." [5] In the fall of the same year Le Gendre made a second visit to the island, in company with a sizeable Chinese force.[6] This time he gained a promise from the leaders of the confederated southern tribes to respect the lives and property of all Americans and Europeans who should thereafter be wrecked on the coast of Formosa.[7] The pledge was kept for several years, but depredations began to be practiced by those outside the confederation and by such tribes as the Botan, who withdrew from the league. Unable to control these savages, the Chinese renounced responsibility for the outrages, and it was not until the Japanese acted in behalf of the Ryūkyūans that the Chinese were forced to confront the situation.[8]

The Japanese government undertook the protection of the Ryūkyūans on the grounds that they were tributary vassals of Japan. Historians point out that, in 1165, Minamoto no Tametomo, a half brother of Minamoto Yoritomo, married a native Ryūkyū princess, and that their male issue later became a ruler of the islands. In 1372 civil disturbances in the islands resulted in the withdrawal of China's claim over the islands. Finally, in 1609, Shimazu Iehisa of Satsuma subdued the islands and established a local government, took census, surveyed lands, passed laws, and collected taxes annually thereafter.[9]

Western writers have substantiated one of the justifications of Japanese interest in the islands by noting that Ryūkyū was peopled by the same race as Japan and that their habits and characteristics are similar to those of the Japanese. The language, except for idioms, is the same.[10] Dr. Bettelheim, who lived for some years in Ryūkyū in the mid-nineteenth century, believed that it was "to all ends and purposes, an integral part of Japan." He gave the following reasons for his conclusion: (1) a Japanese garrison was quartered in Naha; (2) the trade of Ryūkyū was entirely with Japan; (3) the Japanese were present in numbers in Ryūkyū, intermarrying with the natives and owning and cultivating lands;

(4) Ryūkyū officials were controlled by Japanese agents; and (5) "the language, dress, customs, virtues, and vices of Lew Chew correspond to those of Japan, thus establishing a *prima facie* relationship." [11]

The Chinese, however, also claimed the Ryūkyū islands as their own. As Hoshien Tchen notes:

> The dependence of the islands of Ryūkyū *vis-à-vis* China goes back a very long time in the past. It has been formally established that these islands began to pay tribute to China as early as the first year of the reign of Emperor Hung Wu of the Ming dynasty, that is, in 1327 A.D. At the time of the succession of the Ch'ing dynasty, Prince Chang-Tche of Ryūkyū came to Peking in order to offer his congratulations and homage to the representative of the new dynasty and to exchange the seal of the Ming dynasty for that of the new one. After Emperor K'ang Hsi conferred the title of king upon the prince, the annual tribute was to be paid every two years at the imperial court in Peking. And since that time the various kings who succeeded to the Ryūkyū throne have all received their investiture from the emperor of China, considered themselves as his vassals, and paid homage to him. Ryūkyū was one of the most devoted among the vassal countries of China, and one can find proof of it in the title *empire paternel*, a purely Oriental expression, which Ryūkyū was pleased to give to its suzerain.[12]

The Chinese scholar also points out that the Ryūkyū islands were not a part of Japan, but that Japan merely claimed to have the right of protectorate over them.[13] He contends that further evidence of Ryūkyū's recognition of its vassalage to China was presented in 1875 and 1876 when the king and the functionaries of the islands protested Japan's installation of a governor and the stationing of military guards there, its insistence that the king renounce his investiture by, and the payment of tribute to, the Chinese government, and the substitution of the Japanese calendar for the Chinese calendar.[14]

The Ryūkyūans themselves claim to have descended from a divine source whose first ruler was called Offspring of Heaven. The ruler's descendants administered Ryūkyū for 17,802 years when they were succeeded, about A.D. 1200, by a member of a branch of the then-ruling family of Japan.[15] Klaproth's account of the origin of the Ryūkyūans coincides with this. He states further that the race of kings reigning in Ryūkyū is related to the imperial family of Japan, that both China and Japan claim sovereignty, and that the Ryūkyūans pay tribute to both.[16]

The Ryūkyū natives told Commodore Perry that they were "outer dependencies of China" and had "intercourse with a friendly and near nation," that is, Japan.[17]

Whatever the technical relationship between Ryūkyū and its continental and island neighbors, when the Ryūkyū authorities were appealed to by their countrymen to deal with the atrocities involving the Formosans, they turned to Satsuma for succor. But by this time the jurisdiction over Satsuma had been transferred from the Shimazu to the central government, and what was once Satsuma *han* was now merely one of the prefectures of the imperial government, namely, Kagoshima prefecture. Having no power to deal with the situation, the officials in Kagoshima suggested that a commission be sent directly from Ryūkyū to Tōkyō to consider this subject as well as the entire matter of the relationship between the tributary kingdom and the newly established Meiji government. Consequently, a deputation arrived in Tōkyō in the summer of 1872, and the Japanese government agreed to afford full protection to the inhabitants of Ryūkyū and its dependencies. The territory was to be considered a part of the Japanese empire and its ruler to relinquish his sovereign title and become a member of the Japanese nobility.[18]

The Japanese government took immediate action with respect to the Formosan atrocities. Since the western part of Formosa was occupied by the Chinese, the Japanese believed that China would also assume responsibility for maintaining order on the east coast, the area of the aborigines. Japan's protests, however, elicited from China nothing more than the declaration that it could neither punish the tribes outside its own jurisdiction for past crimes nor take steps to prevent them in the future.[19]

American Advice and Counsel

About this time two American officials assigned to posts in the Far East aided and abetted the expansionist cause in Japan by advising the Japanese government to adopt a positive policy toward Formosa. The Saigō-Soejima faction, which controlled the government in the absence of Iwakura, Kido, and Ōkubo, needed no coaxing to accept such a policy. The first of the American officials was Charles E. De Long, the United States minister to Tōkyō (1869-1873). Meeting with Foreign Minister Soejima on October 25, 1872, De Long secretly advised Japan to occupy Formosa, stressing the ideal nature of its climate and the fertility of its soil on which rice, sugar, and yams were being produced in abundance. He also pointed out the existence of rich mineral resources and potential ports and the fact that other countries had their attention focused upon the island. He contended that even if China were to claim jurisdiction over Formosa, the island would be subject to possession by an occupier if the natives themselves ignored Chinese authority. De Long then suggested that Japan send a punitive expedition there to secure a pledge from natives against commiting outrages upon Japanese and Ryūkyūans.[20] Soejima thereupon declared that Formosa was indeed attractive to Japan and asked for De Long's opinion as to Japan's occupying the island.[21] The American diplomat stated that although the United States itself was opposed to taking possession of territory belonging to another country, it nevertheless was partial to its friends who desired to occupy such territory for the purpose of expansion. He offered to use his good offices to obtain, for the Japanese, maps of the Formosan coast, in possession of American naval officers, through the American minister to Peking, Frederick F. Low.[22] Then De Long introduced to Soejima the one man who was undoubtedly more familiar with the details of eastern Formosa than any other foreigner, General Charles W. Le Gendre.

As for the Japanese leaders, they had had aggressive intentions toward China and Formosa for some time. The Chinese historian, Wang Yün-shêng, states objectively that at first Japan was sincere when it sought to establish friendly relations with China. He argues, however, that with the intensification of competition among the Occidental powers in the Far East, the Japanese leaders became apprehensive over their country's safety. Japan's attitude toward China changed when it became apparent that the latter had no farsighted national policy and its internal affairs were disorganized because of the Manchu court's inability to deal effectively with foreign pressures. Japan decided to take advantage of the confused situation to invade Chinese territory. Japan desired, by the exercise of dominant authority in the East, to change the prevailing Western idea that Japan was a weak nation, and in particular to change England's and France's currently contemptuous attitude toward the Japanese.

In support of his thesis, Wang quotes a statement made by Shimazu Nariakira (1810-1858), the able Satsuma *daimyō* and leader of Japanese thought in his day. Nariakira's views are especially germane because they represented the general Satsuma attitude toward foreign affairs in the mid-nineteenth century, and presumably were shared by other Satsuma leaders, including Ōkubo, who monopolized the power in the new Meiji government. Wang quotes Nariakira as saying:

> It was inconceivable that China would deteriorate to such a degree. With its vast territory and population, there could not have been a dearth of loyal and devoted patriots. Yet since the Opium War its administration has been in disorder and ineffective. Internally, it has been plagued by rebellion while England and France have invaded it from without. . . . Japan lies to the east of China, and is in such a position as to necessitate immediate steps to prepare against meeting the same fate as that which has befallen the Chinese; as soon as England achieves its design in China, it will most certainly direct its military might eastward. If we take the initiative, we can dominate; if we do not, we will be dominated. We must prepare defenses with this thought in mind. Considering the present situation, it behooves us first to raise an army, seize a part of China's territory, and establish a base on the Asiatic mainland. We must strengthen Japan without delay and display our military power abroad. This would make it impossible for England and France to interfere in our affairs despite their strength.
>
> Among the coastal regions of China, the one we consider most important from the standpoint of Japanese defense is Foochow. Clearly, its acquisition would greatly facilitate our national defense. . . . We do not advocate the seizure of Foochow with the intention of observing the liquidation of China, but rather to see China awaken and reorganize itself in order that together we might defend ourselves against England and France. But China has always . . . viewed Japan as a tributary state and hence it may be fallacious to believe that coöperation with it for this purpose is possible. Consequently, we must first undertake defensive preparations against foreign encroachment. . . . The initial requirement is the acquisition of both Taiwan and Foochow. . . . Troops from Satsuma and Ōsumi would suffice to seize these two regions, but without warships it is impossible to carry on warfare at sea. It is therefore expedient to provide for military preparations as a means to meeting the present emergency.

This, in essence, was the clarion call for the *fukoku kyōhei* policy which Ōkubo and the Meiji government were now so eager to implement. Fear of foreign aggression motivated Japan to follow a foreign policy that would operate to the detriment of a weakened China. Wang states that the rationale may have been tenable from the Japanese standpoint, but morality is inflexible; there are eternal verities that govern man's actions.

From the standpoint of international morality the rationale of the Japanese cannot be defended.[23]

Le Gendre, the second American destined to influence Japanese foreign policy vis-à-vis Formosa, met with Soejima on October 26, 1872, when he passed through Japan on his way home from Amoy to the United States.[24] He delayed his departure from Japan in order to supply Tōkyō authorities with detailed intelligence from Formosa and to assure the Japanese that they should have no anxiety about Chinese intervention in Taiwan because Peking had neither the desire nor the means of applying force. He was also of the opinion that Formosa could easily be taken with a force of two thousand soldiers.[25] The Saigō faction, already thinking in terms of an expedition, was encouraged by such views, and Le Gendre was immediately appointed an adviser to the Ministry of Foreign Affairs with an annual salary of twelve thousand *yen*.[26] He was, in addition, promised a position as military adviser if an army of subjugation were sent to the island and the governorship of Formosa if Japan acquired the territory.[27]

What was the reaction of the United States government to this matter? Minister De Long, who aided the Japanese in acquiring the services of Le Gendre, was taken to task by his superior, Hamilton Fish, for his unorthodox action.[28] The policy of the United States was to encourage peace in the Orient, as well as to encourage Japan's growth as a modern nation. De Long, however, obsessed with his mission to direct the course of Japan's development, urged its leaders to undertake a punitive campaign, believing that such a move would create a breach between a progressive Japan and a reactionary China, as well as serve as a safety valve to prevent an internal explosion in the form of rebellion that would prove injurious to the new government.[29] But his good intentions were not appreciated by the United States, as they ran counter to the general Far Eastern policy, and as a result he was replaced by John A. Bingham. Le Gendre, however, remained in the employ of the Japanese government, became Ōkubo's adviser on foreign affairs, and contributed his views in the formulation of the Ōkubo-Ōkuma report on Formosa.

The Formosan problem was the outstanding foreign issue after 1872. Prompted by the foreign advisers, Foreign Minister Soejima, accompanied by Le Gendre, went to Peking in the spring of 1873 and obtained a declaration from the Chinese that they were not responsible for the acts of the barbarous tribesmen, and that Peking acquiesced in the Japanese plan to dispatch a mission to Formosa to regulate the affair independently. Soejima, however, neglected to get this avowal in writing, and without documentary evidence the Japanese had great difficulty inducing the Chinese to abide by these initial agreements.[30]

Why did the Chinese commit the diplomatic faux pas of declaring nonresponsibility for the acts of the savages on an island that China occupied, and of consenting to Japan's demands to dispatch troops to the island? The mistake is partly attributable to China's lack of knowledge of international law as practiced in the West; the Chinese diplomats did not have the services of any Western adviser. The Japanese approach, however, was subtle, advised as they were by a former United States consul to Amoy who knew international law and, in addition, understood the idiosyncrasies of the Chinese.

The Japanese explanation to the contrary, Wang, for one, does not make any allusions to any concessions to the Soejima embassy. When Soejima sent Yanagibara to the Tsungli Yamen to discuss the question of chastising the savages with Mao Ch'ang-hsi and Tung Hsun, Mao is reported to have stated:

> We have heard that the savages on Formosa murdered some Ryūkyūans, but we have yet received no intelligence that they killed any Japanese subjects. Both Ryūkyū and Formosa belong to us. When natives within our territories injure each other, the right of arbitrating the wrong devolves upon us. Moreover, we have means of rendering relief to the Ryūkyūans. Consequently, it is not for your country to interfere in the matter.

Yanagibara nevertheless pressed the point that Ryūkyū, the Chinese thesis notwithstanding, lay within the sphere of Japanese influence and as a result the Japanese had more than a passing interest in the question. Yanagibara then asked: "Why did not China, acknowledging the ability to tender justice, chastise the Formosans?" Whereupon the Chinese official retorted that China's temporizing was the result of its effort to investigate the incident thoroughly. He went on to state that simply because a group of people did not come under the direct jurisdiction of a country was no justification for declaring that such a people did not therefore belong to that country. He cited the example of the Ainu in Japan and the American Indians in the United States who, he argued, were universally known to be beyond the direct influence of the governments of Japan and the United States respectively.[31]

While the Soejima embassy was thus wrangling with the Chinese authorities in Peking, a second, but less serious, outrage against shipwrecked Japanese fishermen was reported; and when Soejima returned to Tōkyō the government was more than ever determined to launch the expedition to Formosa.[32] But with the return of the Iwakura mission from abroad and the creation of the Ōkubo government, the Formosan question was relegated to the background.[33]

Continuing Preparations

However, the preparations for a punitive expedition to Formosa had not entirely ceased. They were carried on secretly partly for reasons of domestic policy, but mainly for fear of interference by the representatives of foreign goverments.[34] As early as February 15, 1874, Saigō Tsugumichi was ordered to make a thorough investigation preparatory to the settlement of the pending problem.[35] On April 4, in accordance with his recommendation, the government decided to organize a military force for the expedition with headquarters in the *Dajōkan Seiin* and a branch office at Nagasaki. A Board of Formosan Affairs was established, headed by Ōkuma Shigenobu, who was appointed chief commissioner on April 4, with Saigō Tsugumichi serving as commissioner and commander of the forces.[36] The latter was only twenty-eight years of age at the time. When he expressed his desire to direct military operations in Formosa, Ōkubo hesitated at first to recommend the youthful Tsugumichi's appointment to such a responsible position. He finally did so, however, in deference to Tsugumichi's brother, Saigō Takamori.[37]

The military advisers to the Japanese government were mostly Americans, probably in deference to Le Gendre, an adviser-in-chief on the Board of Formosan Affairs, and also because of the Americans' sympathetic interest in the expedition itself. Lieutenant Commander Douglas Cassel of the U. S. Navy was offered the rank of commodore in the Japanese service, and Lieutenant James R. Wasson, formerly of the U. S. Army Engineers, was commissioned a colonel in the Japanese army.[38]

On the diplomatic front, the Japanese government appointed Yanagibara Sakimitsu as minister to China with orders to leave for Peking on May 19, after the expedition was put underway, to explain Japan's reasons for having dispatched a punitive force to Formosa.[39] In the meantime, numerous transports were engaged to carry the men, several of the largest chartered from foreigners. The "Yorkshire" was secured from the British and the "New York" from the American Pacific Mail Steamship Company.[40]

Mounting Criticisms

When the first ship of the expedition left Tōkyō in mid-April, rumors were circulating among the foreigners in Yokohama about the purpose of the movement. The British viewed it with concern. When, on April 9, Saigō Tsugumichi left Tōkyō with five battleships, Sir Harry Parkes immediately sent the Japanese government a note of inquiry concerning the intent of the fleet headed for Formosa.[41] The following day Parkes and Terajima, the Foreign Minister in the "Ōkubo government," met to discuss the matter. Parkes asked Terajima if China was aware that Japan was beginning a punitive campaign, to which the latter replied that China had not been so informed but that the previous year China had informed Soejima that the aborigines' region in Formosa lay outside the range of Chinese authority and influence.[42] Parkes, however, was suspicious of the Japanese, as indicated in a letter addressed to Sir D. Brooke Robertson and written on April 14. It is quoted in some detail because his analysis of the Japanese and the Formosan situation is admirably made:

> The Japanese have committed the error of believing all that they have been told about themselves and increasing this by their own imagination, and the result is that their own little island is too small to hold them. In this matter they have been led away by their own conceit, and by advice which fitted in exactly with that conceit, and which has been chiefly supplied by that man Le Gendre. . . . He accompanies the expedition as Adviser-in-Chief—for they are too jealous to give him command. . . . The entire possession of Formosa is what is aimed at, but it appears to me that they are calculating without their host if they think that China will brook this. . . . It is an opportunity for Li Hung-Chang and for the ships that the Chinese have been launching at their various arsenals! The Japanese means for war, away from their own country, are very limited.
>
> . . . I suppose the Japanese expedition will land . . . before the Chinese will have had time to rub their eyes. . . . The troops are perhaps 3,000, but they are sending a great number of artificers with framework huts, and in particular a strong corps of 220 sap-

> pers . . . who are to throw up a fort at Shaliaou or Lingkaou, where they propose to land. . . . They claim the right to do all this on the ground that the unsettled parts of Formosa do not belong to China, and because the Chinese disdained responsibility for the acts of the savages. . . . They look forward . . . to acquiring a great sugar colony—a second Cuba, and to command the China coast and the China sea.[43]

Parkes actively protested to the Japanese.[44] However, his concern about Sino-Japanese relations was motivated by more than a desire for justice. The British, it must be remembered, had a vested interest in China, where their trading activities reaped them rich dividends, British trade in China amounting to about two hundred and fifty million dollars at this time. They opposed war over Formosa because it would disrupt their economic endeavors in the Far East. They certainly would have protested less vigorously, if at all, had Japan planned a campaign in Korea; it would have served as a diversionary measure against Russia, which was a real threat to England.

While the British were displaying their anxiety over the movement of the Japanese fleet, the Americans remained silent. Then, on April 18, their minister to Tōkyō (1873-1885), John Bingham, who had previous knowledge of the project and the participation of the Americans in the expedition, protested against the employment by the Japanese government "of any ship or any citizen of the United States in a military or naval expedition hostile to the government or authority of China." [45] The following day Bingham sent another letter protesting the use of any American in Japanese government service unless Japan first obtained the written consent of China to the expedition.[46] However, the Japanese government stood firm. Even the resignation of Kido on the same day in protest over the Formosan campaign failed to prevent the government from carrying out its plan. Yet the remonstrances of the various foreign representatives in Tōkyō, especially those of the United States and Great Britain, were to cause a change in Japan's attitude; she ordered the postponement of the departure of the ships that were assembling at Nagasaki. When asked the reason for this delay, the Japanese government indicated that it was halting the expedition to allow time to inform the Chinese of its plans.[47]

It is apparent from Kido's resignation that the pressure from the foreign governments was not the only factor that caused the Japanese government to alter its attitude. There was an influential element among the leadership which opposed risking a possible war with China. Ironically, Kido had earlier sustained the government's Formosan policy as expressed in the Ōkubo-Ōkuma report of February 6.[48] It is possible that Kido may have agreed to the general principle of the policy, but could not force himself to agree to its implementation.[49]

Later he became a vigorous opponent of the punitive campaign. Like Ōkubo in his debates with Saigō over the Korean issue, Kido argued that a policy based upon expansion and the control of the Far East was premature, contending that Japan should place priority upon internal development. He cautioned that Japan's economy would be strained to a point of danger in financing a military operation in Formosa, and pointed out that the government had no assurance of a quick victory, a premise upon which it had apparently based its decision regarding Formosa. He was certain that Japan would be unable to carry out a protracted war, and pessimistically prophesied that in either victory or defeat such an adventure would bankrupt Japan.[50] His words, like those of the prophet crying in the wilderness, went largely unheeded. It was in these circumstances that Kido resigned on April 18, stating that his decision was not based upon any grievances engendered by the failure to have his views blindly accepted, but rather upon his reluctance to echo a government policy with which he was in disagreement.[51] Kido was undoubtedly convinced that a move southward would prove detrimental to Japan, but there were other considerations as well. The inherent *han* jealousies among the Meiji leaders had not abated, and the fact that the Formosa project was essentially Satsuma-inspired was distasteful to a Chōshū man. Samurai from the various *han* who comprised the government still vied with each other. Some were bound to be hurt. In the case of Kido, his illness, an emotional condition, made him hypersensitive to a situation which obviously would prove advantageous to the Kagoshima clique.[52]

Changing Conviction

Kido's stand was logical and consistent when compared with Ōkubo's. In less than a year the latter had swung around 180 degrees from an anti-expansionist to a proimperialist program. Why did he wait for more than two years after the Formosan incident before calling for its positive settlement? The consensus is that circumstances compelled him to reconsider his original policy of domestic development and noninvolvement abroad. Dissatisfaction with government policy had not abated among the various elements of the country. Saigō Takamori was sulking in Kagoshima while the samurai discontent continued to smolder in the provinces despite the suppression of the Saga rebellion. Their chief grievance was that they received the least benefit from the new government although they had contributed the most to the achievement of the Restoration.[53] In view of this situation Ōkubo was forced to advocate a diversionary campaign to prevent further uprisings within the country. Assured by Le Gendre, he was relatively certain of the success of such a move in Formosa.[54] Furthermore, Ōkubo, being a product of Satsuma, which had traditionally taken a deep interest in the southern region, was especially attracted to Formosa. He realized, moreover, that if the status of the Ryūkyū islands was to be clarified definitely the Formosan problem needed immediate solution. His extreme interest in the southern region has led historians to consider Ōkubo as the pioneer advocate of Japan's southward expansion in the modern era. In this connection, it is interesting to note that he was responsible not only for the clarification of the status of the Ryūkyūs, but also for the acquisition of the Ogasawara islands.[55]

Ōkubo had a vital part in the formation of the Formosan policy. While still in Kyūshū, after the suppression of the Saga revolt, he had received a visit from Saigō Tsugumichi on April 15, six days after the latter had reached Nagasaki with his fleet. The two men discussed the Formosan plans and the political situation in the capital.[56] Saigō had also arranged to contact his brother, Takamori, who gladly consented to contribute a force of approximately three hundred men, referred to as the Chōshūtai, which was ultimately to win plaudits for its bravery on Formosa.[57]

Other events were occurring in Tōkyō which affected the Formosan expedition. On April 19, the day after the Tōkyō government received the American note of protest, it dispatched a telegram to Nagasaki ordering the fleet to remain at anchor. The same day a government official bearing Sanjō's detailed instructions to Ōkuma set out for Nagasaki. For almost a week, until April 25 when the messenger arrived, Ōkuma and Saigō had not been aware of the precise reason for the government's latest order. Meanwhile they had wired to Tōkyō that "the martial spirit among the men is high. It should not be repressed." [58] Hirai's message, however, explained the basis for the decision; it also ordered Ōkuma back to Tōkyō and Saigō to hold the expeditionary forces at Nagasaki until further notice.[59] The order infuriated Saigō, and he was determined to ignore it. Ōkuma on April 26 endeavored to impress upon him the necessity of awaiting instructions before departing for Formosa, but Saigō was not to be persuaded, stating defiantly that "at this late date I would not even obey the orders of the *Dajōdaijin* even if he were to come here personally." [60]

That evening Saigō ordered the fleet to take on supplies, and the following day 270 soldiers were hastened aboard the "Yūkō Maru" which then set its course and sailed for Amoy. Aboard the overloaded vessel were the two American military advisers, Lieutenant Commander Cassel and Colonel Wasson, and Japanese Consul Fukushima Kunari. Saigō, with the aid of Le Gendre, tried to have the "New York" weigh anchor, but its captain, instructed by the American consul in Nagasaki to remain in port, would not comply. The "New York" and the British vessel "Yorkshire" were then detached from the expedition.[61]

Receiving Extraordinary Authority

On April 27, Ōkubo petitioned the proper authorities for permission to proceed as soon as possible to Nagasaki with powers to make decisions as to the future of the expedition.[62] This the council sanctioned the following day.[63] But when Saigō was informed of the telegraphic message telling of Ōkubo's mission, he determined to put the expedition to sea before his arrival. On May 2 he ordered four vessels—the "Nisshin," "Mōshun," "Meikō," and "Sambō"—under the command of Tani Kanjo and Akamatsu Norinaga, to head for Sharyō (Shaliaou) in Formosa. Saigō himself remained behind to await Ōkubo's arrival.[64]

On April 29, five days after his return to Tōkyō after the Saga rebellion, Ōkubo once more directed his course southward, this time for Nagasaki.[65] As on the mission to Saga, he was on this occasion empowered with both civil and military authority.[66] Arriving in the port city on the evening of May 3, he was invited to remain overnight in the home of the sea captain whose ship had borne him there. That night Saigō paid a call.[67] In the party was Major General Nozu Shizuo, allegedly inebriated, who boisterously inquired if vacillation was to be the watchword of the government in the Formosan matter. Ōkubo said sharply, "What did you say?" [68] Taken aback, Nozu remained speechless. There is no doubt that Ōkubo, a civil functionary, commanded considerable respect even from his military colleagues.

Making a Crucial Decision

Confronted with a virtual fait accompli with the major portion of the expedition already headed for its destination, Ōkubo decided to permit the expedition to proceed, and by so doing sanctioned Saigō's arbitrary action which amounted to insubordination. Ōkubo, Saigō, and Ōkuma then proceeded to formulate what was essentially a new Formosan policy. To meet the demands of the United States and England, ships and citizens of the United States were to be detached from the expedition immediately and those of the British were to be detached if war between Japan and China became imminent. The policy, however, did not indicate any departure from Japan's original plan to prosecute its punitive campaign; Saigō was to go directly to Formosa. It did reflect a change in attitude toward China inasmuch as it called for an attempt to reach an understanding with that country over the Formosan issue.[69] On May 4, the three principals at Nagasaki signed an agreement (1) to wire ahead and have Cassel and Wasson (who had left with the first contingent of troops) await the arrival of Saigō; (2) to discharge the two Americans and return them to Japan upon Saigō's arrival; (3) to have Le Gendre return to Tōkyō at the earliest time; (4) to maintain an adequate defense force on Formosa upon the completion of the punitive campaign—until the Formosans agreed to desist from perpetrating outrages and to conform to Japan's will; and (5) to establish relations with China in regard to the settlement of the Formosan question, and, if an incident became imminent, to order the release of English and other foreign employees and the return of foreign ships to Japan.[70]

As far as General Le Gendre was concerned, he abandoned his plan to accompany the mission and, after advising Saigō in detail on landing procedures, conditions in the region of the aborgines, and the geography of the island, returned to Tōkyō to assist in counteracting the hostility of certain foreign diplomatic agents.[71] Le Gendre was critical of the Japanese government for making concessions to the foreign representatives. He contended that the United States Minister John Bingham was fully aware of the employment of the Americans. China, too, he argued, had tacitly agreed to the punitive expedition by its declaration of nonresponsibility regarding Formosa. Japan unwisely prepared for the venture openly, and therefore, when the movement became too obvious and protests were made by the various foreign representatives, the United States could no longer maintain its silence. He implied that the ships should have sailed under a veil of secrecy for Formosa from some port other than Nagasaki.[72]

Ōkubo, Saigō, and Ōkuma at the same meeting also decided (1) to notify Tōkyō by telegraph to dispatch Minister Yanagibara to China immediately; (2) to have Saigō proceed immediately to Sharyō with ships rented or purchased; (3) to have Ōkuma remain in Nagasaki for consultation with Yanagibara upon the latter's arrival; (4) to have Ōkubo leave for Tōkyō the next day (May 5) to report the nature of the decisions arrived at in Nagasaki; and (5) to assign Ōkubo all responsibility for the consequences of these decisions.[73] Ōkubo reëmphasized his determination to bear the responsibility for his actions in a letter forwarded to Sanjō, the *Dajōdaijin*.[74]

In accordance with the agreement concluded at Nagasaki, Ōkubo, accompanied by Le Gendre and an interpreter, left for Tōkyō on May 6.[75] Ōkuma, having the responsibility of replacing the detached American and British ships of the expedition, succeeded in purchasing two foreign vessels—coincidentally an American and an English ship—which happened to arrive in port on May 9. Hastily renaming them "Sharyō Maru" and "Takasa Maru," respectively, Ōkuma ordered them loaded with weapons and stores. It was aboard the flagship "Sharyō Maru" that Saigō sailed for Formosa on May 17.[76]

Rumblings in China

On the diplomatic front, China, after learning of the departure of the Japanese vessels from Nagasaki, on May 11 dispatched a note to the Japanese government signed by Prince Kung and nine other commissioners in the Tsungli Yamen. It reminded Japan that Soejima in his talks with the Chinese government the previous year had made no mention of Japan's intention to utilize troops in dealing with the Formosan problem.[77] The Japanese did not reply officially to this note. They simply informed the Chinese that Minister Yanagibara would be in Peking presently to handle the situation.[78] The Chinese note itself was ill-advised inasmuch as it admitted that China's administrative authority did not extend to the aborigines' region, although China considered it a part of her territory. The Japanese were quick to grasp the admission and use it as a rationale for the invasion.[79] The Chinese government thereupon ordered Shen Pao-chen, director general of ship administration, to prepare for the defense of Formosa. His plan, drawn up together with Li Hu-nien, the Fukien viceroy, recommended to Peking (1) the establishment of communication with the foreign representatives to gain an expression of views regarding the Japanese action and therewith to exert pressure upon the Japanese for the recall of their troops; (2) the storage of military supplies—ships, torpedoes, cannons, and ammunition; (3) the recruitment of personnel; and (4) the establishment of communication between Foochow and Amoy and Formosa.[80] Pan Yu was sent to Taiwan to assist Shen Pao-chen in its defense.[81]

Before long the Japanese on Formosa were to learn of China's interest in their activities. On May 22, the day on which Saigō reached Formosa, two Chinese ships of war arrived with an agent bearing a letter from the Fukien viceroy affirming that his government claimed authority over the territory in question and expressing the wish that Saigō withdraw his troops after they had established order and security. Saigō, however, indicated that he would proceed with his task as a military officer and leave matters of diplomacy to those within whose province they lay.[82] Later, on June 22, Pan Yu arrived to negotiate directly with Saigō in an attempt to have the troops evacuated. As a means of proving that the tribesmen had had tributary relations with China, the Chinese envoy displayed Mexican silver dollars that were supposedly used as tribute. He also had written promises from the aborigines that future outrages would not be perpetrated.[83] Saigō again refused to negotiate.[84]

Earlier, on May 19, the Japanese government had sent Yanagibara as minister to China to assure the Tsungli Yamen that Japan's purpose in the present action in Formosa was to chastise the offenders and restore order.[85] In Shanghai he had a meeting with Pan Yu to discuss matters pertaining to the punishment of the murderers of the Ryūkyūans, the execution of all those who resisted the Japanese army, and a pledge from the aborigines to desist from committing further atrocities. The Chinese official agreed to satisfy the Japanese with respect to these terms, ultimately getting a pledge from the savages as called for.[86] But when informed that the Chinese intended to enter into direct negotiations with Saigō, Yanagibara told the Chinese officials that Saigō had no authority to adjust problems arising between the two countries. Pan Yu nevertheless proceeded with his plans.[87] Subsequently, upon returning from his unsuccessful mission to Formosa, he informed the Japanese minister that Saigō had acceded to the evacuation of his troops and requested Yanagibara to make arrangements for the move. Yanagibara, however, through communication with Saigō on Formosa, had been kept informed of the details of his contacts with the Chinese. The minister realized that Pan Yu was prevaricating and decided he could no longer deal with him. The Japanese minister therefore left Shanghai on July 31 to negotiate directly with the Tsungli Yamen.[88] En route, in Tientsin, he conferred with Li Hung-chang, the Chihli viceroy. Their conversation has been quoted verbatim by both Chinese and Japanese historians because it reveals the points of difference existing between the contending parties at this juncture.[89]

Li could not understand Japan's use of ground forces in Formosa. He conceded that a ship of war could lawfully place men ashore to punish pirates committing violence upon its personnel. He implied, however, that the use of troops was tantamount to the invasion of Chinese territory. Yanagibara argued that this was necessitated by China's apparent indifference toward the rendering of justice; the perpetrators of the murders had not been punished.[90] Li countered by stating that no action was required because the Ryūkyūans were not Japanese, whereupon Yanagibara reminded him that Japan was acting upon the specific request of the Ryūkyū king.[91] With no small degree of logic and sarcasm Li accused Japan of acting in bad faith, of invading Chinese territory while at the same time dispatching an envoy intoning words of peace. "Without being two separate entities," Li queried, "could Japan in this wise engage in military activities on the one hand while enunciating concord on the other?" [92]

A Chinese historian has aptly summarized the situation by noting that the Japanese action constituted a state of hostilities without the declaration of war.[93] This is a tenable argument if it is true that China exercised indisputable jurisdiction over the region of the aborigines on Formosa. Unfortunately for China, the clouded nature of the title to this area contributed to the creation of Sino-Japanese differences. Arriving in Peking, Yanagibara was confronted with the Tsungli Yamen's demand that Japanese troops be evacuated from Formosa.[94]

Opposition at Home

In Tōkyō, there was strong reaction to Ōkubo's arbitrary decision in the Formosan matter. After his return from Nagasaki on May 15, he unsuccessfully attempted to placate the critics among his colleagues, those who were fearful of repercussions from abroad, by apologizing for his action. Sensing his responsibility as a key member of the government, Iwakura accepted the blame for the reversal of the government's decision to halt the expedition temporarily and handed in his resignation.[95] Shimazu Hisamitsu, the *Sadaijin*, advised against accepting the resignation, stating that such a step ought to be considered only if and when a Formosan settlement terminated in failure.[96]

It was at about this time also that, as a consequence of a clash of views between progressive Ōkubo and conservative Hisamitsu, a political crisis occurred. Hisamitsu's palpable antipathy toward Ōkubo and the policy of the government had not lessened despite the position he was given in the central government. Earlier, when Hisamitsu had returned to Kagoshima during the Saga rebellion, he had done so with a twofold purpose: to prevent the spread of insurrectionary fever to that area, and to exert his influence in persuading Saigō Takamori to rejoin the central government. When the scheme to obtain Saigō proved abortive, Hisamitsu used this as a pretext to resign as a member of the government. He was, however, induced to reconsider when he was presented with an imperial order, and he returned to Tōkyō on April 21.[97] Thereupon a plan was evolved to elevate him to the position of *Sadaijin*.[98] Ōkubo could not lend his enthusiastic support to this move, chiefly because it meant relegating Iwakura to a status subordinate to Hisamitsu.[99] Hisamitsu was nevertheless given the high post on April 27 and soon utilized the new vantage point to impede if not arrest the nation's progress toward modernization. On May 23 he petitioned Iwakura on the following points:[100]

1. To reinstate ceremonial attire.[101] This particular demand was obviously a reaction to the abolition of class distinctions by the new Meiji government. Everyone was now free to wear any type of dress, except at court, on ceremonial occasions.[102]

2. To abolish the land tax. Earlier in 1872 the land tax reform of the Meiji government called for a land survey throughout the empire. The basis for the assessment of taxes was found by con-

verting the land's net average produce for five years into its money value, and then the rate of the land tax was fixed at 3 per cent of this. Under the *ancien régime*, however, the land tax based upon the annual yield of rice was submitted in kind. Whether Hisamitsu desired to revert completely to this system is doubtful, but any degree of reversion may have seemed to him a definite easement of the tax burden.

3. To abolish the new miscellaneous taxes, a demand made despite the fact that the Meiji government had, under the land-tax law, wiped out two thousand miscellaneous duties.[103]

4. To abolish the harsh treatment in cases of breaches of etiquette.

5. To restore the *heishi* (samurai), or, in other words, the former military system.[104]

6. To decrease army and increase navy forces. This demand was a logical one, coming as it did from a Kagoshima leader. The Satsuma *han* had stressed naval power while Chōshū had traditionally concentrated upon its army. Subsequently, throughout the Meiji, Taishō, and Shōwa eras until the end of World War II, Satsuma men were to dominate the naval arm and Chōshū men the army branch of Japan's fighting services. The motivation to decrease the army and increase the naval force in this instance may have been Hisamitsu's desire to see the service in which his own associates from Satsuma predominated maintain preëminence over that in which the Chōshū men held superiority.

7. To halt nonurgent public works projects.

8. To construct an imperial palace comparable to the one in Kyōto.

Hisamitsu, moreover, threatened to resign if Ōkubo should object to his demands. This was obviously a direct challenge to Ōkubo who, in deference to his former *han* superior, also offered to resign.[105] But the other members of the Meiji government would not accede to this. In fact, Public Works Minister Itō Hirobumi and Commissioner of Colonization Kuroda Kiyotaka approached Sanjō and Iwakura and had them prevail upon Hisamitsu to withdraw his demands.[106] Iwakura finally persuaded Ōkubo to reconsider his resignation, pointing out that he was needed by both the court and the people during the period of instability.[107] Clearly, the action of Ōkubo's colleagues in the government indicated that, when given a choice of retaining either Hisamitsu, whose presence proved advantageous as a replacement for Saigō Takamori, or Ōkubo, there was no question in their minds. Ōkubo could not be relinquished. He remained. In another sense this represented a victory of the rising class of wealthy farmers and merchants and a defeat for the feudal samurai caste of which Hisamitsu was a symbol.

Besides being confronted with conflicts between personalities, the government was constantly reminded of the unresolved Formosan issue. By the summer of 1874 the Japanese leaders were divided over the matter of troop withdrawal. Some of them argued that, since the objective of the punitive campaign had been achieved with the pacification of the savage tribesmen, there was no further justification for maintaining the forces on Formosa.[108] The proponents of withdrawal were probably influenced by other considerations as well. In July, illness prostrated a large number of troops which necessitated successive reinforcements to replace the casualties. There was also the disquieting report that China was preparing an expedition of some twenty thousand men to be sent to the island.[109] There was, on the other hand, a group composed of such men as Ōkubo, Ōkuma, and Ōki who were strongly opposed to evacuation. They knew through Yanagibara's reports that morale was high among the troops, and that the officers were in favor of war with China, having aspirations of extending Japanese authority throughout its eighteen provinces.[110] The opponents of withdrawal stood firm. Ōkubo emphasized that, with no diplomatic settlement achieved, the troops could not be brought home; to do so would destroy Japan's bargaining power when the time came to demand an indemnity from China. And an indemnity Ōkubo was determined to acquire. The government ultimately accepted his view.[111]

The month of July, 1874, found powerful Home Minister Ōkubo completely absorbed in the problems relating to Formosa. He spent a great deal of his time conferring with his foreign advisers, Boissonade and Le Gendre. Ōkubo in turn counseled Sanjō.[112] After due deliberation the government, on July 8, came to a decision. It would press China for a settlement and go to war if this became inevitable.[113] The decision was transmitted to the two service ministries on the following day.[114] One plan of battle, which was presented to Ōkuma of the Board of Formosan Affairs to be put into operation should the Peking negotiations fail, called for the reinforcement of the forces on Formosa with two fresh battalions and an armored vessel to be anchored at Amoy. When the orders were issued, army and navy forces were to launch an attack upon Formosa while, at the same time, severing communications with Fukien and the adjacent islands. A force of ten thousand was to be transported south aboard several ships of war which would ostensibly head toward Formosa. This group, however, would veer to the mainland at a given point, land, reduce Peking, and overrun the eighteen provinces.[115] These were indeed critical times, but Ōkubo seemed to find time to relax by playing the game of *go*, or Japanese checkers, with friends.[116]

Contemplating a Mission to China

Although outwardly tranquil, Ōkubo did not share the confidence of the military men in the field in Japan's ability to run roughshod over China. China had not been neglecting defensive preparations. She had built gun emplacements on outlying islands adjacent to Formosa, laid a marine cable between Amoy and Formosa, acquired the latest type of German rifles, recruited army and navy personnel, and purchased armored vessels from Denmark.[117] Ōkubo thoroughly comprehended the gravity of the situation. A slight misstep could plunge both nations headlong into war—a war Ōkubo did not want at this particular time. And although Minister Yanagibara was in Peking, he did not possess plenary power and had to refer all important questions to the government in Tōkyō. Obviously the existing situation precluded the making of quick decisions and this could prove disadvantageous to Japan. Ōkubo felt it imperative to have a competent, responsible official of high rank in China to carry on negotiations.[118] Naturally, he considered himself the logical person for the mission.

Again, as on past occasions, Ōkubo, taking the initiative, petitioned the government on July 13 to be appointed as an emissary to deal with China over the Formosan question.[119] Again, there was opposition from his colleagues. Sanjō, Iwakura, and Ōkuma said that he could not be spared at a time when strong leadership was required in Tōkyō.[120] Ōkubo persisted and on July 26 he strongly urged Sanjō and Iwakura to give their consent.[121] Finally, on July 30, the government gave him unofficial sanction to go.[122] Ōkuma, however, continued to resist, threatening to resign if

Ōkubo had his way.[123] Ōkubo nevertheless was officially appointed on August 1 as *benri daijin,* or minister plenipotentiary to China.[124]

An appointment as an envoy plenipotentiary to a large country of high civilization such as China was a signal honor for Ōkubo. Ōkubo may not have been insensible to the prestige factor, but more than this he had a genuine desire to resolve an issue for which he had assumed total responsibility when he made the decision to send Japanese troops to Formosa. Despite his various shortcomings as an individual, there is no question but that he possessed a keen sense of responsibility. Realizing that the reputation of the nation was at stake, he was more than eager to resolve the issue personally.[125]

In his study of Ōkubo's motives for journeying to Peking as a negotiator, Tokutomi concludes that the Japanese statesman was not interested in acquiring a pretext for beginning hostilities against China, but solely in reaching a peaceful settlement.[126] This is true. But at the same time he was not against action that might have gained Formosa for Japan. He gave priority to the attainment of peace because of his knowledge of his nation's actual fighting potential. On August 4, War Minister Yamagata Aritomo notified him of the feeble condition of the military and discouraged any large-scale troop movements abroad. Moreover, he warned that the unstable domestic situation made such a move doubly hazardous for the country.[127] Ōkubo pressed for some assurance that the military branch would lend support to the diplomatic arm of the nation. Finally, on the following day, Yamagata promised Ōkubo that some battalions could be made available in the event of war. This assurance gave Ōkubo a degree of confidence as he looked ahead to his coming confrontation with the Chinese authorities.[128]

Had Japan enjoyed a margin of military superiority over China at this juncture, Ōkubo might have gone to Peking with no thought of concluding peace, but rather to lay down intolerable terms and, following China's protestations, declare war against it. Ōkubo would have had little difficulty convincing the most influential leaders of the feasibility of a war of aggrandizement. The following table indicates the proponents of the various views with respect to foreign policy during the early Meiji era: [129]

Expansion Advocates	Internal Development Advocates
Saigō Takamori	Of Protecting the Northern Approach:
Soejima Taneomi	Kuroda Kiyotaka
Itagaki Taisuke	Enomoto Buyō

Etō Shimpei	Of Protecting the Southern Approach:
Gotō Shōjirō	Ōkubo Toshimichi
Kirino Toshiaki	Ōkuma Shigenobu
	Ōki Takato
	Of Noninvolvenment Abroad:
	Kido Kōin
	Inoue Kaoru

Had Ōkubo expounded a policy of conquering Formosa, the only real opposition would have come from Kido and Inoue. By the summer of 1874, however, Kido had resigned and neither Inoue nor Enomoto were members of the Council of State. Kuroda alone could have done very little to overcome the combined influence of such men as Ōkubo, Ōkuma, and Ōki, all of whom were advocates of safeguarding Japan's southern approach. Had Ōkubo thought the time ripe for war with China, he could without difficulty have had his way, and the Saigō military faction would have supported him gladly. Japan's weakness, however, forced Ōkubo to strive for peace at the conference table.

Preparing for Eventualities

Prior to his departure for China, Ōkubo, in a memorandum to Sanjō, outlined a program designed to put the nation on a war footing should the resolution of Sino-Japanese differences prove impossible.[130] The recommendations were (1) to have imperial rescript issued exhorting the various functionaries to exert their utmost effort in this time of emergency; (2) to issue a similar order to the two service ministries, the purport of which was to ascertain their state of readiness in manpower, weapons, ammunition, and ships; (3) to have the functionaries above the rank of *sangi* go to the imperial palace daily regardless of whether they had any specific business to attend to or not; (4) to encourage the nation to work as though war had actually been decided upon, despite the decision that war would be the last resort; (5) to press the army and navy ministers on matters of military strategy; (6) to have the *Ōkurashō* ascertain the amount of gold and grain available; (7) to have the various ministries limit expenditures to the bare minimum; (8) to send the mission to China aboard the warship "Ryūjō"; (9) to acquire warships, weapons, and ammunition from abroad; (10) to dispatch ministers to Prussia and the United States immediately; (11) to notify ministers abroad of the particulars of the punitive expedition and the state of Japan's relation with China; and (12) to appoint new *sangi*.[131]

One of the interesting features of the plan was the attempt to reach an understanding with Prussia and the United States, no doubt because these powers were more sympathetic to Japanese aspirations in Formosa than were Great Britain, Italy, Russia, and Spain, which had remonstrated strongly against the Formosan campaign. To fill the vacancy created by Ōkubo's absence during his trip to Peking, Army Minister Yamagata Aritomo, Colonization Commissioner Kuroda Kiyotaka, and *Sain* President Ijichi Masaharu were made state councilors on August 2.[132] These officials from Chōshū, Hizen, and Satsuma, respectively, were men upon whom Ōkubo could rely.

The memorandum reflects Ōkubo's analytical capability—his dominant mental trait—which enabled him to outline the ramifications of a specific problem and to provide for the maximum safeguards against contingencies. He was an originator, organizer, and executor—and administrator *par excellence*. Would he stand the test as a negotiator on a major diplomatic mission?

On August 5 Emperor Meiji deigned to receive Ōkubo in audience and exhorted him to do his utmost for the nation.[133] Ōkubo in the meantime had been given extraordinary powers to deal with the existing situation. For example, he could at his discretion depart from the principles outlined in Yanagibara's instructions. And although the primary purpose of the negotiations as far as Ōkubo was concerned was to preserve the peace between the two countries, he nevertheless could decide to take Japan into war if necessary. If circumstances demanded, he could exercise full authority over all Japanese civil and military officials involved in the Formosan affair, including Le Gendre.[134] Japan placed its fate in Ōkubo's hands.

Because of Ōkubo's powerful grip on the government at this time, his colleagues were compelled to tolerate his imperious disposition. Incredible as it may seem, the fact is that no one knew precisely until Ōkubo was ready to leave for Peking on August 6 what his innermost feelings were with respect to war and peace; he felt that as a plenipotentiary it was unnecessary to confide in anyone about such matters. Itō Hirobumi, anxious to ascertain in a general way at least in which direction Ōkubo's mind was inclined, tried to ferret out his thoughts at the Tōkyō station before he took the train to Yokohama, but in this he was unsuccessful.

Later, at the port when Ōkubo and his well-wishers were aboard the American steamer "Costa Rica" just before its departure, the envoy told his friends that he would return home as soon as possible after the settlement of the Formosan problem. Itō later revealed that this was the first inkling he had had of Ōkubo's desire to work for a peaceful settlement.[135]

Such arrogance on the part of an official is unusual in the West, but Japanese functionaries have been noted for their haughtiness, although their attitude has changed remarkably since World War II. Although Confucianism, which served as a pattern for Japanese ethics, spoke of "no foregone conclusion, no obstinacy, and no egotism," the master-servant, father-son relationship that Confucius stressed involved the respect of the inferior for his superior. This philosophy, as has been noted, was utilized by the Tokugawa *shōgun* to instill in the people an attitude of submissiveness to authority. Submissiveness became a virtue, and, as a result, official arrogance increased in inverse ratio to the increasing submissiveness of the people. Ōkubo and the other Meiji leaders, being products of the Tokugawa culture, behaved in the expected arbitrary manner of functionaries. It is interesting to note in this connection that the very individuals who had attacked the authoritarian attitude of the Tokugawa leaders assumed in time the same characteristics as the leaders they displaced.[136]

On the Diplomatic Assignment

Ōkubo and his party, including M. Boissonade, the Japanese envoy's trusted adviser, arrived in Tientsin on September 1 [137] where he was given a progress report of the negotiations that had taken place between Minister Yanagibara and the Tsungli Yamen.[138] The report was not encouraging. Since Yanagibara's arrival in Peking on July 31, he had held a number of meetings with the Chinese government without tangible results. The Chinese persistently refused to recognize Japan's action in Formosa, claiming all the while that the entire island was their possession, while the Japanese minister just as stubbornly adhered to his argument that the region of the aborigines lay outside China's jurisdiction.[139] On September 4, the minister dispatched a messenger to Ōkubo and suggested that he remain in Tientsin a little longer while he made renewed efforts to reach an understanding with the Peking government. Yanagibara made it clear that, should China refuse to accede to Japan's demands, he would withdraw from the capital. This action, he thought, would force the Chinese to concede.[140] Ōkubo was not impressed with the suggestion. He was not one to stand aside and allow a subordinate to carry on negotiations if he were prepared to do so himself. He rejected Yanagibara's idea and on September 5 decided to leave for Peking immediately.[141] On September 10 he arrived in Peking, determined to deal directly, frankly, and firmly with the Tsungli Yamen.[142]

Ōkubo felt that his presence in Peking was imperative if the negotiations were to succeed, an attitude bred of supreme confidence. Although he was fully prepared to have the onus of failure placed upon him should no settlement be reached, he was equally determined to be considered the one person responsible for the success of the mission. He was obviously not a team man and had to be the chief participant in all negotiations that had a direct and fateful bearing upon the government he had helped to found. In many ways he is reminiscent of American Secretary of State John Foster Dulles, whose self-reliance precluded to a high degree his utilization of subordinates in the State Department. Such men are not popular.

By going directly to Peking without first conferring with Li Hung-chang, the Chihli viceroy, Ōkubo, who understood the significance of protocol, broke a Chinese usage of long standing. Li was mortified by such a breach of etiquette.[143] This apparently premeditated action was probably influenced by Le Gendre who, in September, 1872, advised Soejima, then Japan's Foreign Minister, not to deal with secondary Chinese officials, but instead to negotiate directly with the central government authorities.[144] It is very likely that Ōkubo in 1874 was adhering to the day-to-day advice of his foreign aides, M. Boissonade and Le Gendre, the latter having joined the party at Tientsin.[145] As Westerners whose respective governments had reacted unfavorably to China's insistence that international relations be carried on through the intermediary of viceroys and other provincial officials, Boissonade and Le Gendre conceivably hoped to persuade Japan to protest China's policy. Although under the Second Treaty Settlement (1856-1860) the foreign powers extracted from China the promise to allow direct relations with the central government, thereby making it unnecessary for diplomats to deal on the provincial level, Japanese missions had up to this time made it a point to call upon Li Hung-chang before proceeding to Peking. The viceroys generally endeavored to settle problems in international relations themselves if at all possible and were reluctant to have such matters referred to Peking. Under foreign tutelage in diplomatic matters, Ōkubo's strategy during his negotiations with the Chinese were to reflect more than incidentally the philosophy of international relations adhered to by his foreign mentors as well as by their individual prejudices toward a seemingly hopeless and unprogressive China.

Mapping Strategy

Prior to the initial parley with the Chinese on September 14, Ōkubo consulted with Boissonade on the points to be discussed. Then at one o'clock in the afternoon on the appointed day, he and Yanagibara went to the Tsungli Yamen where they were met by Prince Kung and his associates.[146] After the preliminary greetings the talks began in earnest, with Ōkubo serving as the sole spokesman for Japan. The Chinese, on the other hand, had no one advocate, although Wen Hsiang was clearly their outstanding negotiator. In establishing the points of difference between his nation and China, Ōkubo told the Chinese that "your government claims the aborigines' region as its territory while we affirm that it is a region of the aborigines belonging to no one." [147] Ōkubo's aim was to prove that China had not exercised jurisdiction over this portion of Formosa. Hence he argued that a dependency could be considered worthy of that term only insofar as the country claiming it exercised authority therein by the establishment of an administrative system and military facilities. The Chinese were forced to admit that their vast territories precluded the creation of administrative machinery in every corner of its domain.[148] Ōkubo persisted in his argument. He cited *kōhō*, or public law of nations, under which a country laying claim to a wilderness region could not acquire possession without first establishing an administrative structure and deriving benefits from their claim.[149] The Chinese in turn tried to justify their claim under the provisions of public law by indicating that the area in question had been a source of tribute. To this Ōkubo countered with the statement that, according to inquiries made on the island, none of the tribal chieftains were aware of tributes having been tendered to China.[150]

With the verbal sparring obviously leading nowhere, Ōkubo next presented the Chinese with two questions, the answers to which he expected to receive within a few days. They were: (1) The prerequisite for the establishment of a sphere of influence is the ability to furnish tangible evidence that an administrative agency has been created, through which authority is exercised over the region in question. What has been done regarding this jurisdictional matter? (2) Why are the savages permitted to inflict injury upon the persons of those who have been shipwrecked along the Formosan coast without suffering punishment? [151]

The outstanding feature of the first meeting was undoubtedly Ōkubo's well-reasoned argument based upon a law conceived in the West. This indicates his aptness as Boissonade's disciple, and also attests to the care with which the French legalist advised the Japanese envoy.[152] The strategy employed was subtle, placing the Chinese constantly on the defensive. The two questions presented to the Chinese were designed to checkmate the opponent, making it impossible for him to move in the game of diplomatic chess without conceding defeat. Ōkubo intended to discuss the two points in order. If the Chinese conceded that their jurisdiction did not extend over the aborigines' region, he would press his point that Japan thereby had the right to deal freely and independently with the Formosan problem. If, on the other hand, China maintained a claim of ownership over the region, he was prepared to place upon China the blame for actions of its Formosan "subjects." [153] Later, in explaining to Saigō Tsugumichi the reason for centering the negotiations upon these two points, Ōkubo said: "We hoped to have China recognize our worthy objective. We desired to illuminate the merits of the case in the light of the principles of public law as recognized by the nations of the world in order to preserve our reputation, even if the negotiations failed, and to eliminate the cause for future differences with China." [154] Through this cautious approach, Ōkubo hoped not to antagonize world opinion, which would be detrimental to the young and yet unrecognized Japanese nation.

Ōkubo was careful to solicit the goodwill and to understand the viewpoints of the foreign powers that were interested in the Sino-Japanese question. He visited the English, American, and Russian legations on the day after the initial conference with the Chinese.[155] He soon discovered that the foreign representatives, especially the British minister, were just as eager to know the feelings of the Japanese as he was to know theirs. On September 16 Sir Thomas Francis Wade of the British legation called upon Ōkubo at his hotel to gain more specific knowledge of Japan's objective.[156]

On the afternoon of the same day delegates from the Tsungli Yamen arrived at Ōkubo's quarters bearing the reply to the Japanese note of

September 14.[157] In reply to the first question, the Chinese note reiterated that tribute had been received from the savage tribesmen and, as for the question of administration, stated that the region in dispute was under the jurisdiction of the administrative office of the adjacent province. With reference to the second question, the note stated that the Chinese government had never failed to act upon grievances where injuries had been visited upon foreign traders and officials of those countries with which China had treaty relations, if the representative of the country concerned had communicated to the Tsungli Yamen the details of the situation. Had Japan, with regard to the Formosan incident, made a representation to the Chinese government, the Tsungli Yamen would not have failed to investigate.[158]

Making No Progress

The third meeting, which took place on September 19, failed to produce positive results. Ōkubo continued to point out that under public law the territory of southeast Formosa could not be considered as belonging to the Chinese,[159] whereupon Wen Hsiang suggested that the negotiations proceed upon the basis of the first Sino-Japanese treaty of amity, ratified on March 9, 1873, in which the two signatories promised to respect the territorial integrity of each other's possessions.[160] The Chinese negotiator argued that public law was coded in the West in comparatively recent times and therefore did not apply to China. He further charged that for Japan to refer disparagingly to the Chinese administration of Formosa amounted to criticism of the Chinese government in general. He then demanded that matters pertaining to the savage area of Formosa be left entirely in the hands of China.[161] In reply to this bellicose outburst of the Chinese, Ōkubo declared with vigor that, in spite of his desire for peace, his primary duty was to ascertain the status of the disputed territory.[162] The Chinese, however, would not be swayed. All of Formosa was theirs. They pointed out that Japan's questioning of China's jurisdiction over certain portions of Formosa was tantamount to China's questioning Japan's jurisdiction over its port of Nagasaki. Japan would certainly not accede to a similar request from China, said Wen Hsiang. Ōkubo's rejoinder was pointed: "If there were savages living at Nagasaki, the Japanese government would deal with them in such a manner as to prevent their inflicting harm upon mariners."[163] The talks came to a halt with neither side satisfied.

The British minister called upon Ōkubo again on September 26 to discuss Japan's policy toward Formosa. Did Japan mean to retain its forces on the island for an indefinite period or would the troops be withdrawn under certain conditions? Ōkubo, like a seasoned diplomat, equivocated, stating that he was not saying that the troops would not be evacuated under any circumstances.[164] As for the question of war or peace, Ōkubo's mind by this time was made up. Japan would not start a war. In a report to Sanjō dated September 27, 1874, the day after the third meeting with the Chinese, Ōkubo assured his superior that "until they [the Chinese] commence hostilities, I have no intention of declaring war. Even if the negotiations fail, there is no alternative but to await their next move."[165]

The fourth meeting, held on October 5, was no more productive than the earlier parleys. China steadfastly maintained her position while Ōkubo tried vainly to obtain an admission from her representatives that their government had avowed to Soejima in 1873 its nonresponsibility for the acts of the savage tribesmen. The conference finally ended with Ōkubo threatening to return home.[166] The complete breakdown of negotiations was imminent.

Polling His Subordinates

In this extremely grave situation Ōkubo, despite his magisterial tendencies, condescended to poll the opinions of his subordinates. Although his own mind was made up, he was nonetheless interested in knowing the temper of those about him. Among them, the following were in favor of going to war with China: Yanagibara Sakimitsu, Inoue Ki, Takasaki Masakaze, Fukushima Kunari, Kabayama Suenori, and Kodama Toshikuni. Yanagibara was especially provoked by the impertinent tenor of the note from the Chinese government. Those who were for peace included Fukuhara Toshikatsu, Iwamura Takatoshi, Tanabe Taichi, and Yoshihara Shigetoshi. Tanabe argued that further efforts should be made to preserve the peace while Fukuhara and Iwamura believed that there was insufficient justification for a declaration of war.[167] Ōkubo included himself among the peace faction. He would not have been averse to war if complete victory were assured. Being a realist, however, he thought in terms of Japan's military potential, an appraisal of which had indicated that although Japan was prepared to a degree, it still lacked an adequate number of warships and other military accouterments to insure a successful prosecution of war against China.[168]

The British were just as anxiously observing the progress of the Ōkubo negotiations as was the Japanese government. For Japan, the British rightly deduced, time was of the essence. Parkes in Tōkyō aptly described Japan's dilemma when he said that "every day's delay is a gain to China but a loss to Japan, and the latter therefore will hurry on a settlement or a collision." [169] Minister Wade in Peking worked feverishly for a settlement and the avoidance of a collision. On October 9, he suggested to Yanagibara the possibility of arbitrating the controversy in accordance with the practice of the West. Wade stated quite confidently that China would probably not object. Yanagibara, however, rejected the suggestion.[170]

On October 10 Ōkubo forwarded another note to the Tsungli Yamen and was determined to leave the capital if the Chinese reply proved nonconstructive.[171] The Japanese note reiterated Japan's position and censured China's inconsistent attitude. It was strongly worded, but assured the Chinese that "Japan did not send troops to Formosa because it coveted any territory." [172] Ōkubo's diary on October 11 notes that the Chinese had requested an extension of the five-day limit within which they were expected to reply to the Japanese ultimatum.[173]

As the crisis approached, Ōkubo, acutely sensitive to the attitude of the foreign representatives in Peking, made shrewd use of them as agents to contact the Chinese. The English, he perceived, were anxious to mediate and were eager to know whether Japan was ready to reach an understanding on the basis of an indemnity or had already decided upon war.[174] Ōkubo, however, did not manifest any desire for mediation. His strategy was to impress upon all concerned that Japanese public opinion had reached a feverish state with the people demanding a definitive settlement, and it behooved him to return home soon to placate the aroused populace.[175] In a letter to Sanjō written on October 13 he confided that "both England and the United States, because of self-interest, are eager to intercede with a view to preventing war. France has a desire to aid Japan and is more than ready to accept a request for assistance from us." [176]

The British by this time had arrived at the conclusion that Japan might be willing to evacuate its troops if offered sufficient indemnity for its expenditures of men and material in the Formosan campaign. In approaching Ōkubo concerning this matter, Wade resorted to flattery; Ōkubo reported Wade as saying: "Japan has manifested its power to the Chinese government. Until now, I had only heard about Japan through the medium of the newspaper. And having met you I am deeply impressed. I am certain that the Chinese government will indemnify Japan, and if as a result a settlement should be reached, Japan's honor would be heralded throughout Europe. . . ." [177] Then, upon Wade's suggestion, an agent was sent to confer with Robert Hart, the superintendent of customs of the Chinese government, who declared that he would have the Chinese agree to an indemnity.[178] Ōkubo began to disclose his purpose; in his talk with Minister Wade, on October 14, he indirectly referred to an indemnity when he conceded that Japan would withdraw its troops "if we could do so with honor." He went on to point out that Japanese troops had undergone privation and suffered casualties while the government was compelled to expend huge sums of money for the punitive campaign. He asserted that unless the government and the people were given reasonable satisfaction for their sacrifice, the troops could not be withdrawn.[179]

Beginning of Phase Two

Two days later, on October 16, the Chinese replied to the ultimatum of October 10. Their note was conciliatory and showed an inclination to bring the negotiations to a satisfactory conclusion.[180] The second phase of negotiation was opened when, on October 18, another meeting was called and the four Chinese negotiators stated that they would not discuss the question of title to southern Formosa, but were prepared to take cognizance of China's negligence in the Formosan incident as well as Japan's justification in sending a punitive expedition to the island. They were, furthermore, willing to compensate for the murder of the Ryūkyūans. Ōkubo thereupon agreed to continue the negotiations.[181] But on the following day the Chinese sent another note declaring that although they were willing to indemnify Japan for the losses sustained, they could not consent to a written agreement noting the indemnity, its purpose, and its amount. Moreover, they could not deliver the money until after the Japanese troops had evacuated the island.[182]

For the Chinese this was evidently a face-saving device; to have acceded to the Japanese terms would have been an admission of defeat. The Japanese, however, found this unpalatable. Could they accept an oral promise at face value? Ōkubo and Yanagibara went to the Tsungli Yamen on October 20 and presented their rejoinder to what they considered arbitrary propositions. But the Chinese were adamant. They reasoned that since Japan had sent troops into Chinese territory, a payment in the form of an indemnity for their withdrawal would affect China's honor. They therefore insisted that the indemnity would have to be considered as relief money for the families of the murdered Ryūkyūans. Ōkubo demanded a documentary pledge that payment would be made before he could promise the removal of troops from Formosa, but the Chinese refused.[183] Ultimately the Chinese yielded to the extent that they would specify the sum but would not have it documented. Ōkubo could not endorse this.[184] The Japanese on October 23 again presented their demands, but with no success. The negotiations were all but broken off.[185]

Ōkubo was once more ready to leave Peking. He called upon the various foreign representatives on the following day and bade them farewell.[186] On October 25 he sent Fukuhara to Shanghai and Kabayama and Hishijima to Amoy and Formosa, respectively.[187] On the same day he sent his final communication to the Tsungli Yamen in which he expressed regret concerning China's attitude toward Japan and indicated that Japan would continue to work for the pacification and development of the Formosan area under occupation. He concluded his note by informing the Chinese of his inability to pay a personal call upon the Tsungli Yamen prior to his departure from China.[188]

The British minister had continued to work behind the scenes. On the morning of October 23 Wade called upon Ōkubo and asked what Japan was demanding in the way of an indemnity, and was told quite frankly that Japan requested three million *yen*.[189] Earlier, on October 21, a member of the Japanese party had gone to the Tsungli Yamen to discuss Japan's expenditures for the campaign and informed the Chinese that the total was five million *yen*. He reported that, exclusive of two million *yen* spent for the purchase of ships and implements of war, the actual disbursements in Formosa amounted to three million *yen*. The Chinese, however, had been dubious of the figures and inquired: "Does not rumor have it that your actual expenditures amounted to no more than fifty or sixty thousand *yen*?" The Japanese official replied that no one but the Japanese would have knowledge of the exact amount.[190] Wade, in talking with Ōkubo two days later, was obviously eager to repair the breach in Sino-Japanese relations, and again pursued the matter of the indemnity. He asked if Ōkubo had the authority to order the evacuation of the troops if China were to comply with Japan's terms. Ōkubo replied in the affirmative.[191] Thus Ōkubo had reason to believe that British pressure on the Tsungli Yamen would induce the Chinese to relent. He was surprised to meet with resistance when he met with the Chinese later, on the afternoon of October 23, at what was to have been the final meeting before Ōkubo's departure from Peking.

Reaching an Agreement

On October 25, the day before his announced departure, Ōkubo received a visit from Francis Wade who reported that after a lengthy conversation with the Chinese he was asked to notify Ōkubo of China's willingness to make certain concessions. China, he said, would pay five hundred thousand *taels*, one hundred thousand *taels* of which were to be for the relief of the families of the murdered victims and the remainder to be considered as compensation for Japan's miscellaneous expenditures. The initial payment of one hundred thousand *taels* would be paid immediately, Wade said, and the balance after the Japanese forces evacuated Formosa. A documentary pledge was also promised. Ōkubo thanked the British minister profusely for his efforts in behalf of peace.[192] The final settlement was reached on October 31. Under the terms of the Peking Agreement of 1874, China recognized as just and proper Japan's action in Formosa, Japan was to receive five hundred thousand *taels*, the two countries were to annul all official correspondence hitherto exchanged between them, and China agreed to protect navigators in the future against outrages committed by the savages.[193]

War between the two countries was averted.

It is generally conceded by both Japanese and Chinese that the British minister played a key role in bringing about the compromise settlement. There is no doubt that the British minister exerted considerable pressure upon the Chinese government.[194] Prince Kung's report to the Chinese emperor justifying the decisions of the Tsungli Yamen in its relation with the Japanese makes note of the important role played by the British diplomat.[195] The Chinese rationale for concluding the disadvantageous settlement was that inadequate military preparations decreased their bargaining power.[196] It becomes apparent that the settlement was basically the result of the recognition by both sides of the lack of the margin of military strength required to assure either of them victory in a shooting war.

Despite Ōkubo's inability to procure the indemnity he had originally demanded, there is no doubt that the treaty of 1874 represented a diplomatic defeat for the Chinese and a victory for the Japanese. By conceding that Japan had legitimate reason for undertaking the Formosan expedition —securing justice for the Ryūkyūans—China tacitly recognized Japan's suzerainty over the Ryūkyūs. If, as the Chinese contended, the Japanese had been given no prior authorization for the mission to Formosa, the treaty by implication sanctioned Japan's move into Chinese territory without its claimant's acquiescence.[197] Writing to his friend, Sir D. Brooke Robertson, Sir Harry Parkes succinctly summed up the settlement:

> I received yesterday your note of the 5th inst. Since it was written we have both heard of the settlement effected by Wade. I think that he is to be congratulated on his success; so are the Japanese who, thanks to him, have escaped from a very grave difficulty of their own creation; but how to congratulate China I do not know. She appears to fare sadly by the arrangement. I thought it possible that they might in the end agree to cry quits, on condition that the Japanese retire from Formosa, but I certainly did not expect to find China willing to pay for being invaded.[198]

The settlement had various significant aspects. First, it testified to Japan's military and diplomatic skill. One Western observer believed that the Formosan enterprise was prompted by an impulse of humanity and carried through with resolution, spirit, and discretion. Although it was not diplomatically gigantic in proportion, it was as perfect in all the details of its performance as any similar operation up to that time. This observer felt that the enterprise reflected excellent qualities of diplomatic capacity and statesmanship.[199] Although the Japanese motive in going into Formosa was questionable, this tribute to Japanese military efficiency and diplomatic ability is well founded. Ōkuma, in fact, attributed to the Formosan enterprise the early recognition by the foreigners that Japan was capable of preserving law and order within its domain. Consequently, the British and French soon thereafter withdrew their forces from Yokohama.

Another consequence of the Formosan experience was the exposure of

China's general political and military debility.[200] The colonial powers, quick to take note of this condition, within two decades began to make the once-powerful Middle Kingdom the victim of their rapacity: Japan was the first to manifest its desire for territory on the Asiatic mainland when it attacked China in 1894. The various European nations soon thereafter were openly participating in the process of dismantling China.

The Chinese understandably have not been proud of the Formosan episode in their history. Hoshien Tchen is highly critical of those who brought humiliation upon China as the result of their concessions. He charged that "ses [China's] ministres étant à cette époque absolument incapable de traiter les question nationales come l'auraient fait de véritables hommes d'État" (its [China's] ministers at that time were absolutely incapable of dealing with national questions as real statesmen should).[201]

If China's inept statesmen were responsible for the disgraceful Formosan settlement, is it true that Japan's relative success in the bargaining was contingent in large measure upon Ōkubo's genius? He must be credited with playing his role almost unerringly and for good reason. By nature he was a perfectionist, and his arguments were based on hours of preparation and thought. He met daily with Boissonade to discuss points of international law and then practiced argumentation constantly with his colleagues.[202] At the negotiation table he was equipped to press a point with confidence. He was unquestionably Japan's chief advocate, allowing none of his subordinates, outside of Yanagibara on a few occasions, to interject their comments at the conference table.

It is a mistake to give Ōkubo all of the credit for the successful settlement, as some of his Japanese biographers and at least one Western writer have done, but neither is it justified to attribute it entirely to Wade, as Parkes has done.[203] Without Wade's intervention a settlement would have been difficult, if not impossible, but Ōkubo utilized Wade and the other foreign representatives for his own end. Adept at *ruse de guerre*, Ōkubo transferred the art to the realm of diplomacy and through his determined demeanor and speech led others to believe that Japan was prepared to go to war if China did not relent and accept his demands. Also, Japanese newspapers were reporting plans for the settlement of discontented samurai on the island of Formosa, and such information lent credence to Ōkubo's contention that the military elements within his country were restive and desirous of ending the Formosan controversy shortly, either peacefully or by war.[204] Had Ōkubo failed to play his part effectively, the British would not have acted with dispatch in forcing the Chinese to accept most of the Japanese demands. Ōkubo, however, would not have been so successful without the dedicated counsel of such men as Boissonade and Le Gendre. The Chinese, without such advisers, were at a decided disadvantage in a negotiation in which they were compelled to abide by Western rules. Consequently, they were outmaneuvered. Viewed in the light of these facts, the settlement was the result of no one individual but a combination of individuals and circumstances.

Contacting Li Hung-chang

Gratified over the results of the mission, Ōkubo and his party left Peking on November 1 and arrived in Tientsin two days later.[205] There, Ōkubo paid a call upon Li Hung-chang, whom he described as a "great man." [206] Li had been strongly opposed to any compromise with the Japanese.[207] On this occasion, however, the viceroy was cordial. The two men expressed their hope for future amity between their countries. Ōkubo then voiced what was perhaps his aspiration with respect to Japanese foreign policy when he said: "It is my belief that if China and Japan were to coöperate harmoniously, we could extend without difficulty our influence throughout the East. I sincerely hope that this relationship may be realized." [208] The leaders then compared notes on the number of ships and the nature of mineral resources possessed by their respective countries. When Li intimated that China lacked copper, Ōkubo said: "Japan has considerable copper. If you should ever have need for it, I shall see to it that you are supplied." Li inquired if arrangements could be made by merely writing directly to Ōkubo, to which the latter replied in the affirmative. Few leaders other than a dictator would have dared to commit a nation to such an unequivocal agreement.[209]

From Tientsin, on November 4, Ōkubo left for Shanghai, arriving there three days later.[210] On November 10 the Japanese collected the one hundred thousand *taels*, the initial payment of the indemnity, from the collector of customs in Shanghai.[211] The next day Ōkubo boarded the "Shinagawa Maru" for Formosa to inform Saigō of the settlement and authorize the withdrawal of his forces.[212] After spending two days on the island, he left for home on November 18.[213]

Upon arriving in Tōkyō on November 27, Ōkubo was given a rousing welcome by the Japanese people and received by the Emperor.[214] Even

Kido expressed his gratitude to Ōkubo for having preserved the peace, his only regret being, he said, that several hundred soldiers had lost their lives on the field through illness.[215]

But not everyone joined in the acclaim.

Japanese historians have subsequently expressed their dissatisfaction with the settlement. One writer has contended that the Japanese have no reason to feel proud of their diplomacy during this period. He notes that under foreign pressure the government hesitated in implementing its Formosan policy, and that only after Saigō confronted it with a fait accompli did Ōkubo decide to revert to the original policy of dispatching the expedition. He further argues that, instead of vacillating, Japan should have forged ahead with its plans, and if China had objected, their representatives should have been forced to come to Japan to negotiate; it was a mistake for Ōkubo to go to China. He also claims that the indemnity was rightfully owing to Japan for its expenditure of men and material, and hence its acquisition cannot be considered an extraordinary achievement.[216] Another historian is critical of Ōkubo for obtaining merely five hundred thousand *taels* as a condition for the withdrawal of Japanese forces.[217]

Evidence indicates that Ōkubo himself was not so mercenary as his biographers would have one think; he contemplated returning the major portion of the indemnity to China, although his scheme never materialized. This is apparent from a letter to Kuroda Kiyotaka which Ōkubo wrote a few days before leaving the Chinese capital. Dealing with the apportionment of the relief money, Ōkubo suggested that a good sum be paid to those who displayed valor in battle. The remaining four hundred thousand *taels*, he stated, should be returned to China to be spent specifically in Formosa for the administration of the area inhabited by the savage tribesmen and for the protection of navigators against future outrages. Ōkubo's sense of humanity was not the father to the idea. It was based upon political considerations. By this unprecedented move, he hoped to dispel China's suspicion toward Japan, at the same time revealing to the world Japan's magnanimity.[218] He was anxious to reach a *rapprochement* with China, a country with which Japan would have to coöperate if her future prosperity were to be assured.[219] Ōkubo's expression of goodwill toward China, conveyed in the course of his talk with Li Hung-chang, was not mere formality but a genuine declaration of his feelings. He was later to give concrete form to his belief in the practicability of Sino-Japanese coöperation; upon returning to Tōkyō and consulting with the Chinese minister, Ōkubo established language schools offering courses in Chinese. He was confident that through such agencies cultural and commercial intercourse between the two countries could be facilitated.[220]

The Japanese Emperor was highly satisfied with the outcome of the Ōkubo mission, and on December 12 he presented Ōkubo and each member of the embassy with gifts expressive of imperial pleasure.[221] A day later Ōkubo received an imperial grant of ten thousand *yen*.[222] He, however, returned the money, asking that it be expended for the aid of the destitute and other urgent needs.[223] But the Emperor did not honor his request.[224] It was with this sum that Ōkubo later built his large Western-style home in Kōjimachi, Sannen-chō, Tōkyō, which was completed in January, 1876.[225] The house cost more than originally anticipated, and Ōkubo was forced to borrow three thousand *yen*.[226] Critics were to soon take Ōkubo to task for his extravagance. His enemies went so far as to circulate in Kagoshima the picture of the newly erected building of the Government Printing Bureau with the notation that it was Ōkubo's pretentious dwelling! [227]

Some Ōkubo biographers have stressed Ōkubo's frugality; others have justified his extravagance. Itō Nitaro, although stating that Ōkubo did not live extravagantly, does admit that he was an owner of a villa at Nihonenoki.[228] Tokutomi declares that Ōkubo erected his home not for his own comfort, but for the purpose of receiving and entertaining high-ranking foreign dignitaries.[229] Whichever the case may be, it is a truism that when an individual rises in position and has access to wealth, he is usually attracted to and accepts the way of life of the the society to which he has advanced. Ōkubo was no exception.

VIII
Target of the Enemy

By the end of 1874 Ōkubo, partly by virtue of his accomplishments in the realm of diplomacy, had become the most important member of the government, with powers to match his position.[1] But despite his authority he was not oblivious to the fact that support of key leaders was necessary in the successful conduct of affairs of state. At the moment he was deprived of the coöperation of some of the most important among them. Kido Kōin had resigned in protest over the Formosan adventure, Saigō Takamori was quietly rallying around himself the samurai malcontents in the province, and Shimazu Hisamitsu, although a member of the government, was not loyal.[2] This situation weakened the government, and hence Ōkubo looked hopefully in the direction of Kido to whom he was partial in spite of their past differences on matters of policy. Would he rejoin the government? Ōkubo steadfastly maintained that Satsuma and Chōshū, whose sons had founded the new government of Japan, should be actively engaged in directing its course. Recognizing Kido as the most capable representative of Chōshū, Ōkubo was anxious to act in concert with him.[3]

It is apparent that although Ōkubo enjoyed power and used it boldly, he realized that it was necessary to share and thereby limit his own authority for a greater purpose. At the moment he was unquestionably thinking in terms of the welfare of the state. In his eagerness to establish a strong government, Ōkubo was willing to exhaust every means to win Kido's coöperation, even to relegating himself to a subordinate position.[4] To say, however, that he was patriotically motivated would be only partly true; an ambitious man in high position would not fail to appreciate the correlation between the prosperity of the nation and his own well-being as one of its leaders.

Ōkubo's eventual reconciliation with Kido was effected through a prearranged meeting in Ōsaka. The outcome of the historic Ōsaka conference of 1875 was the establishment of a Satsuma-Chōshū-Tosa coalition government with Kido Kōin and Itagaki Taisuke agreeing to rejoin the government, thus laying the groundwork for a more representative national structure.

There are differences of opinion as to who actually initiated the movement to bring Ōkubo and Kido back together. Ōkubo's biographers are inclined to give the credit to their subject.[5] Others imply that it was Itō Hirobumi. It is quite possible that both Ōkubo and Itō had such plans. Itō, according to his biographer, had discussed the scheme with Inoue Kaoru, a Chōshū man who was convinced that national stability could be established only as the autocratic tendencies of the existing administration was restrained, and the groundwork laid for representative institutions. The two men agreed that, if their ideas were to materialize, it would be necessary to have Kido return to Tōkyō and become a member of the government. Consequently, on November 28, 1874, Inoue left Yokohama for Kido's home in Yamaguchi in order to discuss the matter with him.[6]

Coincidentally, on the very day of Inoue's departure for Yamaguchi, Ōkubo visited Itō at his residence and intimated that he was planning to go to Yamaguchi to persuade Kido to rejoin the government. Ōkubo's confidence in the possibility of persuading Kido to accept his invitation was undoubtedly strengthened by the latter's display of friendship toward him after his return from China. Kido had sent an extremely cordial letter congratulating Ōkubo upon his successful mission, addressing him, incidentally, as Kōtō, Ōkubo's first name, and at the same time signing the letter with his own first name, Kōin.[7] Itō, however, was understandably reluctant to encourage Ōkubo to meet Kido immediately. He offered a counterproposal. Allow him, Itō suggested, first to dispatch a letter to Kido to ascertain his mind regarding the idea and, should he be agreeable to it, he, Itō, would arrange the meeting between the two principals in Namba (Ōsaka).[8] Later, on December 12, Iwakura and Sanjō gave their consent to such a conference, and on the following day Ōkubo sent Itō a letter of thanks for consenting to make the necessary arrangements.[9] On December 24 Ōkubo left Tōkyō for Ōsaka.[10]

Agreeing to Compromise

Ōkubo and Kido met for their first series of talks at the Sambashirō on January 8, 1875, at which time the former entreated the latter to take a seat in the government. Kido, however, was not enthusiastic, and the meeting ended with him making no commitment.[11] After giving the matter due consideration, Kido wrote to Ōkubo expressing regret that he could not accept his invitation.[12] Deeply disturbed over Kido's refusal, Ōkubo wrote to Itō on January 11 asking him to come to Ōsaka to lend his weight to the conference.[13] Itō consented without hesitation, arriving in Ōsaka on January 22. He immediately consulted with Ōkubo and received his assent to present to Kido on the following day a compromise political program designed to harmonize with Kido's liberal philosophy. By promising far-reaching reforms the two men hoped to induce Kido to work with them.

Itō's next step was to approach Kido. He did this in a highly confidential manner, as he did not wish to give Kido the impression that Ōkubo had already seen and sanctioned the program and revealed its contents.[14] The most important points read roughly as follows: (1) to prevent the evils of authoritarianism, the opinions of the people shall be consulted in bringing about legislative reforms, and simultaneously a *genrōin* (senate) shall be established to serve as a basis for a future national assembly; (2) to strengthen judicial authority, a *daishinin* (supreme court) shall be established; (3) to ascertain the people's will a *chihōkan kaigi* (conference of prefectural governors) shall be established; and (4) to insure actual imperial rule, the duties of the Council of State shall be separated from those of the various departments, and veteran statesmen such as Ōkubo and Kido shall serve in the main in an advisory capacity with lesser officials appointed to handle administrative duties on the departmental level.[15]

On January 29 all of the principals agreed to these points.[16]

To strengthen his own position within the government he was about to rejoin, Kido expressed his desire to see Itagaki Taisuke offered a place in the Council of State. If this was part of the price to be paid to secure

Kido, Ōkubo would pay it. He raised no objection to the request, and Kido forthwith consented to become once more a member of the central government.[17] On January 30 Kido and Inoue met with Itagaki to acquaint him with the Ōkubo-Itō proposition. The Tosa liberal at first demanded a promise that the reforms would be implemented immediately, but he ultimately yielded to Kido's *zenshinsetsu*, or the doctrine of gradualism.[18] Kido's views with respect to the speed with which the reforms should be implemented are found in his diary entry for February 9:

> Went to see Itō and Ōkubo at a little past 9:00 A.M. As usual I expressed my views on constitutionalism and the establishment of local assemblies by means of which the foundation for a national assembly may gradually be laid. Ōkubo agreed with me. I have recently talked with Itagaki on the same matter and he and the others are all in accord with me. With Ōkubo's concurrence today, the outlook for the country and its people is very bright.[19]

Kido's concept of an ideal administrative system for Japan was introduced to the conference and may be illustrated as follows:

Tennō Heika (Emperor)
Naikaku (council)
Dajōdaijin
Sadaijin
Udaijin
Sangi

Gyōsei (executive) | *Daishinin* (judicial) | *Genrōin* (senate)
Chihōkan Kaigi (Conference of Prefectural Governors)

The governmental structure would consist of three branches: the executive, legislative (senate), and judicial. The legislative branch, with an upper and lower house, would be the basis for a national assembly.[20]

After Kido and Inoue met with Itagaki, another meeting was arranged with Ōkubo and Itō present. Itagaki once again voiced his willingness to join the government and work for gradual reforms.[21] Much relieved, Ōkubo left Ōsaka and returned to Tōkyō on February 18, followed six days later by Itō, Inoue, and Kido. Itagaki, who had made an unsuccessful attempt during the Ōsaka conference to persuade Saigō Takamori to join the coalition government, was the last one to reach the capital, arriving on March 4, 1875.[22] Kido was commissioned a *sangi* on March 8, as was Itagaki four days later.[23]

The success of the Ōsaka conference assured Ōkubo a coalition government, but at considerable expense to himself. In accepting the compromise reform measure he had in effect consented to the circumscription of his own authority. Each provision was designed to prevent the gravitation of power to the strong bureaucrat from Satsuma. The program represented an undisguised reprimand to Ōkubo. This measure to limit his opponent's influence delighted Kido. Without assurance of such checks on Ōkubo, Kido, who acutely sensed the danger of eventual usurpation of power by Satsuma men, would not have considered returning to Tōkyo. The Ōsaka conference signified a victory of no small dimension for the liberals over a bureaucratic authoritarian. Although Ōkubo's objective at the conference was specifically to gain Kido's assent to support the Meiji government, his intermediaries, Itō and Inoue, had an added purpose in making the arrangements for the conference, namely, the attainment of a mutually acceptable policy upon which there could be ultimately erected a constitutional government structure. As Itō and Ōkubo expected, Kido, the "cautious liberal," and later Itagaki, the extreme liberal, were attracted by the relatively democratic features of the proposal. These men felt that, through the agreement reached, an authoritarian, Satsuma-centered government could be liberalized sufficiently to permit voices other than those of Ōkubo and his lieutenants to be heard.

Why did Ōkubo accept the Ōsaka compromise with such graciousness? He must have been aware, for instance, that in allowing Itagaki to share in the government he was tacitly expressing his tolerance for the idea of establishing a national assembly at an early date. In attaining his primary objective would he not endanger his own position in sanctioning measures inimical to power monopolization? In this connection, it should be reëmphasized that Ōkubo was not opposed to constitutionalism and the concomitant representative institutions envisaged by such men as Kido. He was, however, concerned with the time of their establishment. He opposed a premature imposition of such institutions upon a people unprepared to exercise their political responsibilities. At this particular juncture, undoubtedly influenced by the rising clamor for more democracy, he deemed the time propitious to begin laying the groundwork for a more liberal form of government. Furthermore, as one Japanese historian points out, Ōkubo's malleability was also occasioned by the confidence he had in his own ability to determine the general course of the nation despite any significant changes that might be made in its policy.[24] Power begets confidence, and Ōkubo lacked neither. With Kido's resumption of authority in the national government, many of his followers who had been hostile toward Ōkubo would be appeased. The reduction in the number of potentional enemies of the government outweighed, in Ōkubo's estimation, the circumscription of his own power.[25]

Effecting a Major Reform

With the coalition government established, Ōkubo took steps to implement the decisions of the Ōsaka conference. The result was the reform of 1875, one of the important landmarks in Japanese history. A report of the commission—including Ōkubo, Kido, Itagaki, Itō, and Inoue—which was formed to investigate the government structure, recommended on March 28 a polity that retained the features envisaged by Kido.[26] On April 14, 1875, an imperial rescript ordered the establishment of the *Genrōin* "to enact laws for the empire." The rescript, moreover, stated that "by also assembling representatives from the various provinces of the empire, the public mind will be best known and the public interest best consulted. . . ." [27] The *Sain* and the *Uin* were abolished, although the *Dajōkan* was retained.[28] Osatake considers this rescript as ranking alongside the Charter Oath in significance.[29]

As a result of the reorganization of 1875 the Japanese were nominally given a more democratic government, the structure of which suggested an incipient system of checks and balances. But it is doubtful that the oligarchs had any intention of establishing an independent legislature or judiciary when they created the *Genrōin* and *Daishinin*. The Senate had no substantive powers in legislation, and the Supreme Court was subject to the control of the *Dajōkan* through the Ministry of Justice. The control of all affairs of state remained with the *Dajōkan*. These changes were made with the specific purpose of satisfying the demand for a less autocratic form of government, and although new institutions were created, the fact of despotism was to remain.[30]

In May the government announced that the *Chihōkan Kaigi*, or the Conference of Prefectural Governors, which Kido had hoped might develop into the lower house of a national assembly, would be convened on June 20.[31] Home Minister Ōkubo normally would have been the appropriate person to preside over the first meeting of this body, but he stepped aside and encouraged Kido to accept the chairmanship.[32] The initial meeting of the *Chihōkan Kaigi* took place at the Asakusa Higashi Honganji, on which occasion the Emperor read a rescript outlining the purpose of this legislative organ. The assembly deliberated until July 17, during which time it discussed questions pertaining to the maintenance of roads and bridges, local police matters, procedures for the selection of the members of the *chihō minkai*, or local assemblies, poor relief, and the establishment of elementary schools.[33] Like the *Genrōin*, which had no powers of legislation, the *Chihōkan Kaigi* was no more than a debating society. Articles 10 and 11 of its constitution stipulated that the final decision in matters pertaining to taxation and proposals initiated by the members of the conference were to be made by the emperor, or in reality by the oligarchy. Although the membership of this body was composed of able men, they conducted themselves in a manner thoroughly unbecoming legislators. Contention and selfishness ruled. It anticipated in this respect the later Japanese Diet. At least one constitutional historian has stated that the Japanese cannot criticize the unruly behavior of the Diet in recent times if they are aware of the nature of the first meeting of the *Chihōkan Kaigi*.[34]

Suppressing Press Freedom

A significant outgrowth of this conference was the institution of rigid press and libel laws. Journalists attending the conference in large numbers discussed the political issues of the day and criticized the despotic character of the government with such vehemence that on June 28 the government promulgated measures severely restricting freedom of the press. The restrictive press laws did not represent any antipathy of the Japanese government toward the development of the newspaper industry as such; the government itself founded most of the newspapers that were published in the decade 1872-1882—publications that were used to make known the views of Ōkubo and his fellow oligarchs. But when journals advocating reform became numerous and ever more vociferous against the tyranny of the bureaucrats, the government instituted repressive laws to preserve the unity of the country.[35] These laws were authored by Ōkubo. Editorials appearing in opposition newspapers, which had increased in number after 1872, were censored, and writers who continued to criticize the government were either fined or placed under domiciliary arrest. The laws were revised in 1876 and the severity of the punishment increased.[36] These laws were made purposely ambiguous so they could be interpreted as the government willed. For example, they stated in part that "any newspaper or magazine publishing material deleterious to the peace of the nation shall be forbidden to publish. . . ." [37] It is of interest to note that as early as May of 1868 the Meiji government arrested and imprisoned a newspaper editor for having written articles glorifying the victories of the rebel troops. Fukuchi Genichirō, the publisher of the *Kōkō Shimbun*, had waged war against the Sat-Chō leaders, stating at one time that "we cannot be satisfied unless the Ministerialists are overthrown and the sovereign rights are restored to the Emperor in fact as well as in name." [38] The press laws were not popular with the people, and the oligarchy's attempts to suppress all antigovernment press activities eventually ended in failure. There were also those within the government itself who opposed the laws. Minister of Communications Maejima Hisomu was opposed to them, but he was powerless to persuade Ōkubo to abolish them. Home Minister Ōkubo argued that the laws were necessary to cope with the situation at the time, and Maejima himself conceded that there were some grounds for his colleague's stand.[39]

To Ōkubo disunity within the government was a bane. The newly created *Genrōin*, a result of the reform measure adopted as one means of uniting the divergent interests of the various political factions, held its inaugural ceremony on July 5. The *Daishinin* was also established in line with the decision made at Ōsaka. The government's intention was to have Iwakura accept the presidency of this body, but this he refused to do.[40]

Confronting Ministerial Discord

Despite the liberal reforms, dissatisfaction within the government worked against the unity for which Ōkubo strove. Itagaki did not remain contented for long. The *Genrōin*, he contended, was nothing more than a *kansei gikai*, or a government-inspired assembly.[41] He was also bitter over the delay in the implementation of the *naikaku bunri*, or the separation of the councilors from departmental affairs, which was part of the Ōsaka agreement. This particular clause was intended to prevent members of the *Seiin*, composed solely of *sangi*, from concurrently holding positions as department heads.[42] Shimazu Hisamitsu was another member of the government who continued to harbor resentment against Ōkubo and the general policy of the administration, but for entirely different reasons. As an archconservative, he was in disagreement with what was to him an excessively radical course that the nation was following. In March, 1875, he had complained to Sanjō and Iwakura that no reply was made to his petitions of August 2, 1872, and June 6, 1873.[43] Hisamitsu was promised that his suggestions, a series of reactionary proposals, would be considered at the meeting of the *Genrōin* later that year, but he was not satisfied with such an arrangement. When, on May 6 and again on May 15, Yanagibara Sakimitsu was sent to his home especially to prevail upon him to accept the presidency of the *Genrōin*, Hisamitsu refused to comply.[44] He and Itagaki, the two disgruntled officials of the government, gravitated toward each other, and eventually the conservative and the liberal joined together in opposing the government.

Itagaki's undisguised hostility toward the policy of the Meiji government had other repercussions. His eagerness to realize representative government for Japan as rapidly as possible brought him into conflict with Kido.[45] On September 5 Kido noted in his diary that Itagaki had violated the agreement made at the Ōsaka conference to proceed gradually in the creation of representative institutions. Disgusted with the situation, Kido attempted to resign on grounds of ill health, but Ōkubo argued strenuously against such a decision—this despite the fact that relations between the two men were far from cordial, for, once taking his position as a *sangi*, Kido had become uncompromising in adherence to his own political views.[46] Ōkubo and Itō, however, successfully constrained the Chōshū leader to remain in the government.[47]

Despite the retention of Kido, the coalition government was not fated to last much longer. On October 19 Hisamitsu made a final attempt to disrupt the administration when he recommended that Sanjō be ordered to resign. His contention was that Sanjō was irresolute and unable to exercise adequate control over the civil and military officials, and that if he were not removed the empire was in danger of eventually becoming the slave of the Western nations.[48] The recommendation was not honored; Sanjō was retained.[49] The rebuff brought reaction. Hisamitsu indicated that he had no alternative but to leave the government. His ally, Itagaki, also in ill humor, joined Shimazu Hisamitsu and quit Tōykō's official life.[50] Their resignations were accepted on October 27.[51] The departure from the capital of this pair united in a paradoxical political marriage suggests that the Meiji leaders had both little tolerance for the accelerated liberal program advocated by Itagaki and no thought of accepting the conservatism of Hisamitsu. The policy of gradualism in establishing representative government, definitely a Kido policy with which Ōkubo concurred in essence, emerged victorious. Both Ōkubo and Kido were opposed to imposing a representative form of government prematurely. Kido, for example, felt that if the people are insufficiently enlightened it is necessary for the sovereign to anticipate their unanimous desires and act for them in making the decisions pertaining to affairs of state, and to entrust to the officials the execution of their wishes.[52] Ōkubo conceded that nothing was more important at the time than giving thought to Japan's system of government, but advised against haste. He was against imitating the limited monarchies of the West without giving adequate thought to what type of government would best suit Japan.[53]

With the loss of both Itagaki Taisuke and Shimazu Hisamitsu, the oligarchs, although victors in the constitutional issue, were compelled to labor under the disadvantage of a weakened government. Besides these two men, Iwakura at this time was unavailable for service because of illness. Sanjō, moreover, was not in the most ideal position to render effective leadership, having been the target of the recent attack by Hisamitsu. This was indeed a period that perplexed the minds of the leaders.[54] But Ōkubo did not display any signs of anxiety. On October 20 he wrote the bedridden Iwakura a letter full of confidence and determination. He said:

> One must readily accept difficulties of this nature in a period when a nation is being established or it would be impossible to undertake a task of any great magnitude. The next seven or eight years probably will be no better. At a time like this, it would be impossible to realize one's aspiration of establishing a state unless one has sufficient devotion to the cause and the will to carry the burdens of the nation upon one's own shoulders if necessary.[55]

Ōkubo continued by voicing his resolve to carry out his responsibilities. It is clear that this boldness of spirit was not mere magniloquence. It was confidence nurtured by an awareness of his real ability, tested in the crucible of experience. He had successfully met problems of the most complex nature in the past and did not question for a moment his ability to resolve any that might present themselves in the future.

Touring Northeastern Japan

For several months during the summer of 1876 Ōkubo left pressing matters of state behind him while he toured northeastern Japan. His primary purpose for the trip was to make advance preparations for the coming imperial visit to this area. The Emperor, conforming to the new policy of drawing closer to his subjects, was expected to spend about two months visiting the various prefectures as he had done earlier in 1872 on his circuit of the southwest.[56] The itinerary that Ōkubo arranged for the imperial party, which was to include Saigō Tsugumichi and Kido Kōin, comprised visits to the prefectures of Saitama, Tochigi, Fukushima, Yamagata, Miyagi, Akita, Aomori, Iwate, and Hakodate.[57]

The secondary purpose of Ōkubo's trip was to study at firsthand the results of the Westernization program the new government had initiated. In advance of the main party he visited educational institutions and newly established industries. On May 24 he was taken to a girls' school in Tochigi.[58] On June 5 he visited the Kuwano village reclamation area in Fukushima.[59] After observing a display of local products, he was taken to see a silver mine operating in consonance with the government's program to increase the production of precious metals.[60] In Okitama on June 9 he watched sericultural operations and was guided through a silk filature, an industry created to increase Japan's trade potential.[61] He visited a hospital and the prefectural industrial research center at Yamagata on June 11.[62] On June 17 he observed the operation of justice at the Miyagi prefectural court,[63] and on the following day was shown through a food-experiment laboratory.[64] Then on June 23 Ōkubo arrived at the Iwanuma station to await the arrival of the imperial party.[65] After accompanying the group to Hakodate, he was given permission to return to Tōkyō in advance of the imperial entourage. He arrived in Yokohama on July 19, 1876.[66]

In taking the initiative in arranging for this particular tour, Ōkubo had still another objective in mind. Having grand plans for developing the rich natural resources of northeastern Japan, he had recognized that an imperial visit to the area would serve to lessen the people's resistance to such a program when the time came for its inauguration.[67] It is apparent that the Meiji bureaucrats had little scruple in using the revered name of the Emperor in carrying out their policies. This explains in great measure the success they had in implementing the modernization policy. It is more than likely that if they had not had the prestige of the imperial house to rely upon, their reform program, like that of China after 1898, would have been abortive and the country divided among battling factions. The imperial house has been and remains the unifying factor in Japanese national life.

Economic Philosophy

Ōkubo's keen interest in the economic development of Japan as a means of strengthening the country's military power never flagged. Internal and external problems arose to harass the administrators, but these were allowed to interfere in no way with the long-range policy of *fukoku kyōhei.* The economic philosophy of the foremost advocate of government promotion of industrialization is cogently expressed in a proposal Ōkubo presented to the government for consideration in the summer of 1874.

> Generally speaking, a country's strength is dependent upon the prosperity of its people. The prosperity of the people in turn depends upon their productive capacity. And although the amount of production is determined in a large measure by the diligence of the people engaged in manufacturing industries, a deeper probe for the ultimate determinant reveals no instance when a country's productive power was increased without the patronage and the encouragement of the government and its officials.[68]

In referring to state intervention in the promotion of economic strength, Ōkubo very likely had episodes in Chinese history in mind. Li Ssu (d. 208 B.C.) of the Ch'in dynasty (255–206 B.C.), for example, utilized the authority of the state in abolishing feudalism, unifying writing, and implementing legal and economic reforms. He was especially interested in the encouragement of agriculture, in the furtherance of which private trade was discouraged through a government monopoly of basic products such as salt and iron.[69] Moreover, Ōkubo was undoubtedly aware of Wang An-shih (A.D. 1021–1086) of the Northern Sung dynasty, one of the most prominent statesmen of his time, who not only encouraged the farming class and thereby agricultural production through agricultural loans, but strengthened China's military potential through the institution of the conscription system. He also took the initiative in the creation of a government system of education.[70]

But of more direct influence upon Ōkubo's economic thinking was the example of governmental patronization of manufacturing and trade in England. Having observed England's economic policy at firsthand, Ōkubo was much impressed with its efficacy and became increasingly convinced that a similar policy was indispensable for Japan in its present circumstances.

Ōkubo's proposal to the government for the promotion of industry outlined the results of the Restoration, which he felt had effectively destroyed the narrow traditions and abuses of the past. He noted that since then Japan had reformed its life by adopting the finest features of the various nations of the world, and consequently tremendous changes had been wrought as far as the country's strength was concerned. He observed, however, that the internal situation was still in flux, with the people restive and discontented, despite the diligent work of the government officials on all levels.[71] The Saga rebellion and the Formosan campaign were outgrowths of internal unrest; economic conditions, he believed, played an important part in stimulating the disorders among the people. Rebellion did not thrive in prosperity, he declared: "Because of the critical times through which the nation is traversing, it behooves every government official to concentrate upon the encouragement of manufacturing industries and the increase of production generally in view of establishing the basis for wealth and power." [72]

Ōkubo was highly dissatisfied with the existing condition of industrial development; the production of consumer goods was actually decreasing. This, he contended, was due to the unenlightened attitudes of the people who, being unappreciative of the changing times, would not undertake profitable enterprises, and to officials who had not offered them adequate guidance and encouragement in this direction. The government's annual income of a mere fifty million *yen* was sufficient proof of the nation's low earning power.[73]

Ōkubo's report to the government was not entirely pessimistic. To indicate that the future was far from hopeless, he cited the example of England, a small island country comparable to Japan, which had taken advantage of its ports and mineral resources to establish itself as an outstanding nation. He then described in detail England's mercantilistic policy under which it reserved the country's shipping to the native trading fleet.[74] The development of trade stimulated domestic industries, he noted, and went on to explain very knowledgeably the purpose behind the

British Navigation Acts, namely, to build up a merchant marine, to train sailors, and to prevent the unlimited importation of foreign goods, thereby offering protection to home industries. Ōkubo pointed out that, having attained its goal, England then reverted to free trade. This protective policy of the British government, he said, had enabled England to amass wealth and increase her power.[75]

There is no doubt that Ōkubo wished to emulate the British mercantilist policy. He recognized, however, that differences in location, climate, custom, and the temporal setting in which Japan would begin would preclude the development of enterprises exactly like those of the English, and hence he believed it impossible to adhere strictly to their pattern. But he was convinced that England should serve as the model.[76]

Ōkubo had certain misgivings about his countrymen's ability to accomplish for Japan what the British had done for England. He said that "our country's topography and natural resources are similar to those of England, but the character of our people is not as strong. It is the responsibility of the government to encourage them to apply themselves diligently to manufacturing enterprises." [77]

In his conclusion, Ōkubo suggested to the government that a survey be made of regions where natural resources existed, an estimate be drawn up of the available working force to engage in productive endeavors, and a plan be formulated to encourage the development of factories. Proper laws, he suggested, should then be enacted to implement the government's economic policy.[78]

Government intervention in developing Japan's industrial potential was necessitated by the lack of individual initiative among the people, a characteristic stifled during the long period of feudalism. Scarcity of capital also forced government participation in the establishment of large-scale capitalistic enterprises. Still another factor was Japan's meager industrial experience. No one was more aware than Ōkubo that without government aid Japan could not make the transition from a relatively simple economy to the more complex industrial order of the West.[79]

Government control and encouragement of industries in Japan was responsible for the rapid rise of capital holdings of such families as the Mitsui, Mitsubishi, Shimada, and Ono; the ties between such families and the Meiji government were close. The tremendous increase in wealth among these businessmen with political affiliations does not, however, imply that this produced a politically powerful middle class.

Despite the marriage of business and government, the political authority continued to rest with the government, thus checking the growth of liberalism in Japan.[80]

Promoting Economic Development

After his return from the world tour in 1873, Ōkubo had consistently promoted a course of industrial growth despite the disruptions caused by the Korean, Saga, and Formosan incidents.[81] He had accepted the position of Minister of Home Affairs specifically to execute the westernization policy, working through one of the ministry's important bureaus—the *kangyōryō*, or the industrial promotion bureau.

Realizing that agriculture was the basic industry of the land, Ōkubo made plans in 1874 to establish an agricultural school to train young men who would become the teachers and leaders in this industry. Its curriculum was to include veterinary science and agricultural chemistry, among other subjects, with instructors from America and Europe. It was not, however, until 1876 that the institution was actually established. Students were recruited from the various prefectures and attended their first classes in 1877.[82] Besides theory, the students were required to gain practical experience in reclamation work, the use of various farm implements, the handling of horses, and the mixing and use of fertilizers. Eventually the school was to become the College of Agriculture of the Tōkyō Imperial University.[83] Ōkubo marked his interest in the school by donating, in 1877, about fifty-four hundred *yen* to be used for the aid of the needy students of agriculture.[84]

In 1877 he also established the Mita agricultural experimental station, on the site of the former Satsuma residence, where plants obtained from France and elsewhere were grown. His emphasis on agricultural production was based upon the premise that agricultural products were the country's most important trade items, and that an increase in Japan's volume of trade would have an important bearing upon the development of domestic industries. The products of the government experimental station, devoted to seed and plant improvement, were distributed to the areas best suited for their growth and were intended to contribute toward increasing farm productivity.[85]

Ōkubo also had an experimental stock-breeding center established at Shinjuku upon the suggestion of an American who indicated that Japanese livestock needed improvement. Imported cattle and sheep were scientifically bred, and the improved strains were apportioned to the various livestock-raising regions.[86]

Ōkubo's economic program was not to terminate here. To the end of establishing a more favorable balance of trade by decreasing Japan's imports, he advocated in 1876 the erection of a textile factory for the manufacture of woolens, a product which still had to be acquired from abroad.[87] The Satsuma rebellion temporarily halted the plan, and it was not until 1879, a year after Ōkubo's death, that the factory was finally established.[88] It was he who was also responsible for the founding of the silk filature in Gumma prefecture for the reeling of raw silk to be placed in the export trade. The idea for its establishment crystallized in Ōkubo's mind during his visit to a filature in Lyon, France, after the manager told him that the raw silk being used there had come from Japan.[89] If Japan had the raw silk, Ōkubo reasoned, why could she not process it herself?

A statement Ōkubo later made to the manager of the government filature, which was then in the process of being constructed in Gumma, revealed the nature of the government's long-range industrialization policy. The manager was told that, although the plant would initially be controlled by the government, it would ultimately be sold to private interests. Ōkubo therefore urged him to spare no expense in the purchase of the best machinery available. This, he said, would give the private owner who later acquired the filature from the government a better chance of survival than if inferior equipment were installed. He did not wish to see private owners fail in any of the ventures the government had a hand in establishing and was prepared to use the power of the government to insure that they were given a healthy start.[90]

The government policy of aid to agriculture took the form of subsidies and encouragement in the use of new equipment by the farming class.[91] The policy paid dividends; there was to be a tremendous development of agriculture, both in acreage and per-acre productivity. Among other factors that contributed to this progress were the abolition of the feudal land system, the development of internal communication and transportation systems which opened up new markets for farm products, and the growth of the non-agricultural population dependent upon commerce and industry which increased demand for agricultural products.[92]

Ōkubo was also concerned with the development of the shipping industry in Japan because of its importance in both war and peace. In 1875 there were two native shipping firms, the Yūbin Kisen Kaisha and the Mitsubishi Kaisha, which competed so fiercely that freight rates were progressively lowered until they were hovering near the point of no profit. Had this situation been allowed to continue, one or the other company would have inevitably become bankrupt. Ōkubo, who had learned to appreciate the value of shipping during the Formosan expedition, arranged for the establishment of a single strong shipping line. The government then offered the newly reorganized Mitsubishi Kaisha, which was to be the forerunner of the N.Y.K. (Nippon Yūsen Kaisha) line, a subsidy of two hundred and fifty thousand *yen* annually, thirteen government-owned ship, plus eighteen others the government has purchased from the now defunct Yūbin Kisen Kaisha. Iwasaki Yatarō was retained to direct the operation of the new line because he had displayed unusual managerial talent as the head of the old Mitsubishi Kaisha.[93] Private foreign lines, however, could not compete with the type of direct subsidy offered by the Japanese government to the Japanese line. As a result, the American Pacific Mail Steamship Company went out of business, selling to the new Japanese company three of its ships used in the Yokohama-Kōbe-Nagasaki-Shanghai trade, and its warehouses in Kōbe and Shanghai. Because of the policy initiated by Ōkubo and the other Meiji leaders, within sixteen years Japan had taken over much of the shipping trade formerly dominated by the foreign firm. In time, Japan monopolized its intercoastal trade.[94]

Ōkubo then took steps to train an adequate number of seamen to man the merchant marine. On September 15, 1875, a government order was issued to the Mitsubishi Kaisha, directing the company to establish a nautical college to train mariners. For this purpose the firm was given an additional one hundred and fifty thousand *yen* annually.[95] As a result the Yūsen Kisen Mitsubishi Kaisha Shōsen Gakkō was established, and in January, 1876, it began recruiting students, the first class graduating a year later.[96]

Another Ōkubo measure to promote trade was the national exposition of 1877, held to introduce to the world the products of Japan.[97] He had learned the effectiveness of such public exhibitions from past experience. In 1867 Iwashita Masahira took goods produced in Satsuma and the Ryūkyū Islands to the great Paris Exposition.[98] Again, in 1874, Japan accepted an invitation to display its products at a world exposition in the

United States. On this occasion Ōkubo established an office within the Ministry of Home Affairs with himself as director to make preparations for the exhibition. The results of Japan's participation in the Philadelphia Exposition had been highly gratifying; exports to the United States increased considerably. Consequently, in 1876, Ōkubo petitioned Sanjō, asking for government sanction to hold a similar exposition in Tōkyō at Ueno Park between February 15 and June 15, 1877.[99] The suggestion was readily accepted and Ōkubo was directed to supervise the undertaking with the assistance of Matsukata Masayoshi. However, the outbreak early that year of the Satsuma rebellion forced the postponement of the exposition until August, 1877.[100]

Thus, by various means, Ōkubo, adhering generally to the mercantilist philosophy, sowed the seeds of economic modernization. Because, as Japanese economic historians point out, the first decade of the Meiji era was an experimental stage in industrialization, a "sprouting phase," no extraordinary progress was observable in the nation's economic life.[101] Ōkubo had nevertheless planted well. The fruits of his labor, however, were to come after his death. He did not live to see his economic field appearing "white unto harvest." In a fitting tribute to the able innovator and industrializer, an editorial in the Tōkyō *Akebono* of June 3, 1878, eulogized the late Home Minister Ōkubo Toshimichi, stating among other things that he had a deep interest in the promotion of industries, his objective being to make Japan as economically self-sufficient as possible.[102]

Ōkubo believed that through rapid industrialization a long step could be taken to alleviate the economic pressures impinging upon the samurai class; industries could absorb the unemployed former warriors and make them a constructive element in Japanese society. To facilitate the task of finding employment for the samurai, Ōkubo in 1876 established the *jusan kyoku*, an employment bureau within the Ministry of Home Affairs. He also initiated specific programs designed to settle samurai on the land. The government colonization program was to furnish volunteer settlers with tools and the necessary funds with which they could erect their homes and develop virgin lands. Ōkubo selected Fukushima as a suitable site for this program. And for the samurai who wished to engage in farming close to home, Home Minister Ōkubo had a plan for allotting them undeveloped land in their own neighborhoods. Another of his schemes to give employment to the former warriors was through a program of public works, which included government-sponsored river- and harbor-improvement projects.[103] These were obviously steps taken to prevent an internal explosion caused by the most politically active class in Japan, the samurai.

Dealing with Internal Unrest

Although the process of westernization proceeded steadily under the guidance of the government, there was continued resistance to its policies, particularly from the samurai dissidents. When, on March 28, 1876, the central government prohibited the samurai from bearing two swords, the badge of the warrior class, a rumble of indignation became increasingly audible within their ranks.[104] Then, on August 5, 1876, the government issued an edict making compulsory the commutation of all feudal pensions, thus causing further unrest. After the Restoration the new government had assumed the burden of paying the annual rice stipends of the *daimyō* and samurai in order to win their loyalty. The paying of the annual rice stipend, however, had placed a heavy strain upon the impoverished national treasury. By 1871 the government offered to commute these privileges into government bonds, so enabling it to transform immediate cash requirements into long-term obligations. The government would not have to pay annual payments in rice or the cash equivalent but would only be required to pay interest upon the bonds issued. This commutation scheme was devised by Ōkubo, the Finance Minister at the time.[105] Now the decree of 1876 ordained that all former members of the warrior class transform their incomes, if they had not already done so voluntarily, into government bonds at from 5 to 7 per cent interest. The samurai, especially those with small incomes, suffered by the transfer of their perpetual feudal claims into cash or government bonds; their assets were reduced to one-half their original value. Thus a pensioner who had a hereditary income of fifty thousand *yen* was not entitled to a capital sum of twenty-five thousand *yen*, payable at the convenience of the government in the course of thirty years, but would receive interest at 5 per cent on that amount, or only 12,500 *yen*. The *daimyō*, with larger incomes, suffered much less than the average samurai under this measure. Out of the total of over three hundred thousand pensioners at this time, only a little more than 580 had incomes over one thousand *yen*.[106]

The government's decree of 1876 was not only a measure to improve its financial situation, but also an attempt to destroy every vestige of feudalism in Japanese life. It had dire economic as well as social consequences for the samurai. They did not allow the liquidation of their class without a struggle. In Kumamoto two hundred rebels assembled at the Fujisaki shrine on the night of October 24 and, after dividing into seven groups, attacked the government barracks and the prefectural office in that city. The garrison commander, Major General Taneda Masaaki, and the prefectural governor, Yasuoka Yoshitaka, were murdered by the dissidents. The rebellion, however, was shortlived; by the following day it had been quelled by the government troops.[107] Yet this rebellion incited other insurrections.[108] Three days later four hundred samurai of the Akizuki *han* (Fukuoka prefecture) revolted. Then in November came the Hagi rebellion led by Maebara Issei, the former assistant war minister. He had raised the standard of revolt against the government's land tax reform, the Sakhalin-Kurile exchange, and the unfair treatment of the samurai class. By November 11 government forces had succeeded in suppressing this uprising.[109]

The peasant class also had its grievances against the government.[110] Peasant dissatisfaction centered around the land tax; the military conscription system; the abolition of the *eta*, or pariah, class; the change to the solar calendar; the decree to dress their hair in Western fashion; the establishment of elementary schools; the initiation of public hygienic measures, such as the cholera prevention program; and the general rise in the price of consumer goods.[111] Economic factors appear to have been the basis of most complaints. In 1876 there were farmer revolts in Naga-gun, Wakayama prefecture, and several in Ibaragi and Mie prefectures.[112]

To mitigate peasant dissatisfaction, Ōkubo, as director of the land tax revision bureau, which had been established in March, 1875, presented to Sanjō, on December 27, 1876, a proposal for the reduction of the land tax.[113] Ōkubo's petition stated that, in spite of the increased national production and the flourishing state of the commercial community, the farmers had yet to be affected by Japan's economic prosperity. Their impoverishment, it said, caused them to rebel. Pointing out that the land-tax reform of 1873, although a definite improvement over that of 1872, was still unsatisfactory, he requested that the tax be reduced from 3 per cent to 2½ per cent.[114] The proposal received government sanction on December 30, and the new tax law went into effect on January 4, 1877.[115] Agriculture was considered the basic industry upon which the country's economic well-being depended, and the reduction of the land tax was an indication of the steadily growing strength of the land-owning and merchant classes in relation to the samurai caste. The measure to reduce the land tax had a definite relation to the forced commutation of samurai pensions. The latter was effected because the government, anticipating the land-tax reduction and the attendant decrease in revenue, realized it could no longer afford to support a nonproductive warrior class. The decision to revise the land tax therefore implied that the samurai class was to be sacrificed to the peasants who formed the backbone of Japanese agriculture.

Crushing the Satsuma Rebellion

The Satsuma rebellion represented the last serious attempt of a samurai faction to gain control of the government. Inasmuch as the insurrection did not include samurai of provinces other than of Satsuma, it cannot be considered a national resistance movement. It was essentially a Saigō-inspired rebellion of Satsuma samurai.

It will be recalled that after the defeat of the war party in 1873 in the struggle centering around the Korean question, Saigō had returned to Kagoshima. He had settled down there to an apparently passive life, refusing to lend overt support to his samurai compeers who on various occasions thereafter had attempted unsuccessfully to oppose the government leaders they accused of usurping imperial authority. Saigō, however, had in reality not been indifferent to nor inactive in the samurai cause. He was thought to have been implicated indirectly in the Saga rebellion of 1874. It was for the purpose of coaxing him into the government camp that Shimazu Hisamitsu had been ordered back to Kagoshima, a move that proved abortive.[116] Japanese historians contend that Saigō opposed taking advantage of the internal unrest created by the Hagi rebellion led by Maebara Issei, preferring to wait for a more opportune time to strike against the government.[117]

In Kagoshima Saigō had built up his own following. Utilizing the government pension granted to him for his service to the nation in the war of the Restoration, he founded and maintained in the city a so-called *Shigakkō*, or private school. Its objective was to nurture in its students the traditional Satsuma samurai spirit and to defend the nation against the incoming tide of Occidentalism with its stress upon individualism.[118]

Saigō hoped to produce a cadre of well-disciplined young men trained for government service, a group of men who would take over the government under his leadership after a revolution.[119] The school was in essence a military academy to prepare students to devote their lives to forwarding the samurai cause, or essentially the Saigō cause. Pro-Saigō historians have, of course, denied this.[120] Branch schools were eventually established in 124 districts throughout the city of Kagoshima, in which stress was laid upon the military arts and at least one hour each day was spent in the study of Chinese literature.[121] Paradoxically, some foreigners were employed as instructors, and students who proved themselves extraordinarily talented were sent to Europe to study military tactics.[122] By 1875 the *Shigakkō* in Kagoshima alone had seven thousand students while branch institutions with from three hundred to a thousand students had been established in the various towns and villages of the perfecture.[123]

Significantly, the Kagoshima arsenal and powder factories and the textile mill of the prefecture were kept operating at full capacity. Although the arsenal had been transferred to the government, the Kagoshima authorities allowed no one other than native officials within its confines.[124] These facilities were to prove useful in the hands of the *Shigakkō* party.

The authority of the national government in Kagoshima was weak and continued to decrease as the strength of Saigō's private schools increased. By the end of 1876 Kagoshima had become practically an autonomous political entity. Ōyama Tsunayoshi, although a government official, aided and abetted the *Shigakkō* cause.[125] Fully aware of the situation, Home Minister Ōkubo recalled Ōyama in July, 1876, and ordered him to initiate a thorough reform of the prefectural administration. Ōyama, however, begged for the deferment of this move, explaining that the existing situation in the prefecture would not permit such a reform. Therefore, in October, Ōkubo dispatched a subordinate to Kagoshima with orders to undertake whatever reforms were necessary, but his mission was unsuccessful.[126] At this time Kido, always concerned over Satsuma's control in national affairs and now aware of the strength of the *Shigakkō* movement, urged Ōkubo to deal firmly with the dangerous situation in Kagoshima.[127] Ōkubo ordered ten or more members of the *Keishichō,* or the Metropolitan Police Bureau, under Nakahara Hisao, to carry on a secret investigation of the activities of Saigō's followers.[128]

It was a difficult task for Ōkubo to take positive action against his fellow samurai in Satsuma, especially in view of his desire to regain his former popularity among them. On the other hand, if he were to refuse to act on Kido's demands, he would reap the wrath of the Chōshū faction, and would become the target of attack not only from the *Shigakkō* party, but from members within the government as well. Ōkubo chose to take direct action to combat the forces of opposition in his own province.[129] Ōkubo has been criticized for having yielded to *han* jealousy and for advocating positive measures to extend the authority of the national government over Kagoshima; his critic contends that he should have pursued a policy of peace and exerted his effort in guiding the *Shigakkō* movement in the direction of reason.[130]

The national government, in line with Kido's harsh policy toward its opponents, had been increasing its fighting potential. By 1876 its army had been augmented by thirty thousand men, and its navy had nine warships and eight steam transports available for service.[131] And as a precautionary measure, the government, in January, 1877, requisitioned a steam transport from the Mitsubishi Kaisha to the employed specifically for the removal of arms and munitions stored in the Kagoshima arsenal.

When the Kagoshima samurai were informed of this move the members of the *Shigakkō* broke into the powder magazine on the nights of January 29 and 30, and on the following night entered the naval shipyard and carried off large quantities of weapons and other war materials. They occupied the shipyard and gave it the name which it had originally borne during the Shimazu period, the Shūseikan. Here the rebels were to manufacture small arms and ammunition to be used against the government troops.[132] On February 2 the Satsuma insurgents attempted to prevent the government transport from taking aboard the powder in the magazine.[133]

The mood of rebellion was rising. When on February 4 the news of the situation in Kagoshima reached Kyōto, where the majority of the government officials had come to attend the ceremony for the opening of the Ōsaka-Kyōto railway line, an emergency conference was immediately held. As a result, Admiral Kawamura Sumiyoshi, a Satsuma man, was sent to Kagoshima. There Governor Ōyama informed him that the samurai class in Satsuma had taken up arms in the belief that the government was preparing to attack Kagoshima, a conclusion based upon the alleged confession, according to Kawamura's information, of two of the government police agents captured by members of the Saigō faction. Admiral

Kawamura requested a personal interview with Saigō, hoping he could by this means forestall a civil war, but this interview never materialized.[134] Saigō, with fifteen thousand men, had already marched northward, ostensibly to carry on negotiations with the central government officials.[135] On the evening of February 9 Kawamura sent a telegram to the government announcing the failure of his mission and the outbreak of civil war.[136] Ōkubo, who had been in Tōkyō, made immediate plans to join his colleagues in Kyōto as soon as he heard of the latest developments, arriving in Kōbe on February 16. There he conferred with Admiral Kawamura, and on the following day the Meiji leaders decided to send a punitive force against Saigō with Prince Arisugawa as commander-in-chief.[137] On February 19 the central government proclaimed civil war.[138]

In the meantime, the rebels who had reached Kumamoto challenged the imperial garrison troops there. On February 20 Saigō's men laid siege to the castle of Kumamoto, in which the government forces had taken up position. It was saved only by the timely arrival of reinforcements.[139] Finally, on September 24, Saigō was wounded in a fierce battle at Shiroyama, an eminence overlooking the city of Kagoshima. One of his lieutenants performed the friendly office of severing his chief's head from his shoulders to spare him from falling alive into enemy hands.[140]

With the defeat of the rebel forces at Shiroyama the civil war was ended. This was announced by the government on September 25.[141] The losses on both sides were heavy, totaling over thirteen thousand killed and over twenty thousand wounded. Kagoshima was almost entirely destroyed, and the greater portion of Kumamoto reduced to ashes.[142]

The suppression of this large-scale samurai uprising by government forces proved once more the superiority of the modernized conscript army. Even with this force, however, Ōkubo realized that the government would have had difficulty crushing the rebellion had it occurred earlier—say, during the time of the Saga uprising or the Formosan campaign. Writing to Itō during the course of the Satsuma rebellion, he expressed the thought that, although the present difficulty was unquestionably a great misfortune, he was nevertheless grateful from the viewpoint of the court that it was occurring at the time it was and not any earlier.[143]

One of the unanswered historical questions of this period is whether or not Ōkubo sent government agents to Kagoshima with the express order to assassinate Saigō if this were necessary to prevent a war. One pro-Saigō historian points out that Tanaka Naoya, one of the government spies, dispatched a telegram to Tōkyō saying that ordinary means of control would not pacify the restive members of the *Shigakkō* and suggesting that fire be set to the three powder magazines within the city. During the ensuing excitement, he wired, Saigō and forty of his compeers ought to be put to the sword. This message, falling into the hands of the rebels, was responsible for commencement of the civil war. The government, in attempting to explain the telegram, indicated that the term *shisatsu* (to observe), written in *kana*, or Japanese syllabary, in telegraphic messages, was misinterpreted by the Saigō followers as *shisatsu* (to pierce).[144] There is also the allegation that the chief of the Metropolitan Police Bureau had ordered his agents to kill Saigō if he acted suspiciously.[145] These historians point to the confession made by Nakahara in which he admitted that the objectives of the police agents were to create a division within the ranks of the *Shigakkō*, win the members over to the government camp, break up the *Shigakkō*, and, in the event an uprising took place, assassinate Saigō and kill his followers to the man.[146]

On the other side, Mounsey makes the point that the *Shigakkō* party extorted Nakahara's confession by torture in order to afford the people of Kagoshima convincing proof of the existence of a conspiracy to kill Saigō and thus create a *casus belli*.[147] Tanaka Sōgorō argues that circumstances—that is, the growing division between the government and the samurai faction in Kagoshima—made an ultimate clash between these two forces inevitable. He is of the opinion that the rebellion would have occurred with or without Saigō. Ōkubo, he believes, was aware of this. Hence he concludes that there was no logical reason for Ōkubo wanting to have Saigō liquidated.[148] Other Japanese historians have taken the view that sentimentality would keep Ōkubo from wanting to have his friend of childhood days obliterated from the political scene by violent means. They have pointed out that Ōkubo went so far as to volunteer to meet with Saigō in an attempt to avoid a carnage.[149] This scheme was not carried out because (1) there was a strong element within the government that wished to suppress the Satsuma samurai faction with an immediate resort to arms; (2) there were some who were unconvinced that the plan would succeed and moreover feared for Ōkubo's life if he met with Saigō; and (3) there were those who suspected that Ōkubo might ally himself with Saigō.[150]

In summarizing some of the factors that incited the rebellion, mention must be made of the relationship between Ōkubo and Saigō, two men representing incompatible political ideals which finally destroyed their friendship. Disgruntled because he had no position of national prominence from which to champion his cause, Saigō quietly prepared for the day when he could overthrow Ōkubo and the policy for which he stood. He wished to restore a feudal system with the emperor substituted for the *shōgun* and, of course, to have the Satsuma *han* and his colleagues entrusted with the direction of national affairs. The Satsuma samurai blamed Ōkubo and his faction for the loss of social, economic, and political privileges. They supported Saigō in the belief that once in authority he would, among other things, make the civil and military branches of the government a monopoly of the samurai, allow them to wear their swords, and repeal the pension commutation act.[151] When the hated Meiji government began taking steps to extend its rule over the semi-independent state of Kagoshima by attempting to reform the prefectural administration, its people, strongly imbued with the separatist ideas of the Satsuma *han*, drew closer to Saigō. The capture of the government spies further strengthened their resolve to resist. The immediate cause of the rebellion, however, was the government's decision to remove military stores from Kagoshima.

Inasmuch as the hostilities were precipitated by the enthusiasm of the *Shigakkō* members and not by Saigō's orders—he was in Ōsumi when the members of his faction attacked the government military establishments—it is difficult to accept without some qualification the thesis that the rebellion was a personal affair of Saigō, motivated by his frustrations.[152] Rather it was motivated by the frustrations of both Saigō and the Satsuma samurai who were acutely aware that their peculiar position in society was being prejudiced by the policy of the national government. Had the samurai not felt the searing resentment toward Ōkubo and the other Meiji leaders in Tōkyō, Saigō could not have rallied them to his side in such great numbers. The rebellion was in essence a war between the Satsuma samurai and Ōkubo and only secondarily a personal conflict between Saigō and Ōkubo. For example, Watanabe states:

> At first Saigō and Ōkubo belonged to Satsuma, then Satsuma came under the control of Saigō and Ōkubo. Later Ōkubo became a part of the central government, and it eventually came under his control. Saigō and the samurai in the province, acutely aware of their contributions to the Restoration, desired to take possession of the na-

tional government. The conflict between Satsuma and Ōkubo terminated in civil war.[153]

The tremendous ill feeling that the people in Kagoshima harbored toward Ōkubo was expressed during the Satsuma rebellion when his home was destroyed by an angry mob.[154] They considered him a traitor to the *han* because of his aid to its enemy. Did not this statesman have any sentiment toward his fellow samurai? He undoubtedly did, although his feeling toward them had cooled as his popularity among them declined. The fact that he temporized until pressure from Kido prodded him into taking positive steps against Kagoshima indicates his reluctance to antagonize those in his province any more than it was necessary. But Ōkubo was a national leader, persistent in his objective of unifying the country. To have allowed sentiment to interfere on this occasion would have compromised the government's position and defeated his own purpose. It is fortunate for Japan, during a period when divisive forces might easily have rent it asunder, that it possessed a tough-minded man of action such as Ōkubo. He was hated and called evil-hearted, wicked, crafty, calculating, and unapproachable, but without him and men of his caliber at the helm the history of modern Japan might have been entirely different. Had conservatism been allowed to triumph because of government vacillation, Japan, if it had reverted to a feudal state, could never have made its meteoric rise to modernism.

Aiding Korea

During the height of the Satsuma rebellion Ōkubo made a friendly gesture toward Korea. Word that the Korean government had made a request for food to feed its famine-stricken populace reached Japanese leaders while they were meeting in Kyōto. The majority of them were for rejecting the request in view of the existing emergency in Japan. But Ōkubo overruled the majority by arguing that to give aid to Korea in its present situation was Japan's moral responsibility. He had a ship then in military service made available to transport grain to Korea.[155] His action, in this matter at least, reveals his authority in the Council of State if not his sense of humanity. The gesture of cordiality undoubtedly was largely politically motivated; this was an opportunity to lessen the animosity the Koreans had for the Japanese and to bring Korea into friendly relations with Japan.

The gesture would also benefit Japan from the standpoint of her relations with the Western nations.

Home Life

Although Ōkubo in public life was coldly austere, he seems to have shed this manner in the presence of his family. He was married to a woman called Masuko, but very little has been written about her, no doubt in conformity with Japanese custom which relegated women to the background. And, as was the custom among Japanese men of wealth and position, he maintained a concubine, although his biographers have described him as a man of high moral character.[156] A newspaper account on October 29, 1878, reported that the "late Ōkubo Toshimichi's concubine, Oyu, on the sixteenth gave birth to a baby boy who was named Toshikata." [157] His children were Yoshiko, the eldest daughter, who was married to Ishūin Hikokichi; and sons, Hikokuma, whose name was later changed to Toshikazu; Nobukuma, who later adopted his mother's family name and became Makino Shinken; Toshitake; Tatsukuma; Yukuma, who was adopted by the Ishihara family; Shunkuma; Shichikuma; and Toshikata.[158] With these children Ōkubo appears to have been extremely indulgent. As already indicated, he took great interest in their education, placing two of them in American schools in the care of Takahashi Shinkichi, a friend living in the United States. Ōkubo's diversions included *shōgi*, smoking, hunting, and attending *sumō* matches.[159] Men in public life are often judged solely upon the basis of the public's impressions of them. This was particularly true for Ōkubo. His enemies were numerous, and before long he was to become a victim of their hate.

Sacrifice upon the Altar of Progress

At six o'clock on the morning of May 14, 1878, Ōkubo had a conversation with Yamayoshi Morisuke, the governor of Fukushima prefecture, during the course of which Ōkubo told him that thirty years would be required to realize the objectives of the imperial government. The first ten years, the first phase in the development of Japan, constituted a beginning in this direction. The second phase would see the establishment of internal order and the completion of the program of strengthening the nation. This was the period, he intimated to Yamayoshi, into which Japan was moving. He expressed his resolve to overcome whatever obstacles might lie in the future to reach these goals. The third decade would be the period in which the progress made would have to be maintained through the wise direction of the succeeding leaders.[160] His words were prophetic. But little did he realize that these would be among his last utterances.

He left his residence in Kasumigaseki at eight o'clock in a carriage drawn by two horses for an engagement at the imperial palace. The sky was overcast, and there was hardly a soul on the streets. As the coach headed for Shimizudani, Ōkubo glanced over some documents. Suddenly some men with drawn swords leaped out from behind a small building located along the route and hacked at the horses' legs, incapacitating them. They then killed the coachman, and when Ōkubo tried to leave the carriage, Shimada Ichirō, one of the six conspirators, attacked him with his dirk, making a gaping wound from his mid-forehead to below his eyes. The assassin pulled him out of the coach and then applied the coup de grace. When the groom, who had escaped the murderers, returned with aid, the assassins had fled. It was Saigō Tsugumichi who took Ōkubo's body back to the Ōkubo home.[161]

Most Ōkubo biographers have described their subject as having met death with courage. One of them states that Ōkubo was unperturbed when the attackers made their appearance, ordering them to wait while he wrapped his documents in a *furoshiki*.[162] On the other hand, Watanabe notes that according to one description of Ōkubo's final moments, he pleaded with his assassins to spare his life, promising to accede to whatever demands they might make upon him.[163] Ōkubo's attempt to leave the carriage to escape the murderers apparently indicates that he was not as poised under imminent death as some of his admirers would believe. (The death of the Japanese leader might have been averted had the police offered Ōkubo greater protection. A few days prior to the murder an anonymous informant had sent Ōkubo a letter warning him of a possible attempt upon his life, but he placed little credence in the missive.[164])

The six samurai conspirators—five from Ishikawa prefecture and one from Shimane prefecture—under the leadership of Shimada Ichirō, gave themselves up after committing the crime and were eventually tried and executed. During the trial they justified their deed by charging that Ōkubo had (1) suppressed the rights of the people, (2) monopolized administrative affairs, (3) promulgated laws arbitrarily, (4) depleted the national treasury through expenditures upon unnecessary public works projects, (5) fomented disorders by weakening the authority of the patriotic samurai, and (6) prejudiced Japan's national rights through improper handling of foreign relations.[165]

It is evident from the statement of motives that the charges made against Ōkubo represented not merely the grievances of the samurai per se, but also those of all opposition groups who objected to the monopolization of power by the Satsuma strongman. It is probable that the samurai conservatives were most directly concerned with conspiracy inasmuch as Ōkubo's policies were highly prejudicial to the warrior class, but the results of the plot were not discountenanced by the extreme liberals of the Itagaki stamp who were dissatisfied with the government's excessively deliberate progress in the direction of a constitutional government. Hence, although it would be convenient to summarize by stating that Ōkubo was a martyr to progress, such a conclusion would not be precisely true. He was murdered because the opposition, both conservatives and radicals of the day, were jealous of his arbitrary exercise of authority; unless he were removed from the political scene, their own aspirations would continue to be frustrated. Ōkubo's murder set a precedent for subsequent political assassinations of top government officials.

Whether the assassins' principal incentive in murdering Ōkubo was the government's failure to establish representative institutions or the avenging of the death of Saigō has been disputed, but the consensus is that revenge was an important motivation.[166] Ōkubo's murder therefore was a direct consequence of the Satsuma rebellion. These two events taken together had vital political consequences for Japan. Through the suppression of the rebellion, one of the last semi-independent states of the nation was brought under the direct control of the central government. Again the defeat of the samurai elite by government troops vindicated the thesis of the Meiji leaders that a conscript army could be molded into as fine and effective a fighting force as that composed of samurai. Finally, Ōkubo's murder hastened the arrival of constitutional government in Japan. The people looked upon the assassins as champions of a more liberal rule, and increasing discussions of representative institutions were engendered. As a result the government was induced to expedite the establishment of local assemblies, a plan, ironically, which a governors' conference called by Ōkubo just prior to his death had approved. Thus in July, 1878, the Meiji government announced that prefectural assemblies would be established with members elected by a restricted male electorate.[167]

Summary

Ōkubo's career is a classic example of the adage that "power seldom grows old at court." His life was ended at the very prime, at the height of his power. By 1878 he was unquestionably the strongest man in the government, a position to which he had propelled himself, not so much through guile as in his earlier political life, but, after the Restoration, through the display of sheer competence, untiring persistence, and an undeviating dedication to his cause. If unpopular with many outside of the government, he was held in high respect by his colleagues because of his proven ability as an administrator. The successful handling of the Formosan negotiations established him as a capable negotiator and elevated him in political stature, although it is now evident that he could not have succeeded had he relied solely upon his own resources. After receiving the accolade of a generally grateful nation for defeating the empire of China in diplomacy, it was unnecessary for him thereafter to use brazen power tactics to retain his authority. In fact, his success was of such magnitude that he had little or no misgivings as to the future stability of his position when he accepted the compromise at the Ōsaka conference designed to limit his power. Ōkubo's loyalty to the nation remained in general unshaken. In essence, he symbolized the growing concept of nationalism in Japan, a concept that he more than any other single leader in the early Meiji period helped to nurture. The power Ōkubo exerted in court was not of long duration but, fortunately for Japan, by 1878 its basic policies were established and the country was sufficiently along the road to economic maturity so that succeeding leaders could carry on the work he had so successfully begun.

IX
Summary and Conclusions

In the preceding pages an attempt has been made to portray the life of one of the most important and interesting figures in Restoration and early Meiji history. Although Japan was fortunate in having a number of truly great men to guide her destiny during the crucial transition from feudalism to modernism, the selection of one out of a galaxy of outstanding individuals as the greatest leader of the era may lay the writer open to criticism. It is obvious, however, when a comparison is made of the so-called triumvirate of the Restoration, each with his particular genius, that Ōkubo's contributions to the establishment and maintenance of the new order in Japan were among the most fundamental. After sharing in the work of the Restoration, his talent as a statesman was exhibited, and he most confidently and efficiently directed the course of the new government during the subsequent decade. To those who have looked closely at his life he appears to have been the granitic pillar of state, stable and powerful. To conclude that Ōkubo and his contemporaries controlled the events that changed the course of Japanese history would be controvertible, but there is no doubt that in his relatively short life Ōkubo helped to shape history by modifying and directing environmental forces. Writing in 1909, Watanabe Shūjirō, who certainly was not one to eulogize his subject, conceded that "there has been no one to replace Ōkubo." [1] And indeed it is doubtful that Japan has since produced a leader of his caliber.

He was one of the many bright young lower samurai who as *han* officials participated in the political reform movements in the Tempō era. From this group were to emerge the strong leaders who, supported by the dissident groups in general—*kuge, rōnin,* peasants, and *chōnin*—as well as by factors such as external pressures upon the Bakufu and the weakness of the Edo regime itself, accomplished the Restoration. Ōkubo was in the forefront of this movement and subsequently became one of the chief architects of the Meiji government. His peers, the samurai, ran the government on an authoritarian basis.

Ōkubo's constitutional philosophy, however, was neither liberal nor conservative. A gradualist, he was for a limited monarchy with representative institutions. He wisely preached against a hasty, ill-advised move to give a people with no experience in self-government privileges that they could not intelligently utilize. Opinion is varied as to what his gradualism implied. One Japanese historian speculates that, had Ōkubo lived another decade, he and not Itō would have been considered the father of the Japanese constitution.[2] Another writer states that he served as the bulwark against the influx of democratic ideas, thus preventing the alien concepts from taking root prematurely in Japanese soil. The writer continues:

> He lived to be only forty-nine, but with his vigor he might have been influential in politics for at least twenty more years had he not been murdered. If he had lived that long, the promulgation of the Japanese constitution of 1889 might have been delayed another ten years. Since its promulgation was premature, a delay of a decade might have allowed Japan to develop a more mature political party system.[3]

Regardless of Ōkubo's motives, the doctrine of gradualism was well founded in view of the Japanese people's lack of understanding of the democratic concepts and institutions.

As a result of the Iwakura mission, Ōkubo and other government leaders familiarized themselves with political democracy and especially with Western technological advances. Ōkubo himself seems to have been less affected by what he saw in the United States than in the more advanced countries of Europe. Had the United States at the time occupied a position of power equal to that of Prussia and England, the constitutional history of Japan undoubtedly would have been considerably different. As respecters of power and success, the Meiji leaders probably would have looked more to American ideals than to those of Prussia. This, however, was not to be. Prussian governmental structure caught the attention of Ōkubo and his colleagues as did English economic practices. Unfortunately, as a result, the more democratic processes of Western civilization did not leave a profound impression upon these men whose test for institutions was whether they strengthened the power of the state.

Among the leaders of Japan there have been few who could claim successful achievements in as many fields of governmental activity as Ōkubo. Comparing the men of the triumvirate of the Restoration there is none who equals Ōkubo in this respect. Saigō was essentially a soldier. Kido was a thinker. Neither of them possessed the qualities that made Ōkubo a great statesman, one who distinguished himself not only as an administrator, but as a soldier and diplomat as well. Such an unusually versatile leader bears closer evaluation. What were the characteristics that made Ōkubo tower over his contemporaries?

A great leader is intellectually superior to the majority of his followers and colleagues. Knowledge indubitably is power. With high intellectual gifts an individual is better equipped to gain authority over others because of his ability to accomplish feats that may seem extraordinarily difficult to the more mediocre. Ōkubo had a keen mind which he exercised through reading, engaging in debates, and playing the mind-flexing game of *go*. His precosity was apparent early in life, and it was Saigō, three years Ōkubo's senior, who stated on one occasion that his younger friend had no peer in debate. Not only was he on intimate terms with Chinese literature and philosophy, but he also had a profound knowledge of Western political thought, which is reflected in his thesis on constitutional government.

Intellect alone, however, cannot assure one of immortality in the sphere of political leadership; if it could, many of the great thinkers would *ipso facto* have made great leaders. Also, there have been great leaders who were not geniuses. Leadership, which implies the power to inspire devotion, is therefore not based entirely upon intellect. Along with ample mental powers a great leader must have the gift of character. What were the moral qualities that made Ōkubo the singular statesman that he was?

Ōkubo possessed, above all, the quality of fortitude, the power of perseverance. With whatever cause he allied himself, he unreservedly undertook all responsibilities, and there is no evidence to indicate that he ever deserted a task because of discouragement. As an advocate of the *kōbu gattai* policy during his days as a *han* official, he was opposed by an influential samurai element within and without the Satsuma *han*. Despite the unrelenting pressures, Ōkubo adhered to his moderate position until the union between court and Bakufu had been achieved. Again, after shifting to the *tōbaku* policy, he consistently worked to overthrow the Bakufu and did not cease his endeavors until the Restoration was accomplished. In the national government, it was he who held the government together and pressed for the implementation of the Meiji policy of modernization. A willingness to risk his reputation and honor for the achievement of a task can be seen in Ōkubo's assumption of complete responsibility for the suppression of the Saga rebellion and the settlement of the Formosan question.

Ōkubo was a man who was generally patient under setbacks and interference. Unlike Saigō, whose temperament did not brook the obstructive tactics of others, Ōkubo could and did display poise under the most trying circumstances. His strategy in drawing close to Shimazu Hisamitsu for political reasons is an example of the patience he was capable of. Had he been as intemperate and rash as Saigō, the civilian party might not have won its signal victory over the militarists in the conflict revolving around the Korean question. Knowing that he alone could not successfully contend with Saigō and his party over such a thorny issue, Ōkubo wisely waited until his colleagues returned from abroad. The trait of patience allowed him to wait and act at the most opportune moment.

Ōkubo clearly had the sense of the continuity of a great cause. As a *han* official his cause was the reformation of the conservative, tradition-encrusted government of Satsuma, the ultimate objective being to strengthen the *han*'s military, political, and economic structures, and later it was the establishment of a strong imperial government capable of helping Japan to take her place among the nations of the world in both peace and war. This sense of continuity affected his entire outlook as a government official and helped to nurture resilience in defeat as well as an optimistic spirit that enabled him to retain hope in even the bleakest moments of life.

Ōkubo was a courageous man. He had the intellectual courage to face facts squarely and unflinchingly. If a problem called for a solution, he immediately put himself to the task of resolving it. The fact that he seemed unwilling to concede that any task was too large for him accounts in part for his success as a leader. He had the moral courage, furthermore, to voice his convictions even against overwhelming opposition;

it took such courage to break with his own *han* of Satsuma and, as a central government official, to sanction military action against it. And a man of less character might not have had the will to overrule the Council of State in order to assist Korea when the Japanese government was involved in a serious emergency of its own. As for physical courage, there is no evidence to indicate that he was cowardly in the face of physical danger. Ōkubo is said to have pleaded for his life just before he was cut down by the assassin's sword on the morning of May 14, 1878, but it is difficult to place credence in such a report, which was probably a fabrication by those who wished to discredit him. The fact that he refused police protection after he was informed of the plot to kill him would seem to disprove the story. Ōkubo fully realized that he had bitter enemies, and under such circumstances he could not have continued to exercise the type of bold leadership for which he was noted had he feared death. A further analysis of Ōkubo indicates that he was, like all successful politicians, an opportunist who tended to think that "the good end justifies every means."[4] How else can one account for his shifting from one ideology to another whenever circumstances dictated? Originally a *jōi* adherent, he later joined the ranks of the *kaikoku* party when this appeared the necessary and beneficial step to take. A hater of foreigners at one moment, he became an ardent advocate of foreign intercourse the next. Likewise in inter-*han* relations the Satsuma policy reflected Ōkubo's ability to take advantage of circumstances regardless of the moral issues involved. Hence when the Satsuma-Aizu alliance no longer proved useful to the *han*, he unhesitatingly advised the dissolution of the relationship and the formation of the more beneficial Satsuma-Chōshū alliance. In the realm of personal friendship, moreover, Ōkubo reflected this same attitude. After having won the attention of Shimazu Hisamitsu, Ōkubo used his chief's prestige to facilitate the progressive reforms within the *han*, then to force the Tokugawa Bakufu to make similar improvements, and finally to overthrow the Bakufu and restore imperial rule. As Hisamitsu's usefulness diminished, however, so did Ōkubo's reliance upon him; he gradually solicited the favor of other influential individuals, going outside of the *daimyō* class to that of the *kuge*. For example, he chose Iwakura as an ally. In doing so, Ōkubo chose a man with ideals similar to his own, through whom his own ideas and aspirations were naturally channeled to the court. There is no doubt that Ōkubo's meteoric rise to power in the national government was in no small measure facilitated by this friendship. He likewise sought Kido's friendship, but its instability in time induced Ōkubo to draw closer to another Chōshū man, Itō Hirobumi, a move based not only upon a genuine affinity for Itō, but also upon political considerations; Chōshū was needed as a supporter of the central government. Ōkubo's attitude toward his foreign advisers was no different. Among them, he first relied heavily upon Le Gendre who, in the course of time, was relegated to a secondary position after the more prestigious Boissonade.

Ōkubo was willing to resort to extreme means to further his cause. It will be recalled that at one time he even contemplated murdering Hisamitsu, whose life was spared only because Ōkubo realized that he would be more useful to him alive. He also masterminded the strategy to force the Bakufu to concede to reforms, and planned to have the members of the Tokugawa council killed if they should refuse to accept the Satsuma demands.

Was Ōkubo's Machiavellian behavior due to moral weakness? From the standpoint of Judaeo-Christian morality Machiavellianism is abhorrent. Western writers have strongly condemned Orientals for tolerating the breach of moral law. It should be realized, however, that the cultural mores of Japan during the feudal period sanctioned even murder if it were committed with a justifiable end in view. Thus the Japanese have idolized the Forty-seven Rōnin who took justice into their own hands and assassinated Lord Asano in order to avenge the wrong done to their own lord. Ōkubo, consequently, must be judged against the background of his peculiar society. The Japanese have tended to picture his every action as having been motivated solely by a noble purpose, a great cause. He was, according to most of his biographers, moved either by loyalty to the *han*, or, later, to the throne and the nation-state. Even Courant, Ōkubo's French biographer, notes that he was "lacking in personal ambition." [5]

It is difficult to accept the latter thesis in its entirety. Man by nature tends to be selfish. Ōkubo's sense of loyalty was undoubtedly strong; he was dedicated to the cause of unifying and stabilizing the new nation-state. But to assert that he had no personal ambition, that he was prompted to political action, earlier in behalf of the *han* and later in behalf of the imperial house and nation, entirely by a sense of loyalty gives a distorted picture. He was human enough to be concerned with his own interests, with his own self-preservation, his security, his ease, his pleasures, his reputation, his honor, and his glory. He was bound in turn to be concerned with the well-being of the society upon which his own welfare depended. Thus, while an official of the Satsuma *han*, he worked diligently to place the *han* in the position of national prominence. Then, in the name of imperial restoration, he participated actively in the overthrow of the Bakufu, after which he established himself, other members of his own *han*, and a selected number of like-minded individuals from other *han*, in the national government. He was, as Tōyama Shigeki has suggested, one of the "new class of bureaucrats"—authoritarian in tendency—who emerged from the crucible of *han* politics. As a functionary of the central government, he exerted the utmost effort to strengthen the newly erected political edifice. Was he motivated by a profound loyalty to the throne? Yes. But the answer cannot be unqualified. Even the Satsuma *han*, which played a yeoman part in the Restoration movement, did not hesitate to go against imperial orders when expediency dictated. The inference is obvious: personal ambition did motivate Ōkubo and his colleagues as well. In striving to bring honor and glory to Japan, the oligarchy worked for the ruling class and incidentally for the people at large.

It may be said that the economic, political, and social reforms initiated by Ōkubo and the other Meiji leaders generally benefited the people with the exception of the samurai. The reforms, however, were not oriented to benefit the people as such, but to strengthen the nation. The Meiji leaders were dedicated to the task of creating a strong nation-state upon whose prosperity their own prosperity depended and as a consequence the components of the state, the people, received only secondary consideration. To attain their objectives, however, the Meiji leaders were compelled to pay a price to gain the support of the people. The reduction of the land tax, the encouragement given to the commercial and industrial classes, the abolition of the stigma attached to the *eta* class, were certainly not genuine acts of generosity of the Meiji leaders, but sops offered to win the backing of the people. The notable achievements of the Meiji period were dictated by necessity.

Unlike Kido Kōin, Ōkubo was more a doer than a thinker. His strength lay in his ability to implement the great ideas he had acquired through his experiences as a *han* official, his extensive reading, and his personal observations while abroad. He put these ideas into effect with consistency and thoroughness, always with his eye upon the ultimate goal. He was respected by many of his colleagues, but generally disliked. This was owing in part to the fact that he played his role as a bureaucrat too well. As one Japanese historian has said, Ōkubo's unpopularity was attributable to his insistence upon remaining in a neutral official position on most issues, not siding with the samurai as did Saigō, not upholding the cause of the people's rights as did Itagaki. Moreover, his personality militated against his gaining popularity among the people. A strong-willed, coldly courageous authoritarian, he made implacable enemies. Although he did not absolutely lack human sympathy, his demeanor under normal circumstances was severe and seldom expressed warmth. A smile or a laugh was such a rarity for Ōkubo that whenever he broke down his wall of reserve and displayed warmth it was not accepted as being genuine. People usually attached political significance to any of his deviations from his usual emotional expressions.[6]

Popularity, however, should not be the major criterion for judging a leader. Often circumstances dictate that a leader consciously impose his will, assume a dictatorial posture and risk the antagonism of the majority in order to perform a difficult task. Japan in the early Meiji period was weak and rent by division. Internal pressures were liable at any moment to tear down the newly erected governmental structure. It was a time when determined and drastic measures were essential for the continued existence of the Japanese nation. Ōkubo and his colleagues molded the country's institutions to meet the challenge, and in so doing were forced to retain the militant aspects of the earlier feudal society. The first decade of the Meiji period was a time when government policy was oriented exclusively toward national survival. The emphasis was on war and preparation for war, the despotic state, the subordination of the individual to the state, the application of force to compel coöperation. Through the *fukoku kyōhei* policy Japan, in the mid-nineteenth century, endeavored to do what the European powers aimed for during the seventeenth and eighteenth centuries through their mercantilistic policy, the enrichment and strengthening of the fatherland. The followers of this policy in the West were no less concerned with national survival than were the Meiji leaders. Whether there is validity in Spencer's theory of societal development or not, the hard fact remains that, had the Japanese leaders failed to establish military and economic power, Japan most likely would not have been able to achieve its next stage in societal evolution, the industrial society, and could not have warded off the forces operating against it.[7]

Clearly, Ōkubo lived and worked in one of the most exciting and critical periods in Japanese history, a period during which the fate of the nation hung in the balance. The very nature of the times called for strong and determined leadership. A petulant, compulsive leader such as Saigō, although adored by the nation, would not have been adequate for the tremendous challenge of the age; nor would a vacillating, easily-discouraged leader such as Kido. Saigō and Kido had great qualities, but to achieve and maintain the unity and cohesion of the nation, a leader of Ōkubo's caliber and temperament was essential.

With an iron hand, Ōkubo guided the new state along a middle path, veering neither excessively to the right to placate the elements of conservatism nor to the left to solicit the favor of those advocating people's rights, but establishing for Japan the course that would lead her gradually on the road toward modernization in most aspects of Japanese life. Granted that Ōkubo was authoritarian and an ambitious, often seemingly unprincipled leader, he nevertheless was the right man in the right position at the right time as far as Japan was concerned. He utilized many of the reform measures he and his samurai colleagues had conceived in their respective *han* to solidify the national government and thereby assure the future development of the nation. Courant succinctly described the tremendous accomplishment of this Meiji leader when he stated that Ōkubo's work may be summarized in one sentence: In less than a decade he extracted from a complex feudal system a modern, centralized state provided with all of its machinery.[8]

Ōkubo's power, which assisted him in becoming the great state-builder, also, ironically, helped cause his downfall. Not all Ōkubo biographers and writers dealing with the Meiji period have made this fact explicit. Some of them have contended merely that he was murdered by reactionaries who favored the maintenance of the feudal society, the only area of difference among the advocates of this thesis being in the emphasis they have placed upon the primary motivating factor for the assassination. One school has indicated that it was the revenge of Saigō's death.[9] A second has implicitly noted that Ōkubo's assassination was provoked more by a general reaction among the samurai against Ōkubo's antifeudal policy.[10] The holders of the latter view have pointed out that the reactionaries, obviously harmed by the Meiji government's policy of modernization, held Ōkubo, the most influential among the oligarchy, responsible for the progressive destruction of the old order—the institutions of the Bakufu, the *han*, and the like—under which the samurai occupied positions of privilege. This idea was also shared by the reporter for *The Times* of London, who, on May 15, 1878, stated:

> One is sometimes tempted to believe that there is a contagion in evil which spreads with fearful rapidity over the whole world. A short time ago Vera Zasulitch shot General Trepoff, and a few days ago Hödel fired at the Emperor of Germany, and yesterday Okubo, the second Directing Minister of Japan, was murdered in the streets of the capital by five assassins on his way to a Cabinet Council. Okubo was the promoter and defender of all the reforms which have marked the recent rise of Japan. He was one of the conquerors in the last insurrection, and for these reasons was held in special horror by the defenders of the suppressed abuses. The partisans of feudalism knew that in him they would destroy one of their chief adversaries. By a strange contrast, too, while in Europe it is socialism and anarchy which have prompted the assassination, in Japan it is reaction. Okaubo [*sic*], who came to Europe in 1873, left behind him a character for firmness, frankness, and enlightenment. His loss is a public misfortune for Japan. All assassins have been arrested.[11]

Must the reactionaries bear the sole responsibility for the assassination? Another group of scholars has emphasized that Ōkubo was the victim of those who were jealous and resentful of his authority which at the time of his murder was so great that it was almost unchallengeable. Implicit in this thesis is the thought that reaction alone did not prompt the murder, but that all elements who disagreed with Ōkubo's political philosophy were involved.[12]

Ōkubo's assumption of power was closely correlated with the amount of responsibility he accepted. He epitomized authority. By the end of the decade prior to the Restoration he had reached the peak of influence in the Satsuma *han*. By the end of the decade after the Restoration he had attained a position of almost ultimate authority in the Meiji government. It is germane to trace in summary fashion the means by which Ōkubo monopolized authority in the national government.

After the Restoration the power behind the Meiji government was represented by the military might of Satsuma, Chōshū, Tosa, Hizen, and Echizen, among which Satsuma was the most powerful. Among the individuals most influential between the years 1868 and 1871 were the two *kuge*, Sanjō Sanetomi, *Udaijin*, and Iwakura Tomomi, *Dainagon;* the ex-*daimyō* Nabeshima Naomasa, *Dainagon;* and the low-ranking samurai Sasaki Takayuki of Tosa, Soejima Taneomi and Ōkuma Shigenobu of Hizen, Hirozawa Saneomi and Kido Kōin of Chōshū, and Ōkubo Toshimichi of Satsuma. Among the samurai those from Satsuma and Chōshū were the most powerful politically. After 1871 when Saigō and Itagaki joined the government and helped effect the abolition of the *han* and the establishment of the prefectures, the *kuge* and *daimyō* classes rapidly declined in influence. With the administrative reorganization of that year Sanjō became *Dajōdaijin* and Saigō, Kido, Itagaki, and Ōkuma were made *sangi*. Iwakura was appointed Foreign Minister and Ōkubo, relinquishing the position of *sangi*, accepted the post of Finance Minister. In 1873 Gotō Shōjirō, Ōki Takato, and Etō Shimpei were added to the list of *sangi*, but the actual power in the government at this time was in the hands of Ōkubo, Saigō, and Kido. After the Korean debate of the same year Saigō, Itagaki, Soejima, Gotō, and Etō left the government, and as their replacements Itō Hirobumi of Chōshū, Terajima Munenori of Satsuma, Katsu Kaishū, the former Bakufu official, and Ōki Takato Hizen were appointed *sangi*. Ōkubo and Kido who remained in the government were now the most influential political figures. In 1874, with Kido's resignation, Shimazu Hisamitsu of Satsuma was given the post of *Sadaijin* to offset the loss of Saigō, and two other Satsuma men, Ijichi Masaharu and Kuroda Kiyotaka, were installed as *sangi*, as was Yamagata Aritomo of Chōshū. With Kido gone the dominant oligarch was Ōkubo, but as a result of the Ōsaka conference of 1875 Kido and Itagaki rejoined the government. Once more Ōkubo was compelled to share his authority with Kido. Then, with the resignation of Ōkubo's former *han* superior, Shimazu Hisamitsu, in 1875, and of Itagaki and Kido in the following year, Ōkubo became the sole repository of power. With the suppression of the Satsuma rebellion he consolidated the authority of the state and by the same token that of his own. In general, historians are agreed that the years 1873 to 1876 were a period during which Ōkubo progressively monopolized political power.[13]

That Ōkubo during this time possessed unlimited authority no one has denied, and it is true that he exercised all of it to complete his tasks. Writers have contended that if Ōkubo's assassins had understood his purpose in creating what might be termed a "necessary despotism," they might have become his staunch supporters and not his enemies.[14] Ōkubo, however, by exerting his tremendous political strength, successfully prevented the implementation of the policies of both the extreme conservatives and the liberals and consequently became the focus of public hate. It is a foregone conclusion that the reactionaries resented his destruction of their way of life. As for the progressives, on the other hand, the assassins' charges against Ōkubo include the complaints voiced by these very elements. That the government itself realized that the murder was not merely a plot of the feudal party is apparent because soon after the murder it hastened the program of gradual reform, the objective of which was to establish representative institutions.[15]

Power obviously was a constructive as well as destructive force in Ōkubo's life: constructive inasmuch as it made Ōkubo an effective nation-builder, destructive in that it caused his downfall. Was his death a misfortune for Japan? Although he had advocated eventual representative government would he ungrudgingly have sanctioned it even if the time were ripe to do so? Just prior to his death he had been offered the position of *Udaijin*, which he declined, expressing his desire rather to become the Minister of the Imperial Household. What course might the history of the nation have taken had he gained the absolute confidence of the throne? We cannot know. What is certain is that the future government of Japan would not have been any more liberal than it was to become even had Ōkubo lived to participate in public affairs after 1878; it was in the main his disciples, after all, who inherited his philosophy and went on to shape the nation's destiny. Ōkubo's primary task, that of solidifying the shaky structure of the Meiji government, had already been completed by the time of his assassination. Consequently, his death was a public misfortune for Japan to the extent that it lost a shrewd, realistic statesman who had ably fulfilled his mission of giving a feudal country an impetus sufficient to assure it a place in the family of modern nations. Undeniably Ōkubo deserves an eminent position among the great statesmen of Japan on this accomplishment alone.

Notes

Notes

The English titles given in brackets following the Japanese titles are rough translations for the convenience of the reader.

Notes to Chapter I

1. In this connection, one example will suffice to illustrate the action of such external forces impinging upon Meiji Japan. The unification of Japan, although carried out by the Meiji leaders, was aided by other factors inherent in the Tokugawa system itself. The feudal system, the essential characteristic of which is decentralization, was so operated by the Tokugawa authorities as to secure the centralization of power. Under their rule Japan enjoyed a long period of peace which in turn set in motion economic currents of a capitalistic nature. The nationwide circulation of currency under the centralized government resulted in the nationwide circulation of commodities. Commodity circulation was also stimulated by the Tokugawa government's establishment of what amounted to free markets represented by such cities as Edo, Ōsaka, and Nagasaki. The development of a so-called nationwide economy, closely combined with the centralized feudal system, helped to foster in the Tokugawa period the unification of the state along modern lines. It furnished the material basis for the unification of Japan. See Horie Yasuzō, "The Economic Significance of the Meiji Restoration," reprint from *Kyōto University Economic Review*, XII, no. 11 (n.d.), 66.

2. See Sidney D. Brown, "Kido Takayoshi (1833-1877): Meiji Japan's Cautious Revolutionary," in *Pacific Historical Review*, XXV (1956), 151-162.

3. Mushakōji Saneatsu, *Great Saigō: The Life of Saigō Takamori*, adapted and translated by Sakamoto Moriaki (Tōkyō: Kaitakusha, 1942).

4. Maurice Courant, *Ôkoubo* (Paris: Ancienne Librairie Germer Bailliere et Cie, 1904). This book is part of a series of biographies dealing with statesmen who played dominant roles in modern world history. At the time the book was published those who had already been selected as subjects were Bismarck of Prussia, Prim of Spain, Disraeli and Gladstone of England, Metternich of Austria, Cavour of Italy, and Lincoln of the United States. It is noteworthy that the French saw fit to include Ōkubo among these world-renowned political figures and is a significant indication

that there were those in Europe who discerned the unusual stature of this Japanese statesman.

Sidney D. Brown has recently written a valuable article on Ōkubo: "Ōkubo Toshimichi: His Political and Economic Policies in Early Meiji Japan," in *The Journal of Asian Studies*, XXI (February, 1962), 183-197.

5. Courant, *op. cit.*, p. 1.

6. It is gratifying to note that others share this view. Joyce Chapman Lebra has recently completed a dissertation (Radcliffe College, 1957-1958) entitled *Japan's First Modern Popular Statesman; A Study of the Political Career of Ōkuma Shigenobu* (1838-1922). For her article entitled "Ōkuma Shigenobu and the 1881 Political Crisis," see *The Journal of Asian Studies*, XVIII (August, 1959), 475-487.

7. Thomas Jefferson, "Notes on Virginia," Andrew A. Lipscomb, ed., in *The Writings of Thomas Jefferson* (Washington, D.C.: The Thomas Jefferson Memorial Association, 1904), II, 207.

8. The *fudai daimyō* had been Tokugawa Ieyasu's allies before the battle of Sekigahara in 1600, while the *tozama daimyō* were allies who had sworn fealty to him after their defeat by his forces.

9. One *koku* is equivalent to 5.11902 U. S. bushels (dry).

10. Matsudaira Tarō, *Edo Jidai Seido no Kenkyū* [A Study of the Political Institutions of the Edo Period], (Tōkyō: Buke Seido Kenkyūkai, 1919), I, 381-382. *Hatamoto* originally referred to the camp of a *shōgun*. It later designated the samurai who guarded the *shōgun*'s camp. The term then became applicable to retainers in general. Under the Tokugawa the five thousand or so *hatamoto* were the direct vassals of the *shōgun;* that is, lesser lords holding fiefs directly of the *shōgun*. See Asakawa Kanichi, ed. and trans., *The Documents of Iriki* (Tōkyō: Japan Society for the Promotion of Science, 1955), pp. 323, 381.

11. Matsudaira, *op. cit.*, I, 382. Historically the *gokenin* were Minamoto Yoritomo's immediate vassals. He accepted many local chieftains who either came to his aid or who capitulated to him in the war against Taira in the twelfth century. See Asakawa, *op. cit.*, pp. 7, 16, 47.

During the Tokugawa period the *hatamoto* could be received in audience by the *shōgun*, a privilege the *gokenin* did not share. The latter numbered about 17,300 in 1722. See Ishin Shiryō Hensan Jimukyoku, *Ishin Shi* [History of the Restoration] (Tōkyō: Ishin Shiryō Hensan Jimukyoku, 1939), I, 245; hereafter cited as *Ishin Shi.*

12. Takekoshi Yosoburo, *The Economic Aspects of the History of the Civilization of Japan* (New York: The Macmillan Co., 1930), I, 551; hereafter cited as Takekoshi, *Economic Aspects*. The *ryō* was about 37.5 grammes, or 578.7 grains, or nearly one-tenth of a pound troy.

13. The *rōjū* were also called *karō*. They were chosen from among the *daimyō* whose revenue exceeded twenty-five thousand *koku,* the *wakadoshiyori,* and the *sobayōnin*. The Kyōto *shoshidai* and the Ōsaka *jōdai* usually became *rōjū* at the end of their terms.

14. Matsudaira, *op. cit.*, I, 732. The name *wakadoshiyori,* or junior elders, was derived from the fact that originally they were selected from among the sons of *rōjū,* or great elders. Subsequently, they were chosen from among the *fudai daimyō*, but there were occasions when even *tozama daimyō* were made *wakadoshiyori.*

15. *Ibid.*, pp. 767-768. The *ōmetsuke,* or great censors, numbering four or five, were attached to the Council of State; and the *metsuke,* numbering from ten to twenty-four, to the Junior Council. These censors were assisted by a number of sub-

ordinates called *kachi metsuke*. The number of *metsuke* in office at any given time was reflective of the condition of the period. In 1617, when the office of *metsuke* was created, there were fifteen members. The number was thereafter increased to twenty-four in 1631 when political conditions were unsettled. During the third quarter of the seventeenth century it was decreased to twenty, then to ten during the years 1716-1736. At the end of the Tokugawa period, when political conditions were unstable, the number was again increased to twenty.

16. James Murdoch, *A History of Japan* (London: Kegan Paul, Trench, Trubner and Co., Ltd., 1926), III, 12; Matsudaira, *op. cit.*, I, 833-834; Koda Shigetomo, "Edo no Shisei" [City Administration of Edo], in *Iwanami Kōza: Nihon Rekishi*, Kuroita Katsumi, ed., IV (Tōkyō: Iwanami Shoten, 1933), 7.

17. See Kurita Mototsugu, "Edo Bakufu Seiji" [Government of the Edo Bakufu], in *Iwanami Kōza: Nihon Rekishi*, Kuroita Katsumi, ed., IV (Tōkyō: Iwanami Shoten, 1935), 16.

18. See Matsudaira, *op. cit.*, I, 329 ff. and 351 ff. Usually there were from five to seven *sobayōnin*, but Tsunayoshi, the fifth *shōgun*, had over twenty.

19. Murdoch, *op. cit.*, II, 9.

20. William Elliot Griffis, *The Mikado: Institution and Person* (Princeton: Princeton University Press, 1915), p. 55; hereafter cited as Griffis, *The Mikado*. The imperial family received from the *shōgun* incomes in kind, although they were less than those of some of the greater Tokugawa *daimyō*. The sovereign was not allowed to own land. For figures on the Bakufu's rice allotment to the *kuge*, see *Ishin Shi*, I, 26-27.

21. Kurita, "Edo Bakufu Seiji," p. 17; *Ishin Shi*, I, 33-34.

22. Kikuchi Shunsuke, *Tokugawa Kinreikō* [Commentary on the Tokugawa Laws] (Tōkyō: Yoshikawa Kōbunkan, 1931), 1st series, I, 1, 2.

23. Griffis, *The Mikado*, p. 55.

24. For a detailed picture of the disposition of fiefs during the various periods of the history of the Tokugawa Bakufu, see Matsudaira, *op. cit.*, I, 505-672. For an interesting study of the rise of the modern *daimyō* made by an American scholar, see John W. Hall, "Foundations of the Modern Japanese Daimyo," in *The Journal of Asian Studies*, XX (May, 1961), 317-329.

25. Matsudaira, *op. cit.*, I, 409. One of the duties of the *ōmetsuke* was to keep a close watch over the number of guns in the Kantō area. Hunting with firearms was strictly controlled, and only authorized persons were allowed to possess a gun within a radius of ten *ri* (one *ri* = 2.44030 miles) of Edo. Within this restricted area not even hunters were allowed to carry firearms. See also J. C. Hall, "The Tokugawa Legislation," in *Transactions of the Asiatic Society of Japan*, XLI, part 5 (Tōkyō, 1913), 707.

26. Kurita, "Edo Bakufu Seiji," p. 31.

27. For the full text in Japanese, see Kikuchi, *op. cit.*, I, 90-92. An excellent translation of the laws may be found in Tsunoda Ryūsaku, William Theodore de Bary, and Donald Keene, comps., *Sources of the Japanese Tradition* (New York: Columbia University Press, 1958), pp. 335-338.

28. See Kikuchi, *op. cit.*, I, 93-95, for the full text of the *buke hatto* of 1635. For the schedule showing the month during which each *daimyō* was expected to arrive in Edo, see Matsudaira, *op. cit.*, I, 685-692.

29. For an enlightening study of the effects of the development of land and sea communications in the Edo period, see Furuta Ryōichi, "Edo Jidai no Kōtsū" [Com-

munications in the Edo Period], in *Iwanami Kōza: Nihon Rekishi*, Kuroita Katsumi, ed., I (Tōkyō: Iwanami Shoten, 1934), 3 ff. Furuta concludes that the development of communications was owing (1) to the Bakufu policy of facilitating travel for its own agents and the *daimyō* who were required to travel between their fiefs and Edo under the *sankin kōtai* system, (2) to the existence of a long period of internal peace, and (3) to changes in economic conditions. During the later Edo period an increasing number of merchants on business and Shintō votaries traveling from one shrine to another used the various land and sea routes.

The development of communications enabled the cultures of all parts of Japan to intermix and fuse. Hence the effete court culture of Kyōto affected the *bushi*, or warrior, culture of Edo, and by the end of the Tokugawa period the center of Japanese civilization had been transferred from Kyōto to Edo. From Edo, the various *daimyō* and their retainers carried the culture peculiar to the capital city back with them to the provinces and vice versa.

Ports and *shuku*, or post towns, were established as communications developed, and the customs that originated in these centers were ultimately introduced throughout the land, the travelers serving as transmitters. Thus the popular feminine hairstyle of the early Tokugawa period, called the Hyōgo-*mage*, was created by the prostitutes of the port of Hyōgo. The Shimada-*mage*, another well-known coiffure, was first worn by the ladies of pleasure at Shimada and eventually became accepted by women throughout Japan. The natural consequence of the development of communications was the gradual standardization of Japanese culture.

30. Kurita, "Edo Bakufu Seiji," pp. 32-33.

31. See Nakamura Naokatsu, *Kokushi Tsūron* [Treatise on National History] (Kyōto: Hoshino Shoten, 1939), p. 176.

32. See Kurita, "Edo Bakufu Seiji," pp. 52-53.

33. *Ibid.*, p. 53. For Arai Hakuseki's views on foreign trade, see Honjō Eijirō, *Economic Theory and History of Japan in the Tokugawa Period* (Tōkyō: Maruzen Co., Ltd., 1943), pp. 11-12; hereafter cited as Honjō, *Economic Theory.*

34. See Kurita, "Edo Bakufu Seiji," p. 54.

35. For a summary treatment of the samurai class in general, see Kurita Mototsugu, "Seiji oyobi Seido" [Politics and Institutions], in *Nihon Bunka Shi Taikei* [An Outline History of Japanese Culture], Tanaka Kazuhiko, ed., IX (Tōkyō: Seibundō Shinkōsha, 1937), 67-70. The formative period of the samurai caste, including the growth of their code of honor and the cult of the sword, is discussed by G. B. Sansom, *Japan: A Short Cultural History* (New York: Appleton-Century-Crofts, Inc., 1943), pp. 266-269. See also G. B. Sansom, *A History of Japan* (Stanford: Stanford University Press, 1958), I, 234 ff. and 358 ff.

36. For a recent scholarly discussion of the origin and development of the castle-town, or *jōkamachi*, see John Whitney Hall, "The Castle-Town and Japan's Modern Urbanization," in the *Far Eastern Quarterly*, XV (November, 1955), 37-56. See also Nakamura Naokatsu, *op. cit.*, pp. 135-143; and Takekoshi, *Economic Aspects*, I, 288.

37. Samurai class differentiation had its origin in the Muromachi period when civil wars produced victors and vanquished. The victorious samurai integrated their defeated foes into their own ranks but were careful to keep them subordinate to their own retainers. For a short but enlightening discussion of this social phenomenon, see Shirayanagi Takeshi, *Ōkubo Toshimichi* (Tōkyō: Chōbunkaku, 1943), pp. 39-43.

38. Jean Ray, *Le Japon, grande puissance moderne* (Paris: Librairie Plon, 1942), p. 151.

39. See Haruyama Sakuji, "Edo Jidai no Kyōiku" [Education in the Edo Period], in *Iwanami Kōza: Nihon Rekishi*, Kuroita Katsumi, ed., II (Tōkyō: Iwanami Shoten, 1935), 11.

40. See Frank Alonson Lombard, *Pre-Meiji Education in Japan* (Tōkyō: Kyō Bun Kwan, 1914), pp. 76-80; and Haruyama, *op. cit.*, pp. 14-17.

41. *Ibid.*, p. 19; Lombard, *op. cit.*, pp. 84-85.

42. Haruyama, *op. cit.*, pp. 12-13.

43. Yoshida Saburō, "Shisō to Gakumon" [Thought and Learning], in *Nihon Bunka Shi Taikei*, Tanaka Kazuhiko, ed., IX (Tōkyō: Seibundō Shinkōsha, 1937), 136.

44. The use of money, according to Honjō Eijirō, began as early as the Keichō (1596-1614) and the Genna (1615-1623) eras. It was not, however, until the Genroku era (1688-1703) that coins circulated widely in Japan; see Honjō Eijirō, *The Social and Economic History of Japan* (Kyōto: Institute for Research in Economic History of Japan, 1935), pp. 121-122; hereafter cited as Honjō, *Social and Economic History*. See also Takizawa Matsuyo, *The Penetration of Money Economy in Japan* (New York: Columbia University Press, 1927), pp. 30-49.

For a good concise discussion in Japanese of the merchant class during the Tokugawa period, see Nakamura Naokatsu, *op. cit.*, pp. 188-207. Nakamura develops the thesis that the Tokugawa period was the age of the samurai and concurrently an age of the *chōnin*. Reference should also be made to Takekoshi, *Economic Aspects*, especially Volumes II and III, and Nakamura Kōya, "Meiji Ishin to Chōnin Kaikyū" [The Merchant Class and the Meiji Restoration], in *Meiji Ishin Shi Kenkyū*, Tōkyō Teikoku Daigaku Shigakkai, ed. (Tōkyō: Fuzambō, 1929), pp. 478 ff.

45. E. Herbert Norman, *Japan's Emergence as a Modern State* (New York: Institute of Pacific Relations, 1940), p. 18. See also Kanno Watarō, *Nihon Kaisha Kigyō Hassei Shi no Kenkyū* [A Study of the History of the Emergence of Corporate Enterprise in Japan] (Tōkyō: Iwanami Shoten, 1931), Chap. II. Kanno notes that the increased circulation of money during the latter part of the Edo period was due to the greater amount of gold available, to the *sankin kōtai* system, as well as to the growth of cities and the rising standard of living which necessitated the conversion of rice to money.

46. Referring to the low social status of the Japanese merchant class, Courant states that "les marchands étaient dans la situation des juifs au moyen-age." Courant, *op. cit.*, p. 8.

It is interesting to note that in China during this period the merchants occupied a position analogous to their counterparts in Japan. The Chinese had four social strata: the intellectual, the farmer, the artisan, and the merchant. A fifth, the soldier, was sometimes added. Since the soldier neither created nor produced, he was placed at the bottom of the social scale. See Harrison Forman, *Changing China* (New York: Crown Publishers, 1948), p. 173.

In Japan, significantly, the soldier, in contrast to his counterpart in China, has occupied an honored position in society and understandably the Japanese have been more militaristic than the Chinese who have tended to deëmphasize the importance of force. This difference in attitude of the two peoples toward military power was to have an important effect upon the welfare of the two countries in the nineteenth century; Japan withstood the pressures from abroad by building up its defenses while China fell before the onslaught of Western colonialism.

47. Tsuchiya Takao, "Keizai" [Economics], in *Nihon Bunka Shi Taikei*, Tanaka Kuzuhiko, ed., X (Tōkyō: Seibundō Shinkōsha, 1939), 119. For a discussion of the views of economic theorists of the Tokugawa period, such as Kumazawa Banzan and Yamazaki Anzai, regarding the subordination of the feudal lords and samurai to the commercial class, see Honjō, *Economic Theory*, pp. 34 ff.

48. For a discussion of the transformation of class distinctions, see Honjō, *Social and Economic History*, pp. 189-212.

49. The *rōnin* of the Tokugawa period were masterless samurai who for one reason or another had lost their capital pension. They, however, must be differentiated from the *rōnin* of the *Ōchō Jidai*, or the period in Japanese history during which the emperors governed in their own names, specifically from the beginning of Japanese history to the establishment of the Kamakura shōgunate in 1192. The latter were vagrant peasants who left their native villages because of economic distress and wandered throughout the land. These transients were often apprehended and returned to their native provinces, although at other times their services were used in punitive expeditions, defense, and colonization work. See Kurita, "Edo Bakufu Seiji," p. 35.

50. Norman, *op. cit.*, p. 17. The *rōnin* resented being harassed by the Tokugawa government, and evidence indicates that they took active part in the various peasant uprisings that plagued Tokugawa Japan. Maladministration in the domain of the Kii branch of the Tokugawa family incited a revolt of farmers and *rōnin* in 1823 which the central government suppressed with forces under the command of the *machi bugyō* and *kanjō bugyō*. See Hugh Borton, "Peasant Uprisings in Japan of the Tokugawa Period," in *Transactions of the Asiatic Society of Japan*, 2nd series, XVI (Tokyo, 1938), 80-83; hereafter cited as Borton, *Peasant Uprisings*.

51. See Tsuchiya Takao, "Edo Jidai no Keizai" [Economy of the Edo Period], in *Iwanami Kōza: Nihon Rekishi*, Kuroita Katsumi, ed., VIII (Tōkyō: Iwanami Shoten, 1930), 8-10.

52. *Ibid.*, p. 14.

53. *Ibid.*, pp. 15-17. For Kumazawa Banzan's comment on the impoverishment of the agrarian communities, see Honjō, *Economic Theory*, pp. 40-41.

54. Tsuchiya Takao, "Edo Jidai no Keizai," pp. 18-20.

55. *Ibid.*, pp. 21-22.

56. Takekoshi, *Economic Aspects*, III, 175; and Borton, *Peasant Uprisings*, p. 88.

57. Takekoshi, *Economic Aspects*, III, 175.

58. Murdoch describes the *rōnin* as "a sinister figure of dread in the land; a spectre that ever haunts the dreams of the officials making the weaker-kneed among them sweat the cold sweat of terror." He gives them credit for the destruction of the Bakufu by stating that "in truth, on probing into the heart of the political situation of the times, it becomes tolerably plain that it was the *rōnin* and their sympathizers that were chiefly responsible for the fall of the Bakufu." Murdoch, *op. cit.*, III, 704.

59. John Bassett Moore, A *Digest of International Law as Embodied in Diplomatic Discussions, Treaties and Other International Agreements, International Awards, the Decisions of Municipal Courts, and the Writings of Jurists, and Especially in Documents, Published and Unpublished, Issued by Presidents and Secretaries of State of the United States, the Opinions of Attorneys-General, and the Decisions of Courts, Federal and State* (Washington: Government Printing Office, 1906), V, 736-737.

60. For the text of President Fillmore's letter to the Japanese Emperor, see Frank H. Severance, ed., "Millard Fillmore Papers," Buffalo Historical Society, *Publications*, X (1907), 393-396.

61. In a friendly treatment of the thirteenth President of the United States, Griffis describes him as being ambitious to make America great, and states that in foreign relations the President endeavored to impress upon the world that America desired "to do righteousness and to be generous toward the weak." William Elliot Griffis, "Millard Fillmore and His Part in the Opening of Japan," Buffalo Historical Society, *Publications*, IX (1906), 65-66; hereafter cited as Griffis, *Millard Fillmore*.

As a firm believer in Manifest Destiny, Perry hoped to extend the jurisdiction of the United States beyond the limits of the Western continent. He therefore endeavored to acquire Okinawa, Formosa, and the Bonin Islands for his country and desired to have Americans eventually populate all the islands stretching across the central Pacific. His grandiose plan was in essence the acquisition for the United States of strategic control and development of the Pacific Ocean area north of the equator. He dreamed of colonies. But, as Earl Swisher points out, this was essentially Perry's personal scheme and "there was no obstacle to its fulfillment except the indifference of the United States government and the preoccupation of the American people." See Earl Swisher, "Commodore Perry's Imperialism in Relation to America's Present-Day Position in the Pacific," in *Pacific Historical Review*, XVI (February, 1947), 30-40.

62. Tokutomi Iichirō, the eminent Japanese historian, has further subdivided the diverse opinions expressed by thinkers on this question. The *jōi-teki kaikoku* view held by the Mito adherents would have opened Japan only after an initial effort to forcibly expel the foreigners had failed. Shimazu Nariakira of Satsuma and others who held the *kaikoku-teki jōi* opinion contended that it would be foolhardy to fight while knowing that defeat was a certainty. Rather than take such a risk, this group urged that the country should be opened and Western weapons acquired; only then should an attempt be made to expel the foreigners. The *jōi-teki jōi* exponents maintained that the foreigners should be expelled immediately, at any cost. The *kaikoku-teki kaikoku* viewpoint represented the progressives who argued from the premise that it was only natural to associate freely with the outside world. Isolation, they held, was an unnatural situation arbitrarily created by the Tokugawa Bakufu in a country with a long history of international contacts prior to the seventeenth century. The *kōtō-teki kaikoku* opinion was held by the extreme passivists who were willing to kowtow to the foreigners. See Tokutomi Iichirō, *Meiji Ishin no Taigyō* [The Great Task of the Meiji Restoration] (Tōkyō: Minyūsha, 1935), pp. 47-54. For a detailed and scholarly analysis in English of these ideas of foreign policy and their impact on the decisions of the statesmen of the late Tokugawa period, see W. G. Beasley, ed. and trans., *Select Documents on Japanese Foreign Policy*, 1853-1868 (London: Oxford University Press, 1955), pp. 3-93.

63. See Shimada Saburō, *Kaikoku Shimatsu* [Particulars Relating to the Opening of Japan] (Tōkyō: Yoronsha, 1888), pp. 119, 120; Carl Crow, *He Opened the Door of Japan* (New York and London: Harper and Brothers, 1939), pp. 215-216; and Payson Jackson Treat, *The Early Diplomatic Relations between the United States and Japan*, 1853-1865 (Baltimore: The Johns Hopkins Press, 1917), p. 108. Harris warned the Japanese in 1857 of the expediency of concluding an early treaty with the United States if Japan were to avoid the danger of having treaties imposed upon her by England and France. Harris, according to Treat, personally agreed to mediate should trouble arise with the English and the French.

64. Ii Naosuke was bitterly criticized for submitting to the West and was ultimately assassinated on March 3, 1860, by anti-Bakufu elements. For a detailed work attempting to justify Ii's decision, see Shimada, *op. cit.* For a shorter book in English, based upon the *Kaikoku Shimatsu,* see H. Satoh, *Agitated Japan: The Life of Baron Ii Kamon-no-kami Naosuke* (New York: D. Appleton and Co., 1896).

65. G. B. Sansom, *The Western World and Japan* (New York: Alfred A. Knopf, 1950), p. 291.

66. Beasley, *op. cit.*, p. 92.

67. Tōkyō Teikoku Daigaku Shiryō Hensanjo, *Meiji Shiyō* [Essentials of Meiji History] (Tōkyō: Kinkōdō Shoseki Kabushiki Kaisha, 1933), I, 1.

Notes to Chapter II

1. Ōkubo was to bear several names during the course of his life. His *yōmyō,* or childhood name, was Shōkesa, which was before long changed to Shōsuke. Later he was called Ichizō and finally Toshimichi. He also bore the pseudonym Kōtō. Kōtō is simply the combination of the first Chinese character in the compound word Kō-zuki-gawa (Kōzuki River) and the ideograph meaning "east," pronounced *tō.* Thus Kō-tō means the man from the east side of the Kōzuki River. See Itō Nitarō, *Ōkubo Toshimichi* (Tōkyō: Heibonsha, 1941), I, 278-279; Tokutomi Iichirō, *Ōkubo Kōtō Sensei* [Master Ōkubo Kōtō] (Tōkyō: Minyūsha, 1927), p. 5.

2. Katsuda has included in his work a map of Kajiyamachi, *circa* 1848, showing the residences of Satsuma samurai. Katsuda Magoya, *Ōkubo Toshimichi Den* [Biography of Ōkubo Toshimichi] (Tōkyō: Dōbunkan, 1910), I.

3. *Ibid.*, p. 5. See Volume I of Katsuda's work for a map of Kajiyamachi showing the location of the homes of these personalities.

4. Sakai discusses these and other paradoxes and furnishes explanations in terms of the peculiar circumstances created by the very geographical location of Satsuma as well as by the class structure of its samurai. Robert K. Sakai, "Feudal Society and Modern Leadership in Satsuma-han," *The Journal of Asian Studies,* XVI (1957), 365-376.

5. John Harington Gubbins, "Hideyoshi and the Satsuma Clan in the Sixteenth Century," *Transactions of the Asiatic Society of Japan,* VIII (1880), 96-97; hereafter cited as Gubbins, "Hideyoshi and Satsuma."

6. Asakawa Kanichi, ed. and trans., *The Documents of Iriki* (Tōkyō: Japan Society for the Promotion of Science, 1955), p. 1.

7. Gubbins, "Hideyoshi and Satsuma," p. 94.

8. Francis Ottiwell Adams, *The History of Japan* (London: Henry S. King and Co., 1874), I, 150.

There is no lack of evidence as to the traditional military might of the Satsuma *han.* For example, during the Meiji Boshin, the civil war of 1868, out of the hundred or more *han* that rallied to the imperial standard and contributed forces for the government expedition against the Tokugawa insurgents, the Kagoshima *han* played a leading and distinguished part. Ōtsuka Takematsu, ed., *Sappan Shutsugun Senjō* [Satsuma Han's Military Situation] (Tōkyō: Nihon Shiseki Kyōkai, 1932), I, 1.

9. Yoshi S. Kuno, *Japanese Expansion on the Asiatic Continent* (Berkeley: University of California Press, 1937-1940), I, 123; Maurice Courant, *Ôkoubo* (Paris:

Ancienne Librairie Germer Bailliere et Cie, 1904), p. 35. In the sixteenth century, numerous voyages of trade, discovery, or piracy were made as far west as India and the Kuriles to the north. The Japanese adventurers gave the island of Luzon (Rōson in Japanese) in the Philippines its name. William Elliot Griffis, *The Mikado's Empire* (New York: Harper and Brothers, 1886), p. 246.

10. James Murdoch, *A History of Japan* (London: Kegan Paul, Trench, Trubner and Co., Ltd., 1925), I, 419. See also Itō, *op. cit.*, I. The author devotes the first several chapters of the volume to a detailed description of the love affair between Yoritomo and his mistress.

11. Asakawa, *op. cit.*, pp. 8-10.

12. *Ibid.*, p. 11. In October, 1576, Shimazu Yoshihisa, together with his brothers Yoshihiro and Iehisa, led a huge army raised from the whole of Ōsumi and Satsuma and from a portion of Hyūga and defeated Itō Yoshisuke, who had established control over a large portion of northern Hyūga and Ōbi. Two years later, on December 18, 1578, Ōtomo of Bungo, in central Kyūshū, was defeated by the Shimazu when he answered Itō's plea for aid in reëstablishing himself at Sadowara in Hyūga. In this engagement Ōtomo lost half of his forces, and the Shimazu annexed Sadowara. See *ibid.*, pp. 314-315; Gubbins, "Hideyoshi and Satsuma," p. 101.

The method of assessment for military service that was employed by the Shimazu during these campaigns is of interest. Holders of one *chō* (2.45 acres) were required to furnish two men, the master and a follower; holders of two *chō*, three men, master and followers; holders of three *chō*, four men, master and followers; and so on. Churches and temples were required to furnish one attendant laborer, referred to as *tsumefu*, as well as three draft horses. Draft horses were also assessed upon widows.

The fighters were required to carry the following implements: one broad axe, one chisel, one log six *shaku* long (one *shaku* = 0.994194 foot), one sickle, one adze, one *tekabushi* (hand cover), one hoe, one saw, one dirt-carrier, and one coil of rope. See Asakawa, *op. cit.*, pp. 315-316.

13. The Ōtomo appealed to Hideyoshi for succor upon learning of Shimazu's preparation in 1585 for the conquest of Bungo. On November 12, 1585, Hideyoshi wrote to Shimazu Yoshihisa in the name of the emperor ordering him to cease hostilities with Ōtomo pending a boundary settlement, an order that was rejected. Yoshihisa likewise turned down a Hideyoshi offer of half of Chikugo and Higo in addition to the Yoshihisa's proper holdings in southern Kyūshū if hostilities ceased. On January 20, 1587, Shimazu attacked Ōtomo at Toshimitsu, winning a decisive victory. Meanwhile, in May, Hideyoshi's army, under his younger brother, Hidenaga, pushed on into Hyūga. On June 1 Hideyoshi himself arrived from Higo by sea and established headquarters in the Taiheiji, a Buddhist temple. Asakawa, *op. cit.*, p. 323; Gubbins, "Hideyoshi and Satsuma," pp. 102-136.

14. Asakawa, *op. cit.*, pp. 323-324; Gubbins, "Hideyoshi and Satsuma," p. 141. *Kōri* was an administrative division of a province.

15. Asakawa, *op. cit.*, p. 332. For a more detailed account in Japanese of the military service rendered by Shimazu in this expedition, see Matsushita Shigesuke, *Kagoshima-ken Kyōdō Keitō Shi* [History of Kagoshima Prefecture] (Kagoshima: Kagoshima Insatsu Kabushiki Kaisha, 1930), I, 138 ff. See Asakawa, *op. cit.*, document no. 150, A and B, pp. 333-334, for details concerning the military service of Shimazu in the Korean expedition.

16. *Ibid.*, p. 335. See also Matsushita, *op. cit.*, I, 150-163. In 1617 the assessed productive power of the land of the three provinces were: Satsuma, 314,805

koku; Ōsumi, 170,833 *koku;* Hyūga, 119,967 *koku;* total, 605,607 *koku.* Asakawa, *op. cit.*, p. 337, document no. 151, B.

17. No direct trade with China was possible after Hideyoshi's Kyūshū expedition until the overthrow of the Ming in 1643. See Murdoch, *op. cit.*, II, 512-513; Asakawa, *op. cit.*, p. 337, document no. 151, C; and Takekoshi Yosoburo, *The Economic Aspects of the History of the Civilization of Japan* (New York: The Macmillan Co., 1930), III, 223-226.

The precise relation the Ryūkyūs bore to China and Japan, respectively, was a point of dispute. See Francis L. Hawks, comp., *Narrative of the Expedition of an American Squadron to the China Seas and Japan, Performed in the Years 1852, 1853, and 1854, under the Command of Commodore M. C. Perry, United States Navy, by Order of the Government of the United States* (United States House of Representatives, 33rd Congress, 2nd Sess., Exec. Doc. 97; Washington: A. O. P. Nicholson, 1856), p. 221. For a scholarly work on the history of the Ryūkyū islands, see George H. Kerr, *Okinawa* (Tōkyō: Charles E. Tuttle Co., 1959).

18. Matsushita, *op. cit.*, I, 269.

19. *Ibid.*, pp. 270-271.

20. See Frank Alanson Lombard, *Pre-Meiji Education in Japan* (Tōkyō: Kyō Bun Kwan, 1914), pp. 86-88.

21. The Japanese had respect for the written character, as did the Chinese. Han Yu-shan, writing about Chinese passion for the written word, says: "Chinese passion for the written characters of their language furthered a desire to make records of men and events. This devotion had almost a religious nature; whether a Chinese could read or not the characters were sacred and even the use of modern newspapers for wrapping paper was frowned upon by the common people and scholars alike. 'Heaven rejoiced' when characters were invented since they 'established contact between the human and the divine'; in like manner 'Hades was made to tremble.' As late as the 1930's men still went about the streets, gathering scraps of paper bearing any signs of writing or printing to be placed in bamboo baskets bearing the inscription, Chin-hsi-tzu-chih (Reverence-love-charactered-paper). Such papers were then burned at Buddhist, Taoist, or Confucian temples." Han Yu-shan, *Elements of Chinese Historiography* (Hollywood: W. M. Hawley, 1955), p. 1.

22. Matsushita, *op. cit.*, I, 272.

23. Lombard, *op. cit.*, p. 89.

24. G. B. Sansom, *Japan: A Short Cultural History* (New York: Appleton-Century-Crofts, Inc., 1943), p. 508.

25. Kishio Satomi, *Discovery of Japanese Idealism* (London: Kegan Paul, Trench, Trubner and Co., Ltd., 1924), p. 72.

26. *Ibid.*, p. 77.

27. Akiyama Kenzō, *The History of Nippon* (Tōkyō: Kokusai Bunka Shinkōkai, 1941), pp. 231-232.

28. *Ibid.*, p. 217. As early as the fifteenth century it was customary for the Shimazu family to invite to their domain scholars from Kyōto and Kamakura. Thus Keian, a Zen monk, lectured in Satsuma upon Chinese philosophy of the Sung school and introduced into Japan and had printed at his patrons' expense the commentaries of Chu Hsi upon the works in the Confucian canon. See Sansom, *Japan: A Short Cultural History*, p. 380.

29. Prior to his invasion, Hideyoshi sent a Shin sect abbot, Kennyō Kōsa, with a retinue of fifty-six persons, including two Hideyoshi emissaries, to live at Shishi-

jima in Satsuma to learn the secrets of the province. Under cover of clerical disguise the agents circulated freely throughout the province and acquainted themselves with the geography and affairs of the *han*. Later these men acted as guides for Hideyoshi's invasion army. After the war the priests of Shishijima were crucified, and all Shin adherents were forced to renounce their creed. See Gubbins, "Hideyoshi and Satsuma," pp. 124-125, 127, 142-143.

30. C. R. Boxer, *The Christian Century in Japan*, 1549-1650 (Berkeley and Los Angeles: University of California Press, 1951), p. 98.

31. Pierre Francois Xavier de Charlevoix, *Histoire du Japon* (Paris: Chez Rollin, 1754), II, 36.

32. *Ibid.*, p. 46; Murdoch, *op. cit.*, II, 53.

33. Charlevoix, *op. cit.*, IV, 125, 187. Japan felt that Christianity could not be of any real practical value to her.

34. Matsushita, *op. cit.*, I, 126.

35. Gubbins, "Hideyoshi and Satsuma," p. 97.

36. Ishigami Konta, ed., *Kōtō Sensei Itsuwa* [Anecdotes Concerning Kōtō] (Kagoshima: Kagoshima-ken Kyōikukai, 1938), p. 4.

37. Tokutomi notes that although it had been thought that the family was descended from Hatakeyama Shigetaka, a Heishi, the Ōkubos are definitely Fujiwara in stock. Tokutomi, *Ōkubo Kōtō Sensei*, p. 4. See also Katsuda, *Ōkubo Toshimichi Den*, I, 5.

38. Ishigami, *op. cit.*, pp. 2-3. There were seventeen or eighteen *hōgiri* (each *hōgiri* comprising several *machi*, or blocks of residence) within the castle-town of Kagoshima.

39. Ōkubo's father was also called Toshio and Shirō, the latter being a pseudonym.

40. Tanaka Sōgorō, *Ōkubo Toshimichi* (Tōkyō: Chikura Shobō, 1938), p. 14.

41. Katsuda, *Ōkubo Toshimichi Den*, I, 16.

42. Ishigami, *op. cit.*, pp. 19-20.

43. The social stratification in Japan was distinct, with the nobility at the top followed by the warrior, peasant, and merchant classes, in that order.

44. Ishigami, *op. cit.*, p. 20.

45. Shirayanagi Takeshi, *Ōkubo Toshimichi* (Tōkyō: Chōbunkaku, 1943), p. 63.

46. See Katsuda, *Ōkubo Toshimichi Den*, I, 31.

47. *Ibid.*, pp. 13-14.

48. Tanaka Sōgorō, *op. cit.*, p. 13.

49. Shirayanagi, *op. cit.*, p. 69. Tokugawa Ieyasu's decree of 1615, "one *han*, one castle," resulted in the destruction of all fortifications except the central castle of each *han*. Satsuma, however, defied these orders and continued to maintain a *tojō seido*, or a pattern of outer castles. See Sakai, *op. cit.*, pp. 366-367.

50. Ishigami, *op. cit.*, pp. 6-8, 12-13.

51. Tanaka Sōgorō, *op. cit.*, p. 15. Among Toshimichi's childhood associates there were a number of boys who later became important personalities in Japanese history, the most famous of whom was Saigō Takamori. As schoolmates and close boyhood friends, Saigō and Toshimichi swam and fished in the river and visited in each other's homes. They were inseparable until political and personal differences eventually ended their close association. It is significant to note that most of Ōkubo's childhood friends were two or three years his senior, a fact that attests to his unusual mental maturity even at this early phase of life.

52. Tokutomi, *Ōkubo Kōtō Sensei*, p. 6.

53. August Karl Reischauer, *Studies in Japanese Buddhism* (New York: Macmillan Co., 1917), p. 115; E. Steinilber-Oberlin, *Les sectes bouddhiques japonaises* (Paris: Les Editions G. Crès et Cie, 1930), p. 129.

54. Daisetz Teitarō Suzuki, *Zen Buddhism and Its Influence on Japanese Culture* (Kyōto: The Eastern Buddhist Society, 1938), p. 10.

55. *Ibid.*, pp. 34-37.

56. A. K. Reischauer, *op. cit.*, p. 122.

57. For an excellent biographical sketch of Wang Yang-ming, see Frederick Goodrich Henke, *The Philosophy of Wang Yang-ming* (London and Chicago: The Open Court Publishing Co., 1916), pp. 3-44. A detailed treatment of the Wang Yangming philosophy to be found in Wang Tch'ang-tche, "La philosophie morale de Wang Yang-ming," *Variétés sinologiques*, XLII, no. 63 (Paris: Librairie Orientaliste P. Geuthner, 1936).

58. Much of his training in Japanese history and literature was acquired from Kumaoka Gōsuke, a venerable scholar who was also versed in Chu Hsi philosophy. See Katsuda, *Ōkubo Toshimichi Den*, I, 19-20.

59. Tanaka Inahiko, *Ketsujin Ōkubo Kōtō* [The Eminent Ōkubo Kōtō] (Tōkyō: Shūbunkan, 1911), p. 19.

60. Katsuda, *Ōkubo Toshimichi Den*, I, 36, 50; Ishigami, *op. cit.*, pp. 22-24.

61. Katsuda Magoya and Usui Yoshiharu, eds., *Ōkubo Toshimichi Monjo* [Papers of Ōkubo Toshimichi] (Tōkyō: Nihon Shiseki Kyōkai, 1927-1929), I, 1-2; hereafter cited as *Ōkubo Toshimichi Monjo*.

62. Katsuda, *Ōkubo Toshimichi Den*, I, 36-37.

63. Shirayanagi, *op. cit.*, p. 24.

64. Tanaka Sōgorō, *op. cit.*, p. 18; Katsuda, *Ōkubo Toshimichi Den*, I, 46.

65. Matsushita, *op. cit.*, I, 278. See also Tōyama Shigeki, *Meiji Ishin* [Meiji Restoration] (Tōkyō: Iwanami Shoten, 1951), p. 40.

66. Matsushita, *op. cit.*, p. 279.

67. *Ibid.*, pp. 280-282; Ishin Shiryō Hensan Jimukyoku, *Ishin Shi* [History of the Restoration] (Tōkyō: Ishin Shiryō Hensan Jimukyoku, 1939-1942), II, 156; hereafter cited as *Ishin Shi*.

68. Matsushita, *op. cit.*, p. 279. *Vide* Chap. I, footnote 62.

69. See W. G. Beasley, ed. and trans., *Select Documents on Japanese Foreign Policy, 1853-1868* (London: Oxford University Press, 1955), document 5, pp. 112-114; Tanaka Sōgorō, *op. cit.*, p. 32.

70. Walter Wallace McLaren, *A Political History of Japan During the Meiji Era* (New York: Charles Scribner's Sons, 1916), p. 61.

In this respect the study of the personnel of the *Sanshoku* (three offices of the central government), the new interim government set up in Kyōto on January 3, 1868, is of interest; even then it was apparent that certain *han* dominated important governing bodies, a tendency that continued through most of the Meiji period. The *sanyo* (junior councilors), one of the most influential offices, was dominated by Satsuma samurai. The following table shows *han* representation (it should be noted that the terms were staggered and not of equal duration) in the position of *sanyo* from January 3, 1868, when the *Sanshoku* was created, to June 11, 1868, when the *Shichi Ka* (Seven Administrative Offices) was organized:

Satsuma	9	Hizen	3	Yanagawa	1	Tsuwano	1
Echizen	6	Tosa	3	Ogaki	1	Akita	1

Kumamoto	6	Aki	3	Takatoku	1	Inuyama	1
Chōshū	5	Inaba	2	Uwajima	1	Oka	1
Owari	5	Bizen	2	Takanabe	1		

Robert A. Wilson, *Genesis of the Meiji Government in Japan, 1868-1871* (Berkeley and Los Angeles: University of California Press, 1957), pp. 105-107. See also *Ishin Shi*, V, 376-380.

71. Charles Lanman, *Leading Men of Japan* (Boston: D. Lathrop and Company, 1883), p. 163.

72. Tanaka Sōgorō, *op. cit.*, pp. 19-20.

73. Katsuda, *Ōkubo Toshimichi Den*, pp. 49-50.

74. Tanaka Sōgorō, *op. cit.*, p. 20.

75. O-Yura, Narioki's mistress and the mother of his illegitimate son, Hisamitsu, served as a symbol of the conservative party from the time of the Takasaki incident. It will be recalled that at that time the progressives backed Nariakira and the conservatives gave their support to Hisamitsu.

76. *Ishin Shi, op. cit.*, II, 400; Tanaka Sōgorō, *op. cit.*, p. 28.

77. Matsushita, *op. cit.*, p. 279. For a succinct discussion of dualism as a political tradition in Japan, see Paul M. A. Linebarger, Djang Chu, and Ardath W. Burks, *Far Eastern Governments and Politics* (New York: D. Van Nostrand Co., Inc., 1956), pp. 289-310.

78. Matsushita, *op. cit.*, p. 289.

79. From the end of 1856 the *jōi* party attempted to influence the Bakufu policy by reinforcing its own popularity with the appeal of *sonnō* ideas, and by 1858 the two groups were firmly allied. Using the slogan "*sonnō jōi*," the antiforeign elements now insisted that only under the aegis of imperial prestige could reform and unity be achieved. See Beasley, *op. cit.*, pp. 37-38.

80. Tanaka Sōgorō, *op. cit.*, p. 30.

81. Marius B. Jansen, *Sakamoto Ryōma and the Meiji Restoration* (Princeton: Princeton University Press, 1961), pp. 36, 41; Albert M. Craig, *Chōshū in the Meiji Restoration* (Cambridge: Harvard University Press, 1961), pp. 56 ff.; Tōyama Shigeki, *Meiji Ishin* [Meiji Restoration] (Tōkyō: Iwanami Shoten, 1951), pp. 33 ff.

82. *Ibid.*, pp. 37-38.

83. Beasley, *op. cit.*, p. 44.

84. Murdoch, *op. cit.*, III, 715.

85. Katsuda, *Ōkubo Toshimichi Den*, I, 98.

86. See Murdoch, *op. cit.*, III, 715-716 for details.

Notes to Chapter III

1. Katsuda Magoya, *Ōkubo Toshimichi Den* [Biography of Ōkubo Toshimichi] (Tōkyō: Dōbunkan, 1910-1911), I, 105.

2. On February 4, 1859, Ijichi Rūemon delivered Ōkubo's letter to Saigō whose ship was in the port of Yamagawa taking on supplies before its departure for Ōshima. Apparently Saigō's reply was dispatched by the same messenger. See Ōkawa Nobuyoshi, ed., *Dai Saigō Zenshū* [Complete Works of Saigō] (Tōkyō: Heibonsha, 1926), I, 146-148; hereafter cited as *Dai Saigō Zenshū*.

3. *Ibid.*, pp. 138-139.

4. *Ibid.*, pp. 144-146.

5. For a list of the members of the Seichū Gumi, see Katsuda Magoya and Usui Yoshiharu, eds., *Ōkubo Toshimichi Monjo* [Papers of Ōkubo Toshimichi] (Tōkyō: Nihon Shiseki Kyōkai, 1927-1929), I, 32-34; hereacter cited as *Ōkubo Toshimichi Monjo.*

6. This elevation to a high position of nominal leadership of prestigious persons exemplifies in microcosm Japanese organizational practice in government. History reveals that dichotomy and even trichotomy of leadership in government have been traditional to the Japanese.

7. See Katsuda, *Ōkubo Toshimichi Den,* pp. 120-121.

8. See Tōyama Shigeki, *Meiji Ishin* [Meiji Restoration] (Tōkyō: Iwanami Shoten, 1951), pp. 35-36; Marius B. Jansen, *Sakamoto Ryōma and the Meiji Restoration* (Princeton: Princeton University Press, 1961), pp. 41-42; and Albert M. Craig, *Chōshū in the Meiji Restoration* (Cambridge: Harvard University Press, 1961), pp. 69-73.

9. *Ōkubo Toshimichi Monjo,* I, 39-40; Ishin Shiryō Hensan Jimukyoku, *Ishin Shi* [History of the Restoration] (Tōkyō: Ishin Shiryō Hensan Jimukyoku, 1939-1942), II, 708; hereafter cited as *Ishin Shi.*

10. *Ōkubo Toshimichi Monjo,* I, 34-39.

11. Katsuda Magoya and Usui Yoshiharu, eds., *Ōkubo Toshimichi Nikki* [Diary of Ōkubo Toshimichi] (Tōkyō: Nihon Shisheki Kyōkai, 1927), I, 41; hereafter cited as *Ōkubo Toshimichi Nikki.*

12. *Ibid.,* pp. 41, 44.

13. See Itō Nitarō, *Ōkubo Toshimichi* (Tōkyō: Heibonsha, 1941), II, 258.

14. Tanaka Inahiko, *Ketsujin Ōkubo Kōtō* [The Eminent Ōkubo Kōtō] (Tōkyō: Shūbunkan, 1911), pp. 30-34; *Ishin Shi,* II, 709.

15. *Ōkubo Toshimichi Nikki,* I, 44.

16. Katsuda, *Ōkubo Toshimichi Den,* I, 140.

17. Tokutomi Iichirō, *Ōkubo Kōtō Sensei* [Master Ōkubo Kōtō] (Tōkyō: Minyūsha, 1927), p. 12.

18. Ishigami Konta, ed., *Kōtō Sensei Itsuwa* [Anecdotes Concerning Kōtō] (Kagoshima: Kagoshima-ken Kyōikukai, 1938), pp. 40-41; Tanaka Sōgorō, *Ōkubo Toshimichi* (Tōkyō: Chikura Shobō, 1938), pp. 37-38; Itō, *op. cit.,* II, 222-226.

19. Itō, *op. cit.,* II, 225.

20. *Ibid.,* p. 248.

21. See Tanaka Sōgorō, *op. cit.,* p. 36.

22. For the text of the petition sent to Hisamitsu in the second month of the first year of Manen (1860), see *Ōkubo Toshimichi Monjo,* I, 55-56.

23. The names of the conspirators are listed in *Ōkubo Toshimichi Nikki,* I, 86-87. For a detailed discussion in English of events leading up to and including the assassination, see James Murdoch, A *History of Japan* (London: Kegan Paul, Trench, Trubner, and Co., Ltd., 1925-1926), III, 663-710. A graphic description in Japanese of the incident is given by Shimada Saburō, *Kaikoku Shimatsu* [Particulars Relating to the Opening of Japan] (Tōkyō: Yoronsha, 1888), pp. 402 ff.; and in *Ishin Shi,* I, 718-720.

24. *Ōkubo Toshimichi Nikki,* I, 57-58.

25. Shimada, *op. cit.,* pp. 430-431.

26. *Ōkubo Toshimichi Nikki,* I, 80.

27. For Arimura Yūsuke's account as told to Ōkubo, see *ibid.,* pp. 59-67.

28. *Ibid.,* p. 68.

29. *Ibid.*, p. 75; Ishigami, *op. cit.*, pp. 52-53.
30. *Ōkubo Toshimichi Nikki*, I, 69.
31. *Ibid.*, p. 70.
32. *Ibid.*, p. 53.
33. Itō, *op. cit.*, II, 252.
34. Yamaguchi Uji, *Kinse Shiriaku* [Outline of History of Modern Japan], translated by Sir Ernest Mason Satow (Tōkyō: The Naigwai Shuppan Kyōkai, 1906), p. 20; hereafter cited as *Kinse Shiriaku.*
35. Itō, *op. cit.*, II, 253.
36. Tokutomi, *Ōkubo Kōtō Sensei*, p. 15.
37. Itō, *op. cit.*, II, 247.
38. Ishigami, *op. cit.*, p. 56. It was after Ōkubo became a *soba yaku* that he changed his first name from Shōsuke to Ichizō.
39. Tanaka Inahiko, *op. cit.*, p. 39.
40. *Ōkubo Toshimichi Monjo*, I, 36.
41. Ishigami, *op. cit.*, p. 59.
42. See Tanaka Sōgorō, *op. cit.*, pp. 50-51.
43. Robert K. Sakai, "Feudal Society and Modern Leadership in Satsuma-han," *The Journal of Asian Studies*, XVI (1957), 367.
44. Tōyama Shigeki, *Meiji Ishin*, pp. 35-36.
45. Ishigami, *op. cit.*, p. 59.
46. Delmer Brown, *Nationalism in Japan* (Berkeley and Los Angeles: University of California Press, 1955), p. 76.
47. *Vide*, pp. 47-48.
48. Early in its history, as it will be noted later, the Meiji government abolished the semiautonomous fiefs and replaced them with prefectures under the control of the central government.
49. See Tanaka Sōgorō, *op. cit.*, pp. 70, 74-75.
50. *Ibid.*, pp. 64-65.
51. *Ōkubo Toshimichi Monjo*, I, 62. The phrase *ichi kisaku* alludes to the secret scheme to burn the Shiba *hantei*, or the *han* residence in the Shiba district of Tōkyō.
52. *Ishin Shi*, III, 65-66; Katsuda, *Ōkubo Toshimichi Den*, I, 204 ff.
53. Unfortunately there is no entry in the Ōkubo diary between January 15, 1862, and April 4, 1862, a period roughly covering the duration of Ōkubo's stay in Kyōto.
54. *Ōkubo Toshimichi Nikki*, I, 46.
55. *Dai Saigō Zenshū*, I, 183, and "Explanation," p. 185.
56. Itō, *op. cit.*, II, 262; *Ishin Shi*, III, 69.
57. Tokutomi, *Ōkubo Kōtō Sensei*, p. 17.
58. *Ibid.*, p. 16; *Ishin Shi*, III, 70.
59. *Kinse Shiriaku*, pp. 22-23; Murdoch, III, 717-718.
60. Katsuda, *Ōkubo Toshimichi Den*, I, 228-229.
61. *Kinse Shiriaku*, pp. 13-15.
62. For a short but scholarly discussion of one phase of the Restoration movement in Chōshū, see Albert M. Craig, "The Restoration Movement in Chōshū," *The Journal of Asian Studies*, XVIII (1959), 187-197. See also Craig, *Chōshū in the Meiji Restoration.*
63. Murdoch, *op. cit.*, III, 719.
64. *Kinse Shiriaku*, pp. 24-25.
65. *Ōkubo Toshimichi Nikki*, I, 103; *Ishin Shi*, III, 71.

66. *Ōkubo Toshimichi Nikki,* I, 111.
67. *Ibid.,* p. 113.
68. *Ibid.,* p. 116.
69. *Ibid.,* pp. 116-117.
70. *Ibid.,* p. 117
71. *Ibid.,* pp. 117-118.
72. Tanaka Sōgorō, *op. cit.,* p. 92; Katsuda, *Ōkubo Toshimichi Den,* I, 242.
73. *Ōkubo Toshimichi Nikki,* I, 118.
74. Katsuda, *Ōkubo Toshimichi Den,* I, 245-246.
75. *Dai Saigō Zenshū,* I, 191-193. While interned on the island, Saigō lived in a small hut and spent most of his time reading, practicing calligraphy, and writing poetry. He took time from these activities to teach some of the children on the island the rudiments of reading and writing. Thus during this period he acquired considerable cultural polish. Also, he was not unmindful of the situation in Satsuma and elsewhere in Japan; when, in 1863, he heard the news of the bombardment of Kagoshima by English warships, he impressed upon the island authorities the seriousness of the situation and made plans to build ships and participate in any emergency if it became necessary.
76. *Ōkubo Toshimichi Nikki,* I, 120.
77. For the full text of Hisamitsu's proposal to the *kuge,* see Nakane Yukie, *Saimu Kiji* [Second Dream Record] (Tōkyō: Nihon Shiseki Kyōkai, 1927), pp. 20-22.
78. *Ishin Shi,* III, 81-82; Nakane, *Saimu Kiji,* pp. 22-24.
79. See Tanaka Sōgorō, *op. cit.,* pp. 99-100.
80. *Ishin Shi,* III, 80.
81. *Ōkubo Toshimichi Nikki,* I, 123-124.
82. *Ibid.,* p. 124.
83. *Ibid.,* p. 131.
84. Tanaka Sōgorō, *op. cit.,* p. 101.
85. *Ōkubo Toshimichi Nikki,* I, 133.
86. Ishigami, *op. cit.,* pp. 89 ff.
87. *Ōkubo Toshimichi Nikki,* I, 139.
88. *Ishin Shi,* III, 98-101.
89. *Ibid.,* p. 103.
90. *Kinse Shiriaku,* p. 29.
91. *Ishin Shi,* III, 103-104.
92. *Ōkubo Toshimichi Nikki,* I, 153.
93. *Ibid.,* p. 160.
94. Shibuzawa Eiichi, *Tokugawa Keiki Kō Den* [Biography of Tokugawa Keiki] (Tōkyō: Fuzambō, 1918), II, 54. For details of the negotiations between Ōhara and the Bakufu agents, see Nakane, *Saimu Kiji,* pp. 111 ff.
95. *Ōkubo Toshimichi Nikki,* I, 163, 165.
96. *Ibid.,* p. 178.
97. A highly detailed account in English of the Richardson affair (the Japanese refer to this as the *Namamugi no hen*) can be found in Francis Ottiwell Adams, *The History of Japan* (London: Henry S. King and Co., 1874), I, 189 ff.
98. Katsuda, *Ōkubo Toshimichi Den,* I, 321.
99. Tanaka Inahiko, *op. cit.,* pp. 44-46.
100. Adams, *op. cit.,* I, 155-173; *Kinse Shiriaku,* pp. 28-29.
101. *Ishin Shi,* III, 260-261.

102. *Ibid.*, pp. 554-555.
103. *Ōkubo Toshimichi Nikki*, I, 199.
104. *Ibid.*, p. 204. The gifts included such traditional items as the Japanese sword.
105. *Ibid.*, p. 206.
106. *Ōkubo Toshimichi Nikki*, I, 210-211.

Notes to Chapter IV

1. See Ishin Shiryō Hensan Jimukyoku, *Ishin Shi* [History of the Restoration] (Tōkyō: Ishin Shiryō Hensan Jimukyoku, 1939-1942), III, 329-331; hereafter cited as *Ishin Shi*. See also Katsuda Magoya, *Ōkubo Toshimichi Den* [Biography of Ōkubo Toshimichi] (Tōkyō: Dōbunkan, 1910-1911), I, 363.
2. *Ishin Shi*, III, 531.
3. *Ibid.*, p. 532.
4. *Ibid.*, pp. 532-533; Shibuzawa Eiichi, *Tokugawa Keiki Kō Den* [Biography of Tokugawa Keiki] (Tōkyō: Fuzambō, 1918), II, 266. See sketch of Yoshida Shōin in Robert Louis Stevenson, "Yoshida-Torajiro," in *The Travels and Essays of Robert Louis Stevenson; Familiar Studies of Men and Books—Miscellaneous Papers* (New York: Charles Scribner's Sons, 1903), XIV, 150-165.
5. *Ishin Shi*, III, 533-534; Shibuzawa, *Tokugawa Keiki Kō Den*, II, 265-266.
6. *Ishin Shi*, III, 535.
7. *Ibid.*, pp. 334-335; Tokutomi Iichirō, *Kinsei Nihon Kokumin Shi* [Modern History of the Japanese Nation] (Tōkyō: Minyūsha, 1918-1941), XLIX, 79; hereafter cited as Tokutomi, *Kokumin Shi*.
8. *Ibid.*, p. 70.
9. Nakane Yukie, *Zoku Saimu Kiji* [Second Dream Record Continued] (Tōkyō: Nihon Shiseki Kyōkai, 1927), I, 336; Katsuda, *Ōkubo Toshimichi Den*, I, 363.
10. Nakane, *Zoku Saimu Kiji*, I, 336-339; Tokutomi, *Kokumin Shi*, XLIC, 93.
11. See Tanaka Sōgorō, *Ōkubo Toshimichi* (Tōkyō: Chikura Shobō, 1938), p. 117.
12. Katsuda Magoya and Usui Yoshiharu, eds., *Ōkubo Toshimichi Monjo* [Papers of Ōkubo Toshimichi] (Tōkyō: Nihon Shiseki Kyōkai, 1927-1929), I, 132; hereafter cited as *Ōkubo Toshimichi Monjo*.
13. Nakane, *Zoku Saimu Kiji*, I, 346; *Ishin Shi*, III, 335. For a detailed account of Ōkubo's activities while in Edo, see Tokutomi, *Kokumin Shi*, XLIX, 97 ff.
14. Nakane, *Zoku Saimu Kiji*, I, 347.
15. *Ishin Shi*, III, 335.
16. *Ōkubo Toshimichi Monjo*, I, 158-161; Tanaka Sōgorō, *op. cit.*, p. 120.
17. *Ōkubo Toshimichi Monjo*, I, 150.
18. Katsuda, *Ōkubo Toshimichi Den*, I, 398.
19. *Ibid.*, p. 400.
20. Yamaguchi Uji, *Kinse Shiriaku* [Outline History of Modern Times], translated by Sir Ernest Mason Satow (Tōkyō: The Naigwai Shuppan Kyōkai, 1908), p. 34; hereafter cited as *Kinse Shiriaku*.
21. Nakane, *Zoku Saimu Kiji*, I, 372. See also W. G. Beasley, ed. and trans., *Select Documents on Japanese Foreign Policy, 1853-1868* (London: Oxford University Press, 1955), p. 234. On March 29, 1863, Tokugawa Keiki and others had informed the court that the Bakufu intended to effect the withdrawal of the foreigners within twenty days after Tokugawa Iemochi returned from Edo, it being the

understanding that the court would issue instructions limiting the *shōgun*'s stay in Kyōto to ten days.

22. *Kinse Shiriaku*, p. 36; *Ishin Shi*, III, 347.

23. James Murdoch, A *History of Japan* (London: Kegan Paul, Trench, Trubner and Co., Ltd., 1925-1926), III, 727-728. See also Francis Ottiwell Adams, *The History of Japan* (London: Henry S. King and Co., 1874-1875), I, 239-250.

24. *Kinse Shiriaku*, p. 41.

25. See Adams, *op. cit.*, I, 276. At one o'clock on the morning of the twenty-fourth of June, Colonel St. John Neale was verbally informed that the Bakufu proposed to pay the indemnity at once, and asked at what hour the money might be brought to the legation. He replied that he would be prepared to accept the money at six o'clock, provided the whole amount of four hundred and forty thousand Mexican dollars was brought at one time. The whole sum was eventually loaded in equal parts aboard three English warships.

26. Murdoch, *op. cit.*, III, 732-733.

27. Katsuda, *Ōkubo Toshimichi Den*, I, 408.

28. Nakane, *Zoku Saimu Kiji*, I, 419; Katsuda, *Ōkubo Toshimichi Den*, I, 408-409.

29. See Murdoch, *op. cit.*, III, 733; *Kinse Shiriaku*, pp. 35-36; and *Ishin Shi*, III, 345-346.

30. The term *hatamoto* has usually been used to designate the close retainers of the Tokugawa *shōgun*. It is apparent, however, that the *daimyō* sometimes used the term in referring to their own samurai counterparts. In his diary Ōkubo has used the character *hata* (flag), the first ideograph in the compound term *hata-moto*, with the addition of a *take kammuri* (bamboo crown), that is, with a radical not ordinarily used in this particular character. In the past, battle standards in Japan were commonly attached to bamboo poles and in the light of this Ōkubo's character for *hata* becomes more meaningful.

31. See Ōkubo's letter to Hisamitsu and also the explanatory remarks in *Ōkubo Toshimichi Monjo*, I, 173-176.

32. See *Ishin Shi*, III, 549-580; Adams, *op. cit.*, I, 342-353. Japanese historians refer to this coup d'etat as the *Hachi-ichi-hachi Jihen*, or the 8-1-8 Incident, as it occurred in the eighth month and on the eighteenth day of the third year of Bunkyū (September 30, 1863).

33. *Ōkubo Toshimichi Monjo*, I, 163.

34. The murderers were never apprehended.

35. Adams, *op. cit.*, I, 308-309. For added details of the Kagoshima bombardment, see John R. Black, *Young Japan* (London: Trubner and Co., 1880-1881), I, Chapter XIX; and also Tokutomi, *Kokumin Shi*, L, 231 ff.

36. Adams, *op. cit.*, I, 310-311.

37. *Ibid.*, p. 312. See also Tanaka Sōgorō, *op. cit.*, p. 130; *Ishin Shi*, III, 495-496. The precautionary measures were warranted. The Satsuma men had plans to attack the British aboard ship while delivering requested provisions to them. The beginning of hand-to-hand combat was to be the signal for the shore batteries to open fire upon the ships.

38. Adams, *op. cit.*, I, 318.

39. *Ibid.*, p. 319.

40. *Ibid.*, p. 320.

41. *Ibid.*, p. 321.

42. Quoted in Itō Nitarō, *Ōkubo Toshimichi* (Tōkyō: Heibonsha, 1941), II, 264-265.
43. *Ibid.*, pp. 265-266.
44. *Ishin Shi,* III, 500; Adams, *op. cit.*, I, 326. See also Kimura Kaishū, ed., *Sanjūnen Shi* [Thirty-Year History of Japan] (Tōkyō: Kōshunsha, 1892), pp. 567-569, for details of the Kagoshima bombardment as reported by the *Yokohama Shimbun* on August 21, 1863.
45. Murdoch, *op. cit.*, III, 735.
46. *Ishin Shi,* III, 501-503. See also Tokutomi, *Kokumin Shi,* L, 248-249; Ernest Satow, *A Diplomat in Japan* (London: Seeley, Service and Co., 1921), p. 89. Tokutomi believes that Admiral Kuper's decision not to land troops on the mainland was a wise one. In fact, he voices the opinion that, had the British landed, they might have been decimated by the Satsuma forces. He also takes note of Sir Ernest Satow's view that Kuper may have decided against a landing party because this had been advocated by Minister Neale, whose insistence upon effecting the venture riled the Admiral. The latter felt that military decisions were in his province and not in that of the diplomatic agent. Satow also notes that the dwindling supply of coal, stores, and ammunition may have been an added factor in motivating Kuper to withdraw.
47. Tokutomi Iichirō, *Ōkubo Kōtō Sensei* [Master Ōkubo Kōtō] (Tōkyō: Minyūsha, 1927), p. 26.
48. Adams, *op. cit.*, I, 328.
49. Shirayanagi Takeshi, *Ōkubo Toshimichi* (Tōkyō: Chōbunkaku, 1943), p. 116.
50. Watanabe Shūjirō, *Ōkubo Toshimichi Genkōroku* [Words and Deeds of Ōkubo Toshimichi] (Tōkyō: Naigai Shuppan Kyōkai, 1892), p. 9.
51. Tanaka Sōgorō, *op. cit.*, p. 132.
52. Watanabe Shūjirō, *op. cit.*, p. 9.
53. Tōyama Shigeki, *Meiji Ishin* [Meiji Restoration] (Tōkyō: Iwanami Shoten, 1951), pp. 160-161.
54. Tanaka Sōgorō, *op. cit.*, p. 133; Murdoch, *op. cit.*, III, 735.
55. *Ishin Shi,* III, 507.
56. Katsuda, *Ōkubo Toshimichi Den,* I, 496.
57. Black, *op. cit.*, I, 235-237.
58. *Ōkubo Toshimichi Monjo,* I, 182.
59. Tanaka Sōgorō, *op. cit.*, p. 137.
60. Katsuda Magoya and Usui Yoshiharu, eds., *Ōkubo Toshimichi Nikki* [Diary of Ōkubo Toshimichi] (Tōkyō: Nihon Shiseki Kyōkai, 1927), I, 213; hereafter cited as *Ōkubo Toshimichi Nikki.*
61. *Ibid.*, p. 231.
62. Katsuda, *Ōkubo Toshimichi Den,* I, 504.
63. Tanaka Sōgorō, *op. cit.*, p. 139.
64. *Ibid.*, p. 140.
65. Katsuda, *Ōkubo Toshimichi Den,* I, 510-511.
66. Tanaka Sōgorō, *op. cit.*, p. 141.
67. *Ōkubo Toshimichi Monjo,* I, 208. In this report Tokugawa Keiki, otherwise known as Hitotsubashi Yoshinobu, is referred to as Hitoki.
68. Tanaka Sōgorō, *op. cit.*, p. 143.
69. Katsuda, *Ōkubo Toshimichi Den,* I, 547-548.
70. *Ibid.*, pp. 548-549; Tanaka Sōgorō, *op. cit.*, pp. 143-144.

71. Ōkawa Nobuyoshi, ed., *Dai Saigō Zenshū* [Complete works of Saigō] (Tōkyō: Heibonsha, 1925-1927), I, 318-319; hereafter cited as *Dai Saigō Zenshū*.
72. Tokutomi, *Ōkubo Kōtō Sensei*, p. 32.
73. *Ōkubo Toshimichi Monjo*, I, 207.
74. Tanaka Sōgorō, *op. cit.*, p. 141.
75. Katsuda, *Ōkubo Toshimichi Den*, I, 552.
76. *Dai Saigō Zenshū*, I, 323; Katsuda, *Ōkubo Toshimichi Den*, I, 555.
77. Murdoch, *op. cit.*, III, 740.
78. Tanaka Sōgorō, *op. cit.*, p. 148.
79. *Ishin Shi*, IV, 87-92; Murdoch, *op. cit.*, III, 743.
80. *Ibid.*, p. 744.
81. *Ōkubo Toshimichi Monjo*, I, 219-220. The Satsuma note to the court is not signed by Ōkubo, but he nevertheless drafted it.
82. Ishigami Konta, *Kōtō Sensei Itsuwa* [Anecdotes Concerning Kōtō] (Kagoshima: Kagoshima-ken Kyōikukai, 1938), pp. 73-76.
83. Katsuda, *Ōkubo Toshimichi Den*, I, 574-576. For an interesting account of Nakahama Manjirō, see Hisakazu Kaneko, *Manjiro, the Man Who Discovered America* (Boston: Houghton Mifflin Co., 1956).
84. Katsuda, *Ōkubo Toshimichi Den, I*, 572-573.
85. Tokutomi, *Ōkubo Kōtō Sensei*, p. 33.
86. See Tanaka Sōgorō, *op. cit.*, pp. 158-159; *Ōkubo Toshimichi Nikki*, I, 235.
87. *Ibid.*, pp. 238, 239.
88. *Ibid.*, pp. 240-241.
89. See Tanaka Sōgorō, *op. cit.*, pp. 163-164.
90. *Ōkubo Toshimichi Nikki*, I, 242.
91. *Ōkubo Toshimichi Monjo*, I, 278.
92. *Ibid.*, p. 274.
93. *Ibid.*, p. 276. The Shūseikan was a military and naval training institute and shipyard.
94. *Ōkubo Toshimichi Monjo*, I, 276; *Ishin Shi*, IV, 448; Tōyama Shigeki, *Meiji Ishin*, pp. 168-169.
95. *Ōkubo Toshimichi Nikki*, I, 250.
96. *Ōkubo Toshimichi Monjo*, I, 279-280.
97. *Ibid.*, p. 280.
98. *Ibid.*, p. 278. Ōkubo makes the request for greater freedom in the matter of decision-making in the opening sentence of this letter.
99. Katsuda, *Ōkubo Toshimichi Den*, I, 640; Tanaka Sōgorō, *op. cit.*, p. 169.
100. *Ishin Shi*, IV, 454.
101. Katsuda, *Ōkubo Toshimichi Den*, I, 643; Tanaka Sōgorō, *op. cit.*, p. 170.
102. *Ōkubo Toshimichi Monjo*, I, 298. Ōkubo's reference to "Chōshū war" undoubtedly refers to the bombardment of Shimonoseki, a port of the Chōshū fief, by the combined British, Dutch, and French squadron in June of 1864.
103. *Ibid.*, p. 300.
104. S. Lane-Poole and F. V. Dickins, *The Life of Sir Harry Parkes* (London: Macmillan and Company, 1894), II, 43; hereafter cited as Lane-Poole, *Harry Parkes*. See also Nakane, *Zoku Saimu Kiji*, IV, 253.
105. *Ibid.*, p. 263; Adams, *op. cit.*, II, 21; Shibuzawa, *Tokugawa Keiki Kō Den*, III, 244.
106. *Ōkubo Toshimichi Nikki*, I, 267; Nakane, *Zoku Saimu Kiji*, IV, 283; Shibuzawa, *Tokugawa Keiki Kō Den*, III, 245.

107. *Kinse Shiriaku,* pp. 78-79; Shibuzawa, *Tokugawa Keiki Kō Den,* III, 266; Murdoch, *op. cit.*, III, 759; Katsuda, *Ōkubo Toshimichi Den,* I, 675.

108. *Ishin Shi,* IV, 291-292.

109. Murdoch, *op. cit.*, III, 762. See also *Kinse Shiriaku,* p. 78.

110. See Tanaka Sōgorō, *op. cit.*, p. 185.

111. *Ishin Shi,* IV, 462.

112. *Ōkubo Toshimichi Monjo,* I, 335.

113. *Ishin Shi,* IV, 455.

114. *Ibid.*, pp. 456-457; Tōyama Shigeki, *Meiji Ishin,* pp. 160-163. An authoritative work in English on Sakamoto Ryūma is Marius B. Jansen, *Sakamoto Ryōma and the Meiji Restoration* (Princeton: Princeton University Press, 1961). See also Tōyama Shigeki, *Meiji Ishin,* pp. 172-173.

115. *Ishin Shi,* IV, 463-467.

116. *Ibid.*, pp. 468-469. Jansen, *op. cit.*, pp. 220-221.

117. Katsuda, *Ōkubo Toshimichi Den,* II, 24.

118. Tanaka Sōgorō, *op. cit.*, pp. 192-193.

119. Watanabe Shūjirō, *op. cit.*, p. 22.

120. Horie Yasuzō, "The Economic Significance of the Meiji Restoration," reprint from *Kyōto University Economic Review,* XII, no. 11 (n.d.), 67; Tanaka Sōgorō, *op. cit.*, p. 212. See also Tōyama Shigeki, *Meiji Ishin,* pp. 166-168.

121. Katsuda, *Ōkubo Toshimichi Den,* II, 33-34; *Ishin Shi,* IV, 501-502. The term *tenri,* or laws of nature, has Western overtones; it is used repeatedly in the Declaration of Independence by Jefferson who was influenced by Rousseau and the contemporary thinking prevalent on the European continent. It would be of interest to see if there were any influences from the West which induced Japanese political thinkers to use the term so frequently. The Japanese concept of *tenri,* however, is no doubt basically Chinese in origin. That the Chinese were long familiar with this concept may be inferred from such phrases as the "Ordinances of Heaven" contained in the *Doctrine of the Mean* and "Does Heaven Speak?" in the *Analects* of Confucius. See James Legge, *The Four Books* (Shanghai: Commercial Press, Ltd., n.d.), pp. 266, 407.

122. Katsuda, *Ōkubo Toshimichi Den,* II, 35; Maurice Courant, *Ôkoubo* (Paris: Librairie Germer Bailliere et Cie, 1904), p. 94. Courant states that Ōkubo replied: "Si le clan de Nagato a commis des acte qui enfassent un ennemi de l'Empire, que le Bakou-hou articule les faits: mais notre clan n'a connaisance de rien de tel. Notre politique est fixée. Si vous nous traitez un ennemis publics, nous vous attendrons."

There is no evidence at hand outside of what has been quoted by biographers of Ōkubo to prove or disprove the veracity of this episode. It occurred, but the description of it by Japanese writers seems to have been embellished and exaggerated. The *Ishin Shi* (IV, 502) verifies Ōkubo's personal meeting with Itakura but gives no further details. It is unfortunate that there are no entries in Ōkubo's diary between the middle of November, 1865, and September 15, 1866, the period during which the episode took place.

123. *Dai Saigō Zenshū,* I, 746-747, 757 ff.

124. *Ishin Shi,* IV, 505. For an outline of the second punitive campaign against Chōshū, see *Ishin Shi,* IV, 474 ff. A more detailed record of matters pertaining to the Bakufu's punitive expedition covering the period between August, 1864, and May, 1865, is to be found in Hayakawa Junsaburō, ed., *Bakufu Seichō Kiroku* [Record of the Bakufu's Punitive Expedition against Chōshū] (Tōkyō: Nihon Shiseki Kyōkai,

1919). See also Murdoch, *op. cit.*, III, 754. Murdoch states that it was nearly two years after Chōshū had been declared a rebel and eighteen months after the first punitive expedition had been disbanded, specifically on July 23, 1866, that the real hostilities began.

The Chōshū *han* had been declared a rebel in August, 1864. Having achieved the purpose of the expedition without a shot being fired, the commander of the Bakufu forces, on January 30, 1865, ordered the disbandment of the army of chastisement. This was an unwise move; Takasugi Shinsaku, a radical loyalist, seized Shimonoseki on the very day the punitive army was ordered disbanded. Thereafter the Chōshū *han* backed the radicals and strengthened its defenses against the anticipated move by the Bakufu. The Tokugawa government announced the second expedition against the rebels in May, 1865, when Chōshū failed to submit to the sentence (confiscation of a hundred thousand *koku* of Chōshū land and the seclusion for life of the Mōris) that a Bakufu council had imposed upon the *han*. See also Albert M. Craig, *Chōshū in the Meiji Restoration* (Cambridge: Harvard University Press, 1961), pp. 251 ff.

125. See Saigō's letter to Ōkubo dated August 19, 1866, making specific reference to France and to the Bakufu in *Dai Saigō Zenshū,* I, 779-780. See also Takekoshi Yosoburo, *The Economic Aspects of the History of the Civilization of Japan* (New York: The Macmillan Co., 1930), III, 360, regarding the French agreement to give the Bakufu military aid against Chōshū.

126. Tanaka Sōgorō, *op. cit.*, pp. 202-203.

127. Lane-Poole, *Harry Parkes,* II, 65.

128. Shibuzawa, *Tokugawa Keiki Kō Den,* III, 354-355.

129. *Ibid.*, pp. 376-379; Tanaka Sōgorō, *op. cit.*, pp. 204-205.

130. *Ōkubo Toshimichi Monjo,* I, 410.

131. Edouard Chavannes, trans. and ed., *Les mémoires historiques de Se-ma Ts'ien* (Paris: Ernest Leroux, 1895-1905), I, 275.

132. Ōtsuki Fumihiko, *Daigenkai* [Encyclopedia of Great Words] (Tōkyō: Fuzambō, 1932-1937), I, 831-832.

133. Ishii Takashi, *Meiji Ishin no Kokusai-teki Kankyō* [The International Circumstances of the Meiji Restoration] (Tōkyō: Yoshikawa Kōbunkan, 1957), p. 461.

134. Murdoch, *op. cit.*, III, 764; Ishigami, *op. cit.*, p. 89.

135. *Ibid.*, pp. 90 ff.

136. Watanabe Shūjirō, *op. cit.*, pp. 11-12.

137. See Tanaka Inahiko, *Ketsujin Ōkubo Kōtō* [The Eminent Ōkubo Kōtō] (Tōkyō: Shūbunkan, 1911), pp. 54-55.

138. Tokutomi, *Ōkubo Kōtō Sensei,* pp. 45-46; Murdoch, *op. cit.*, III, 764. For details of Emperor Kōmei's funeral, see Nakane, *Zoku Saimu Kiji,* VI, 147-148.

139. Murdoch, *op. cit.*, III, 765. The question of opening Hyōgo, Ōsaka, and Edo to foreign trade had been deferred in 1862 with the consent of the treaty powers until January 1, 1868. The new *shōgun* had memorialized the court for the opening of Hyōgo on April 9, 1867, but had received a negative reply. He had then begged for a reconsideration on April 16.

140. Nakane, *Zoku Saimu Kiji,* VI, 257-258; Murdoch, *op. cit.*, III, 766-767; *Ishin Shi,* IV, 634 ff.

141. *Ibid.*, p. 658.

142. *Ōkubo Toshimichi Monjo,* I, 475-478.

143. *Ibid.*, pp. 478-479; *Ishin Shi,* IV, 664.

144. *Ibid.*, pp. 668-669. The Sat-Chō alliance of 1866 did not commit Satsuma to joint military action with Chōshū. See Craig, *Chōshū in the Meiji Restoration*, pp. 340-341. For an English translation of the agreement, see Jansen, *op. cit.*, pp. 299-301.
145. *Ōkubo Toshimichi Monjo*, I, 480.
146. *Ōkubo Toshimichi Nikki*, I, 391; *Ishin Shi*, IV, 678-679.
147. *Ibid.*, pp. 679-682; *Ōkubo Toshimichi Nikki*, I, 391-397.
148. *Ishin Shi*, IV, 686, 698-699, 700.
149. *Ōkubo Toshimichi Nikki*, I, 398.
150. *Ōkubo Toshimichi Monjo*, II, 11.
151. For the full text of the memorial, see *ibid.*, pp. 12-17.
152. *Ishin Shi*, IV, 706-708.
153. *Ibid.*, pp. 709-710; Tada Kōmon and Kagawa Keizō, comps., *Iwakura Kō Jikki* [Authentic Chronicle of Prince Iwakura] (Tōkyō: Iwakura Kō Koseki Hozonkai, 1927), II, 70 ff.; hereafter cited as *Iwakura Kō Jikki*.
154. *Ōkubo Toshimichi Nikki*, I, 401-402; *Ishin Shi*, IV, 714 ff.; Murdoch, *op. cit.*, III, 769-770.
155. *Iwakura Kō Jikki*, II, 84-85.
156. *Ishin Shi*, V, 37-38.
157. *Ōkubo Toshimichi Nikki*, I, 405.
158. *Ibid.*, p. 406.
159. For the text of the communication, see *Ishin Shi*, V, 43-44.
160. *Ōkubo Toshimichi Nikki*, I, 406.
161. Tanaka Sōgorō, *op. cit.*, p. 239.
162. *Ibid.*, p. 240.
163. *Ishin Shi*, V, 54.
164. *Ōkubo Toshimichi Nikki*, I, 407; *Ishin Shi*, V, 55.
165. *Ibid.*, pp. 55-56.
166. *Ibid.*, p. 56.
167. Murdoch, *op. cit.*, III, 772.
168. *Ishin Shi*, V, 57; *Dai Saigō Zenshū*, III, 547-548.
169. *Ishin Shi*, V, 57.
170. Ōtsuka Takematsu, ed., *Iwakura Tomomi Kankei Monjo* [Papers Relating to Iwakura Tomomi] (Tōkyō: Nihon Shiseki Kyōkai, 1930), III, 400; hereafter cited as *Iwakura Tomomi Kankei Monjo*.
171. *Ibid.*, p. 398.
172. For the full text of the proclamation, see *Ishin Shi*, V, 73; *Iwakura Kō Jikki*, II, 148-150.
173. Takahashi Kamekichi, *Nihon Shihonshugi Hattatsu Shi* [The History of the Development of Japanese Capitalism] (Tōkyō: Nihon Hyōronsha, 1928), pp. 8-10.
174. Hani Gorō, *Meiji Ishin* [The Meiji Restoration] (Tōkyō: Iwanami Shoten, 1946), pp. 55-65.
175. *Ibid.*, p. 66.
176. *Ibid.*, pp. 52-53.
177. Horie Yasuzō, "The Economic Significance of the Meiji Restoration," reprint from *Kyōto University Economic Review*, XII, no. 11 (n.d.), 69-70.
178. Thomas C. Smith, *The Agrarian Origins of Modern Japan* (Stanford: Stanford University Press, 1959), pp. 176-179, 204-205.
179. Tōyama Shigeki and Sato Shinichi, eds., *Nihon Shi Kenkyū Nyūmon* [A

Guide to the Study of Japanese History] (Tōkyō: Tōkyo Daigaku Shuppankai, 1956), pp. 243-245.

180. Hattori Shisō, *Meiji Ishin ni okeru Shidō to Dōmei* [Leadership and Alliances of the Meiji Restoration] (Tōkyō: Nihon Hyōronsha, 1949), pp. 30-31.

181. Tōyama Shigeki, *Nihon Shi Kenkyū Nyūmon*, p. 242.

182. *Ibid.* See also Tsuchiya Takao, *The Development of Economic Life in Japan* (Tōkyō: Kokusai Bunka Shinkōkai, 1936), pp. 16-18.

183. *Ibid.*, p. 21.

184. See Tōyama Shigeki, *Nihon Shi Kenkyū Nyūmon*, pp. 235 ff.

185. See Tōyama Shigeki, *Meiji Ishin*, pp. 186-187; also Craig, *Chōshū in the Meiji Restoration*, pp. 51-53.

186. Tōyama Shigeki, *Meiji Ishin*, p. 210.

187. Hani, *op. cit.*, pp. 79-81. See also Itazawa Takeo, "Rangaku no Hattatsu" [Development of Dutch Learning], in *Iwanami Kōza: Nihon Rekishi*, Kuroita Katsumi, ed., III (Tōkyō: Iwanami Shoten, 1933), 3 ff. Dutch learning served (1) to introduce not only Dutch but also European science and arts, (2) to give the Japanese an entirely new world outlook, and (3) to leave an imprint upon the Japanese language. Such terms, for example, as *kampan* (deck), *tarapu* (steps), and *mesu* (knife) are derived from the Dutch words *kampanges*, *trap*, and *mes*, respectively.

For a more complete discussion of the intellectual currents in Tokugawa Japan, refer to G. B. Sansom, *Japan: A Short Cultural History* (New York: Appleton-Century-Crofts, Inc., 1943), pp. 500-513. The fact to bear in mind with reference to the intellectual developments in the late eighteenth and early nineteenth centuries is that, with the rise to prominence of the national scholars and Dutch scholars, there came two currents of thought, one looking into the past to the original polity of Japan and the other looking outward to the West, causing intellectuals to realize that the future of the country depended upon acquiring the knowledge of Western science.

Politically for Japan the significance of the existence of these two currents of thought was obvious. The consequence of the work of the national scholars, delving as they did into the history of Japan, was to nurture the *fukko*, or restoration, concept used by the Meiji Restoration leaders, men such as Ōkubo, Kido, and Saigō, to justify their attempts to overthrow the Tokugawa government. On the other hand, the Dutch scholars who studied Western science were to leave their imprint upon the thinking of the leaders of the mid-nineteenth century; the knowledge of the advanced civilization of the West, which the leaders of Japan acquired by way of the Dutch scholars, was to motivate them to adopt and adapt those aspects of Western civilization that would best serve to strengthen and modernize the country.

For further discussions of these influences, see Nakayama Kyūjirō, "Kinsei Shina yori Ishin Zengo no Nihon ni oyoboshitaru Shoshū no Eikyō" [The Influence of Modern China upon Japan during the Restoration Era], Takeoka Katsuya, "Kokugaku no Hatten to Meiji Ishin" [The Development of Japanese Classical Studies and the Meiji Restoration], and Kure Shūzō, "Yōgaku no Hatten to Meiji Ishin" [The Development of Western Studies and the Meiji Restoration], in *Meiji Ishin Shi Kenkyū*, Tōkyō Teikoku Daigaku Shigakkai, ed. (Tōkyō: Fuzambō, 1929), pp. 329-458.

188. Asai Kiyoshi, *Meiji Ishin to Gun-ken Shisō* [The Meiji Restoration and the County-Prefecture Concept] (Tōkyō: Ganshōdō Shoten, 1939), p. 9.

189. *Ibid.*, p. 14. Asai maintains that the *gun-ken* concept is closely related to the

ōsei fukko idea inasmuch as both are incompatible with feudalism with its inherent concept of administrative decentralization. The restoration of the country to imperial rule implied the abolition of local political entities that existed under the Tokugawa in the form of semiautonomous *han* and replacement with *gun-ken,* or local administrative units responsible to the will of a central government. See *ibid.*, pp. 72-73.

190. Watanabe Ikujirō, *Meiji Shi Kōwa* [Lectures on Meiji History] (Tōkyō: Yoshikawa Kōbunkan, 1935), pp. 6-12.

191. Tōyama Shigeki, *Meiji Ishin,* pp. 67-70.

192. Watanabe Ikujirō, *op. cit.*, p. 5.

193. *Ibid.*, p. 73.

194. Horie, *op. cit.*, p. 70.

195. Takahashi, *Nihon Shihon Shugi Hattatsu Shi,* pp. 39-57.

196. Marius B. Jansen, *Sakamoto Ryōma and the Meiji Restoration* (Princeton: Princeton University Press, 1961), pp. 48-49.

197. Hirao Michio, "Bakumatsu Rōnin to sono Hogo oyobi Tōsei" [The Protection and Control of the *Rōnin* in the Bakumatsu Period], in *Meiji Ishin Shi Kenkyū,* Tōkyō Teikoku Daigaku Shigakkai, ed. (Tōkyō: Fuzambō, 1929), pp. 527-529. See also Jansen, *op. cit.*, p. 101.

198. Hirao Michio, *op. cit.*, p. 530.

199. E. Herbert Norman, *Japan's Emergence as a Modern State* (New York: Institute of Pacific Relations, 1940), p. 49.

200. *Ibid.*, p. 51; Hirao Michio, *op. cit.*, pp. 527-529.

201. Tōyama Shigeki, *Meiji Ishin,* p. 143.

202. *Ibid.*, p. 92.

203. Nakamura Kōya, "Meiji Ishin to Chōnin Kaikyū" [The Merchant Class and the Meiji Restoration], in *Meiji Ishin Shi Kenkyū,* Tōkyō Teikoku Daigaku Shigakkai, ed. (Tōkyō: Fuzambō, 1929), pp. 499-500.

204. *Ōkubo Toshimichi Nikki,* I, 414-415; Tokutomi, *Ōkubo Kōtō Sensei,* p. 47; Murdoch, *op. cit.*, III, 773-776; *Ishin Shi,* V, 77 ff.

205. According to Robert A. Wilson, the offices of *gijō* and *sanyo* were not originally conceived to be composed of ten and twenty members, respectively, as Western writers have repeatedly indicated. The source of the mistaken notion is a document contained in the *Hōrei Zensho* dated January 3, 1868, a translation of which appears in Walter Wallace McLaren, ed., "Japanese Government Documents," *Transactions of the Asiatic Society of Japan,* XLII, pt. 1 (Tōkyō, 1914), 4. See Robert A. Wilson, *The Genesis of the Meiji Government, 1868-1871* (Berkeley and Los Angeles: University of California Press, 1957), p. 14.

206. *Ibid.*, pp. 11-19, 105-107.

207. Watanabe Shūjirō, *op. cit.*, p. 56.

208. Tokutomi, *Ōkubo Kōtō Sensei,* p. 50.

209. Wilson, *op. cit.*, pp. 105-107.

210. Tanaka Inahiko, *op. cit.*, pp. 83-84.

211. *Ibid.*, p. 84; Watanabe Shūjirō, *op. cit.*, p. 47.

212. *Ōkubo Toshimichi Nikki,* I, 421-425. For a description of the battle, see Adams, *op. cit.*, II, 95-101. The cannonading of the Satsuma residence at Mita in Edo was directed by a French officer. Subsequently, on February 18, the representatives of the foreign powers in Kōbe issued a declaration of neutrality. See *Kinse Shiriaku,* p. 111.

213. Itō, *op. cit.*, II, 271.
214. *Ōkubo Toshimichi Nikki*, I, 427.
215. *Ibid.*, p. 428.
216. Tanaka Inahiko, *op. cit.*, pp. 74-75.
217. *Ishin Shi*, V, 56.

Notes to Chapter V

1. Katsuda Magoya and Usui Yoshiharu, eds., *Ōkubo Toshimichi Nikki* [Diary of Ōkubo Toshimichi] (Tōkyō: Nihon Shiseki Kyōkai, 1927), I, 418; hereafter cited as *Ōkubo Toshimichi Nikki*. See also Ishigami Konta, ed., *Kōtō Sensei Itsuwa* [Anecdotes Concerning Kōtō] (Kagoshima: Kagoshima-ken Kyōikukai, 1938), pp. 112-113.

2. See Robert A. Wilson, *Genesis of the Meiji Government in Japan, 1868-1871* (Berkeley and Los Angeles: University of California Press, 1957), pp. 11-19; Naikaku Kampō Kyoku, *Hōrei Zensho, 1868* [Complete Collection of Laws and Ordinances, 1868] (Tōkyō: Naikaku Kampō Kyoku, 1887), pp. 15-16; hereafter cited as *Hōrei Zensho*.

3. Wilson, *op. cit.*, p. 22; Tōkyō Teikoku Daigaku Shiryō Hensanjo, *Meiji Shiyō* [Essentials of Meiji History] (Tōkyō: Kinkōdō Shoseki Kabushiki Kaisha, 1933), I, 17; hereafter cited as *Meiji Shiyō*.

4. Wilson, *op. cit.*, p. 108.

5. Katsuda Magoya and Usui Yoshiharu, eds., *Ōkubo Toshimichi Monjo* [Papers of Ōkubo Toshimichi] (Tōkyō: Nihon Shiseki Kyōkai, 1927-1929), II, 193; hereafter cited as *Ōkubo Toshimichi Monjo*. See also Tada Kōmon and Kagawa Keizō, comps., *Iwakura Kō Jikki* [Authentic Chronicle of Prince Iwakura] (Tōkyō: Iwakura Kō Koseki Hozonkai, 1927), II, 283-284; hereafter cited as *Iwakura Kō Jikki*.

6. *Ōkubo Toshimichi Nikki*, I, 433, 436-437; Ishigami, *op. cit.*, pp. 121-122; Ishin Shiryō Hensan Jimukyoku, *Ishin Shi* [History of the Restoration] (Tōkyō: Ishin Shiryō Hensan Jimukyoku, 1939-1942), V, 431-434; hereafter cited as *Ishin Shi*. For the full text of Ōkubo's memorial, see *Ōkubo Toshimichi Monjo*, II, 191-195.

7. James A. B. Scherer, *Young Japan* (Philadelphia and London: J. B. Lippincott Co., 1905), pp. 216-217; Maurice Courant, *Ôkoubo* (Paris: Ancienne Librairie Germer Bailliere et Cie, 1904), p. 124. Courant quotes a portion of the memorial of February 16:

> L'Empereur, restant enfermé dans la routine de Kyôto, ne pourra ni profiter de la défaite des rebelles, ni organizer l'État, ni établer des relations satisfaisantes avec l'etranger, Osaka, ville maritime, riche et commerçante, située an coeur du pays, est un lieu unique pour le développement diplomatique, militaire et naval, économique du l'Etat. L'Empereur doit s'y transporter pour quelque temps et craindre, s'il tarde, de perdre l'occasion d'inaugurer les réformes indispensable.

8. *Ōkubo Toshimichi Nikki*, I, 438.
9. Scherer, *op. cit.*, pp. 217-218.
10. *Ōkubo Toshimichi Nikki*, I, 448.
11. *Meiji Shiyō*, I, 41.

12. For Ōkubo's proposal dealing with the disposition of the ex-*shōgun*, see *Ōkubo Toshimichi Monjo*, II, 253-254.

For added details on the surrender of the Edo castle as reported in the Japanese press, see Ishida Bunjirō, ed., *Shimbun Kiroku Shūsei Meiji Daijiken Shi* [History of Great Events of the Meiji Era Compiled from Newspaper Records] (Tōkyō: Kinseisha, 1954), pp. 29-30.

13. Ishigami, *op. cit.*, pp. 130-131.

14. *Ōkubo Toshimichi Nikki*, I, 467.

15. *Meiji Shiyō*, I, 77. For the text of the imperial decree, see *Iwakura Kō Jikki*, II, 504.

16. Tanaka Inahiko, *Ketsujin Ōkubo Kōtō* [The Eminent Ōkubo Kōtō] (Tōkyō: Shūbunkan, 1911), p. 98; Ishida, *op. cit.*, p. 39; *Ishin Shi*, V, 442-444. The original advocates for the transference of the capital from Ōsaka to Edo were Etō Shimpei and Ōki Takato. Ōkubo, though not the originator of the plan, accepted the idea and was, furthermore, the most active in working for its realization.

17. See Imai Toshiki, "Edo yori Tōkyō e no Suii" [The Change from Edo to Tōkyō], in *Meiji Ishin Shi Kenkyū* [Studies in Meiji Restoration History], Tōkyō Teikoku Daigaku, Shigakkai, ed. (Tōkyō: Fuzambō, 1929), pp. 761-767.

18. Osatake Takeshi, *Nihon Kensei Shi Taikō* [Outline of Japanese Constitutional History] (Tōkyō: Nihon Hyōronsha, 1938), I, 84-86.

19. Francis Ottiwell Adams, *The History of Japan* (London: Henry S. King and Co., 1874-1875), II, 105; *Meiji Shiyō*, I, 16.

20. Adams, *op. cit.*, II, 103-107.

21. *Ōkubo Toshimichi Nikki*, I, 441-443; Roy Hidemichi Akagi, *Japan's Foreign Relations*, 1542-1936 (Tōkyō: Hokuseidō Press, 1936), p. 58. For details in English of the Sakai incident, see John R. Black, *Young Japan* (London: Trubner and Co., 1880-1881), II, 162-168.

22. Wilson, *op. cit.*, pp. 24-25; *Meiji Shiyō*, I, 23.

23. Wilson, *op. cit.*, p. 110.

24. For the full text in Japanese, see *Hōrei Zensho*, 1868, pp. 63-64.

25. Fujii Jintarō and Moriya Hidesuke, *Sōgō Nihon Shi Taikei: Meiji Jidai Shi* [A Synthesis of Japanese History: History of the Meiji Period] (Tōkyō: Naigai Shoseki Kabushiki Kaisha, 1939), I, 209; hereafter cited as Fujii and Moriya, *Meiji Jidai Shi*. See also *Meiji Shiyō*, I, 34.

26. *Ōkubo Toshimichi Nikki*, I, 447.

27. Cf. Ōtsu Junichirō, *Dai Nippon Kensei Shi* [Constitutional History of Japan] (Tōkyō: Hōbunkan, 1927-1928), I, 213 ff.; Osatake, *op. cit.*, I, 116 ff.

28. *Ibid.*, p. 111.

29. *Ibid.*, p. 112; George M. Beckmann, *The Making of the Meiji Constitution* (Lawrence: University of Kansas Press, 1957), p. 7.

30. Osatake, *op. cit.*, I, 112-113.

31. Beckmann, *op. cit.*, p. 7.

32. Tōyama Shigeki, *Meiji Ishin* [Meiji Restoration] (Tōkyō: Iwanami Shoten, 1951), pp. 226-227.

33. See Tokutomi Iichirō, *Ōkubo Kōtō Sensei* [Master Ōkubo Kōtō] (Tokyo: Minyūsha, 1927), pp. 75-80.

34. *Ōkubo Toshimichi Nikki*, I, 451.

35. *Ibid.*, p. 452.

36. *Ōkubo Toshimichi Monjo*, II, 370.

37. *Ishin Shi*, V, 549.
38. *Ibid.*, p. 552.
39. Ōtsuka Takematsu, ed., *Iwakura Tomomi Kankei Monjo* [Papers Relating to Iwakura Tomomi] (Tōkyō: Nihon Shiseki Kyōkai, 1927-1935), III, 499-500; *Ōkubo Toshimichi Monjo*, II, 304-305.
40. *Meiji Shiyō*, I, 61; *Ishin Shi*, I, 553.
41. *Ibid.*, p. 556.
42. *Ōkubo Toshimichi Monjo*, II, 369; Tanaka Sōgorō, *Ōkubo Toshimichi* (Tōkyō: Chikura Shobō, 1938), p. 295.
43. Sawada Akira, *Meiji Zaisei no Kisoteki Kenkyū* [A Fundamental Study of Meiji Finance] Tōkyō: Hōbunkan, 1934), pp. 240-242.
44. *Ishin Shi*, V, 554-556.
45. Tanaka Sōgorō, *op. cit.*, pp. 301-302.
46. *Ibid.*, pp. 302-303.
47. *Ibid.*, p. 304.
48. Tsumaki Chūta, ed., *Kido Kōin Nikki* [Diary of Kido Kōin] (Tōkyō: Nihon Shiseki Kyōkai, 1932-1933), I, 159; hereafter cited as *Kido Kōin Nikki*.
49. Tanaka Sōgorō, *op. cit.*, pp. 305-306.
50. *Ibid.*, p. 306. See Adams, *op. cit.*, II, 181.
51. Watanabe Shūjirō, *Ōkubo Toshimichi Genkōroku* [Words and Deeds of Ōkubo Toshimichi] (Tōkyō: Naigai Shuppan Kyōkai, 1909), pp. 59-61; Tanaka Inahiko, *op. cit.*, I, 99-102; Katsuda Magoya, *Ōkubo Toshimichi Den* [Biography of Ōkubo Toshimichi] (Tōkyō: Dōbunkan, 1910-1911), II, 611-612; *Kido Kōin Nikki*, I, 99-100.
52. *Meiji Shiyō*, I, 120. For the memorial in English presented by the *daimyō* of Satsuma, Chōshū, Hizen, and Tosa, offering to surrender their fiefs to the throne, see John Harington Gubbins, *The Progress of Japan*, 1853-1871 (Oxford: Clarendon Press, 1911), p. 313.
53. For Kido's memorial, see Tsumaki Chūta, ed., *Kido Kōin Monjo* [Papers of Kido Kōin] (Tōkyō: Nihon Shiseki Kyōkai, 1929-1931), VIII, 25-26; hereafter cited as *Kido Kōin Monjo*. See also Adams, *op. cit.*, II, 181-184.
54. *Ibid.*, p. 185.
55. Katsuda, *Ōkubo Toshimichi Den*, II, 609.
56. *Ibid.*, p. 610.
57. With reference to the abolition of the feudal form of government, the Meiji leaders were faced with a very real problem, an insight into which may be gained by noting what one Japanese economic historian has to say:

> . . . One difficulty arose from the fact that although the leaders of the new Government were generally inspired by the ideal of achieving the unification of the country into a modern State, they themselves were, on the other hand, *samurai* of various clans and received fiefs from their feudal lords. Thus, while their ideal was to secure the restoration of the rule of the land and people to the Emperor, in fact as well as in name, their personal sentiment was rather against a course designed to reduce the authority of their former lords. Another difficulty was that not all feudal lords and their *samurai* understood in full the true aims of the Meiji Restoration; many of them desired the existence of the feudal regime unchanged. In such circumstances, it was difficult to eliminate the feudal form of gov-

ernment all at once, and a half-measure called *Hanseki-Hokan* (the return of the ruling power to the Imperial Court by all feudal lords), had to be taken to begin with. Although feudal lords all surrendered their feuds to the Imperial Court in this way and these former feudal lords were appointed *Chihanji* or governors, the political organization thus made was as if Japan was a federal state founded upon the clan system. Stated more concretely, the *Chihanji* retained their former sway over their land and people unimpaired; with their former retainers as their subordinate officials, they carried on administration and directed their efforts chiefly to the development of their own clans. In short, all clans formed independent and separate political districts. In such circumstances, it was absolutely impossible for the Central Government either to secure the sources of national revenue or to centralize political and military power.

See Horie Yasuzō, "The Economic Significance of the Meiji Restoration," reprint from *Kyōto University Economic Review*, XII, no. 11 (n.d.), 72-73.

58. *Ōkubo Toshimichi Monjo*, II, 493.

59. *Ibid.*, p. 494.

60. Ishigami, *op. cit.*, pp. 148-149. For a discussion of Saionji's trip abroad, see Takekoshi Yosaburo, *Prince Saionji* (Kyōto: Ritsumeikan University, 1933), pp. 79-84.

61. Walter Wallace McLaren, ed., "Japanese Government Documents," *Transactions of the Asiatic Society of Japan*, XLII (Tōkyō, 1914), 22. See also Wilson, *op. cit.*, p. 43.

62. McLaren, "Japanese Government Documents," p. 25; *Ishin Shi*, V, 527, 528. The term *kōmunin* was later changed to *kōginin*.

63. *Ibid.*, p. 679.

64. *Ibid.*; McLaren, "Japanese Government Documents," p. 26.

65. *Ishin Shi*, V, 747-749.

66. *Ōkubo Toshimichi Monjo*, III, 33, 34.

67. *Ōkubo Toshimichi Nikki*, II, 21.

68. *Ibid.*, pp. 22-23.

69. Ōkawa Nobuyoshi, ed., *Dai Saigō Zenshū* [Complete Works of Saigō] (Tōkyō: Heibonsha, 1926-1927), II, 424; hereafter cited as *Dai Saigō Zenshū*. See also *Ōkubo Toshimichi Nikki*, II, 23-25.

70. *Dai Saigō Zenshū*, II, 425.

71. *Ōkubo Toshimichi Nikki*, II, 28, 29.

72. *Ōkubo Toshimichi Monjo*, III, 152-154; Tanaka Sōgorō, *op. cit.*, p. 324. The *Seitaisho* was proclaimed on June 11, 1868. Under the structure of government based upon this document, Ōkubo, a *sanyo*, was a member of the *Giseikan*, or the upper chamber of the legislative department. For authoritative accounts of the *Seitaisho*, consult Wilson, *op. cit.*, pp. 34-65; McLaren, "Japanese Government Documents," pp. 7-15; Walter Wallace McLaren, *A Political History of Japan During the Meiji Era, 1867-1912* (New York: Charles Scribner's Sons, 1916), pp. 62-67; and Osatake, op. cit., I, 136-146.

73. *Hōrei Zensho*, 1869, p. 171; Osatake, *op. cit.*, II, 154-157; *Ōkubo Toshimichi Nikki*, II, 39; *Iwakura Kō Jikki*, II, 721-726; *Meiji Shiyō*, I, 142. For Ōkubo's memorial to Iwakura upon which this reform was based, see *Ōkubo Toshimichi Monjo*, III, 161-166.

74. Osatake, *op. cit.*, I, 151.
75. Tanaka Sōgorō, *op. cit.*, p. 325.
76. Beckmann, *op. cit.*, p. 8.
77. Osatake, *op. cit.*, I, 158.
78. *Meiji Shiyō*, I, 145.
79. George Etsujirō Uyehara, *The Political Development of Japan, 1867-1909* (London: Constable and Co., Ltd., 1910), p. 57.
80. *Ishin Shi*, V, 539.
81. *Hōrei Zensho*, 1869, p. 221. For a list of the new *chihanji* and the revenue of each *han*, see *ibid.*, pp. 221-229.
82. *Hōrei Zensho*, 1869, p. 198; *Ishin Shi*, V, 540.
83. Wilson, *op. cit.*, pp. 66-86; *Hōrei Zensho*, 1869, pp. 249, 156.
84. Beckmann, *op. cit.*, p. 10.
85. *Ōkubo Toshimichi Monjo*, III, 197.
86. Wilson, *op. cit.*, pp. 49-54. The principal duty of the *Kōgisho* established on January 17, 1869, was the enactment of laws. Some twenty proposals were submitted to it for discussion during its short existence. The body considered such matters as the *hanseki hōkan* (return of feuds to the throne), *goyōkin* (forced loan), abolition of *tsūshō* (common name) and the substitution of *jitsumyō* (true name) for official purposes, recruitment of government officials based upon China's examination system, development of foreign trade and commerce, ban on Roman Catholicism, abolition of ceremonial suicide, samurai's right to carry swords, granting of charters and regulating joint-stock companies, and prohibition of tattooing.
87. *Ōkubo Toshimichi Nikki*, II, 50; *Kido Kōin Nikki*, I, 243. See also Kido's letter to Ōkubo in *Kido Kōin Monjo*, III, 391.
88. Tanaka Sōgorō, *op. cit.*, p. 331.
89. *Iwakura Tomomi Kankei Monjo*, IV, 294-295.
90. *Ōkubo Toshimichi Nikki*, II, 54.
91. Katsuda, *Ōkubo Toshimichi Den*, II, 701.
92. *Ōkubo Toshimichi Nikki*, II, 51. See also Wilson, *op. cit.*, p. 120.
93. Tanaka Sōgorō, *op. cit.*, p. 332.
94. *Ishin Shi*, V, 740-741.
95. *Ōkubo Toshimichi Monjo*, III, 247-249.
96. Adams, *op. cit.*, II, 195-196; Katsuda, *Ōkubo Toshimichi Den*, II, 709-713; *Meiji Shiyō*, I, 157.
97. *Ōkubo Toshimichi Nikki*, II, 57; Ishigami, *op. cit.*, p. 161; S. Lane-Poole and F. V. Dickins, *The Life of Sir Harry Parkes* (London: Macmillan and Co., 1894), II, 141-147; hereafter cited as Lane-Poole, Harry Parkes.
98. *Ōkubo Toshimichi Nikki*, II, 49; *Hōrei Zensho*, 1869, p. 237.
99. See Lane-Poole, *Harry Parkes*, II, 121.
100. *Ishin Shi*, V, 613.
101. *Ōkubo Toshimichi Monjo*, V, 335-336; *Ōkubo Toshimichi Nikki*, II, 75.
102. *Ibid.*, p. 76.
103. *Ōkubo Toshimichi Monjo*, III, 346; *Ōkubo Toshimichi Nikki*, II, 78; *Kido Kōin Nikki*, I, 302.
104. *Ōkubo Toshimichi Monjo*, III, 347-348.
105. *Ibid.*, p. 355.
106. *Loc. cit.*
107. *Ōkubo Toshimichi Nikki*, II, 82, 83; *Kido Kōin Nikki*, I, 310.

108. *Ōkubo Toshimichi Nikki,* II, 83.
109. *Ibid.,* p. 84.
110. *Ibid.,* p. 87.
111. *Loc. cit.*
112. Katsuda, *Ōkubo Toshimichi Den,* II, 760.
113. *Ibid.,* pp. 761-762.
114. *Ōkubo Toshimichi Nikki,* II, 90.
115. Tanaka Sōgorō, *op. cit.,* p. 347.
116. McLaren, "Japanese Government Documents," p. 16.
117. Ōkuma Shigenobu, *Fifty Years of New Japan* (London: Smith Elder and Co., 1910), I, 418.
118. Smimasa Idditti, *The Life of Marquis Shigenobu Ōkuma* (Tōkyō: Hokuseidō Press, 1940), pp. 123-126; *Ishin Shi,* V, 588-590.
119. *Ōkubo Toshimichi Monjo,* III, 56.
120. *Ishin Shi,* V, 617.
121. *Ibid.,* pp. 618-619.
122. *Ōkubo Toshimichi Monjo,* IV, 48, 49.
123. *Ibid.,* pp. 54-55.
124. *Ibid.,* p. 56.
125. *Ishin Shi,* V, 409; Wilson, *op. cit.,* p. 73.
126. See Ishigami, *op. cit.,* pp. 174-176.
127. *Ōkubo Toshimichi Monjo,* IV, 116.
128. *Ibid.,* pp. 127-129.
129. *Ōkubo Toshimichi Nikki,* II, 142.
130. *Ibid.,* p. 144.
131. *Ibid.,* p. 145.
132. Tokutomi, *Ōkubo Kōtō Sensei,* pp. 103-104.
133. *Ōkubo Toshimichi Nikki,* II, 148.
134. *Ibid.,* p. 149.
135. *Ibid.,* p. 148.
136. *Ibid.,* pp. 150-151.
137. *Ibid.,* p. 152.
138. *Ibid.,* p. 153; Ishigami, *op. cit.,* p. 181.
139. *Ōkubo Toshimichi Nikki,* II, 154.
140. *Dai Saigō Zenshū,* II, 502-503; *Dai Saigō Zenshū,* III, 673. Chōshū was to contribute three infantry battalions and Tosa two infantry battalions, two artillery units, and two cavalry troops.
141. *Ibid.,* pp. 672-673.
142. Tokutomi, *Ōkubo Kōtō Sensei,* p. 109.
143. Tanaka Sōgorō, *op. cit.,* p. 353.
144. *Ōkubo Toshimichi Nikki,* II, 128.
145. *Kido Kōin Nikki,* I, 460-461.
146. Ishigami, *op. cit.,* p. 182.
147. *Ōkubo Toshimichi Nikki,* II, 168; *Kido Kōin Nikki,* II, 41.
148. *Ōkubo Toshimichi Nikki,* II, 171-173; *Ishin Shi,* V, 772-773.
149. *Ibid.,* p. 774; *Ōkubo Toshimichi Nikki,* II, 174.
150. Tanaka Sōgorō, *op. cit.,* p. 360.
151. *Kido Kōin Nikki,* II, 57; *Ōkubo Toshimichi Monjo,* IV, 311-312; Fujii and Moriya, *Meiji Jidai Shi,* I, 331-332.

152. Cf. Tokutomi, *Ōkubo Kōtō Sensei,* p. 114; Shirayanagi Takeshi, *Ōkubo Toshimichi* (Tōkyō: Chōbunkaku, 1943), p. 168.
153. Watanabe Shūjirō, *op. cit.*, p. 69; Wilson, *op. cit.*, p. 77.
154. Tanaka Inahiko, *op. cit.*, p. 112.
155. Fujii and Moriya, *Meiji Jidai Shi,* I, 334-335; *Ōkubo Toshimichi Nikki,* II, 177; *Meiji Shiyō,* I, 251; *Hōrei Zensho,* 1871, p. 283.
156. *Kido Kōin Nikki,* II, 67.
157. Ōtsu, *op. cit.*, I, 453.
158. American policy-makers who planned the occupation of Japan after World War II recognized the Japanese attitude toward authority. Consequently, they wisely used the prestige of the imperial house to facilitate the achievement of their objectives. Had the imperial symbol been destroyed, it is highly unlikely that the occupation would have been as successful as it was.
159. Horie, *op. cit.*, p. 74.
160. *Ibid.*
161. Wilson, *op. cit.*, p. 99.
162. Ōtsu, *op. cit.*, I, 428.
163. Cf. Lane-Poole, *Harry Parkes,* II, 164.
164. Ōtsu, *op. cit.*, I, 449.
165. *Meiji Shiyō,* I, 253.
166. Katsuda, *Ōkubo Toshimichi Den,* II, 867.
167. *Ishin Shi,* V, 784; *Meiji Shiyō,* I, 256; Adams, *op. cit.*, II, 301-302.
168. *Meiji Shiyō,* I, 255.
169. Adams, *op. cit.*, II, 287, 289.
170. *Ibid.*, p. 292.
171. *Meiji Shiyō,* I, 258.
172. *Ibid.*, p. 259; Adams, *op. cit.*, II, 293, 294, 296.
173. Ōtsu, *op. cit.*, I, 451.
174. *Ōkubo Toshimichi Monjo,* IV, 351.

Notes to Chapter VI

1. Watanabe Shūjirō, *Ōkubo Toshimichi Genkōroku* [Words and Deeds of Ōkubo Toshimichi] (Tōkyō: Naigai Shuppan Kyōkai, 1909), pp. 70-71.
2. Roy Hidemichi Akagi, *Japan's Foreign Relations,* 1542-1936 (Tōkyō: Hokuseidō Press, 1936), p. 86.
3. Charles Lanman, ed., *Leaders of the Meiji Restoration in America* (Tōkyō: Hokuseidō Press, 1931), pp. 2-3. See also Ishin Shiryō Hensan Jimukyoku, *Ishin Shi* [History of the Restoration] (Tōkyō: Ishin Shiryō Hensan Jimukyoku, 1939-1942), V, 824; hereafter cited as *Ishin Shi.*
4. Katsuda Magoya and Usui Yoshiharu, eds., *Ōkubo Toshimichi Nikki* [Diary of Ōkubo Toshimichi] (Tōkyō: Nihon Shiseki Kyōkai, 1927), II, 185; hereafter cited as *Ōkubo Toshimichi Nikki.*
5. *Ibid.*, pp. 188-189.
6. Inoue Kaoru Kō Denki Hensankai, ed., *Segai Inoue Kō Den* [Biography of Inoue Segai] (Tōkyō: Naigai Shoseki Kabushiki Kaisha, 1933), I, 457-458; hereafter cited as *Inoue Kō Den.* See also *Ōkubo Toshimichi Nikki,* II, 192-195.
7. *Inoue Kō Den,* I, 463-464.
8. Katsuda Magoya and Usui Yoshiharu, eds., *Ōkubo Toshimichi Monjo* [Papers

of Ōkubo Toshimichi] (Tōkyō: Nihon Shiseki Kyōkai, 1927-1929), IV, 354-355; hereafter cited as *Ōkubo Toshimichi Monjo.*

9. *Ibid.*, pp. 380-381, 382.

10. *Ibid.*, p. 381.

11. *Ōkubo Toshimichi Nikki,* II, 194-195.

12. Tada Kōmon and Kagawa Keizō, comps., *Iwakura Kō Jikki* [Authentic Chronicle of Prince Iwakura] (Tōkyō: Iwakura Kō Koseki Hozonkai, 1927), II, 951-952; hereafter cited as *Iwakura Kō Jikki.* The following signatures were affixed to the covenant: *Dajōdaijin* Sanjō Sanetomi; *Udaijin* Iwakura Tomomi; *Sangi* Saigō Takamori, Kido Kōin, Ōkuma Shigenobu, Itagaki Masanari; *Gichō* Gotō Motoaki; *Jingi Tayū* Fukuba Yoshikiyo; *Gaimu Kyō* Soejima Taneomi; *Ōkura Kyō* Ōkubo Toshimichi; *Ōkura Tayū* Inoue Kaoru; *Hyōbu Tayū* Yamagata Aritomo; *Mombu Kyō* Ōki Takato; *Kōbu Tayū* Itō Hirobumi; *Shihō Tayū* Sasaki Takayuki; *Shihō Tayū* Shishido Tamuki; *Kunai Kyō* Tokudaiji Sanenori; *Kaitaku Jikan* Kuroda Kiyotaka.

13. *Iwakura Kō Jikki,* II, 948-950.

14. Ishigami Konta, ed., *Kōtō Sensei Itsuwa* [Anecdotes Concerning Kōtō] (Kagoshima-ken Kyōikukai, 1938), pp. 194-195.

15. See Lanman, *Leaders of the Meiji Restoration in America,* pp. 4-5; Nakayama Yasumasa, ed., *Shimbun Shūsei Meiji Hennen Shi* [Chronological History of Meiji Compiled from Newspaper Records] (Tōkyō: Zaisei Keizai Gakkai, 1934-1936), I, 402. See *ibid.*, pp. 423-425, for newspaper accounts concerning the mission from November 12, 1872, to July 26, 1873.

16. For details of the education of the five Japanese girls in American schools, see Lanman, *Leaders of the Meiji Restoration in America,* pp. 44-48.

17. Katsuda Magoya, *Ōkubo Toshimichi Den* [Biography of Ōkubo Toshimichi] (Tōkyō: Dōbunkan, 1910-1911), III, 26.

18. Lanman, *Leaders of the Meiji Restoration in America,* pp. 6-7.

19. *Ibid.*, pp. 13-15.

20. *Ibid.*, p. 15.

21. *Ibid.*, p. 16.

22. *Ōkubo Toshimichi Nikki,* II, 199-200.

23. Lanman, *Leaders of the Meiji Restoration in America,* p. 19.

24. *Ōkubo Toshimichi Nikki,* II, 200-201.

25. Lanman, *Leaders of the Meiji Restoration in America,* pp. 20-21.

26. *Ibid.*, p. 22.

27. *Ibid.*, p. 28.

28. *Ibid.*, p. 29. For the texts of the greetings in Japanese between President Grant and Ambassador Iwakura, see *Iwakura Kō Jikki,* II, 990-993.

29. Lanman, *Leaders of the Meiji Restoration in America,* p. 32. For the text in Japanese of Blaine's speech and that of Iwakura made before the Congress of the United States, see *Iwakura Kō Jikki,* II, 993-994.

30. Six members comprised the Ōkubo party, including an American doctor. See Nakayama, *Shimbun Shūsei Meiji Hennen Shi,* I, 445.

31. See Akagi, *op. cit.*, pp. 88-89; Katsuda, *Ōkubo Toshimichi Den,* III, 37-41.

32. *Ōkubo Toshimichi Monjo,* IV, 448.

33. *Ibid.*, p. 449.

34. Ishigami, *op. cit.*, pp. 209-212.

35. *Ibid.*, p. 199.

36. *Ibid.*, pp. 204-205.

37. *Ibid.*, p. 207.
38. Katsuda, *Ōkubo Toshimichi Den,* III, 52-53.
39. *Ōkubo Toshimichi Monjo,* IV, 492.
40. Tōkyō Teikoku Daigaku Shiryō Hensanjo, *Meiji Shiyō* [Essentials of Meiji History] (Tōkyō: Kinkōdō Shoseki Kabushiki Kaisha, 1933), I, p. 272; hereafter cited as *Meiji Shiyō.*
41. *Ibid.*, p. 273.
42. *Ibid.*, p. 276.
43. *Ibid.*, p. 277.
44. *Ibid.*, p. 284.
45. *Ibid.*, p. 285.
46. *Ibid.*, p. 286.
47. *Ibid.*, p. 287.
48. *Ibid.*, p. 288.
49. *Ibid.*, p. 289.
50. *Ibid.*, p. 303.
51. *Ibid.*, p. 304.
52. *Ibid.*, p. 309.
53. *Ibid.*, p. 311.
54. *Ibid.*, p. 314.
55. *Ibid.*, p. 316.
56. *Ibid.*, p. 319.
57. *Ibid.*, p. 330.
58. Ōkawa Nobuyoshi, ed., *Dai Saigō Zenshū* [Complete Works of Saigō] (Tōkyō: Heibonsha, 1926-1927), III, 690-691; hereafter cited as *Dai Saigō Zenshū.*
59. *Meiji Shiyō,* I, 301.
60. See *Inoue Kō Den,* I, 527-538; *Meiji Shiyō,* I, 334.
61. Kyūgorō Obata, *An Interpretation of the Life of Viscount Shibusawa* (Tōkyō: Daiyamondo Jigiyō Kabushiki Kaisha, 1937), pp. 79-80; Takekoshi Yosaburo, *Japanese Rule in Formosa* (London: Longmans, Green, and Co., 1907), p. 76.
62. See *Inoue Kō Den,* I, 549-561 for the full text of the memorial.
63. See *Inoue Kō Den,* I, 547-548.
64. Smimasa Idditti, *The Life of Marquis Shigenobu Ōkuma* (Tōkyō: Hokuseidō Press, 1940), pp. 146-147.
65. See Tokutomi Iichirō, *Ōkubo Kōtō Sensei* [Master Ōkubo Kōtō] (Tōkyō: Minyūsha, 1927), pp. 141-145.
66. Tsumaki Chūta, ed., *Kido Kōin Nikki* [Diary of Kido Kōin] (Tōkyō: Nihon Shiseki Kyōkai, 1932-1933), II, 336; hereafter cited as *Kido Kōin Nikki.*
67. Nakayama, *Shimbun Shūsei Meiji Hennen Shi,* II, 43; *Meiji Shiyō,* I, 338.
68. *Kido Kōin Nikki,* II, 406.
69. Ōtsu Junichirō, *Dai Nippon Kensei Shi* [Constitutional History of Japan] (Tōkyō: Hōbunkan, 1927-1928), I, 485; *Meiji Shiyō,* I, 352.
70. Ōtsu, *op. cit.*, I, 485-486.
71. Tanaka Inahiko, *Ketsujin Ōkubo Kōtō* [The Eminent Ōkubo Kōtō] (Tōkyō: Shūbunkan, 1911), pp. 114-115.
72. See Tokutomi, *Ōkubo Kōtō Sensei,* p. 140.
73. *Ōkubo Toshimichi Monjo,* IV, 521-522.
74. John Harington Gubbins, *The Making of Modern Japan* (London: Seeley, Service and Co., Ltd., 1922), pp. 120-121.

75. *Ibid.*, pp. 121-122.
76. Tanaka Inahiko, *op. cit.*, pp. 128-129; Kiyozawa Kiyoshi, *Gaiseika to shite no Ōkubo Toshimichi* [Ōkubo as an International Statesman] (Tōkyō: Chūōkōronsha, 1942), p. 15.
77. *Dai Saigō Zenshū*, III, 732.
78. Tanaka Sōgorō, *Ōkubo Toshimichi* (Tōkyō: Chikura Shobō, 1938), pp. 382-383; Kiyozawa, *op. cit.*, p. 14.
79. Tanaka Inahiko, *op. cit.*, pp. 125-126; Kiyozawa subscribes to this thesis, and he, furthermore, points out that Gotō of Tosa concurred with Etō's idea. See Kiyozawa, *op. cit.*, pp. 15-16.
80. *Dai Saigō Zenshū*, II, 738-739.
81. *Ibid.*, p. 737.
82. *Dai Saigō Zenshū*, III, 726-727.
83. *Ibid.*, p. 728.
84. *Ōkubo Toshimichi Monjo*, V, 15.
85. Vide, p. 125.
86. *Kido Kōin Nikki*, II, 420.
87. Kiyozawa, *op. cit.*, p. 19.
88. *Ōkubo Toshimichi Monjo*, V, 28.
89. *Ibid.*, p. 27.
90. *Meiji Shiyō*, I, 354.
91. *Iwakura Kō Jikki*, III, 65.
92. For a detailed description of this momentous meeting, see *Dai Saigō Zenshū*, III, 739-745.
93. For the full text of the memorial, see *Dai Saigō Zenshū*, II, 790-791. The memorial which is contained in the *Dai Saigō Zenshū* is dated October 17, but this copy is believed to have been the one Saigō later duplicated to present to Sanjō. The original copy was presented to the Council of State on October 15.
94. *Ōkubo Toshimichi Nikki*, II, 203-204.
95. *Ibid.*, p. 204.
96. *Ōkubo Toshimichi Monjo*, V, 53 ff. For a translation in English, see Ryūsaku Tsunoda, William Theodore De Bary, and Donald Keene, comps., *The Sources of the Japanese Tradition* (New York: Columbia University Press, 1958), pp. 658 ff.
97. *Ōkubo Toshimichi Monjo*, V, 54; Tsunoda, *op. cit.*, p. 658.
98. *Ibid.*, p. 658; *Ōkubo Toshimichi Monjo*, V, 54-55.
99. *Ibid.*, p. 55; Tsunoda, *op. cit.*, pp. 658-659.
100. *Ibid.*, p. 659; *Ōkubo Toshimichi Monjo*, V, 56.
101. *Ibid.*, p. 57; Tsunoda, *op. cit.*, p. 659.
102. *Ibid.*, p. 660; *Ōkubo Toshimichi Monjo*, V, 58.
103. *Ibid.*, p. 59; Tsunoda, *op. cit.*, p. 660.
104. *Ibid.*, p. 660; *Ōkubo Toshimichi Monjo*, V, 60.
105. *Ibid.*, pp. 62-63; Tsunoda, *op. cit.*, pp. 661-662.
106. *Ibid.*, p. 662; *Ōkubo Toshimichi Monjo*, V, 63-64.
107. Kiyozawa, *op. cit.*, p. 31.
108. Tokutomi, *Ōkubo Kōtō Sensei*, p. 297.
109. See Tanaka Inahiko, *op. cit.*, p. 140; Ishigami, *op. cit.*, pp. 225-226; Kiyozawa, *op. cit.*, p. 11.
110. *Ōkubo Toshimichi Nikki*, II, 204.
111. *Ibid.*, p. 205.

112. *Meiji Shiyō*, I, 356.
113. *Ōkubo Toshimichi Nikki*, II, 206; Tokutomi, *Ōkubo Kōtō Sensei*, p. 221.
114. *Dai Saigō Zenshū*, III, 759.
115. *Ibid.*, p. 758.
116. *Ōkubo Toshimichi Monjo*, V, 105.
117. *Ōkubo Toshimichi Nikki*, II, 208.
118. *Ibid.*, p. 209.
119. Ōtsu, *op. cit.*, I, 682-683.
120. *Ibid.*, p. 684.
121. *Meiji Shiyō*, I, 358; *Ōkubo Toshimichi Nikki*, II, 217; Tanaka Inahiko, *op. cit.*, p. 147.
122. Tokutomi, *Ōkubo Kōtō Sensei*, p. 249; Ishigami, *op. cit.*, p. 228.
123. Paul M. A. Linebarger, Djang Chu, and Ardath W. Burks, *Far Eastern Governments and Politics* (New York: D. Van Nostrand Co., Inc., 1956), p. 400.
124. *Meiji Shiyō*, I, 365.
125. See Ishigami, *op. cit.*, pp. 228-230, 216-217. Also, see *Ōkubo Toshimichi Monjo*, V, 296-304, for an outline of the organizational structure and the responsibilities of the officials of the *Naimushō* as drawn up by Ōkubo.
126. Linebarger, *op. cit.*, p. 354.
127. Tokutomi, *Ōkubo Kōtō Sensei*, p. 252.
128. Sidney D. Brown, "Kido Takayoshi (1833-1877): Meiji Japan's Cautious Revolutionary," in *Pacific Historical Review*, XXV (May, 1956), 151. The definition of autocracy is governmental authority founded in itself, not dependent on any outside source, and embodied in governmental machinery of such a type as to give the actual governor or ruler the supreme power in the state and to enable him to govern the state without subjection to any external control, politically speaking. See Ellen Deborah Ellis, "Autocracy," Edwin R. A. Seligman, ed., in *Encyclopaedia of the Social Sciences* (New York: The Macmillan Co., 1937), II, 321.
129. Brown, "Kido Takayoshi," p. 159.
130. *Ibid.*, p. 152.
131. With respect to the motivation for the organization of some form of representative government, the existence of unequal treaties was a factor. The Japanese felt that a governmental structure with some Western touches, in addition to the building up of an adequate army and navy, would hasten the day when these treaties could be changed.
132. Osatake Takeshi, *Nihon Kensei Shi Taikō* [Outline of Japanese Constitutional History] (Tōkyō: Hyōronsha, 1938), I, 310. See also Ishigami, *op. cit.*, p. 274.
133. Osatake, *op. cit.*, I, 317.
134. *Ibid.*, pp. 318-319. Fukuzawa Yūkichi, a political independent, worked for representative government. One of his articles to the press favoring the opening of a national diet gave impetus to the movement for representative government. See Yūkichi Fukuzawa, *The Autobiography of Fukuzawa Yūkichi*, translated by Eiichi Kiyooka (Tōkyō: Hokuseidō Press, 1934), pp. 342-344.
135. *Ibid.*, p. 346.
136. *Ōkubo Toshimichi Monjo*, V, 182-203. A portion of it is translated into English in Tsunoda, *op. cit.*, p. 666, and a fine translation of the text in its entirety is to be found in George M. Beckmann, *The Making of the Meiji Constitution* (Lawrence: University of Kansas Press, 1957), pp. 111 ff.
137. *Ibid.*, p. 111; *Ōkubo Toshimichi Monjo*, V, 182-183.

138. *Ibid.*, p. 183; Beckmann, *op. cit.*, pp. 111 ff.
139. *Ibid.*, p. 112; *Ōkubo Toshimichi Monjo,* V, 184-185.
140. *Ibid.*, pp. 185, 186, 187; Beckmann, *op. cit.*, pp. 112, 113.
141. *Ibid.*, p. 113; *Ōkubo Toshimichi Monjo,* V, 188.
142. *Ibid.*, pp. 198-200; Beckmann, *op. cit.*, p. 117.
143. *Ibid.*, p. 118; *Ōkubo Toshimichi Monjo,* V, 200-201.
144. Tsunoda, *op. cit.*, p. 665.
145. *Ōkubo Toshimichi Nikki,* II, 234.
146. *Ibid.*, p. 229; Akagi, *op. cit.*, pp. 64-65.
147. *Ōkubo Toshimichi Nikki,* II, 234.
148. *Ōkubo Toshimichi Nikki,* II, 237.
149. *Ōkubo Toshimichi Monjo,* V, 371-374.
150. See *Iwakura Kō Jikki,* III, 99-106, for the text of the memorial. For an English translation, see Walter Wallace McLaren, ed., "Japanese Government Documents," *Transactions of the Asiatic Society of Japan,* XLII, Pt. I (Tōkyō, 1914), 426-432.
151. Ōkuma Shigenobu, *Fifty Years of New Japan* (London: Smith, Elder and Co., 1910), I, 145.
152. McLaren, "Japanese Government Documents," p. lix.
153. *Ōkubo Toshimichi Nikki,* II, 236. For an account of the Saga rebellion, see *Iwakura Kō Jikki,* III, 106 ff.; Ishida Bunjirō, ed., *Shimbun Kiroku Shūsei Meiji Daijiken Shi* [History of Great Events of the Meiji Era Compiled from Newspaper Records] (Tōkyō: Kinseisha, 1954), pp. 55-59. The period of the 1870's was one in which discontent among the farmers and samurai with the new government policies found expression in uprisings. A fairly detailed overview of this opposition to the Meiji government is contained in Fujii Jintarō and Moriya Hidesuke, *Sōgō Nihon Shi Taikei: Meiji Jidai Shi* [A Synthesis of Japanese History: History of the Meiji Period] (Tōkyō: Naigai Shoseki Kabushiki Kaisha, 1939-1940), II, 522 ff.
154. *Ōkubo Toshimichi Nikki,* II, 237.
155. Itō Nitarō, *Ōkubo Toshimichi* (Tōkyō: Heibonsha, 1941), II, 278.
156. *Iwakura Kō Jikki,* III, 107-108.
157. *Ōkubo Toshimichi Monjo,* V, 365-366.
158. Itō, *op. cit.*, p. 278.
159. *Meiji Shiyō,* I, 371; Tanaka Sōgorō, *op. cit.*, p. 396.
160. The term Saikaidō designates one of the main highways of Japan and can also be used to refer to the Kyūshū area.
161. Tanaka Inahiko, *op. cit.*, pp. 153-154; *Ōkubo Toshimichi Nikki,* II, 240.
162. *Ibid.*, p. 241.
163. *Loc. cit.*
164. *Ibid.*, p. 242.
165. *Ibid.*, p. 245.
166. *Ibid.*, p. 246.
167. *Ibid.*, p. 248.
168. *Ibid.*, p. 251.
169. *Ibid.*, p. 254. The *Yūbin Hōchi Shimbun* reported on April 6 that the rebels had been captured on April 3.
170. *Ōkubo Toshimichi Nikki,* II, 258.
171. *Ibid.*, p. 257.
172. Ishigami, *op. cit.*, p. 233.

Notes to Chapter VII

1. Katsuda Magoya and Usui Yoshiharu, eds., *Ōkubo Toshimichi Nikki* [Diary of Ōkubo Toshimichi] (Tōkyō: Nihon Shiseki Kyōkai, 1927), II, 262; hereafter cited as *Ōkubo Toshimichi Nikki.*

2. Kiyozawa Kiyoshi, *Gaiseika to shite no Ōkubo Toshimichi* [Ōkubo as an International Statesman] (Tōkyō: Chūōkōronsha, 1942), p. 46. Hayashi's statement concerning Itō, as Kiyozawa indicates, was an anachronism. The significance of the conversation between Itō and Ōkubo lies in the fact that Ōkubo exuded confidence that the problem, serious as it was, could be settled.

3. Edward H. House, *The Japanese Expedition to Formosa* (Tōkyō, 1875), p. 1. House was pro-Japanese. Another writer who took the Japanese point of view was F. Brinkley, "The Story of the Riu-Kiu (Loo-choo) Controversy," in *Chrysanthemum and Phoenix,* III, pt. 3 (1878-1879), 122-153. For the Chinese view of the Formosan affair, see T. F. Tsiang, "Sino-Japanese Diplomatic Relations, 1870-1894," *The Chinese Social and Political Science Review,* XVII, no. 1 (April, 1933), 16-53. The most comprehensive work in English on the subject is the one by George H. Kerr, *Okinawa* (Tōkyō: Charles E. Tuttle Co., 1959).

4. *Ibid.,* p. 2.

5. *Ibid.,* p. 3.

6. *Ibid.,* p. 4.

7. *Ibid.,* p. 5.

8. *Ibid.,* p. 6.

9. Roy Hidemichi Akagi, *Japan's Foreign Relations, 1542-1936* (Tōkyō: Hokuseidō Press, 1936), pp. 58-59. In this autonomous capacity the Ryūkyū Islands concluded treaties with the United States in 1854, with France in 1854, and with the Netherlands in 1858. See also Kerr, *Okinawa,* pp. 56-59, 157-169.

10. House, *op. cit.,* pp. 7-8. See Kerr, *Okinawa,* pp. 26 ff.

11. Francis L. Hawks, comp., *Narrative of the Expedition of an American Squadron to the China Seas and Japan, Performed in the Years 1852, 1853, and 1854, under the Command of Commodore M. C. Perry, United States Navy, by Order of the Government of the United States* (United States House of Representatives, 33rd Congress, 2nd Sess., Exec. Doc. 97; Washington, A. O. P. Nicholson, 1856), I, 222.

12. Hoshien Tchen, *Les relations diplomatiques entre la Chine et la Japon de 1871 à nos jours; traites, conventions, echange de lettres, etc.* (Paris: Éditions de "la vie universitaire," 1921), p. 24. See also Kerr, *Okinawa,* pp. 130 ff.

13. Hoshien Tchen, *op. cit.,* p. 22.

14. *Ibid.,* pp. 24-25.

15. Hawks, *op. cit.,* I, 221. For a more detailed description of Okinawan origin myths, see Kerr, *Okinawa,* pp. 35 ff.

16. Hawks, *op. cit.,* I, 221.

17. *Ibid.,* p. 222.

18. House, *op. cit.,* p. 9. The Ryūkyū king was given an annual stipend of thirty thousand *yen,* and Japan undertook the handling of the kingdom's foreign relations.

19. *Ibid.,* p. 10. For a more recent account of Formosan incident in relation to Okinawa, see Kerr, *Okinawa,* pp. 356 ff.

20. Kiyozawa, *op. cit.,* pp. 55-56.

21. *Ibid.,* p. 56.

22. For a full report of the meeting, see Gaimushō Chōsabu, ed., *Dai Nippon*

Gaikō Bunsho [Japanese Diplomatic Documents] (Tōkyō: Nihon Kokusai Kyōkai, 1936——), VII, 5-8; hereafter cited as *Dai Nippon Gaikō Bunsho*. See also Kiyozawa, *op. cit.*, p. 56. For Minister De Long's account of this meeting, see his dispatch to Secretary of State Hamilton Fish in the United States Congress, House of Representatives, *Papers Relating to the Foreign Relations of the United States, 1873-1874*, 43rd Congress, 1st sess., Vol. I (Washington: Government Printing Office, 1874), 554; hereafter cited as *Foreign Relations of the United States, 1873-1874*.

23. See Wang Yün-shêng, *Liu shih nien lai Chung Kuo yu Jih Pen* [China and Japan in the Last Sixty Years] (Tientsin: Ta Kung Pao, 1932-1934), I, 57-58; Nagano Isao and Hatano Kenichi, eds. and trans., *Nisshi Gaikō Rokujūnen Shi* [Sino-Japanese Sixty-Year Diplomatic History] (Tōkyō: Kensetsusha, 1933), pp. 82-84.

24. *Dai Nippon Gaikō Bunsho*, VIII, 8-13.

25. *Ibid.*, p. 14.

26. Kiyozawa, *op. cit.*, p. 57; House, *op. cit.*, p. 10.

27. Kiyozawa, *op. cit.*, p. 58.

28. *Foreign Relations of the United States, 1873-1874*, I, 567-568. Secretary Fish's dispatch of December 30, 1872, to De Long stated:

> The part which you have taken in the negotiations for the employment of General Le Gendre by the Japanese, with a distinct reference to the use of his services as an adviser in military operations, should they become necessary, would appear to be inconsistent with the peaceful policy thus wisely recommended. Your dispatch bears witness that you are not unaware of the provision contained in the Statute of the United States (Act of 18th August, 1856, sec. 19; 11 Statutes at Large, 59) which, in distinct terms, prohibits the diplomatic officers of the United States both from recommending any person at home or abroad for any employment of trust or profit under the government of the country in which they reside, and also for asking for any person any emolument, pecuniary favor, office, or title of any kind from such government. . . .

29. Kiyozawa, *op. cit.*, p. 59.

30. For details of the Soejima mission, see Taishi Korosha Denki Hensankai, comp., *Taishi Kaikoroku* [Relations with China in Retrospect] (Tōkyō: Taishi Korosha Denki Hensankai, 1936), I, 43-50; hereafter cited as *Taishi Kaikoroku*. See also House, *op. cit.*, pp. 12-13.

31. See Wang Yün-shêng, *op. cit.*, I, 58-59; Nagano and Hatano, *op. cit.*, I, 84-85; and *Taishi Kaikoroku*, I, 49.

32. *Ibid.*, p. 52; House, *op. cit.*, pp. 13-14.

33. *Ibid.*, p. 14.

34. *Ibid.*, p. 15.

35. *Taishi Kaikoroku*, I, 55.

36. *Ibid.*, p. 56; Ōkuma Kō Hachijūgonen Shi Hensankai, ed., *Ōkuma Kō Hachijūgonen Shi* [Eighty-five Year History of Marquis Ōkuma] (Tōkyō: Nisshin Insatsu Kabushiki Kaisha, 1926), I, 552; House, *op. cit.*, p. 17; *Dai Nippon Gaikō Bunsho*, VII, 17, 29, 42; Kokuryūkai Hombu, ed., *Seinan Kiden* [History of the Saigō Rebellion] (Tōkyō: Kokuryūkai Hombu, 1909-1911), I, 595-596; hereafter cited as *Seinan Kiden*. For Saigō's commission and instructions, see Watanabe Ikujirō, ed., *Ōkuma Shigenobu Kankei Monjo* [Papers Relating to Ōkuma Shige-

nobu] (Tōkyō: Nihon Shiseki Kyōkai, 1932-1935), II, 291-296; hereafter cited as *Ōkuma Shigenobu Kankei Monjo.*

37. *Seinan Kiden,* I, 596.

38. *Dai Nippon Gaikō Bunsho,* VII, 18, 21; House, *op. cit.*, p. 16; Kiyozawa, *op. cit.*, p. 62.

39. *Taishi Kaikoroku,* I, 59.

40. House, *op. cit.*, p. 17.

41. For the text of the letter in English, see *Dai Nippon Gaikō Bunsho,* VII, 23.

42. For the Japanese report of the conversation, see *ibid.*, pp. 24-28.

43. S. Lane-Poole and F. V. Dickins, *The Life of Sir Harry Parkes* (London: Macmillan and Co., 1894), II, 190-192; hereafter cited as Lane-Poole, *Harry Parkes.*

44. See Kiyozawa, *op. cit.*, pp. 63-66; *Dai Nippon Gaikō Bunsho,* VII, 37. The last British note to the Japanese government before the expedition was halted was sent on April 16. It questioned Japanese claims that "the territory in question . . . is beyond the jurisdiction of the Chinese government." Sir Harry stated that during his twenty years in China he had always heard that the whole of Formosa was claimed by China.

45. *Ibid.*, pp. 39-40.

46. *Ibid.*, pp. 45-46; House, *op. cit.*, pp. 19; *Taishi Kaikoroku,* I, 63. For general diplomatic correspondence between Minister Bingham and the State Department regarding the Formosan issue, see *Foreign Relations of the United States, 1873-1874,* I, 677 ff.

47. Kiyozawa, *op. cit.*, p. 69; *Taishi Kaikoroku,* I, 66.

48. Tsumaki Chūta, ed., *Kido Kōin Nikki* [Diary of Kido Kōin] (Tōkyō: Nihon Shiseki Kyōkai, 1932-1933), II, 488; hereafter cited as *Kido Kōin Nikki.*

49. Tokutomi Iichirō, *Ōkubo Kōtō Sensei* [Master Ōkubo Kōtō] (Tōkyō: Minyūsha, 1927), p. 289.

50. *Taishi Kaikoroku,* I, 55; Kiyozawa, *op. cit.*, p. 60.

51. *Kido Kōin Nikki,* III, 18-19; Kiyozawa, *op. cit.*, pp. 60-61. See also Kido's letter to Itō Hirobumi in Tsumaki Chūta, ed., *Kido Kōin Monjo* [Papers of Kido Kōin] (Tōkyō: Nihon Shiseki Kyōkai, 1929-1931), V, 246-247.

52. Tanaka Sōgorō, *Ōkubo Toshimichi* (Tōkyō: Chikura Shobō, 1938), p. 397.

53. Fujii Jintarō and Moriya Hidesuke, *Sōgō Nihon Shi Taikei: Meiji Jidai Shi* [A Synthesis of Japanese History: History of the Meiji Period] (Tōkyō: Naigai Shoseki Kabushiki Kaisha, 1939-1940), II, 526; hereafter cited as Fujii and Moriya, *Meiji Jidai Shi.*

54. Kiyozawa, *op. cit.*, p. 61; Hugh Borton, *Japan's Modern Century* (New York: Ronald Press Co., 1955), p. 97.

55. Kiyozawa, *op. cit.*, p. 51.

56. *Ōkubo Toshimichi Nikki,* II, 259.

57. Kiyozawa, *op. cit.*, p. 62.

58. *Taishi Kaikoroku,* I, 66.

59. See Sanjō's letter to Ōkuma in *Ōkuma Shigenobu Kankei Monjo,* II, 305.

60. *Taishi Kaikoroku,* I, 67.

61. *Ibid.*; Kiyozawa, *op. cit.*, p. 71; House, *op. cit.*, pp. 21-22. The text of Fukushima's letter may be found in Tada Kōmon and Kagawa Keizō, comps., *Iwakura Kō Jikki* [Authentic Chronicle of Prince Iwakura] (Tōkyō: Iwakura Kō Koseki Hozonkai, 1927), III, 148; hereafter cited as *Iwakura Kō Jikki.*

62. *Ōkubo Toshimichi Nikki,* II, 263.

63. *Ibid.*, p. 264.
64. *Taishi Kaikoroku*, I, 67-68.
65. *Ōkubo Toshimichi Nikki*, II, 264.
66. Katsuda Magoya and Usui Yoshiharu, eds., *Ōkubo Toshimichi Monjo* [Papers of Ōkubo Toshimichi] (Tōkyō: Nihon Shiseki Kyōkai, 1927-1929), V, 498-499; hereafter cited as *Ōkubo Toshimichi Monjo*.
67. *Ōkubo Toshimichi Nikki*, II, 266.
68. Kiyozawa, *op. cit.*, p. 73.
69. See *Ōkubo Toshimichi Nikki*, II, 266; Kiyozawa, *op. cit.*, p. 75.
70. *Ōkubo Toshimichi Monjo*, V, 499-500. Besides Cassel and Wasson, there were several other foreigners attached to the expedition, among them Edward Howard House, a correspondent for the *New York Herald*, who presented a graphic description of the campaign in English. For the names of other foreigners, see Kiyozawa, *op. cit.*, p. 62. See also Cassel's reports to Le Gendre in *Dai Nippon Gaikō Bunsho*, VII, 115-125.
71. House, *op. cit.*, p. 25.
72. Kiyozawa, *op. cit.*, p. 79. In all subsequent wars the Japanese took to heart Le Gendre's early advice and sprang upon their enemies after creeping up on them stealthily. The zenith of secrecy in ship movements was, of course, attained in World War II when the Japanese struck out at Pearl Harbor from Japan's island holdings in the Kuriles.
73. *Ōkubo Toshimichi Monjo*, V, 500.
74. *Ibid.*, p. 504.
75. *Ōkubo Toshimichi Nikki*, II, 267.
76. *Taishi Kaikoroku*, I, 70.
77. Wang Yün-shêng, *op. cit.*, I, 61; Nagano and Hatano, *op. cit.*, I, 88. For the text of the Chinese note in English, see *Dai Nippon Gaikō Bunsho*, VII, 75-77.
78. Wang Yün-shêng, *op. cit.*, I, 62; Nagano and Hatano, *op. cit.*, I, 89.
79. *Ibid.*; Wang Yün-shêng, *op. cit.*, I, 61.
80. *Ibid.*, p. 62; Nagano and Hatano, *op. cit.*, I, 90.
81. *Ibid.*; Wang Yün-shêng, *op. cit.*, p. 63.
82. See House, *op. cit.*, pp. 74-79.
83. Wang Yün-shêng, *op. cit.*, I, 65; Nagano and Hatano, *op. cit.*, I, 93.
84. House, *op. cit.*, p. 164.
85. *Dai Nippon Gaikō Bunsho*, VII, 21.
86. Wang Yün-shêng, *op. cit.*, I, 67; Nagano and Hatano, *op. cit.*, I, 96.
87. House, *op. cit.*, pp. 161-162.
88. *Taishi Kaikoroku*, I, 72-73.
89. *Ibid.*, pp. 73-74; Wang Yün-shêng, *op. cit.*, I, 67-71.
90. *Ibid.*, p. 67; Nagano and Hatano, *op. cit.*, I, 98.
91. *Ibid.*, p. 101; Wang Yün-shêng, *op. cit.*, I, 69.
92. *Ibid.*, p. 68; Nagano and Hatano, *op. cit.*, I, 99. In the light of subsequent history, wherein Japanese diplomacy displayed evidence of bad faith caused by the military arm of the government often deciding to act independently of its civil branch, as with Formosa, Li's charge of Japanese duplicity seems to be defensible. Such mendacity represents Machiavellianism at its worst and cannot be condoned, but Machiavellian tactics have been utilized as a part of statecraft among Orientals as well as among Occidentals throughout world history. The United States, founded as it was on the principles of Puritan morality, has generally adhered to the policy

of straightforwardness in international relations, although even her history has chapters which tend to denigrate her reputation.

93. Wang Yün-shêng, *op. cit.*, I, 71.

94. Kiyozawa, *op. cit.*, p. 101.

95. *Iwakura Kō Jikki*, III, 154-155.

96. *Ibid.*, p. 158.

97. Katsuda, *Ōkubo Toshimichi Den*, III, 259-260.

98. *Ibid.*, p. 262.

99. See *Ōkubo Toshimichi Nikki*, II, 263. Ōkubo's entry for April 26 notes that, during a meeting with Iwakura, he expressed his opinions on the Hisamitsu matter. It is believed that Ōkubo advised against Hisamitsu's appointment as *Sadaijin*.

100. *Iwakura Kō Jikki*, III, 158-159.

101. For a complete set of illustrations of ceremonial attire worn by the military caste during the Tokugawa period, see Ono Kiyoshi, *Tokugawa Seido Shiryō* [Historical Materials on the Tokugawa Institutions] (Tōkyō: Toppan Insatsu Kabushiki Kaisha, 1927), Pt. II, 6.

102. Ōkuma Shigenobu, *Fifty Years of New Japan* (London: Smith Elder and Co., 1910), pp. 447-448.

103. *Ibid.*, p. 367. For an enumeration of some of these taxes imposed during the Tokugawa period, see Yosoburo Takekoshi, *The Economic Aspects of the History of the Civilization of Japan* (New York: The Macmillan Co., 1930), II, 315-316.

104. Fujii and Moriya, *Meiji Jidai Shi*, II, 501.

105. *Ōkubo Toshimichi Nikki*, II, 272. For Ōkubo's letter of resignation addressed to Sanjō and Iwakura, see *Ōkubo Toshimichi Monjo*, V, 523.

106. *Ibid.*, p. 535.

107. *Ibid.*, p. 536.

108. For details in English of the Japanese campaign against the Formosan brigands, see Edward H. House, *The Japanese Expedition to Formosa* (Tokyo, 1875).

109. Wang Yün-shêng, *op. cit.*, I, 73; Nagano and Hatano, *op. cit.*, I, 108.

110. Kiyozawa, *op. cit.*, p. 101.

111. *Ibid.*, pp. 101-102.

112. *Ōkubo Toshimichi Nikki*, II, 284.

113. *Ibid.*, p. 286.

114. *Dai Nippon Gaikō Bunsho*, VII, 150.

115. See Kiyozawa, *op. cit.*, p. 103.

116. *Ōkubo Toshimichi Nikki*, II, 286.

117. Wang Yün-shêng, *op. cit.*, I, 71; Nagano and Hatano, *op. cit.*, I, 106; Kiyozawa, *op. cit.*, p. 107. Despite her preparations for war, China was diffident and hopeful that a peaceful settlement could be reached.

118. *Iwakura Kō Jikki*, III, 186.

119. *Ōkubo Toshimichi Nikki*, II, 287.

120. *Iwakura Kō Jikki*, III, 186; *Ōkubo Toshimichi Nikki*, II, 288.

121. *Ibid.*, p. 291.

122. *Ibid.*, p. 292.

123. *Ibid.*, p. 293.

124. *Loc. cit.* For his writ of appointment, see Kanai Yukiyasu, ed., *Shishin Benri Shimatsu* [The Results of the Mission to China], in *Meiji Bunka Zenshū: Gaikō Hen* [Anthology of Meiji Culture: Diplomacy], Yoshino Sakuzō, ed., VI (Tōkyō: Nihon Hyōronsha, 1928-1930), 81; hereafter cited as *Shishin Benri Shimatsu*. The *Shishin Benri Shimatsu* is also included in *Ōkubo Toshimichi Monjo*, X, 195-414.

125. Tanaka Sōgorō, *op. cit.*, p. 405.
126. Tokutomi, *Ōkubo Kōtō Sensei*, p. 303.
127. *Ōkubo Toshimichi Nikki*, II, 294-295.
128. *Ibid.*, p. 296.
129. Kiyozawa, *op. cit.*, p. 49.
130. On July 9, the government had outlined a course of action in the event war was declared. See *Ōkubo Toshimichi Monjo*, VI, 34-45.
131. *Ibid.*, pp. 19-22. The memorandum was forwarded to Sanjō sometime between the middle and the end of July, 1874.
132. *Ōkubo Toshimichi Monjo*, VI, 22; Tōkyō Teikoku Daigaku Shiryō Hesanjo, *Meiji Shiyō* [Essentials of Meiji History] (Tōkyō: Kinkōdō Shoseki Kabushiki Kaisha, 1933), I, 385.
133. *Ōkubo Toshimichi Nikki*, II, 295.
134. *Ōkubo Toshimichi Monjo*, VI, 28-29.
135. Katsuda Magoya, *Kōtō Itsuwa* [Anecdotes Concerning Kōtō] (Tōkyō: Fuzambō, 1928), pp. 118-119; Kiyozawa, *op. cit.*, p. 119.
136. James Legge, *The Four Books* (Shanghai: The Commercial Press, Ltd., n.d.), p. 109.
137. *Ōkubo Toshimichi Nikki*, II, 306. For a list of those in Ōkubo's suite, see *ibid.*, pp. 298-299; *Dai Nippon Gaikō Bunsho*, VII, 172-173; *Shishin Benri Shimatsu*, pp. 81-82.
138. *Ōkubo Toshimichi Nikki*, II, 306-307.
139. Kiyozawa, *op. cit.*, p. 126. For the activities of Minister Yanagibara in Peking up to the time of the arrival of Ōkubo in China, see the report of the Board of Formosan Affairs, edited by Noguchi Tsunetomo, entitled *Shoban Shushisho* [Report of the Purpose of the Chastisement of the Aborigines], in *Meiji Bunka Zenshū: Gaiko Hen* [Anthology of Meiji Culture: Diplomacy], Yoshino Sakuzō, ed., VI (Tōkyō: Nihon Hyōronsha, 1928-1930), 158-161; hereafter cited as *Shoban Shushisho*. This report is also in *Ōkubo Toshimichi Monjo*, X, 415-486.
140. *Ōkubo Toshimichi Nikki*, II, 307-308; Kiyozawa, *op. cit.*, p. 127.
141. *Ōkubo Toshimichi Nikki*, II, 308.
142. *Ōkubo Toshimichi Nikki*, II, 310; Tokutomi, *Ōkubo Kōtō Sensei*, p. 308.
143. Katsuda, *Ōkubo Toshimichi Den*, III, 306.
144. Kiyozawa, op. cit., pp. 127-128.
145. The name Le Gendre has appeared prominently in this phase of Japanese history, and it would be remiss to allow him to fade away, as it were, into oblivion. After his recall from Nagasaki to Tōkyō, Le Gendre did not settle down to a passive life. On August 1 he arrived in Hong Kong, probably sent there by the Japanese government to gather information on the state of Chinese military preparations in south China. On August 5 he reached Amoy where on the following day the marshal of the United States consulate placed him under arrest. Apparently the Chinese viceroy of Fukien charged Le Gendre with planning the Japanese punitive expedition and the American consul at Amoy, J. J. Henderson, ordered his arrest specifically for violating the laws of neutrality. He was sent to Shanghai and immediately released. After serving as an adviser to Ōkubo, Le Gendre returned to Japan and married a Japanese woman, Ikeda Itako of the Fukui *han*. In 1890 he became an adviser in the service of the Korean government, dying in Seoul (Keijō) in 1899. See Kiyozawa, *op. cit.*, pp. 128-131; House, *op. cit.*, pp. 173, 177, 179-180, 189-191.
146. *Ōkubo Toshimichi Nikki*, II, 310-311. For the names of those in attendance, see *Shishin Benri Shimatsu*, pp. 84-85.

147. *Ibid.*, p. 85.
148. *Loc. cit.*
149. *Ibid.*, p. 86.
150. *Loc. cit.*
151. *Ibid.*, p. 87; Kiyozawa, *op. cit.*, p. 139.
152. Tokutomi, Ōkubo Kōtō Sensei, p. 310.
153. Kiyozawa, *op. cit.*, p. 140.
154. *Ōkubo Toshimichi Monjo,* VI, 185; *Shishin Benri Shimatsu,* p. 150.
155. *Ōkubo Toshimichi Nikki,* II, 311.
156. *Ibid.*, p. 312.
157. *Ibid.*, p. 311.
158. *Shishin Benri Shimatsu,* p. 91; *Shoban Shushisho,* pp. 162-163.
159. *Shishin Benri Shimatsu,* p. 93.
160. See Hoshien Tchen, *op. cit.*, pp. 13-20; Akagi, *op. cit.*, pp. 67-68. The Treaty of Tientsin, as this agreement is called, was signed in 1871 by Li Hung-chang and Date Muneki. For the complete texts of the treaty and trade regulations as well as the Chinese and Japanese tariffs annexed to the Treaty of Tientsin, see Inspectorate General of Customs, *Treaties, Conventions, etc., between China and Foreign States,* misc. series no. 30 (Shanghai: Statistical Department of the Inspectorate General of Customs, 1917), II, 507-584; hereafter cited as Inspectorate General of Customs, *Treaties.*
161. *Shishin Benri Shimatsu,* p. 93.
162. Tanaka Sōgorō, *op. cit.*, p. 408; *Shishin Benri Shimatsu,* p. 93.
163. *Ibid.*, p. 95.
164. *Ibid.*, p. 100.
165. *Ōkubo Toshimichi Monjo,* VI, 82.
166. *Shishin Benri Shimatsu,* p. 110; *Ōkubo Toshimichi Nikki,* II, 316.
167. *Ibid.*, p. 318.
168. *Ibid.*, p. 319.
169. Lane-Poole, *Harry Parkes,* II, 194.
170. *Dai Nippon Gaikō Bunsho,* VII, 258-260.
171. *Ōkubo Toshimichi Nikki,* II, 320. For the full text in Chinese of the Japanese note, see *Shishin Benri Shimatsu,* pp. 110-112; and for the summary of the same in Japanese, see *Shoban Shushisho,* p. 169.
172. *Shishin Benri Shimatsu,* p. 112.
173. *Ōkubo Toshimichi Nikki,* II, 320.
174. Ibid., p. 320; Kiyozawa, op. cit., p. 155.
175. *Ōkubo Toshimichi Nikki,* II, 320-321.
176. *Ōkubo Toshimichi Monjo,* VI, 115.
177. *Ōkubo Toshimichi Nikki,* II, 321.
178. *Ibid.*, p. 322.
179. *Shishin Benri Shimatsu,* p. 116.
180. *Ōkubo Toshimichi Nikki,* II, 325; *Shishin Benri Shimatsu,* pp. 119-120; *Shoban Shushisho,* p. 170.
181. For the transcript of the talks, see *Shishin Benri Shimatsu,* pp. 121-124.
182. *Shoban Shushisho,* p. 172.
183. *Shishin Benri Shimatsu,* p. 127.
184. See Tanaka Sōgorō, *op. cit.*, p. 411.
185. *Shishin Benri Shimatsu,* pp. 131-133.

186. *Shoban Shushisho*, p. 174.
187. *Ōkubo Toshimichi Nikki*, II, 328.
188. *Shishin Benri Shimatsu*, pp. 137-139; *Shoban Shushisho*, pp. 174-175; House, *op. cit.*, p. 201.
189. *Shishin Benri Shimatsu*, p. 134; *Ōkubo Toshimichi Nikki*, II, 327.
190. *Shishin Benri Shimatsu*, pp. 129-130.
191. *Ibid.*, pp. 133-134.
192. *Ibid.*, p. 139.
193. *Ibid.*, p. 145; Yosaburo Takekoshi, *Japanese Rule in Formosa* (New York: Longmans, Green and Co., 1907), p. 78. For the complete text of the Peking Agreement in both Chinese and English, see Inspectorate General of Customs, *Treaties*, II, 585-587.
194. Kiyozawa, *op. cit.*, p. 181.
195. Wang Yün-shêng, *op. cit.*, I, 76; Nagano and Hatano, *op. cit.*, I, 112.
196. *Ibid.*, pp. 113-114; Wang Yün-shêng, *op. cit.*, I, 76-77.
197. *Ibid.*, pp. 79-80; Nagano and Hatano, *op. cit.*, I, 116.
198. Lane-Poole, *Harry Parkes*, II, 194.
199. House, *op. cit.*, p. 224.
200. Kiyozawa, *op. cit.*, p. 254. For details of the evacuation of foreign troops from Yokohama on February 25, 1875, see *Iwakura Kō Jikki*, III, 227-231.
201. Hoshien Tchen, *op. cit.*, p. 28.
202. Tokutomi, *Ōkubo Kōtō Sensei*, pp. 336-337.
203. See *ibid.*, p. 355; House, *op. cit.*, p. 211.
204. See Wang Yün-shêng, *op. cit.*, I, 77-78; Nagano and Hatano, *op. cit.*, I, 114.
205. *Ōkubo Toshimichi Nikki*, II, 337-338.
206. *Ibid.*, p. 339.
207. Robert K. Douglas, *Li Hung-chang* (London: Bliss, Sands and Foster, 1895), p. 123.
208. *Ōkubo Toshimichi Nikki*, II, 340.
209. *Ibid.*, pp. 341-342.
210. *Ibid.*, pp. 343, 344.
211. *Ibid.*, p. 346.
212. *Ibid.*, p. 347. A special messenger of rank was sent from Japan on November 13 to order the return of the troops.
213. *Ibid.*, p. 350.
214. *Ibid.*, pp. 353-354. For the text of the imperial rescript issued on the occasion of Ōkubo's return, see *Iwakura Kō Jikki*, III, 210.
215. *Kido Kōin Nikki*, III, 113. For Kido's congratulatory letter to Ōkubo, see *Kido Kōin Monjo*, V, 424-426.
216. Watanabe Shūjirō, *Ōkubo Toshimichi Genkōroku* [Words and Deeds of Ōkubo Toshimichi] (Tōkyō: Naigai Shuppan Kyōkai, 1909), pp. 111-112.
217. *Seinan Kiden*, I, 783.
218. *Ōkubo Toshimichi Monjo*, VI, 158-160.
219. Kiyozawa, *op. cit.*, p. 243; Maurice Courant, *Ôkoubo* (Paris: Ancienne Librairie Germer Bailliere et Cie, 1904), p. 165. Courant states that "il [Ōkubo] espérait préparer un rapprochement des deux puissances de l'Extrême-Orient."
220. Ishigami Konta, ed., *Kōtō Sensei Itsuwa* [Anecdotes Concerning Kōtō] (Kagoshima: Kagoshima-ken Kyōikukai, 1938), pp. 265 ff.
221. *Ōkubo Toshimichi Nikki*, II, 359.

222. *Ibid.*, p. 361.
223. *Ibid.*, p. 362; *Ōkubo Toshimichi Monjo*, VI, 240-241.
224. *Ōkubo Toshimichi Nikki*, II, 364.
225. *Ibid.*, p. 466.
226. Ishigami, *op. cit.*, p. 303.
227. Tokutomi, *Ōkubo Kōtō Sensei*, p. 394.
228. Itō Nitarō, *Ōkubo Toshimichi* (Tōkyō: Heibonsha, 1941), II, 277.
229. Tokutomi, *Ōkubo Kōtō Sensei*, p. 392.

Notes to Chapter VIII

1. Tanaka Sōgorō, *Ōkubo Toshimichi* (Tōkyō: Chikura Shobō, 1938), p. 414.

2. Fujii Jintarō and Moriya Hidesuke, *Sōgō Nihon Shi Taikei: Meiji Jidai Shi* [A Synthesis of Japanese History: History of the Meiji Period] (Tōkyō: Naigai Shoseki Kabushiki Kaisha, 1939-1940), II, 504-505; hereafter cited as Fujii and Moriya, *Meiji Jidai Shi.*

3. Tokutomi Iichirō, *Ōkubo Kōtō Sensei* [*Master Ōkubo Kōtō*] (Tōkyō: Minyūsha, 1927), pp. 362-363; Ōtsu Junichirō, *Dai Nippon Kensei Shi* [Constitutional History of Japan] (Tōkyō: Hōbunkan, 1927-1928), I, 851.

4. Tokutomi, *Ōkubo Kōtō Sensei,* p. 363.

5. Cf. Ishigami Konta, ed., *Kōtō Sensei Itsuwa* [Anecdotes Concerning Kōtō] (Kagoshima: Kagoshima-ken Kyōikukai, 1938), p. 269; Tokutomi, *Ōkubo Kōtō Sensei,* p. 364; Katsuda Magoya, *Ōkubo Toshimichi Den* [Biography of Ōkubo Toshimichi] (Tōkyō: Dōbunkan, 1910-1911), III, 403; Ōtsu, *op. cit.*, I, 851; and Watanabe Shūjirō, *Ōkubo Toshimichi Genkōroku* [Words and Deeds of Ōkubo Toshimichi] (Tōkyō: Naigai Shuppan Kyōkai, 1909), pp. 112-113.

6. Shumbō Kō Tsuishōkai, *Itō Hirobumi Den* [Biography of Itō Hirobumi] (Tōkyō: Shumbō Kō Tsuishōkai, 1940), I, 889-890; hereafter cited as *Itō Hirobumi Den.*

7. Katsuda Magoya and Usui Yoshiharu, eds., *Ōkubo Toshimichi Monjo* [Papers of Ōkubo Toshimchi] (Tōkyō: Nihon Shiseki Kyōkai, 1927-1929), VI, 220-221; hereafter cited as *Ōkubo Toshimichi Monjo.*

8. *Itō Hirobumi Den,* I, 888-889. For Itō's report of Ōkubo's visit to his home to discuss the meeting with Kido, see Komatsu Midori, ed., *Itō Kō Zenshū* [Complete Works of Itō] (Tōkyō: Itō Kō Zenshū Kankōkai, 1927), I, 172-174.

9. *Ōkubo Toshimichi Monjo,* VI, 231-232. See also *Itō Hirobumi Den,* I, 893-894.

10. Katsuda Magoya and Usui Yoshiharu, eds., *Ōkubo Toshimichi Nikki* [Diary of Ōkubo Toshimichi] (Tōkyō: Nihon Shiseki Kyōkai, 1927), II, 365; hereafter cited as *Ōkubo Toshimichi Nikki.*

11. Tsumaki Chūta, ed., *Kido Kōin Nikki* [Diary of Kido Kōin] (Tōkyō: Nihon Shiseki Kyōkai, 1932-1933), III, 139-140; hereafter cited as *Kido Kōin Nikki.* See also *Ōkubo Toshimichi Nikki,* II, 368.

12. Tsumaki Chūta, ed., *Kido Kōin Monjo* [Papers of Kido Kōin] (Tōkyō: Nihon Shiseki Kyōkai, 1929-1931), VI, 15-16; *Itō Hirobumi Den,* I, 900-901.

13. *Ōkubo Toshimichi Monjo,* VI, 247-248.

14. Tokutomi, *Ōkubo Kōtō Sensei,* p. 372.

15. *Itō Hirobumi Den,* I, 906.

16. *Ibid.*, pp. 908-909.

17. *Ōkubo Toshimichi Nikki*, II, 373; *Itō Hirobumi Den*, I, 909.
18. *Itō Hirobumi Den*, I, 909.
19. *Kido Kōin Nikki*, III, 151.
20. See Osatake Takeshi, *Nihon Kensei Shi Taikō* [Outline of Japanese Constitutional History] (Tōkyō: Nihon Hyōronsha, 1938), II, 387-388; Ōtsu, *op. cit.*, I, 855.
21. Ōtsu, *op. cit.*, I, 855.
22. See *Ōkubo Toshimichi Nikki*, II, 377; *Itō Hirobumi Den*, I, 913, 915.
23. Tōkyō Teikoku Daigaku Shiryō Hensanjo, *Meiji Shiyō* [Essentials of Meiji History] (Tōkyō: Kinkōdō Shoseki Kabushiki Kaisha, 1933), I, 406; hereafter cited as *Meiji Shiyō*. The addition of Kido and Itagaki to the government increased the number of *sangi* to eleven: Ōkubo, Kuroda, Ōkuma, Ōki, Katsu, Terajima, Ijichi, Yamagata, Kido, and Itagaki.
24. Tanaka Sōgorō, *op. cit.*, p. 416.
25. Tokutomi, *Ōkubo Kōtō Sensei*, p. 375.
26. Osatake, *op. cit.*, II, 390. The structure of the Japanese government after the reorganization of 1875 is clearly outlined in Paul M. A. Linebarger, Djang Chu, and Ardath W. Burks, *Far Eastern Governments and Politics* (New York: D. Van Nostrand Co., 1956), p. 351.
27. Walter Wallace McLaren, ed., "Japanese Government Documents," *Transactions of the Asiatic Society of Japan*, XLII, pt. 1 (Tōkyō, 1914), 43-51.
28. *Ibid.*, p. 42. See *ibid.*, pp. 51-53, for the constitution and rules for the conduct of business of the *Dajōkan*.
29. Osatake, *op. cit.*, II, 391.
30. McLaren, "Japanese Government Documents," pp. lxxv-lxxvi.
31. Osatake, op. cit., II, 426. For the history of the *Chihōkan Kaigi* and its constitution, see *ibid.*, pp. 418-426; Ōtsu, op. cit., I, 863 ff.
32. Ishigami, *op. cit.*, p. 284.
33. Osatake, *op. cit.*, II, 429-430; Ōtsu, *op. cit.*, I, 868.
34. Osatake, *op. cit.*, II, 432.
35. Fujii and Moriya, *Meiji Jidai Shi*, II, 544; *Meiji Shiyō*, I, 417. For a study of the contention between the Japanese press and the Meiji bureaucracy, see Harry Emerson Wildes, *Social Currents in Japan* (Chicago: University of Chicago Press, 1927), pp. 27-49; Ono Hideo, *Nihon Shimbun Hattatsu Shi* [History of the Development of the Japanese Press] (Ōsaka: Ōsaka Mainichi Shimbunsha, 1922), pp. 50 ff.
36. Kawabe Kisaburō, *The Press and Politics in Japan* (Chicago: University of Chicago Press, 1921), p. 66.
37. *Meiji Shiyō*, I, 449-450.
38. Kawabe, op. cit., p. 62. See also Ono Hideo, *op. cit.*, pp. 32-33.
39. Kanesada Hanazono, *The Development of Japanese Journalism* (Ōsaka: The Ōsaka Mainichi, 1924), pp. 36-37.
40. Osatake, *op. cit.*, II, 392.
41. Tanaka Sōgorō, *op. cit.*, p. 418.
42. Fujii and Moriya, *Meiji Jidai Shi*, II, 514-515.
43. Ōtsu, *op. cit.*, I, 887-889. See also Augustus H. Mounsey, *The Satsuma Rebellion* (London: John Murray, 1879), pp. 73-74. The petition of June 6, 1873, protested against the substitution of Western dress for the traditional ceremonial court costume of the Emperor; the use of the solar calendar; the adoption of Western dress in the departments of the government; the employment of foreigners by the

government and the adoption of their ideas; the want of ability in the Emperor's instructions; the number of sycophants around the Emperor; the near approach of common soldiers to the person of the Emperor; the multitude of insolvent and dissipated officials; the continued allowance of idle pleasures of the nobles; the adoption of foreign rules and practices in schools; the excessive strictness of regulations in the capital; the failure to appoint a fencing instructor for the Emperor; the erection of unnecessary buildings, regardless of the financial condition of the treasury; the adoption of foreign drill; the increase of unnecessary officials; the nonprohibition of evil doctrines, namely, Christianity; the allowance of intermarriage with foreigners; the creation of a board of religion, which dealt with Buddhism and Shintoism without sufficiently differentiating between them; the union of the departments of home affairs and treasury; the adoption of the foreign manner of dressing the hair; and the abandonment of the practice of wearing two swords.

44. Fujii and Moriya, *Meiji Jidai Shi,* II, 512-513.

45. *Ibid.,* pp. 519-520.

46. See *Kido Kōin Nikki,* III, 232-233; *Ōkubo Toshimichi Nikki,* II, 427; Ōtsu, *op. cit.,* I, 895-896.

47. *Ōkubo Toshimichi Nikki,* II, 429.

48. The full text of the petition is found in Tada Kōmon and Kagawa Keizō, comps., *Iwakura Kō Jikki* [Authentic Chronicle of Prince Iwakura] (Tōkyō: Iwakura Kō Koseki Hozonkai, 1927), III, 285-287.

49. *Ibid.,* p. 290.

50. Fujii and Moriya, *Meiji Jidai Shi,* II, 517. In connection with the resignation of Hisamitsu and Itagaki, it is significant to note that Article 4 of the Ōsaka proposal, that pertaining to the divorcement of the *sangi* from concurrent duties as department heads, a proposition that Itagaki strongly advocated, was rejected on October 19 by imperial order.

51. *Ibid.,* p. 518; *Ōkubo Toshimichi Nikki,* II, 445.

52. McLaren, "Japanese Government Documents," pp. 572-573.

53. George M. Beckmann, *The Making of the Meiji Constitution* (Lawrence: University of Kansas Press, 1957), p. 114; *Ōkubo Toshimichi Monjo,* V, 188.

54. Tokutomi, *Ōkubo Kōtō Sensei,* p. 382.

55. *Ibid.; Ōkubo Toshimichi Monjo,* VI, 489-490.

56. *Ōkubo Toshimichi Nikki,* II, 497; Ishigami, *op. cit.,* p. 303.

57. *Ibid.,* pp. 303-304.

58. *Ōkubo Toshimichi Nikki,* II, 497.

59. *Ibid.,* p. 503.

60. *Ibid.,* p. 504.

61. *Ibid.,* p. 505.

62. *Ibid.,* p. 507.

63. *Ibid.,* p. 508.

64. *Ibid.,* p. 509.

65. *Ibid.,* p. 511.

66. *Ibid.,* p. 522.

67. Tokutomi, *Ōkubo Kōtō Sensei,* p. 404.

68. *Ōkubo Toshimichi Monjo,* V, 561.

69. Derk Bodde, *China's First Unifier, A Study of the Ch'in Dynasty as Seen in the Life of Li Ssu* (280?-208 B.C.) (Leiden: E. J. Brill, 1938), p. 171.

70. H. R. Williamson, *Wang An-Shih, A Chinese Statesman and Educationalist*

of the Sung Dynasty (London: Arthur Probsthain, 1935), I, 142-146, 177-178, 322 ff.

71. *Ōkubo Toshimichi Monjo,* V, 561.
72. *Ibid.,* p. 562.
73. *Ibid.,* pp. 562-563.
74. *Ibid.,* p. 563. For an authoritative description of England's shipping policy, see Eli F. Heckscher, *Mercantilism* (London: George Allen and Unwin, Ltd., 1955), II, 34-39, 49.
75. *Ōkubo Toshimichi Monjo,* V, 564.
76. *Loc. cit.*
77. *Ibid.,* p. 565.
78. *Loc. cit.*
79. John E. Orchard, *Japan's Economic Position* (New York: McGraw-Hill Book Co., Inc., 1930), pp. 77-79.
80. Tōyama Shigeki, *Meiji Ishin* [Meiji Restoration] (Tōkyō: Iwanami Shoten, 1951), pp. 304 ff.
81. Ishigami, *op. cit.,* p. 312. For an excellent and succinct discussion in English of Ōkubo's economic programs, see Sidney D. Brown, "Okubo Toshimichi: His Political and Economic Policies in Early Meiji Japan," *The Journal of Asian Studies,* XXI (February, 1962), 183-197.
82. *Ibid.,* p. 314; *Ōkubo Toshimichi Monjo,* IX, 5.
83. Ishigami, *op. cit.,* pp. 314-315.
84. *Ibid.,* p. 318.
85. *Ibid.,* pp. 323-325.
86. *Ibid.,* pp. 326-327.
87. *Ibid.,* p. 329.
88. *Ibid.,* p. 331.
89. *Ibid.,* p. 332.
90. *Ibid.,* pp. 332-333.
91. Makino Terutomo, *Meiji Taishō Shi: Keizai Hen* [History of the Meiji and Taishō Eras; Economics] (Vol. III of the Meiji Taishō Shi) (Tōkyō: Asahi Shimbunsha, 1930-1931), p. 261.
92. Takahashi Kamekichi, *Meiji Taishō Nōson Keizai no Hensen* [Changes in Agrarian Economy During the Meiji and Taishō Eras] (Tōkyō: Tōyō Keizai Shimpōsha Shuppambu, 1926), pp. 3-71.
93. Ishigami, *op. cit.,* pp. 342-344; Makino, *op. cit.,* III, 223-225; *Ōkubo Toshimichi Monjo,* VI, 415-416.
94. Hugh Borton, *Japan's Modern Century* (New York: Ronald Press Co., 1955), p. 115.
95. *Ōkubo Toshimichi Monjo,* V, 416-423.
96. Nihon Kōgakkai and Keimeikai, *Meiji Kōgyō Shi: Zōsen Hen* [Meiji Industrial History: Shipbuilding] (Vol. III of the *Meiji Kōgyō Shi,* Kōgakkai and Keimeikai, eds., Tōkyō: Meiji Kōgyō Shi Hakkōjo, 1904-1931), pp. 415-416.
97. Ishigami, *op. cit.,* p. 344; Nihon Kōgakkai and Keimeikai, *Meiji Kōgyō Shi: Kagaku Kōgyō Hen* [Meiji Industrial History: Chemical Industry] (Vol. IX of the *Meiji Kōgyō Shi,* Kōgakkai and Keimeikia, eds., Tōkyō: Meiji Kōgyō Shi Hakkōjo, 1904-1931), p. 1110.
98. Ishigami, *op. cit.,* pp. 344-345.
99. *Ōkubo Toshimichi Monjo,* VII, 45-49.

100. *Ibid.*, p. 49. For the text of Ōkubo's speech delivered at the opening ceremony, see Nakayama Yasumasa, ed., *Shimbun Shūsei Meiji Hennen Shi* [Chronological History of Meiji Compiled from Newspaper Records] (Tōkyō: Zaisei Keizai Gakkai, 1934-1936), III, 278-279.

101. Takahashi Kamekichi, *Meiji Taishō Sangyō Hattatsu Shi* [History of Industrial Development in the Meiji and Taishō Eras] (Tōkyō: Kaizōsha, 1929), p. 125.

102. Nakayama, *Shimbun Shūsei Meiji Hennen Shi,* III, 399.

103. For a detailed discussion of Ōkubo's interest in the samurai unemployment situation, see Kitsukawa Hidezō, *Shizoku Jusan no Kenkyū* [Study of the Provision of Employment for the Samurai] (Tōkyō: Keizai Shi Kenkyūjo, 1935), pp. 281-289.

104. *Meiji Shiyō,* I, 439, Fujii and Moriya, *Meiji Jidai Shi,* II, 537.

105. *Meiji Shiyō,* I, 452; Borton, *Japan's Modern Century,* p. 83.

106. Mounsey, *op. cit.*, pp. 88-89.

107. Fujii and Moriya, *Meiji Jidai Shi,* II, 537-538. For a more detailed study of the revolt, see Kokuryūkai Hombu, ed., *Seinan Kiden* [History of the Saigō Rebellion], II, 543 ff; hereafter cited as *Seinan Kiden.*

108. Fujii and Moriya, *Meiji Jidai Shi,* II, 538.

109. *Ibid.*, pp. 539-542.

110. For a list of peasant revolts occurring between the years 1871 and 1879, see Takahashi, *Meiji Taishō Sangyō Hattatsu Shi,* pp. 112-114; Ono Takeo, *Nōson Shi* [Agricultural History] (Vol. IX of *Gendai Nihon Bummei Shi* [History of Modern Japanese Civilization], Tōkyō: Tōyō Keizai Shimpōsha Shuppambu, 1940-1944), pp. 195-198.

111. Takahashi, *Meiji Taishō Sangyō Hattatsu Shi,* p. 112; Ono Takeo, *Nōson Shi,* pp. 185-186.

112. Fujii and Moriya, *Meiji Jidai Shi,* II, 524.

113. *Ōkubo Toshimichi Monjo,* VII, 441.

114. *Ibid.*, pp. 438-441.

115. *Meiji Shiyō,* I, 467; *Ōkubo Toshimichi Monjo,* VII, 461; Katsuda, *Ōkubo Toshimichi Den,* III, 566.

116. Mounsey, *op. cit.*, p. 71.

117. See *Seinan Kiden,* II, 696-697.

118. *Ibid.*, p. 652.

119. Borton, *Japan's Modern Century,* p. 100.

120. *Seinan Kiden,* II, 652.

121. *Ibid.*, p. 653.

122. *Seinan Kiden,* II, 654.

123. Mounsey, *op. cit.*, p. 85.

124. *Ibid.*, pp. 78-79.

125. Fujii and Moriya, *Meiji Jidai Shi,* II, 550.

126. *Ibid.*, p. 551.

127. *Ibid.*, pp. 551-552.

128. *Ibid.*, p. 554.

129. *Seinan Kiden,* III, 10-11.

130. *Seinan Kiden,* II, 744.

131. Mounsey, *op. cit.*, p. 87.

132. Fujii and Moriya, *Meiji Jidai Shi,* II, 554.

133. Mounsey, *op. cit.*, p. 122.

134. *Ibid.*, pp. 123-125, 126.

135. Borton, *Japan's Modern Century,* p. 100.

136. Mounsey, *op. cit.*, p. 126.

137. *Ōkubo Toshimichi Nikki*, II, 537; Fujii and Moriya, *Meiji Jidai Shi*, II, 558.

138. Mounsey, *op. cit.*, pp. 138-139.

139. Borton, *Japan's Modern Century*, p. 101; Fujii and Moriya, *Meiji Jidai Shi*, II, 560.

140. Mounsey, *op. cit.*, pp. 214-215.

141. *Ibid.*, p. 218.

142. *Ibid.*, p. 233.

143. *Ōkubo Toshimichi Monjo*, VII, 489.

144. Cf. Ōkawa Nobuyoshi, ed., *Dai Saigō Zenshū* [Complete Works of Saigō] (Tōkyō: Heibonsha, 1926-1927), III, 830; Watanabe Shūjirō, *op. cit.*, p. 118. *Shisatsu* (to observe) and *shisatsu* (to pierce) are homonyms which can readily be differentiated in meaning if written in Chinese characters; different characters comprise the two unrelated terms.

145. *Ibid.*, p. 119.

146. Mounsey, *op. cit.*, p. 277.

147. *Ibid.*, p. 130.

148. Tanaka Sōgorō, *op. cit.*, p. 430.

149. Fujii and Moriya, Meiji Jidai Shi, II, 555-556. Tanaka Sōgorō, however, refutes this, saying that Itō fabricated the story.

150. *Seinan Kiden*, III, 150.

151. Mounsey, *op. cit.*, pp. 112-113.

152. Borton, *Japan's Modern Century*, p. 101. See also Fujii and Moriya, *Meiji Jidai Shi*, II, 556-557. Some Japanese historians imply that Saigō was not responsible for starting the Satsuma rebellion and that he decided to sacrifice himself for the samurai cause only after realizing that civil war was inevitable.

153. Watanabe Shūjirō, *op. cit.*, pp. 121-122.

154. *Ibid.*, pp. 122-123.

155. See Ishigami, *op. cit.*, pp. 374-378.

156. Itō Nitarō, *Ōkubo Toshimichi* (Tōkyō: Heibonsha, 1941), II, 276.

157. Nakayama, *Shimbun Shūsei Meiji Hennen Shi*, III, 468.

158. Itō, *op. cit.*, II, 276. Ōkubo Toshitake has written a short article concerning his father's style of calligraphy. See Yūzankaku Sho no Tomo, ed., *Bakumatsu Ishin Iboku Shinkō* [New Compilation of Late Tokugawa and Restoration Calligraphy] (Tōkyō: Yūzankaku, 1940), pp. 226-229. For further details concerning Ōkubo's family life, see Ishigami, *op. cit.*, pp. 450 ff.

159. *Ibid.*, pp. 470 ff.; Itō, *op. cit.*, II, 377.

160. Katsuda, *Ōkubo Toshimichi Den*, III, 769-770; Tokutomi, *Ōkubo Kōtō Sensei*, pp. 430-431.

161. For a detailed account of Ōkubo's death as reported by the *Nichi Nichi Shimbun* of Tōkyō under the dateline of May 15, 1878, see Ishida Bunjirō, ed., *Shimbun Kiroku Shūsei Meiji Daijiken Shi* [History of Great Events of the Meiji Era Compiled from Newspaper Records] (Tōkyō: Kinseisha, 1954), pp. 99-102. See also Watanabe Shūjirō, *op. cit.*, pp. 126-129; Katsuda, *Ōkubo Toshimichi Den*, III, 770.

162. *Ibid.*, p. 770; Tokutomi, *Ōkubo Kōtō Sensei*, p. 431.

163. Watanabe Shūjirō, *op. cit.*, p. 127.

164. *Ibid.*, pp. 131-132.

165. For the full text of the assassins' accusations against Ōkubo, see Itō, *op. cit.*, pp. 289-298.

166. See Borton, *Japan's Modern Century*, p. 105; Mounsey, *op. cit.*, p. 269; and F. Brinkley, *History of the Japanese People* (New York: Encyclopaedia Britannica Co., 1914), p. 690.

167. Borton, *Japan's Modern Century*, p. 105.

Notes to Chapter IX

1. Watanabe Shūjirō, *Ōkubo Toshimichi Genkōroku* [Words and Deeds of Ōkubo Toshimichi] (Tōkyō: Naigai Shuppan Kyōkai, 1909), p. 171. See also Kawasaki Saburō, *Ōkubo Kōtō* (Tōkyō: Shunyōdō, 1898), p. 4.

2. Tokutomi Iichirō, *Ōkubo Kōtō Sensei* [Master Ōkubo Kōtō] (Tōkyō: Minyūsha, 1927), p. 457.

3. Tanaka Sōgorō, *Ōkubo Toshimichi* (Tōkyō: Chikura Shobō, 1938), pp. 4-5.

4. See Leo Strauss, *Thoughts on Machiavelli* (Glencoe, Illinois: The Free Press, 1958), p. 14.

5. Maurice Courant, *Ôkoubo* (Paris: Ancienne Libraire Germer Bailliere et Cie, 1904), p. 202.

6. See Tanaka Sōgorō, *op. cit.*, pp. 6-7.

7. Spencer applied the biological scheme of evolution to society and expounded the thesis that a society evolved from a lower militant type to a higher industrial form. He believed that among the nations as in nature only the strongest and best survive, a concept that some of the more rugged individualists of this day still accept. See Herbert Spencer, *The Principles of Sociology* (New York: D. Appleton and Co., 1900), II, chaps. 27-28; Richard Hofstadter, *Social Darwinism in American Thought* (New York: George Braziller, Inc., 1959), chap. 2.

8. Courant, *op. cit.*, p. 202.

9. Cf. Tokutomi, *op. cit.*, p. 433; Courant, *op. cit.*, p. 198; Augustus H. Mounsey, *The Satsuma Rebellion* (London: John Murray, 1879), p. 269; Hugh Borton, *Japan's Modern Century* (New York: Ronald Press Co., 1955), p. 105.

10. Cf. Katsuda Magoya, *Ōkubo Toshimichi Den* [Biography of Ōkubo Toshimichi] (Tōkyō: Dōbunkan, 1910-1911), III, 768; Watanabe, *op. cit.*, p. 124; Itō Nitarō, *Ōkubo Toshimichi* (Tōkyō: Heibonsha, 1941), II, 284; J. Morris, *Makers of Japan* (London: Methuen and Co., 1906), p. 194.

11. News item in *The Times* (of London), May 16, 1878.

12. Fujii Jintarō and Moriya Hidesuke, *Sōgō Nihon Shi Taikei: Meiji Jidai Shi* [A Synthesis of Japanese History: History of the Meiji Period] (Tōkyō: Naigai Shoseki Kabushiki Kaisha, 1939-1940), II, 585; Ōtsu Junichirō, *Dai Nippon Kensei Shi* [Constitutional History of Japan] (Tōkyō: Hōbunkan, 1927-1928), II, 134; Kawasaki Saburō, *Ōkubo Kōtō* (Tōkyō: Shunyōdō, 1898), pp. 167-168.

13. Ōtsu, *op. cit.*, II, 161-162.

14. Katsuda, *Ōkubo Toshimichi Den,* II, 783-784; Itō, *op. cit.*, II, 287.

15. See G. B. Sansom, *The Western World and Japan* (New York: Alfred A. Knopf, 1950), p. 344.

Glossary

Glossary

Ake no koromo	朱の衣	Red robe.
Anzaisho	行在所	The emperor's temporary headquarters.
Bakumatsu	幕末	The closing period of Bakufu rule, 1853-1868.
Benji	辨事	Officials of the third rank who served in the executive department of the *Seitaisho* government.
Benri daijin	辨理大臣	Minister plenipotentiary.
Boshin no eki	戊辰の役	The civil war of 1868 in which the imperial forces defeated the Tokugawa diehards.
Bugyō	奉行	A high commissioner of the Bakufu.
Buke (sho) hatto	武家〔諸〕法度	Laws governing the military (*daimyō*) houses.
Bushi	武士	A term designating a warrior; a samurai.

Cha-ire	茶入れ	Tea canister.
Chihanji	知藩事	The title given to former *daimyō* who were made imperial governors over the fiefs they had surrendered to the national government in 1869.
Chihōkan Kaigi	地方官会議	The assembly of prefectural (*ken* and *fu*) governors established in 1875.
Chihō minkai	地方民会	Local assemblies.
Chiseijo	知政所	Satsuma *han*'s administrative office after 1869.
Chō	町	Measure of land: 2.45 acres.
Chōgi sanyo	朝議参與	Court councilor.
Chōnin	町人	Townspeople; merchant class.
Chōshū	長州	The fief in southwestern Honshū belonging to the Mōri family.
Chūnō	中農	A middle-class peasant.
Daigaku	大学	A university.
Daikan	代官	A Tokugawa governor; also an official of a *han* district office.
Daimyō	大名	A feudal lord with an annual rice revenue of 10,000 *koku* or more.
Dainagon	大納言	A chief councilor of state who assisted the senior officer in the Two *Kan* Six *Shō* government, 1869.
Daishinin	大審院	The Supreme Court established in 1875 following the Osaka conference.
Daitai	大隊	An infantry battalion.

Dajōdaijin 太政大臣 The highest ranking minister in the *Dajōkan*. Cf. *Dajōkan*.

Dajōkan 太政官 The new government structure created under the *Seitaisho*; also the title of the imperial government in prefeudal times.

Danjōdai 彈正台 The board of censors of the early Meiji government, 1869-1871.

Dejō 出城 An outer castle (Satsuma).

Dōjō 道場 An exercise hall.

Eki 駅 A post station.

Eta 穢多 An outcast.

Fu 府 A municipal or urban prefecture.

Fudai daimyō 譜代大名 A *daimyō* whose forebears had supported the Tokugawa before 1600 (Battle of Sekigahara).

Fukoku kyōhei 富國强兵 "Rich country, strong army."

Fukko 復古 Restoration.

Furoshiki 風呂敷 A large kerchief used to wrap and carry various items.

Gaikoku bugyō 外國奉行 A Tokugawa commissioner of foreign relations.

Gaimushō 外務省 Foreign Office.

Gakkan 学館 A school; an academy.

Gakkō 学校 A school.

Gakumonjo 学問所 A pre-Meiji term for school.

Genrōin 元老院 The Senate created in 1875, following the Osaka conference.

Gichō	議長	A speaker or chairman.
Gijō	議定	A senior councilor in the new Meiji government.
Go	碁	Japanese checkers.
Gōchū	郷中	An association for young boys in Satsuma.
Gokajō no Goseimon	五箇條の御誓文	The Charter Oath of five articles.
Gokanjōkata kogashirakaku	御勘定方小頭格	An assistant treasurer of the Satsuma *han.*
Gokenin	御家人	Tokugawa retainers who were ranked below the *hatamoto* and with incomes of less than 10,000 *koku.*
Gōnō	豪農	A wealthy peasant.
Gōshi	郷士	A farmer-samurai.
Gōso	強訴	An appeal by irregular process.
Goyō toritsugi	御用取次	A liaison officer between council and *shōgun* in the Tokugawa government; and between council and *daimyō* in the *han* government.
Goyōkin	御用金	Forced loans imposed upon merchants.
Goyō toritsugi minarai	御用取次見習	A *goyō toritsugi* trainee. Cf. *goyō toritsugi* above.
Gundai	郡代	A governor of a Tokugawa holding yielding more than 100,000 *koku* of rice.
Gun-ken	郡縣	"County-prefecture."
Gun kubariyaku (gumbu yaku)	軍配役	A *han* official in charge of all military supplies and funds.
Gunyaku kata	軍役方	A *han* official in charge of military affairs.

Hachi-ichi-hachi Jihen	八一八事変	"8-1-8 Incident"; the September 30, 1863, coup d'etat when the Satsuma-Aizu forces drove Chōshū radicals out of Kyōto.
Hachikyoku	八局	The "Eight Offices"; the administrative structure established on February 5, 1868.
Haihan chiken	廃藩置縣	"Abolition of *han*, establishment of prefectures" (the reform of 1871).
Hambaku	反幕	"Anti-Bakufu."
Han	藩	The domain of a *daimyō*. The various *han* in the Tokugawa period were classified as *dai han* (400,000 *koku*), *chū han* (100,000 to 400,000 *koku*), and *shō han* (below 100,000 *koku*).
Hanji	判事	A departmental official of the Meiji government (*Hachi Kyoku*).
Hanseki hōkan	版籍奉還	"Restoration of the fiefs to the throne."
Hanshu	藩主	A *daimyō*.
Hara kiri	腹切り	Disembowelment.
Hatamoto	旗本	Tokugawa vassals ranking above the *gokenin* and below the *fudai daimyō*; the direct retainers of the *daimyō* were sometimes also referred to as *hatamoto*.
Heishi	兵士	A soldier.
Hōgiri	方限	A term designating a "district," eighteen of which were to be found within the city of Kagoshima.

Hōkentō	封建黨	The feudal party that opposed the imperial government during the Saga rebellion.
Hoshō	輔相	Joint executive officers of the executive department of the *Seitaisho* government.
Hyakushō ikki	百姓一揆	Peasant revolt.
Hyōbushō	兵部省	The Ministry of War in the Two *Kan* Six *Shō* (early Meiji) government structure.
Hyōbu tayū	兵部大輔	A vice-minister of a department in the Two *Kan* Six *Shō* (early Meiji) government.
Hyōgo-mage	兵庫髷	A hair style, originally worn by prostitutes of Hyōgo, which later became popular throughout Japan.
Jichō ron	自重論	The doctrine of prudence, caution, circumspection.
Jimu kakari	事務掛	A departmental official in the *Shichi Ka* government. Cf. *Shichi Ka.*
Jimu kantoku	事務監督	A supervisor of administrative affairs.
Jingikan	神祇官	The Department of Shintō in both the *Seitaisho* and Two *Kan* Six *Shō* (early Meiji) structures of government.
Jitō	地頭	During the Tokugawa period, the collective name for the *hatamoto* and *gokenin.*
Jitsumyō	実名	"True name."
Jōdai	城代	A *han* official in charge of his

		daimyō's castle; also a Bakufu official in charge of the *shōgun*'s castle.
Jōi	攘夷	"Expel the barbarian."
Jōi-teki jōi	攘夷的攘夷	A view of the die-hard expulsionists who advocated expelling the foreigners at any cost.
Jōi-teki kaikoku	攘夷的開國	A view of foreign policy held by the Mito school which advocated opening Japan to foreign intercourse only after expulsion efforts had failed.
Jōka no shi	城下の士	A *han* samurai attached to the main castle as opposed to those in the outer castles.
Jōkyoku Kaigi	上局会議	The meeting of the upper chamber of the legislative department in the *Seitaisho* structure of the Meiji government.
Jōshu	城主	A *daimyō* owning a castle.
Jōyaku kaisei goyōkakari	條約改正御用掛	The official in charge of treaty revision.
Jūdō	柔道	The Japanese art of self-defense.
Jūjutsu	柔術	Cf. *jūdō*.
Juku	塾	A private school in the Tokugawa period.
Jusan kyoku	授産局	The employment bureau established by Ōkubo in the Home Ministry.
Kachi metsuke	徒目附	A Tokugawa censor, ranking below the *metsuke*, who kept the warrior class under surveillance.

Kaigun Kyō	海 軍 卿	The title of the Minister of the Navy until 1885.
Kaikoku	開 國	"Open the country."
Kaikoku ron	開 國 論	"Open the country" doctrine; the viewpoint of those who favored treaties with the West in the period 1854-1858.
Kaikoku-teki jōi	開國的攘夷	Shimazu Nariakira's position on foreign policy which stressed intercourse with the West for the express purpose of acquiring Occidental military techniques and weapons; he believed that only after Japan gained strength should any attempt be made to expel the foreigners.
Kaikoku-teki kaikoku	開國的開國	The policy of opening Japan to foreign intercourse unconditionally.
Kaiseijo	開 成 所	A Satsuma military academy.
Kakiyakujo	書 役 助	An archivist's aide.
Kakurō	閣 老	A *rojū;* a term coined by the specialists in Chinese learning.
Kamme	貫 目	Measure of weight. 1 *kan* = 8.26720 pounds.
Kammon	関 門	Barriers set up throughout Japan to regulate movement of traffic.
Kampaku	関 白	A senior official of the imperial court; a regent.
Kangaku juku	漢 学 塾	A private school in the pre-Meiji era in which Chinese learning was emphasized.

Kangakusha	漢学者	Specialists in Chinese studies.
Kangyōryō	勧業寮	The industrial promotion bureau established in Ōkubo's Home Ministry.
Kanjō bugyō	勘定奉行	A Bakufu financial officer.
Kantō	関東	In the Tokugawa period, the term applied to the city of Edo and the eight surrounding provinces.
Karō	家老	The chief minister of the Bakufu (called *tairō* after 1638); the chief minister of the *han*, sometimes known also as *toshiyori*.
Kaseijo	家政所	The Satsuma *han* office which dealt with Shimazu family affairs; redesignated *Naimukyoku* in 1869.
Katte gata	勝手方	A Tokugawa financial officer.
Keihōryō	警保寮	The police bureau in Ōkubo's Home Ministry.
Keishichō	警視廳	Metropolitan Police Board.
Ken	縣	Prefecture.
Kendō	劍道	Fencing.
Kinai	畿内	The Kyōto metropolitan district.
Kinki	近畿	The Ōsaka-Kyōto district.
Kinnō	勤王	"Loyalism."
Kinnōka	勤王家	"Loyalist."
Kinnō ron	勤王論	"Loyalist" doctrine.
Kirishitan bugyō	吉利支丹奉行	The Bakufu commissioner dealing with Christians.
Kirokusho	記錄所	The Satsuma *han* archives.

Kōbu gattai	公武合體	"Court-Bakufu union."
Kōginin	公議人	A delegate from the fiefs to the assembly established under the *Seitaisho*.
Kōgisho	公議所	The deliberative assembly established under the *Seitaisho*.
Kokka fuchū	國家不忠	"Disloyalty to the state."
Koku	石	Measure of capacity: 4.9629 bushels; one-tenth of a ton in reference to ships.
Kokugakusha	國学者	Japanese scholars (*wagakusha*).
Kokuji goyōgakari	國事御用掛	Court advisers, 1863-1868.
Komon	顧問	An adviser, counselor.
Komononari	小物成	Miscellaneous feudal taxes.
Kōmunin	公務人	A *han* delegate to the lower chamber of the legislative department of the *Seitaisho*.
Konoe hei	近衛兵	Imperial guards.
Kōri	郡	The administrative division of a province.
Koshōgumi	小姓組	Bodyguards or attendants to the *daimyō* or *shōgun*.
Kōtō-teki kaikoku	叩頭的開國	The foreign policy of the extreme passivists who would kowtow to foreigners and accede to their demands.
Kuge	公家〔公卿〕	A court noble.
Kuge hatto	公家法度	Laws governing the court nobles.
Kuji gata	公事方	A Tokugawa judicial officer.
Kunaishō	宮內省	Imperial Household Ministry.
Kuni	國	Country; nation. The term is also used to refer to a province.

Kura yaku	藏役	*Han* official in charge of receiving, storing, and distributing grain.
Kyōbushō	教部省	The Ministry of Moral Instruction dealing with religion in general, established by the Meiji government in 1872 and abolished in 1877.
Kyōwa	共和	"Republicanism."
Kyōwa seijishū	共和政治州	A republic.
Mabiki	間引	"Thinning," applied to population-reduction in the Tokugawa period.
Machi bugyō	町奉行	A Bakufu commissioner of such cities as Kyōto and Ōsaka.
Metsuke	目附	A Bakufu censor who kept the *hatamoto* under surveillance for the Junior Council.
Mimbu Kyō	民部卿	A Minister of Civil Affairs.
Mimbushō	民部省	The Ministry for Civil Affairs of the Two *Kan* Six *Sho* (early Meiji) government.
Mimbu shoyū	民部少輔	The official third in line of responsibility in the *Mimbushō*.
Mombushō	文部省	The Ministry of Education after 1871.
Naichi dai-ichi shugi ron	内地第一主義論	The viewpoint of those who advocated devoting primary consideration to domestic affairs as opposed to external expansion (Ōkubo *vs.* Saigō).
Naikaku bunri	内閣分離	The policy calling for the separation of the councilors from

		departmental duties of the Meiji government.
Naimu Kyō	内務郷	The title of the Minister of Home Affairs in the Meiji government prior to 1885.
Naimushō	内務省	The Ministry of Home Affairs.
Namamugi no hen	生麦の変	The Richardson affair of 1862.
Nisaishū	二才衆	Youths aged seventeen to twenty-three who advised and taught younger boys of the Satsuma boys' association, the *gōchū*.
Ōchō jidai	王朝時代	The "Monarchical Age," from the earliest times to A.D. 1192.
Ōdō	王道	"Monarchical rule."
Okonando	御小納戸	Officials in both the Bakufu and *han* governments who dealt with their masters' hairdressers, food-handlers, gardeners, stable hands, and so on.
Okonando tōdori	御小納戸頭取	The chief *okonando*.
Ōkura Kyō	大藏郷	The title of the Minister of Finance under the Two *Kan* Six *Shō* (early Meiji) structure of government.
Ōkurashō	大藏省	The Ministry of Finance.
Ōkura tayū	大藏大輔	The title of the vice-minister of finance in the early Meiji government.
Ōmetsuke	大目附	A Bakufu censor who kept the *daimyō* and officials of *daimyō* status under surveillance.

Osegumi	年長組	The men twenty-four years of age and older who served as advisers to the Satsuma boys' association.
Ōsei fukko	王政復古	Restoration of imperial rule.
Osso	越訴	An appeal to higher authority by bypassing regular channels.
Rangakusha	蘭学者	Dutch scholars.
Ri	里	Measure of distance: 2.45 English miles.
Rōjū	老中	A senior Bakufu official who was a member of the council of elders.
Rōnin	牢人〔浪人〕	Masterless samurai.
Ryō	両	Unit of currency: 78 *ryō* = roughly 100 Mexican dollars.
Sadaijin	左大臣	The Minister of the Left.
Saikaidō	西海道	One of the eight great divisions of Japan which included Satsuma.
Sain	左院	The Board of the Left of the early Meiji government.
Sake	酒	Rice wine.
Sangi	参議	A councilor of state.
Sanke	三家	The three senior branch houses of the Tokugawa family: Owari, Kii, Mito.
Sankin kōtai	参勤交代	The Bakufu system of forced alternate residence of the *daimyō* in Edo.
Sankyō	三卿	The three Tokugawa branch houses—Tayasu, Hitotsubashi, and Shimizu—who were de-

		scended from either Tokugawa Yoshimune or Ieshige.
Sansei	参 政	The officials who ranked below the *rōjū* (in the Bakufu) and below the *karō* (in the *han* government); also *han* officials who served under a *chihanji*.
Sanshoku	三 職	The three offices of government established on January 3, 1868: the Executive, Senior Council, and Junior Council.
Sanyo	参 與	A junior councilor in the *Sanshoku* and *Seitaisho* structures of government.
Satsuma-yaki	薩 摩 燒	Satsuma porcelain.
Seichū Gumi	精 中 組	The Satsuma loyalist group formed around Ōkubo.
Seichū shi	精 中 士	"Loyal retainer."
Seiin	正 院	The Central Board of the Meiji government, 1871-1877.
Seii taishōgun	征夷大將軍	"Barbarian-subduing generalissimo," the full title of the office of *shōgun*.
Seikan ron	征 韓 論	The doctrine of invading Korea.
Seikantō	征 韓 黨	"Conquer Korea" party.
Seitaisho	政 体 書	"Document on the Structure of Government," the so-called Constitution of 1868 which established the *Dajōkan*.
Seitei no kawazu	井底の蛙	Literally "frog in a well," meaning an individual with narrow views.

Sengoku jidai	戰國時代	The "Age of Warring States," 1480-1570.
Sesshō	攝政	A regent.
Shaku	尺	Linear measure: 0.994194 foot.
Shichika	七科	The government composed of seven administrative offices established on February 10, 1868.
Shigakkō	私学校	The private schools established in Satsuma by Saigō and his followers after his resignation from the central government.
Shijuku	私塾	A private school.
Shimada-mage	島田髷	Shimada hair style.
Shimpei	親兵	The court guards, later redesignated *konoe hei*.
Shisatsu	視察	"To observe."
Shisatsu	刺殺	"To pierce."
Shishinden	紫宸殿	The audience chamber of the imperial palace in Kyōto.
Shissei	執政	A senior minister of a *han* who served under a *chihanji*.
Shōen	莊園	A manor.
Shōgi	將棋	Japanese chess.
Shoshidai	所司代	The *shōgun*'s representative in Kyōto.
Shōtai	小隊	Platoon (infantry); section (artillery); troop (cavalry).
Shoyū	少輔	A departmental official in the Two *Kan* Six *Shō* (early Meiji) government.
Shūgiin	集議院	The new name for the *Kōgisho*, the legislative body of the new Meiji government.

		which met on October 11, 1869.
Shugo	守護	A military commissioner.
Shuku	宿	A post town; post station.
Shūseikan	集成館	The Satsuma naval shipyard.
Shuseki sangi	主席参議	A senior *sangi*.
Soba yaku	側役	An adviser to a *daimyō*.
Sobayōnin	側用人	See *goyō toritsugi*.
Sōjaban	奉者番	A Bakufu superintendent of ceremony and etiquette.
Sokkō ron	卽行論	"Immediate action" doctrine.
Sonnō jōi	尊王攘夷	"Revere the emperor, expel the foreigner."
Sōsai	総裁	The senior executive officer of the *Sanshoku*.
Sumō	相撲	Japanese wrestling.
Tairō	大老	A "great elder," or regent, of the Bakufu.
Taishōin	待詔院	An organ of the Meiji government dealing with petitions.
Taishōin gakushi	待詔院学士	An officer in the *Taishōin*.
Taishōkyoku	待詔局	The original nomenclature of the *Taishōin*.
Tama wo ubau	王を奪ふ	"To steal the jewel," or to usurp the throne.
Tayū	大輔	An administrative assistant to the head of a department in the Two *Kan* Six *Shō* (early Meiji) government; a vice-minister.
Tekabushi	手かぶし	"Hand cover," or glove.
Tempō jidai	天保時代	The period 1830-1868.

Tenchō gokōfuku	天朝御興復	Imperial restoration.
Tennō heika	天皇陛下	The emperor.
Tenri	天理	Natural laws.
Terakoya	寺小屋	A temple school.
Tōbaku	倒幕	"Overthrow the Bakufu."
Tōbaku ron	倒幕論	"Overthrow the Bakufu" doctrine.
Tojō	外城	Outer castles (Satsuma).
Tojō no shi	外城の士	Samurai connected with the outer castles.
Tōkaidō	東海道	The great road leading from Kyōto to Edo (Tōkyō).
Tonya	問屋	Commission merchants.
Tōsan	逃散	To flee.
Tozama daimyō	外様大名	A *daimyō* whose ancestors had not submitted to Tokugawa rule until after 1600 (Sekigahara). Cf. *fudai daimyō*.
Tsuke yaku	附役	A Satsuma *han* office that Toshimichi's father held in the department dealing with Ryūkyū affairs.
Tsumefu	詰夫	An attendant laborer.
Tsūshō	通称	"Common name."
Uchiharai rei	打ち拂ひ令	The Tokugawa expulsion decree.
Uchikowashi	打ちこわし	The practice of dissident peasants and townspeople of destroying houses of landlords and usurers.
Udaijin	右大臣	The Minister of the Right in the early Meiji government.

Uin	右院	The Board of the Right. Cf. *Sain.*
Wagakusha	和学者	A Japanese classical scholar.
Waka	和歌	A 31-syllable Japanese poem.
Wakadoshiyori	若年寄	A junior elder.
Yari	槍	A spear.
Yashiki	屋敷	A residence.
Yōkōha	洋行派	The progressives in the Meiji government who had been exposed to Western influences.
Yōmyō	幼名	"Childhood name."
Zenshinsetsu	漸進説	A doctrine of gradualism.
Zettai shugi kanryō	絶体主義官僚	An absolute bureaucracy.

Bibliography

Bibliography

The English titles given in brackets following the Japanese titles are rough translations for the convenience of the reader.

Bibliographic Note

Because of his importance in Restoration and Meiji history, Japanese scholars have focused considerable attention upon Ōkubo and have produced numerous volumes discussing eulogistically the achievements of the man. Most of the published works on Ōkubo have been included in this bibliography. Among them, the following have proved of particular interest and value. (1) Tokutomi Iichirō, *Ōkubo Kōtō Sensei* [Master Ōkubo]: Tokutomi, a historian, political critic, and voluminous writer, quotes extensively from source materials. He concentrates on Ōkubo's post-Restoration political activities and presents an analysis of Ōkubo's character, in the process of which he tends to be excessively laudatory of Ōkubo. (2) Tanaka Sōgorō, *Ōkubo Toshimichi:* Tanaka, a university professor of political science and a specialist in Restoration history, tends to have a Marxian orientation, but he attempts to be objective. Tanaka has relied heavily on the classic work on Ōkubo, of which mention will be made next. (3) Katsuda Magoya, *Ōkubo Toshimichi Den* [Biography of Ōkubo Toshimichi]: Katsuda's biography of Ōkubo is undoubtedly the most complete of any work on the subject. An educator, Katsuda has written a three-volume study that is especially valuable inasmuch as he has had access to materials on the Restoration because of his close connection with the bureau within the Ministry of Education which was commissioned to edit historical documents of that period. Quoting extensively from primary sources, Katsuda presents a detailed description of Ōkubo's political career but makes no attempt to analyze Ōkubo's character. Like most other biographers of Ōkubo, Katsuda is inordinately eulogistic. A very important feature of his work is the inclusion of a bibliography, something not common in older Japanese publications. He lists the titles of 157 source materials. Another work which should be mentioned because its tone contrasts with the aforementioned publications is (4) Watanabe Shūjirō, *Ōkubo Toshimichi Genkōroku* [Words and Deeds of Ōkubo Toshimichi]. Watanabe is comparatively unorthodox in his treatment of Ōkubo as he refrains from being unduly eulogistic. A final work deserving comment is (5) Kiyozawa Kiyoshi, *Gaiseika to shite no Ōkubo Toshimichi* [Ōkubo Toshimichi as an International Statesman]. A newspaper reporter and a recognized critic of diplomacy and politics, Kiyozawa has presented a succinct description of one of several facets of the adroit Meiji leader, that of an international statesman.

Primary sources indispensable for the study of Ōkubo, and available in the United States, include the *Ōkubo Toshimichi Nikki* [Diary of Ōkubo Toshimichi], compiled in two volumes, the *Ōkubo Toshimichi Monjo* [Papers of Ōkubo Toshimichi], in ten volumes, the *Shishin Benri Shimatsu,* which consists of documents relating to the Sino-Japanese negotiations over the Formosan question, and the *Shoban Shushisho,* a report of the Board of Formosan Affairs.

Furthermore, important sources pertaining to the lives of Ōkubo's colleagues are readily accessible in American libraries that have Far Eastern collections. The *Kido Kōin Nikki* [Diary of Kido Kōin], *Kido Kōin Monjo* [Papers of Kido Kōin], *Iwakura Tomomi Kankei Monjo* [Documents Relating to Iwakura Tomomi], and *Dai Saigō Zenshū* [Complete Works of Saigō], to mention a few, are works in this category.

There are, in addition, other valuable sources which the researcher studying the Restoration and Meiji periods may tap. Nakane Yukie's diary entitled *Sakumu Kiji,* covering the years from 1853 to 1858, is a useful work in four volumes as is his *Saimu Kiji,* which deals with the eventful years between 1858 and 1862. The *Zoku Saimu Kiji,* a work based upon the documents of the Fukui *han,* in the writing of which Nakane is involved, describes political happenings from the year 1862 to 1867.

As for general works on the Restoration period, the most valuable in Japanese is the six-volume compilation by the Ishin Shiryō Hensan Jimukyoku entitled *Ishin Shi* [History of the Restoration]. On the Meiji period, the joint efforts of Fujii Jintarō and Moriya Hidesuke have produced a concise delineation in two volumes (part of the *Sōgō Nihon Shi Taikei*) entitled *Meiji Jidai* (Meiji Period). Tōyama Shigeki, a representative leftist writer, has an interesting study entitled *Meiji Ishin* [Meiji Restoration].

In this study I have drawn freely from these and other sources. Works are listed in the following order: Japanese, Chinese, French, and English.

Works in Japanese

Aoyama Kaikan, ed. *Kōtō Sensei Ibokushū* [Collection of Kōtō's Calligraphy]. Tōkyō: Kōgeisha, 1927.

Asahi Shimbunsha. *Meiji Taishō Shi* [History of the Meiji and Taishō Eras]. Tōkyō: Asahi Shimbunsha, 1930-1931. 6 vols.

Asashina Chisen, ed. *Meiji Kōshinroku* [Record of Meiji Heroes]. Tōkyō: Shimpōsha, 1918. 4 vols.

Asai Kiyoshi. *Meiji Ishin to Gun-ken Shisō* [The Meiji Restoration and the County-Prefecture Concept]. Tōkyō: Ganshodō Shoten, 1939.

Dajōkan, ed. *Fukko-Ki* [Records Concerning the Meiji Restoration]. Tōkyō: Naigai Shoseki Kabushiki Kaisha, 1930-1931. 15 vols.

Fujii Jintarō and Moriya Hidesuke. *Sōgō Nihon Shi Taikei: Meiji Jidai Shi* [A Synthesis of Japanese History: History of the Meiji Period]. Tōkyō: Naigai Shoseki Kabushiki Kaisha, 1939-1940. 2 vols.

Furuta Ryōichi. "Edo Jidai no Kōtsū" [Communications in the Edo Period], in *Iwanami Kōza: Nihon Rekishi,* Kuroita Katsumi, ed. Vol. I. Tōkyō: Iwanami Shoten, 1933-1935.

Gaimushō Chōsabu, ed. *Dai Nippon Gaikō Bunsho* [Japanese Diplomatic Documents]. Tōkyō: Nihon Kokusai Kyōkai, 1936——. 9 vols.
Hani Gorō. *Meiji Ishin* [Meiji Restoration]. Tōkyō: Iwanami Shoten, 1946.
Haruyama Sakuji, "Edo Jidai no Kyōiku" [Education in the Edo Period], in *Iwanami Kōza: Nihon Rekishi*, Kuroita Katsumi, ed. Vol. II. Tōkyō: Iwanami Shoten, 1935.
Hattori Shisō. *Meiji Ishin ni okeru Shidō to Dōmei* [Leadership and Alliances of the Meiji Restoration]. Tōkyō: Nihon Hyōronsha, 1949.
Hayakawa Junsaburō. *Bakufu Seichō Kiroku* [Record of the Bakufu's Punitive Expedition Against Chōshū]. Tōkyō: Nihon Shiseki Kyōkai, 1919.
Hirao Michio. "Bakumatsu Rōnin to sono Hogo oyobi Tōsei" [The Protection and Control of the *Rōnin* in the Bakumatsu Period], in *Meiji Ishin Shi Kenkyū*, Tōkyō Teikoku Daigaku Shigakkai, ed. Tōkyō: Fuzambō, 1929.
Imai Toshiki. "Edo yori Tōkyō e no Suii" [The Change from Edo to Tōkyō], in *Meiji Ishin Shi Kenkyū*, Tōkyō Teikoku Daigaku Shigakkai, ed. Tōkyō: Fuzambō, 1929.
Inoue Kaoru Kō Denki Hensankai, ed. *Segai Inoue Kō Den* [Biography of Inoue Segai]. Tōkyō: Naigai Shoseki Kabushiki Kaisha. 1933-1934. 5 vols.
Ishida Bunjirō, ed. *Shimbun Kiroku Shūsei Meiji Daijiken Shi* [History of Great Events of the Meiji Era Compiled from Newspaper Records]. Tōkyō: Kinseisha, 1954.
Ishigami Konta, ed. *Kōtō Sensei Itsuwa* [Anecdotes Concerning Kōtō]. Kagoshima: Kagoshima-ken Kyōikukai, 1938.
Ishii Takashi. *Meiji Ishin no Kokusai-teki Kankyō* [The International Circumstances of the Meiji Restoration]. Tōkyō: Yoshikawa Kōbunkan, 1957.
Ishin Shiryō Hensan Jimukyoku, *Ishin Shi* [History of the Restoration]. Tōkyō: Ishin Shiryō Hensan Jimukyoku, 1939-1942. 6 vols.
———. *Ishin Shiryō Kōyō* [Outline of Historical Materials on the Restoration]. Tōkyō: Ishin Shiryō Hensan Jimukyoku, 1937-1939. 10 vols.
Itazawa Takeo. "Rangaku no Hattatsu" [Development of Dutch Learning], in *Iwanami Kōza: Nihon Rekishi*, Kuroita Katsumi, ed. Vol. III. Tōkyō: Iwanami Shoten, 1933-1935.
Itō Nitarō. *Ōkubo Toshimichi*. Tōkyō: Heibonsha, 1941. 2 vols.
Kanai Yukiyasu, ed., *Shishin Benri Shimatsu* [The Results of the Mission to China], in *Meiji Bunka Zenshū: Gaikō Hen*, Yoshino Sakuzō, ed. Vol. VI. Tōkyō: Nihon Hyōronsha, 1928-1930.
Kanda Chūgaku Kōyūkai. *Kōshitsu no Hampei* [Bulwark of the Imperial House]. Tōkyō: Kōshitsu Hampeisha, 1904.
Kanno Watarō. *Nihon Kaisha Kigyō Hassei Shi no Kenkyū* [A Study of the History of the Emergence of Corporate Enterprises in Japan]. Tōkyō: Iwanami Shoten, 1931.
Katsuda Magoya. *Kōtō Itsuwa* [Anecdotes Concerning Kōtō]. Tōkyō: Fuzambō, 1928.
———. *Ōkubo Toshimichi Den* [Biography of Ōkubo Toshimichi]. Tōkyō: Dōbunkan, 1910-1911. 3 vols.
Katsuda Magoya and Usui Yoshiharu, eds. *Ōkubo Toshimichi Monjo* [Papers of Ōkubo Toshimichi]. Tōkyō: Nihon Shiseki Kyōkai, 1927-1929. 10 vols.
———. *Ōkubo Toshimichi Nikki* [Diary of Ōkubo Toshimichi]. Tōkyō: Nihon Shiseki Kyōkai, 1927. 2 vols.

Kawasaki Saburō. *Ōkubo Kōtō*. Tōkyō: Shunyōdō, 1898.

Kikuchi Shunsuke. *Tokugawa Kinreikō* [Commentary on Tokugawa Laws]. Tōkyō: Yoshikawa Kōbunkan, 1931.

Kimura Kaishu. *Sanjūnen Shi* [Thirty-Year History]. Tōkyō: Kōshunsha, 1892.

Kitsukawa Hidezō. *Shizoku Jusan no Kenkyū* [Study of the Provision of Employment for the Samurai]. Tōkyō: Nihon Keizai Shi Kenkyūjo, 1935.

Kiyozawa Kiyoshi. *Gaiseika to Shite no Ōkubo Toshimichi* [Ōkubo as an International Statesman]. Tōkyō: Chūōkōronsha, 1942.

Koda Shigetomo. "Edo no Shisei" [City Administration of Edo], in *Iwanami Kōza: Nihon Rekishi,* Kuroita Katsumi, ed. Vol. IV. Tōkyō: Iwanami Shoten, 1933-1935.

Kojima Tokumi. *Shin Nippon no Kensetsu to Jimbutsu* [Personalities and the Construction of a New Japan]. Tōkyō: Kyōbunsha, 1940.

Kokuryūkai Hombu, ed. *Seinan Kiden* [History of the Saigō Rebellion]. Tōkyō: Kokuryūkai Hombu, 1909-1911. 6 vols.

Komatsu Midori, ed. *Itō Kō Zenshū* [Complete Works of Itō]. Tōkyō: Itō Kō Zenshū Kankōkai, 1927. 3 vols.

Kure Shūzō. "Yōgaku no Hatten to Meiji Ishin" [The Development of Western Studies and the Meiji Restoration], in *Meiji Ishin Shi Kenkyū,* Tōkyō Teikoku Daigaku Shigakkai, ed. Tōkyō: Fuzambō, 1929.

Kurita Mototsugu. "Edo Bakufu no Seiji" [Government of the Edo Bakufu], in *Iwanami Kōza: Nihon Rekishi,* Kuroita Katsumi, ed. Vol. IV. Tōkyō: Iwanami Shoten, 1933-1935.

———. "Seiji oyobi Seido" [Politics and Institutions], in *Nihon Bunka Shi Taikei,* Tanaka Kazuhiko, ed. Vol. IX. Tōkyō: Seibundō Shinkōsha, 1937-1942.

Kuroita Katsumi, ed. *Iwanami Koza: Nihon Rekishi* [Iwanami Lectures: Japanese History]. Tōkyō: Iwanami Shoten, 1933-1935. 9 vols.

Makino Terutomo. *Meiji Taishō Shi: Keizai Hen* [History of the Meiji-Taishō Eras: Economics]. Vol. III. Tōkyō: Asahi Shimbunsha, 1930-1931. 6 vols.

Matsubara Munetoshi. *Ōkubo Toshimichi.* Tōkyō: Shinchōsha, 1912.

Matsudaira Tarō. *Edo Jidai Seido no Kenkyū* [A Study of the Political Institutions of the Edo Period]. Tōkyō: Buke Seido Kenkyūkai, 1919.

Matsushita Shigesuke. *Kagoshima Ken Kyōdo Keitō Shi* [History of Kagoshima Prefecture]. Kagoshima: Kagoshima Insatsu Kabushiki Kaisha, 1930. 15 vols.

Meiji-Taishō Shi [History of the Meiji and Taishō Eras]. Tōkyō: Asahi Shimbunsha, 1930-1931. 6 vols.

Miyake Torata. *Ōkubo Toshimichi Kō no Den* [Biography of Ōkubo Toshimichi]. Tōkyō: Bummeidō, 1878.

Murakami Naojirō. "Kirishitan Shumon no Kōhai" [Rise and Decline of Christianity], in *Iwanami Kōza: Nihon Rekishi,* Kuroita Katsumi, ed. Vol. V. Tōkyō: Iwanami Shoten, 1933-1935.

Nagano Isao and Hatano Kanichi, eds. and trans. *Nisshi Gaikō Rokujūnen Shi* [Sino-Japanese Sixty-Year Diplomatic History]. Tōkyō: Kensetsusha, 1933. 4 vols.

Nagasaka Kaneo, ed. *Denki Dai Nippon Shi* [Biographical History of Japan]. Tōkyō: Yūzankaku. 1935-1936.

———. *Denki Dai Nippon Shi: Seijika Hen* [Biographical History of Japan: Statesmen]. Vol. IX. Tōkyō: Yūzankaku. 1935-1936.

Naikaku Kampō Kyoku. *Hōrei Zensho* [Complete Collection of Laws and Ordinances, 1867-1926]. Tōkyō. Naikaku Kampō Kyoku, 1887——.

Nakamura Kōya. "Meiji Ishin to Chōnin Kaikyū" [The Merchant Class and the Meiji Restoration], in *Meiji Ishin Shi Kenkyū,* Tōkyō Teikoku Daigaku Shigakkai, ed. Tōkyō: Fuzambō, 1929.

———. "Seiji oyobi Seido" [Politics and Institutions], in *Nihon Bunka Shi Taikei,* Tanaka Kazuhiko, ed. Vol. X. Tōkyō: Seibundō Shinkōsha, 1939.

Nakamura Naokatsu. *Kokushi Tsūron* [Treatise on National History]. Kyōto: Hoshino Shoten, 1939.

Nakamura Tokugorō. *Ōkubo Kyō no Ikun wo Shinobite* [Recalling the Great Achievements of Minister Ōkubo]. Ōsaka: Mitsukoshi Shiten, 1927.

Nakane Yukie. *Saimu Kiji* [Second Dream Record]. Tōkyō: Nihon Shiseki Kyōkai, 1927.

———. *Zoku Saimu Kiji* [Second Dream Record Continued]. Tōkyō: Nihon Shiseki Kyōkai, 1927-1928. 6 vols.

———. *Sakumu Kiji* [Records of Yesterday's Dreams]. Tōkyō: Nihon Shiseki Kyōkai, 1920-1921. 4 vols.

Nakayama Kyūjirō. "Kinsei Shina yori Ishin Zengo no Nihon ni oyoboshitaru Shoshū no Eikyō" [The Influence of Modern China upon Japan during the Restoration Years], in *Meiji Ishin Shi Kenkyū,* Tōkyō Teikoku Daigaku Shigakkai, ed. Tōkyō: Fuzambō, 1929.

Nakayama Yasumasa, ed. *Shimbun Shūsei Meiji Hennen Shi* [Chronological History of Meiji Compiled from Newspaper Records]. Tōkyō: Zaisei Keizai Gakkai, 1934-1936. 15 vols.

Nihon Eiyū Den Hensanjo. *Nihon Eiyū Den* [Biographies of Japan's Great Personalities]. Tōkyō: Hibonkaku, 1936. 10 vols.

Nihon Kindai Shi Kenkyūkai. *Kindai Nihon Jimbutsu Seiji Shi* [A History of Personal Politics of Modern Japan]. Tōkyō: Tōyō Keizai Shimpōsha, 1955. 2 vols.

Nihon Kōgakkai and Keimeikai, eds. *Meiji Kōgyō Shi* [Meiji Industrial History]. Tōkyō: Nihon Kōgyō Shi Hakkōjo, 1904-1931. 10 vols.

———. *Meiji Kōgyō Shi: Kagaku Kōgyō Hen* [Meiji Industrial History: Chemical Industry]. Nihon Kōgakkai and Keimeikai, eds. Vol. IX. Tōkyō: Nihon Kōgyō Shi Hakkōjo, 1904-1931.

———. *Meiji Kōgyō Shi: Zōsen Hen* [Meiji Industrial History: Shipbuilding]. Nihon Kōgakkai and Keimeikai, eds. Vol. III. Tōkyō: Nihon Kōgyō Shi Hakkōjo, 1904-1931.

Noguchi Tsunetomo. "Shoban Shushisho" [Report of the Purpose of the Chastisement of the Aborigines], in *Meiji Bunka Zenshū: Gaikō Hen,* Yoshino Sakuzō, ed. VI, 152-178. Tōkyō: Nihon Hyōronsha, 1928-1930.

Ogawa Taichirō, ed. *Meiji Dai Nempyō* [Chronological Table of Meiji]. Tōkyō: Yoshikawa Kōbunkan, 1914.

Ōkawa Nobuyoshi, ed. *Dai Saigō Zenshū* [Complete Works of Saigō]. Tōkyō: Heibonsha, 1926-1927. 3 vols.

Ōkuma Kō Hachijūgonen Shi Hensankai, ed. *Ōkuma Kō Hachijūgonen Shi* [Eighty-five Year History of Marquis Ōkuma]. Tōkyō: Nisshin Insatsu Kabushiki Kaisha, 1926. 3 vols.

Ono Hideo. *Nihon Shimbun Hattatsu Shi* [History of the Development of the Japanese Press]. Ōsaka: Ōsaka Mainichi Shimbunsha, 1922.

Ono Kiyoshi. *Tokugawa Seido Shiryō* [Historical Materials on the Tokugawa Institutions]. Tōkyō: Toppan Insatsu Kabushiki Kaisha, 1927.

Ono Takeo. *Nōson Shi* [Agricultural History]. Vol. IX of the *Gendai Nihon Bum-*

mei Shi [History of Modern Japanese Civilization]. Tōkyō: Tōyō Keizai Shimpōsha, 1940-1944.

Osatake Takeshi. *Meiji Ishin* [Meiji Restoration]. Tōkyō: Hakuyōsha, 1942-1949. 4 vols.

———. *Nihon Kensei Shi Taikō* [Outline of Japanese Constitutional History]. Tōkyō: Nihon Hyōronsha, 1938. 2 vols.

Ōtsu Junichirō. *Dai Nippon Kensei Shi* [Constitutional History of Japan]. Tōkyō: Hōbunkan, 1927-1928. 10 vols.

Ōtsuka Takematsu, ed. *Hyakkan Rireki* [Curricula Vitae of Government Officials]. Tōkyō: Nihon Shiseki Kyōkai, 1927-1928. 2 vols.

———. *Iwakura Tomomi Kankei Monjo* [Papers Relating to Iwakura Tomomi]. Tōkyō: Nihon Shiseki Kyōkai, 1927-1935. 8 vols.

———. *Saga Sanenaru Nikki* [Diary of Saga Sanenaru]. Tōkyō: Nihon Shiseki Kyōkai, 1929-1931. 3 vols.

———. *Sappan Shutsugun Senjō* [Satsuma *Han*'s Military Situation]. Tōkyō: Nihon Shiseki Kyōkai, 1932-1933. 2 vols.

———. *Shoshidai Nikki* [Shoshidai Diary]. Tōkyō: Nihon Shiseki Kyōkai, 1928. 2 vols.

Sawada Akira. *Meiji Zaisei no Kisoteki Kenkyū* [A Fundamental Study of Meiji Finance]. Tōkyō: Hōbunkan, 1934.

Shibuzawa Eiichi. *Tokugawa Keiki Kō Den* [Biography of Tokugawa Keiki]. Tōkyō: Fuzambō, 1918. 8 vols.

Shimada Saburō. *Kaikoku Shimatsu* [Particulars Relating to the Opening of Japan]. Tōkyō: Yoronsha, 1888.

Shirayanagi Takeshi. *Ōkubo Toshimichi*. Tōkyō: Chōbunkaku, 1943.

Shumbō Kō Tsuishōkai. *Itō Hirobumi Den* [Biography of Itō Hirobumi]. Tōkyō: Shumbō Kō Tsuishōkai, 1940. 3 vols.

Sobu Rokurō. *Meiji Shi Sōran* [Complete Survey of Meiji History]. Tōkyō: Meiji Shi Kankōkai, 1936-1939. 4 vols.

Tabohashi Kiyoshi. "Meiji Gaikō Shi" [Meiji Diplomatic History], in *Iwanami Kōza: Nihon Rekishi,* Kuroita Katsumi, ed. Vol. VIII. Tōkyō: Iwanami Shoten, 1933-1935.

Tada Kōmon and Kagawa Keizō, comps. *Iwakura Kō Jikki* [Authentic Chronicle of Prince Iwakura]. Tōkyō: Iwakura Kō Koseki Hozonkai, 1927. 3 vols.

Taishi Korosha Denki Hensankai, comp. *Taishi Kaikoroku* [Relations with China in Retrospect]. Tōkyō: Taishi Korosha Denki Hensankai, 1936. 2 vols.

Takahashi Kamekichi. *Meiji Taishō Nōson Keizai no Hensen* [Changes in the Agrarian Economy During the Meiji and Taishō Eras]. Tōkyō: Tōyō Keizai Shimpōsha Shuppambu, 1926.

———. *Meiji Taishō Sangyō Hattatsu Shi* [History of Industrial Development in the Meiji and Taishō Eras]. Tōkyō: Kaizōsha, 1929.

———. *Nihon Shihonshugi Hattatsu Shi* [History of the Development of Japanese Capitalism]. Tōkyō: Nihon Hyōronsha, 1928.

Takeoka Katsuya. "Kokugaku no Hatten to Meiji Ishin" [The Development of Japanese Classical Studies and the Meiji Restoration], in *Meiji Ishin Shi Kenkyū,* Tōkyō Teikoku Daigaku Shigakkai, ed. Tōkyō: Fuzambō, 1929.

Tanaka Inahiko. *Ketsujin Ōkubo Kōtō* [The Eminent Ōkubo Kōtō]. Tōkyō: Shūbunkan, 1911.

Tanaka Kazuhiko, ed. *Nihon Bunka Shi Taikei* [Survey of Japanese Cultural History]. Tōkyō: Seibundō Shinkōsha, 1937-1942. 12 vols.

Tanaka Kōken, ed. *Mito Bakumatsu Fūunroku* [Record of the Situation in Mito in the Latter Days of the Bakufu]. Tōkyō: Fuzambō, 1933.

Tanaka Sōgorō. *Ōkubo Toshimichi*. Tōkyō: Chikura Shobō, 1938.

Tokutomi Iichirō. *Kinsei Nihon Kokumin Shi* [Modern History of the Japanese Nation]. Tōkyō: Minyūsha, 1918-1941. 66 vols.

———. *Meiji Ishin no Taigyō* [The Great Task of the Meiji Restoration]. Tōkyō: Minyūsha, 1935.

———. *Ōkubo Kōtō Sensei* [Master Ōkubo Kōtō]. Tōkyō: Minyūsha, 1927.

Tōkyō Teikoku Daigaku Shigakkai. *Meiji Ishin Shi Kenkyū* [Study of the History of the Meiji Restoration]. Tōkyō: Fuzambō, 1929.

Tōkyō Teikoku Daigaku Shiryō Hensanjo. *Meiji Shiyō* [Essentials of Meiji History]. Tōkyō: Kinkōdō Shoseki Kabushiki Kaisha, 1933. 2 vols.

Tōyama Shigeki. *Meiji Ishin* [Meiji Restoration]. Tōkyō: Iwanami Shoten, 1951.

Tōyama Shigeki and Satō Shinichi, eds. *Nihon Shi Kenkyū Nyūmon* [A Guide to the Study of Japanese History]. Tōkyō: Tōkyō Daigaku Shuppankai, 1956.

Tōyama Shigeki and Adachi Yoshiko, eds. *Kindai Nihon Seiji Shi Hikkei* [A Manual of Modern Japanese Political History]. Tōkyō: Iwanami Shoten, 1961.

Tsuchiya Takao. "Edo Jidai no Keizai" [Economy of the Edo Period], in *Iwanami Kōza: Nihon Rekishi,* Kuroita Katsumi, ed. Vol. VIII. Tōkyō: Iwanami Shoten, 1930.

———. "Keizai" [Economics], in *Nihon Bunka Shi Taikei,* Tanaka Kazuhiko, ed. Vol. X. Tōkyō: Seibundō Shinkōsha, 1939.

———. "Keizai Seisakuka to Shite no Ōkubo Toshimichi" [Ōkubo Toshimichi as a Formulator of Economic Policy], in *Chūō Kōron,* LX (April, 1935), 95-110.

———. "Ōkubo Naimukyō Jidai no Shokusan Kōgyō Seisaku" [The Industrialization Policy During Ōkubo's Term as Home Minister], in *Keizai Gaku Ronshū,* IV (September, 1934), 1193-1252.

Tsumaki Chūta, ed. *Kido Kōin Monjo* [Papers of Kido Kōin]. Tōkyō: Nihon Shiseki Kyōkai, 1929-1931. 8 vols.

———. *Kido Kōin Nikki* [Diary of Kido Kōin]. Tōkyō: Nihon Shiseki Kyōkai, 1932-1933. 3 vols.

Watanabe Ikujirō. *Meiji Gaikō Shiwa* [Talks on Meiji Diplomatic History]. Tōkyō: Nihon Hōsō Shuppan Kyōkai, 1940.

———. *Meiji Shi Kōwa* [Lectures on Meiji History]. Tōkyō: Yoshikawa Kōbunkan, 1935.

———, ed. *Ōkuma Shigenobu Kankei Monjo* [Papers Relating to Ōkuma Shigenobu]. Tōkyō: Nihon Shiseki Kyōkai, 1932-1935. 6 vols.

Watanabe Shūjirō. *Ōkubo Toshimichi Genkōroku* [Words and Deeds of Ōkubo Toshimichi]. Tōkyō: Naigai Shuppan Kyōkai, 1909.

———. *Ōkubo Toshimichi no Isshō* [Life of Ōkubo Toshimichi]. Tōkyō: Daigakkan, 1900.

Yamamoto Yūzō. *Saigō to Ōkubo* [Saigō and Ōkubo]. Tōkyō: Nipponsha, 1947.

Yoshida Saburō. "Shisō to Gakumon" [Thought and Learning], in *Nihon Bunka Shi Taikei,* Tanaka Kazuhiko, ed. Vol. IX. Tōkyō: Seibundō Shinkōsha, 1937-1942.

Yoshino Sakuzō, ed. *Meiji Bunka Zenshū* [Anthology of Meiji Culture]. Tōkyō: Nihon Hyōronsha, 1928-1930. 24 vols.

Yūzankaku Sho no Tomo, ed. *Bakumatsu Ishin Iboku Shinkō* [New Compilation of Late Bakufu and Restoration Period Calligraphy]. Tōkyō: Yūzankaku, 1940.

Work in Chinese

Wang Yün-shêng, *Liu shih nien lai Chung Kuō yu Kuō yu Jih Pen* [China and Japan in the Last Sixty Years]. Tientsin: Ta Kung Pao, 1932-1934. 7 vols.

Works in French

Charlevoix, Pierre Francois Xavier de. *Histoire du Japon*. Paris: Chez Rollin, 1754. 6 vols.

Chavannes, Edouard, ed. and trans. *Les mémoires historiques de Se-Ma Ts'ien*. Paris: Ernest Leroux, 1895-1905. 5 vols.

Courant, Maurice. *Ôkoubo*. Paris: Ancienne Librairie Germer Bailliere et Cie, 1904.

Ray, Jean. *Le Japon, grande puissance moderne*. Paris: Librairie Plon, 1942.

Steinilber-Oberlin, E. *Les sectes bouddhiques japonaises*. Paris: Les Editions G. Crès et Cie, 1930.

Tchen Hoshien. *Les relations diplomatiques entre la Chine et le Japon de 1871 à nos jours traités, conventions, échange de lettres, etc.* Paris: Editions de "la vie universitaire," 1921.

Wang Tch'ang-tche. "La philosophie morale de Wang Yang-ming," in *Variétés sinologiques*, XLII, no. 63. Paris: Librairie Orientaliste P. Geuthner, 1936.

Works in English

Adams, Francis Ottiwell. *The History of Japan*. London: Henry S. King and Co., 1874-1875. 2 vols.

Akagi, Roy Hidemichi. *Japan's Foreign Relations, 1542-1936*. Tōkyō: Hokuseidō Press, 1936.

Akiyama, Kenzō. *The History of Nippon*. Toshirō Shimanouchi, trans. Tōkyō: Kokusai Bunka Shinkōkai, 1941.

Asakawa, Kanichi, ed. and trans. *The Documents of Iriki*. Tōkyō: Japan Society for the Promotion of Science, 1955.

Aston, W. George. *A History of Japanese Literature*. New York: D. Appleton-Century Co., Inc., 1933.

Beasley, W. G., ed. and trans. *Select Documents on Japanese Foreign Policy, 1853-1868*. London: Oxford University Press, 1955.

Beckmann, George M. *The Making of the Meiji Constitution*. Lawrence: University of Kansas Press, 1957.

Black, John R. *Young Japan*. London: Trubner and Co., 1880-1881. 2 vols.

Bodde, Derk. *China's First Unifier: A Study of the Ch'in Dynasty as Seen in the Life of Li Ssu* (280?-208 B.C.). Leiden: E. J. Brill, 1938.

Borton, Hugh. *Japan's Modern Century*. New York: Ronald Press Co., 1955.

———. "Peasant Uprisings in Japan of the Tokugawa Period," in *Transactions of the Asiatic Society of Japan*. 2nd series, Vol. XVI. Tōkyō, 1938.

Boxer, Charles R. *The Christian Century in Japan, 1549-1650*. Berkeley and Los Angeles: University of California Press, 1951.

Brinkley, F. *History of the Japanese People*. New York: Encyclopaedia Britannica, Co., 1914.
Brown, Delmer M. *Nationalism in Japan*. Berkeley and Los Angeles: University of California Press, 1955.
Brown, Sidney D. "Kido Takayoshi (1833-1877): Meiji Japan's Cautious Revolutionary," in *Pacific Historical Review*, XXV (May, 1956), 151-162.
———. "Ōkubo Toshimichi: His Political and Economic Policies in Early Meiji Japan," in *The Journal of Asian Studies*, XXI (February, 1962), 183-197.
Chung, Henry. *The Case of Korea*. New York: Fleming H. Revell Co., 1924.
Craig, Albert M. *Chōshū in the Meiji Restoration*. Cambridge: Harvard University Press, 1961.
———. "The Restoration Movement in Chōshū," in *The Journal of Asian Studies*, XVIII (February, 1959), 187-197.
Crow, Carl. *He Opened the Door of Japan*. New York and London: Harper and Brothers, 1939.
Curtis, William Elroy. *The Yankees of the East*. New York: Stone and Kimball, 1896. 2 vols.
Dennett, Tyler. *Americans in Eastern Asia*. New York: Barnes and Noble, Inc., 1941.
Douglas, Robert K. *Li Hung-chang*. London: Bliss, Sands and Foster, 1895.
Ellis, Ellen Deborah. "Autocracy," *Encyclopaedia of the Social Sciences*, Vol. II. New York: The Macmillan Co., 1937.
Embree, John F. *The Japanese Nation*. New York: Farrar Rhinehart, Inc., 1945.
Forman, Harrison. *Changing China*. New York: Crown Publishers, 1948.
Fukuzawa, Yūkichi. *The Autobiography of Fukuzawa Yūkichi*. E. Kiyooka, trans. Tōkyō: Hokuseidō Press, 1934.
Gaimushō. *Treaties and Conventions Concluded between the Empire of Japan and Foreign Countries, 1854-1874*. Tōkyō: Nisshūsha, 1874.
Griffis, William Elliot. *The Mikado: Institution and Person*. Princeton: Princeton University Press, 1915.
———. *The Mikado's Empire* (5th ed.). New York: Harper and Brothers, 1886.
———. "Millard Fillmore and His Part in the Opening of Japan," *Buffalo Historical Society Publications*, IX, 55-79.
Gubbins, John Harington. "Hideyoshi and the Satsuma Clan in the Sixteenth Century," in *Transactions of the Asiatic Society of Japan*, Vol. VIII, Pt. I, pp. 92-143. Yokohama, 1880.
———. *The Making of Modern Japan*. London: Seeley, Service and Co., Ltd., 1922.
———. *The Progress of Japan, 1853-1871*. Oxford: Clarendon Press, 1911.
Hall, John C. "The Tokugawa Legislation," in *Transactions of the Asiatic Society of Japan*, Vol. XLI, Pt. V. Tōkyō, 1913.
Hall, John Whitney. "The Castle-Town and Japan's Modern Urbanization," in *The Far Eastern Quarterly*, XV (November, 1955), 37-56.
———. "Foundations of the Modern Japanese Daimyo," in *The Journal of Asian Studies*, XX (May, 1961), 317-329.
Hamada, Kengi. *Prince Itō*. Tōkyō: Sanseidō Co., Ltd., 1936.
Han, Yu-shan. *Elements of Chinese Historiography*. Hollywood: W. M. Hawley, 1955.
Hanazono, Kanesada. *The Development of Japanese Journalism*. Ōsaka: The Ōsaka Mainichi, 1924.
Hawks, Francis L., comp. *Narrative of the Expedition of an American Squadron to*

the China Seas and Japan, Performed in the Years 1852, 1853, and 1854, under the Command of Commodore M. C. Perry, United States Navy, by Order of the Government of the United States. (U. S. House of Representatives, 33rd Congress, 2nd Session, Exec. Doc. 97.) Washington: A. O. P. Nicholson, 1856. 4 vols.

Heckscher, Eli F. *Mercantilism.* London: George Allen and Unwin, Ltd., 1955. 2 vols.

Henke, Frederick Goodrich. *The Philosophy of Wang Yang-ming.* London and Chicago: The Open Court Publishing Co., 1916.

Heusken, Henry. *Japan Journal, 1855-1861.* Jeannette C. van der Corput and Robert A. Wilson, trans. and eds. New Brunswick, New Jersey: Rutgers University Press, 1964.

Hofstadter, Richard. *Social Darwinism in American Thought.* New York: George Braziller, Inc., 1959.

Honjō, Eijirō. *The Social and Economic History of Japan.* Kyōto: Institute for Research in Economic History of Japan, 1935.

———. *Economic History and Theory of Japan in the Tokugawa Period* Tōkyō: Maruzen Co., Ltd., 1943.

Horie, Yasuzō. "The Economic Significance of the Meiji Restoration." Reprint from *Kyōto University Economic Review*, Vol. XII, no. 11. Kyōto, n.d.

House, Edward H. *The Japanese Expedition to Formosa.* Tōkyō, 1875.

Idditti, Smimasa. *The Life of Marquis Shigenobu Ōkuma.* Tōkyō: Hokuseidō Press, 1940.

Ike, Nobutake. *The Beginnings of Political Democracy in Japan.* Baltimore: Johns Hopkins Press, 1950.

Inspectorate General of Customs. *Treaties, Conventions, etc., between China and Foreign States,* Vol. III, misc. series: no. 30. Shanghai: Statistical Department of the Inspectorate General of Customs, 1917. 2 vols.

Jansen, Marius B. *Sakamoto Ryōma and the Meiji Restoration.* Princeton. Princeton University Press, 1961.

Jefferson, Thomas. "Notes on Virginia," in *The Writings of Thomas Jefferson,* Andrew A. Lipscomb, ed. Vol. II. Washington, D.C.: The Thomas Jefferson Memorial Association, 1903-1904. 20 vols.

Kaneko, Hisakazu. *Manjirō, the Man Who Discovered America.* Boston: Houghton Mifflin Co., 1956.

Kawabe, Kisaburō. *The Press and Politics in Japan.* Chicago: University of Chicago Press, 1921.

Kerr, George H. *Okinawa.* Tōkyō: Charles E. Tuttle Co., 1959.

———. *A Survey of Literature in Japan before 1868.* Tōkyō, 1936.

Kikuchi, Dairoku. *Japanese Education.* London: John Murray, 1909.

Kishimoto, Hideo, comp. and ed., *Japanese Religion in the Meiji Era.* J. F. Howes, trans. Vol. II of the Centenary Culture Council Series. Tōkyō: Ōbunsha, 1956. 14 vols.

Kuno, Yoshi S. *Japanese Expansion on the Asiatic Continent.* Berkeley: University of California Press, 1937-1940. 2 vols.

Lane-Poole, S., and F. V. Dickens. *The Life of Sir Harry Parkes.* London: Macmillan and Co., 1894. 2 vols.

Lanman, Charles. *Leading Men of Japan.* Boston: D. Lothrop and Co., 1883.

Lanman, Charles, ed. *Leaders of the Meiji Restoration in America.* Tōkyō: Hokuseidō Press, 1931.

Lebra, Joyce Chapman. "Ōkuma Shigenobu and the 1881 Political Crisis," in *The Journal of Asian Studies*, XVIII (August, 1959), 475-487.
Legge, James. *The Four Books*. Shanghai: The Commercial Press, Ltd., n.d.
Linebarger, Paul M. A., Djang Chu, and Ardath W. Burks. *Far Eastern Governments and Politics*. New York: D. Van Nostrand Co., Inc., 1956.
Lombard, Frank Alonson. *Pre-Meiji Education in Japan*. Tōkyō: Kyō Bun Kwan, 1914.
McGovern, William M. *Modern Japan*. London: T. Fisher Unwin, Ltd., 1920.
McLaren, Walter Wallace, ed. "Japanese Government Documents," in *Transactions of the Asiatic Society of Japan*, Vol. XLII, Pt. I. Tōkyō, 1914.
———. *A Political History of Japan During the Meiji Era 1867-1912*. New York: Charles Scribner's Sons, 1916.
Minagawa, Masataka. *A History of Japanese Literature*. Tōkyō: Gansuidō, 1936.
Moore, John Bassett. *A Digest of International Law as Embodied in Diplomatic Discussions, Treaties and Other International Agreements, International Awards, The Decisions of Municipal Courts, and the Writings of Jurists, and Especially in Documents, Published and Unpublished, Issued by Presidents and Secretaries of State of the United States, the Opinions of Attorneys-General, and Decisions of Courts, Federal and State*. Washington: Government Printing Office, 1906. 8 vols.
Morris, J. *Advance Japan*. London: W. H. Allen and Co., Ltd., 1895.
———. *Makers of Japan*. London: Methuen and Co., 1906.
Morse, Edward S. *Japan Day by Day*. New York: Houghton Mifflin Co., 1917.
Mounsey, Augustus H. *The Satsuma Rebellion*. London: John Murray, 1879.
Murdoch, James. *A History of Japan*. London: Kegan Paul, Trench, Trubner and Co., Ltd., 1925-1926. 3 vols.
Mushakōji, Saneatsu. *Great Saigō: The Life of Saigō Takamori*, Sakamoto Morishi, trans. Tōkyō: Kaitakusha, 1942.
Norman, Herbert E. *Japan's Emergence as a Modern State*. New York: Institute of Pacific Relations, 1940.
Obata, Kyūgorō. *An Interpretation of the Life of Viscount Shibusawa*. Tōkyō: Daiyamondo Jigyō Kabushiki Kaisha, 1937.
Ōkuma, Shigenobu. *Fifty Years of New Japan*. London: Smith, Elder and Co., 1910. 2 vols.
Orchard, John E. *Japan's Economic Position*. New York: McGraw-Hill Book Co., Inc., 1930.
Quigley, Harold S. *Japanese Government and Politics*. New York: The Century Co., 1932.
Reischauer, August Karl. *Studies in Japanese Buddhism*. New York: The Macmillan Co., 1917.
———. *Early Japanese History*. Princeton: Princeton University Press, 1937. 2 vols.
Reischauer, Robert K. *Japan, Government and Politics*. New York: Thomas Nelson and Sons, 1939.
Rockhill, William W. *China's Intercourse with Korea from the XVth Century to 1895*. London: Luzal and Co., 1905.
Sakai, Robert K. "Feudal Society and Modern Leadership in Satsuma-han," in *The Journal of Asian Studies*, XVI (May, 1957), 365-376.
Sansom, George B. *Japan: A Short Cultural History*. New York: Appleton-Century-Crofts, Inc., 1943.

———. *The Western World and Japan*. New York: Alfred A. Knopf, 1950.

———. *A History of Japan*. Stanford: Stanford University Press, 1958-1963. 3 vols.

Satoh, H. *Agitated Japan: The Life of Baron Ii Kamon-no-kami Naosuke*. New York: D. Appleton and Co., 1896.

Satomi, Kishio. *Discovery of Japanese Idealism*. London: Kegan Paul, Trench, Trubner, and Co., Ltd., 1924.

Satow, Ernest. *A Diplomat in Japan*. London: Seeley, Service and Co., 1921.

Scherer, James A. B. *Young Japan*. Philadelphia and London: J. B. Lippincott Co., 1905.

Seligman, Edwin R. A., ed. *Encyclopaedia of the Social Sciences*. New York: The Macmillan Co., 1937. 15 vols.

Severance, Frank H., ed. "Millard Fillmore Papers," in Buffalo Historical Society *Publications*, Vols. X, XI. Buffalo, 1907.

Smith, Thomas C. *The Agrarian Origins of Modern Japan*. Stanford: Stanford University Press, 1959.

Spencer, Herbert. *The Principles of Sociology*. New York: D. Appleton and Co., 1900. 3 vols.

Stevenson, Robert Louis. "Yoshida-Torajirō," in *The Travels and Essays of Robert Louis Stevenson; Familiar Studies of Men and Books—Miscellaneous Papers*. Vol. XIV, 150-165. New York: Charles Scribner's Sons, 1903.

Strauss, Leo. *Thoughts on Machiavelli*. Glencoe, Illinois: The Free Press, 1958.

Suzuki, Daisetz Teitarō. *Zen Buddhism and Its Influence on Japanese Culture*. Kyōto: The Eastern Buddhist Society, 1938.

Swisher, Earl. "Commodore Perry's Imperialism in Relation to America's Present-Day Position in the Pacific," in *Pacific Historical Review*, XVI (February, 1947), 30-40.

Takekoshi, Yōsaburō. *Japanese Rule in Formosa*. New York: Longmans, Green, and Co., 1907.

———. *Prince Saionji*. Kyōto: Ritsumeikan University, 1933.

Takekoshi, Yosoburo [Yosaburo]. *The Economic Aspects of the History of the Civilization of Japan*. New York: The Macmillan Co., 1930. 3 vols.

Takizawa, Matsuyo. *The Penetration of Money Economy in Japan, and Its Effects upon Social and Political Institutions*. Columbia University Studies in History, Economics and Public Law, no. 285. New York: Columbia University Press, 1927.

Treat, Payson Jackson. *The Early Diplomatic Relations Between the United States and Japan, 1853-1865*. Baltimore: The Johns Hopkins Press, 1917.

———. *Japan and the United States, 1853-1921*. Stanford: Stanford University Press, 1928.

Tsuchiya, Takao. *The Development of Economic Life in Japan*. Tōkyō: Kokusai Bunka Shinkōkai, 1936.

———. "An Economic History of Japan," N. Skene Smith trans., in *Transactions of the Asiatic Society of Japan*. 2nd series, Vol. XV. Tokyo, 1937.

Tsunoda, Ryūsaku, William Theodore de Bary, and Donald Keene, comps. *The Sources of the Japanese Tradition*. New York: Columbia University Press, 1958.

United States, Congress, House of Representatives, *Papers Relating to the Foreign Relations of the United States, 1873-1874*. (43rd Congress, 1st session, Vol. I.) Washington: Government Printing Office, 1874.

Uyehara, George Etsujirō. *The Political Development of Japan, 1867-1909*. London: Constable and Co., Ltd., 1910.

Webb, Herschel. *An Introduction to Japan*. New York: Columbia University Press, 1955.
Wildes, Harry Emerson. *Social Currents in Japan*. Chicago: University of Chicago Press, 1927.
Williamson, H. R. *Wang An-Shih, A Chinese Statesman and Educationalist of the Sung Dynasty*. London: Arthur Probsthain, 1935. 2 vols.
Wilson, Robert Arden. *Genesis of the Meiji Government in Japan, 1868-1871*. Berkeley and Los Angeles: University of California Press, 1957.
Yamaguchi, Uji. *Kinse Shiriaku* [Outline History of Modern Times]. Ernest Satow trans. Tōkyō: Naigai Shuppansha, 1906.
Yamashita, Tokuji. *Education in Japan*. Tōkyō: Kenkyūsha, 1938.
Yanaga, Chitoshi. *Japan since Perry*. New York: McGraw-Hill Book Co., Inc., 1949.

Index

Index